Group Dynamics in Sport, 5th Edition

Group Dynamics in Sport
5th Edition

Mark Eys
Wilfrid Laurier University

M. Blair Evans
Pennsylvania State University

Alex Benson
Western University

PUBLISHING

A Division of the International Center for Performance Excellence
West Virginia University
375 Birch Street, WVU-CPASS
PO Box 6116
Morgantown, WV 26506-6116

Copyright © 2020, West Virginia University
All rights reserved.

Reproduction or use of any portion of this publication by any mechanical, electronic, or other means is prohibited without written permission of the publisher.

Library of Congress Card Catalog Number: 2020940625

ISBN: 9781940067520

Cover Design: Wendy Lazzell
Front cover photo: © Shutterstock.com
Back cover photo: ID 531171694 © SWKrulllmaging | istockphoto.com
Production Editor: Kassi Roberts

10 9 8 7 6 5 4 3 2 1

FiT Publishing
A Division of the International Center for Performance Excellence
West Virginia University
375 Birch Street, WVU-CPASS
PO Box 6116
Morgantown, WV 26506-6116
800.477.4348 (toll free)
304.293.6888 (phone)
304.293.6658 (fax)
Email: fitcustomerservice@mail.wvu.edu
Website: www.fitpublishing.com

Special Dedication

Dr. Bert Carron

Dr. Bert Carron was an internationally recognized expert in group dynamics in sport and exercise contexts, and within the broader field of sport psychology. The first edition of *Group Dynamics in Sport* was initiated by Bert in 1988, and he led the three subsequent editions. It is important to us to highlight some of his accomplishments, particularly for those who are new to the field and/or did not have a chance to meet him over the course of their careers. In addition to his accomplishments, he greatly valued his colleagues and the work they conducted along with their graduate students. His career highlights include

- EdD from the University of California–Berkeley; undergraduate and master's degrees from the University of Alberta.
- Over 40-year career at the University of Western Ontario, London, Ontario, Canada (37 years) and the University of Saskatchewan, Saskatoon, Saskatchewan, Canada.
- Published over 200 articles, books, and chapters.
- The Carron Lecture, instituted by the Canadian Society for Psychomotor Learning and Sport Psychology in 2004, is delivered each fall at the society's conference by experts in the field of sport psychology.
- Canadian Society for Psychomotor Learning and Sport Psychology Fellow.
- North American Society for the Psychology of Sport and Physical Activity Distinguished Scholar (2007).
- National Academy of Kinesiology International Fellow (1992).
- Awarded the International Council of Sport Science and Physical Education's Prize and Sport Science Award of the International Olympic Committee President (1996).

Contents

Special Dedication v
Table of Contents vii
Acknowledgments xiii
Preface xv

Section 1   Introduction 1

Chapter 1   The Nature of Groups 3
            The Reality of Groups 5
            The Utility of Groups 7
            Definitional Issues in the Study of Groups 9
                What a Group is Not 10
                What a Group Is 10
                A Sport Team Defined 12
                Group Dynamics Defined 13
            Conceptual Frameworks for Groups 13
                A Conceptual Framework for Group Effectiveness 14
                A General Conceptual Framework for the Nature of Groups 16
                A Conceptual Framework for Sport Teams 18

Chapter 2   The Study of Groups 19
            Commonsense versus Science 19
            The Scientific Method 20
                Generating a Research Question 21
                Formulating a Hypothesis 21
                Hypothesis Testing 21
                Ruling out Alternative Explanations and Replication 22
            Special Considerations in the Study of Sport Teams 22
            Research Protocols in the Study of Sport Teams 24
                Nonexperimental Protocols 24
                Experimental Protocols 28
            Summary 29

Chapter 3   Group Development 31
Group Development Defined 31
Theories of Group Development 32
    The Sequential Stage (Linear) Perspective 32
    The Repeating Cycles (Pendulum) Perspective 34
    Additional Models of Group Development 38
Group Membership Changes 39
    Managing the Integration of New Members 39
    Advantages and Disadvantages of Membership Turnover 40
Athlete Turnover and Team Success 40
The Replacement of Managers and Coaches 42
    Manager Turnover and Team Success 43
    Cause versus Effect Interpretations 45

Section 2   Foundations of Groups in Sport 47

Chapter 4   Group Environment 49
Group Size 49
    Optimal Sport Team Size 50
    Outcomes Related to Group Size 52
Group Territory 57
    Types of Territories 58
    Marking Group Territory 60
    The Home Advantage in Sport 60
    Understanding the Causes of the Home Advantage 63
    Can Home Territory Be a Disadvantage? 71

Chapter 5   Member Attributes 75
Group Composition 76
Amount of Group Resources 77
    The Amount of Individual Ability 78
    The Amount of Psychosocial Attributes of Members 79
Diversity of Group Resources 83
    Variety, Separation, and Disparity 84
    Diversity in Sex 85
    Diversity in Age and Team Tenure 85
    Diversity in Racial Identity/Ethnicity 86
    Diversity in Social Psychological Characteristics 86
    Diversity in Ability 87
Compatibility of Group Resources 88
    Compatibility of Member Abilities 90
    Compatibility with Group Roles 91
    Compatibility Between the Coach and the Athlete 91

Section 3 Group Structure 95

Chapter 6 Group Position 99
- The Importance of Positions in Groups 100
  - Spatial Centrality..100
  - Interactional Centrality..100
- The Importance of Positions in Sport Teams 101
- Group Position and Group Processes..105
- Positional Stacking by Race/Ethnicity..106

Chapter 7 Group Roles.. 109
- Types of Group Roles 110
  - Formal vs Informal Roles 110
  - Task vs Social Roles 111
- How Roles Develop.. 112
  - Communicating Formal Role Responsibilities in Sport.................... 114
  - The Emergence of Informal Roles in Sport.. 115
- The Nature and Correlates of the Elements of Role Involvement............... 116
  - Role Performance... 116
  - Role Clarity/Ambiguity.. 116
  - Role Conflict..120
  - Role Efficacy 122
  - Role Commitment and Acceptance..122
  - Role Satisfaction..123
- Enhancing Role Performance 124

Chapter 8 Group Norms 127
- Types of Team Norms 129
- Emergence of Team Norms 131
- The Function of Team Norms 132
- The Stability of Norms 133
- Factors Influencing Conformity to Group Norms 134
  - Personal Factors 136
  - Situational Factors 138
- The Nature of Group Norms in Sport 139
  - Norms within Sport Teams...139
  - Norms Beyond the Sport Group 141
- Modifying Team Norms 143
  - The Source of the Communication 143
  - The Nature of the Communication...145
  - The Nature of the Target 145
  - Dynamic Norms 146

Chapter 9 Social Hierarchy in Groups ... 147

The Nature of Social Hierarchy ... 148
  Status and Power as the Bases of Social Hierarchy ... 148
  A Functional Perspective on Social Hierarchy ... 149
  A Conflict Perspective on Social Hierarchy ... 151
  When Social Hierarchy is Beneficial versus Detrimental ... 152
  Personal Attributes Associated with Social Rank ... 154
  Situational Characteristics and Social Rank ... 155
Sport Involvement and Social Status ... 156

Section 4 Group Processes and Emergent States ... 159

Chapter 10 Group Leadership ... 161

Universal Approaches to Leadership ... 162
  Universal Trait Approach ... 162
  Universal Behavior Approach ... 163
Situational Approaches to Leadership ... 165
  Contingency Theory ... 165
  Life Cycle Theory ... 166
  Multidimensional Model of Leadership ... 168
Transformational Leadership Theory ... 170
Peer Leadership ... 171
The Leadership Process Model: The Role of Followership ... 172
Gender and Leadership ... 174
  Gender and Leadership Emergence ... 174
  Gender and Leadership Behavior ... 175
  Gender and the Evaluation of Leadership ... 176
Leader Decision Styles ... 177
  Cohesion and Team Decision-Making ... 179
  The Normative Model of Decision Making ... 180

Chapter 11 Competition and Cooperation in Groups ... 183

Studying Competition and Cooperation ... 184
Competition and Cooperation Within Groups ... 185
  Competition and Cooperation as a Group Structure ... 186
  Competition and Cooperation as a Group Process ... 187
  Consequences of Competition and Cooperation within Groups ... 190
Individual Level of Competition and Cooperation ... 190
Intergroup Competition ... 191
  Intergroup Processes ... 192
Promoting Cooperation at Within- and Between-Group Levels ... 194
  Within-Group Cooperation ... 194
  Between-Group Cooperation ... 194

Chapter 12 Team Goals 197

Goal-Setting Effects in Organizations 198
    Goal-Setting Effectiveness 198
    Performance and Group Goals 199
    Components of Effective Individual Goals 199
Why Does Goal Setting Work? 200
Goal-Setting Effects in Sport: Individual Goals 201
    Outcome, Performance, and Process Goals 202
    Goal-Setting and Youth Development 203
Goal-Setting Effects in Sport: Team Goals 203
Individual Goals versus Team Goals..204
Applied Insight: Implementation Intentions 207

Chapter 13 Communication and Coordination in Groups....................................209

Describing Group Communication 210
Effective Group Communication 211
    Perceived Effectiveness 211
    Communication and Coordination 212
    Transactive Memory and Shared Mental Models 213
Downfalls of Group Communication...214
    Groupthink 215
    Decision-Making Flaws in Groups 216
    Group Polarization 217
Enhancing Group Communication 220
    Creating a Positive Environment 220
    Proactive Approaches 220
    Strategic Ways to Convey Information 220
    Double-Checking Decisions to Account for Biases 221
    Training in Group Situations 221
    Design Transactive Memory Systems 221

Chapter 14 Cohesion in Sport Groups 223

Definitions of Cohesion in Social and Work Groups 224
Definition of Cohesion in Sport Teams 225
The Measurement of Cohesion in Sport Teams 226
    Historical Perspectives..226
    The Group Environment Questionnaire (GEQ) 227
Correlations of Cohesion in Sport Teams 231
    Situational Factors and Cohesion 233
    Personal Factors and Cohesion 234
    Leadership Factors and Cohesion 238
    Team Factors and Cohesion 239
Team Success and Cohesion 241
    Historical Perspective 241

Meta-Analyses of Cohesion and Performance Relationships 242
Moderators of the Cohesion-Performance Relationship 242
Negative Aspects of Cohesion 244

Chapter 15 Collective Efficacy 247
The Nature of Collective Efficacy 248
Collective Efficacy and Performance 249
Mechanisms Linking Collective Efficacy to Performance 250
Sources of Collective Efficacy 250
Prior Performance 250
Vicarious Experiences 253
Verbal Persuasion 253
Group-Specific Sources of Collective Efficacy 253
Overlaps between Self-Efficacy and Collective Efficacy 255

Chapter 16 Developing Effective Sport Teams 257
The Nature of Developing Effective Teams 257
Defining Team Development 259
Benefits of Team Development 259
Team Building Programs in Sport 261
Carron and Colleagues' Indirect Team Building Approach 264
The Effectiveness of Team Building 266

References 269
Index 309
About the Authors 321

Acknowledgments

It is our hope that the 16 chapters in this book will serve to introduce readers to the complexity and simplicity, as well as the practical and theoretical significance, of group dynamics in sport teams. Interest in understanding the dynamics of sport groups has grown considerably over the past three decades. It is our hope that our book will stimulate even more interest in the future. As has been the tradition in the previous editions, we as authors recognize that we owe a debt of gratitude to a number of people, which can only be done individually.

Mark Eys: My experiences in life and in academia have been made extremely enjoyable and enlightening through my involvement in and exposure to a number of different groups. First, I would not be investigating issues in group dynamics without the initial encouragement and guidance of Drs. Bert Carron, Neil Widmeyer, Larry Brawley, and Steve Bray. Sadly, Bert (June 2014) and Neil (December 2015) passed away in recent years, and I hope they understood what a positive impact they had on my life in and out of academia. Second, I have benefited from my associations with numerous graduate students and colleagues, many of whom I also consider as trusted friends. These individuals have made my work-life much less work-like. Certainly, the opportunity to work with Blair and Alex on this edition has been valuable because they are experts in this area of study, but also meaningful because of our past connections. Finally, a special acknowledgement to the two most important groups in my life who continue to support me: my parents Shirley and Adrian, and my wonderful wife Stephanie and daughters Abby and Lena. It took three editions for my kids to become teenagers. Time flies, and I couldn't be prouder of them.

M. Blair Evans: I was thrilled for the chance to contribute to this book and looked forward to working on my contributions whenever I sat at a keyboard with free time. Similar to Alex, my passion for group dynamics was ignited when taking this course as an undergraduate with Mark as instructor. I was not aware of the satisfaction I would gain studying groups, nor the community of researchers, teachers, and students that I would enter. This community became most evident when I've faced trials that come along in life—when colleagues were there to rely on. I am thankful for Alex and Mark, along with the academic community that provides me with the chance to flourish. Of course, I am grateful for my wife Brianne, as well as our children Aubrey and Ellis—the environment for me to be humbled, hopeful, and happy as a peach.

Alex Benson: Contributing to this book has been exciting, challenging, but most of all, deeply rewarding. Although groups and the people within them have always fascinated me, it was not until taking Mark's advanced sport psychology course that I began to develop a passion for studying groups. This passion continued to grow after I had the good fortune of being accepted into Mark's lab as a graduate student. Fast forwarding to present day, I feel incredibly grateful for the opportunity to work with Mark and Blair on this book—two individuals who continue to have an immeasurable impact on my academic career through their mentorship, support, and friendship. Outside of academia, my family and friends continue to be an unending reservoir of both joy and support. To my parents Allan and Mary Beth, thank you for all the ways you have supported me—there are simply far too many things to list. To my wonderful wife Sara, I am so incredibly lucky and thankful to be navigating life with you as my teammate.

Preface

It is exciting to be able to offer the fifth edition of *Group Dynamics in Sport*. However, the decision to continue this book is bittersweet given that the lead author of the first four editions, Dr. Bert Carron, passed away in June 2014. Bert was a friend, mentor, and preeminent scientist whose name is inextricably linked with group dynamics in sport and exercise. To be crystal clear, this is Bert's book. After contemplating the project and having several discussions with colleagues, we feel that Bert would be pleased to see his efforts continued in this manner, and we are honored to attempt to live up to the impact that the previous editions have had on the topic of group dynamics and, more broadly, the field of sport psychology. To quote Bert from the preface of the 1998 edition: "What can be said about such a topic? Well, for one thing, it isn't rocket science—but not for the reasons that you might think. For most of us, understanding groups is far more important." Although it is tough to encapsulate his career, we provided some highlights in the special dedication and commit to recognizing his work in this and any future editions of the book.

Based on the amount of research that has been conducted on group dynamics in sport in the last decade, an update was overdue. Group dynamics continues to be a focus for many scholars around the world. Whereas the moniker sport group dynamics was most commonly used by researchers in North America and the United Kingdom in past decades, there are thriving research groups who embrace this approach to studying sport from many countries around the world. This interest and available research afforded us the opportunity to significantly revise the content areas, while maintaining the general topics to allow for some consistency for those who have developed course content around this text. However, there are several changes to the text that should be outlined. First, Dr. Blair Evans (Penn State University, United States) and Dr. Alex Benson (Western University, Canada) have joined as coauthors and have provided fresh perspectives and creativity throughout the book chapters.

A second change is that several of the chapters have been reorganized and/or streamlined. For example, in previous editions, literature pertaining to group size and group territory were presented across two chapters. In the current edition, we have streamlined this information such that it is now contained within one chapter (Chapter 4, "Group Environment"). A similar approach was taken for content focused on the amount, variability, and compatibility of group resources (previously four shorter chapters streamlined into one comprehensive chapter—Chapter 5, "Member Attributes"), as well as cohesion (two chapters into one; Chapter 14). Finally, to be consistent with current definitions and approaches, we decided to recategorize the topic of leadership (Chapter 10) as a process, though we continue to recognize the structural implications of both coach- and athlete-centered leadership.

Updated examples to illustrate the concepts are a third change within the book. To some degree, there is a Toronto Raptor-centric feel in certain chapters; especially descriptions of their NBA championship-winning team in 2018–2019. We couldn't help our Canadian selves, and you never know how long it might take for the organization to win another championship.

What hasn't changed in the current edition are the core constructs and seminal theories that helped define our field. Overall, the current edition utilizes the same strategy as previous revisions, in that it maintains a focus on particular topics while profiting from several years of new research and insights. In this edition, there are 16 chapters presented in four sections. In the first section (Introduction), general issues associated with the nature of groups and group dynamics are introduced, then protocols used for the study of groups are outlined, and, in the third chapter, the development of groups is discussed. In the next three sections, research associated with foundational group inputs (i.e., group environment and member attributes) and group structure (i.e., roles, norms, and status), as well as group processes (i.e., leadership, cooperation/competition, team conflict/division, team goals, communication, and building/working in teams) and emergent states (i.e., group cohesion, collective efficacy) is presented. In the final chapter (building and working in teams), the types of interventions used to develop more effective teams are outlined.

It is also worth noting the approximately 30-year evolution of this text for the interested reader, and to recognize the efforts of Dr. Heather Hausenblas (Jacksonville University) who had a big impact on the second and third editions:

> First edition: *Group Dynamics in Sport: Theoretical and Practical Issues* (Carron, 1988)
> Second edition: *Group Dynamics in Sport* (Carron & Hausenblas, 1998)
> Third edition: *Group Dynamics in Sport* (Carron, Hausenblas, & Eys, 2005)
> Fourth edition: *Group Dynamics in Sport* (Carron & Eys, 2012)
> Fifth and current edition: *Group Dynamics in Sport* (Eys, Evans, & Benson, 2020)

Section 1

Introduction

It takes much more than one supremely talented skinny man to win the Tour de France. That man matters, certainly, but....it's easy to lose sight of the importance of teammates in cycling. The Tour goes out of its way to make itself seem like an individual competition, giving the race leader a bright yellow jersey that can be seen from helicopters and propping him up on a podium after each stage to wave flowers and a plush lion at the cameras. But don't be fooled. Cycling is about much more than pure physical effort. Yellow jersey contenders need teammates to make sure they use their energy as efficiently as possible while climbing some of the biggest mountains in the world. And in perhaps no other sport are the support staff—the team directors, soigneurs, mechanics, and chefs—so critically important to the mission, too. Every Tour de France team is an intricate machine that could collapse if any part of it fails. (Bien, 2018, para. 1–4)

It might seem counterintuitive to kick-start a group dynamics book with an example of what is traditionally viewed as an independent sport. However, the above quote illustrates that groups are pervasive across sport types. Readers may typically associate the study of groups with more traditional contexts such as basketball, soccer, and volleyball. But, as will become clear throughout this book, athletes and coaches must contend with group scenarios in a lot of different ways. Team sport athletes coordinate their efforts against the actions of their opponents. Tennis players both train with and compete against members of their own club. Curlers decide on the leadership structure and throwing order of their group, and must constantly communicate regarding the conditions of the ice and the path of the rock. Youth sport coaches contend with and manage several different groups in their environment (e.g., athletes, coaching staff, parents, sport organization). These, of course, are just a few examples. As such, it is very important to set the stage before examining specific topics of sport group dynamics. In the chapters within this first section, the nature of groups and group dynamics (Chapter 1), how one studies groups (Chapter 2), and general ideas about group development (Chapter 3) are presented.

1

The Nature of Groups

[United States Women's Soccer Head Coach Jill] Ellis concurs with her captain that the squad's cohesiveness will be an invaluable team weapon once the US hits the pitch for the start of the Women's World Cup next June. 'This group is a tight group. They genuinely enjoy playing together,' Ellis said. 'There's a fun about how we play, and they enjoy it, and they feed off of that.' (Hunt, 2018, para. 8–9)

Membership and involvement in groups are pervasive characteristics of our society. We enter life as a member of society's strongest and most significant group—the family. As we grow and develop, we become members of, and are influenced by, other important groups in social and work settings. We attend school in groups, worship in groups, socialize in groups, and carry out business in groups. Also, play, exercise, and sport are often group activities. Even so-called individual sports like wrestling, badminton, and tennis are group activities since at least two people (the minimum number of people necessary to constitute a group) are required for competition (see Chapter 11 for greater elaboration on how individual sports are important group environments to understand). In group settings, we influence the behaviors, cognitions, and attitudes of other people and, in turn, are influenced ourselves. Overall, the groups to which we belong have a powerful impact on our lives (see Exhibit 1.1).

Although membership in groups is not always associated with positive outcomes, our involvement in groups seems inevitable. Baumeister and Leary (1995), drawing on research evidence from a wide cross section of areas in psychology, stated that the need to belong—the desire for interpersonal attachments—is a fundamental human motivation. Baumeister and Leary (1995) noted that a number of conditions must be present before a state, need, or condition is truly fundamental. The desire for interpersonal attachments satisfies all of these in that it:

Exhibit 1.1. Reasons Groups Are Influential and Important to Understand

Concept	Support	Implications for Sport
Groups are everywhere!	"No one knows for certain how many groups exist at this moment, but given the number of people on the planet and their groupish proclivities, 30 billion is a conservative estimate" (Forsyth, 2019, p. 5).	Whether one participates in team or individual sports, group membership is a given, for both task and social objectives.
We evolved to form and rely on groups.	"Tribal warfare and raiding are hypothesized to have selected for mechanisms that motivate individuals to identify with, form, and defend one's in-group, and also the cognitive capacity to discriminate 'us' versus 'them'" (Balish, Eys, & Schulte-Hostedde, 2013, p. 415).	If people have embedded social responses to groups, these are critical for understanding behaviors in team situations that involve stress, hierarchies, and competition.
Belonging to groups satisfies a fundamental human need.	"Human beings have a pervasive drive to form and maintain at least a minimum quantity of lasting, positive, and impactful interpersonal relationships" (Baumeister & Leary, 1995, p. 497).	Sport involvement with others has the potential to be rewarding beyond achieving the objectives of the activity itself. If sport groups are designed to be appealing, this may be useful to encourage greater participation.
Groups shape how we see ourselves.	"A person's feelings of state self-esteem are an internal, subjective index or marker of the degree to which the individual is being included versus excluded by other people" (Leary, Tambor, Terdal, & Downs, 1995, p. 518).	Sport groups are likely to have a substantial impact on how people see and value themselves.
Being left out of groups hurts.	"Ostracism can lead to a variety of responses, including (a) behaviors that reflect the desire to be liked and get re-included, (b) antisocial and aggressive behaviors, (c) a stunned and affectless state, and (d) attempts to flee the situation" (Williams, 2007, p. 445).	Deselection, clique development, and the value we attach to athletic achievements make sport a prominent context through which exclusion is experienced.
Groups make us behave in unusual ways.	"Potential reasons for engaging in [hazing] behaviors have been reported, such as an opportunity to show commitment to the sport and/or build group cohesion, and a desire to be accepted by the team" (Mishna, Kerr, McInroy, & MacPherson, 2019, p. 56).	Conformity to groups can be useful (e.g., participating and training together) or harmful (e.g., hazing). We need to understand groups to harness the positive aspects of groups in sport.

(a) is present across a wide variety of situations,
(b) has an important influence on thought and emotion,
(c) leads to health or adjustment problems if it is not satisfied,
(d) stimulates behavior designed to satisfy it,
(e) is present in all people,
(f) is not a product of some other motive (such as the need for safety), and
(g) has an influence on a large number of behaviors.

Because the need to belong is a fundamental motivation, it cannot be satisfied through mere social contact with strangers or individuals we dislike. Neither can it be satisfied through

Exhibit 1.2. Teamwork Is Considered Important for Individual and Team Success in Sport

General Manager George McPhee on the improbable 2017–2018 inaugural year success of the National Hockey League's Vegas Golden Knights:

> *It's a real team approach; we don't rely on certain individuals or certain stars. We are a team in every sense....What we wanted to do was acquire the most talented players we could, while making sure they were the right personalities for this team....We were still able to come up with the proper team construction, because that was not easy to get the right alignment of forwards, centers, defensemen, and goaltenders, while getting the very best assets. (Rybaltowski, 2018, para. 7, 9)*

Coach Steve Dolan on the University of Pennsylvania's first women's distance medley team victory at the Penn Relays:

> *'It's an historic moment... What I'm so proud of is sometimes you think it's possible but you actually have to capture the moment and do it, and to watch all four of them run to the best of their ability and put it together as a team was fantastic. I think they'll remember this for life.' [Runner Uchechi] Nwogwugwu echoed those sentiments, adding, 'I really wanted to do something special with these beautiful, lovely ladies and I'm so proud of everything we've accomplished today.' (Juliano, 2019, para.4, 8)*

Sveinn Asgeirsson, a board member of the Tolfan supporters' club, on the Iceland National Soccer Team upcoming challenge in the 2018 World Cup:

> *'We've been talking about Argentina...They don't play as a team. They're just 11 individuals, and we've got that over them—an Icelandic team who will do anything for each other on the pitch. If we can keep [Lionel] Messi down, anything is possible.' As Iceland have shown already, it really is. (Ames, 2018, para. 41)*

---

pleasant social interactions with strangers. Baumeister and Leary (1995) emphasized that "first, people need frequent personal contacts or interactions with the other person [and] second, people need to perceive that there is an interpersonal bond or relationship marked by stability, affective concern, and continuation into the foreseeable future" (p. 500).

Sport is one of the primary aspects of society that satisfies our need to belong. What do we know about the group in sport? Possibly not as much as we know about the family, army unit, or work group, but that picture is changing. One general purpose in writing this book was to review the body of research literature about group dynamics in sport groups given its practical importance. Exhibit 1.2 highlights some examples of the importance team dynamics have for sport performance. Before we enter into the specifics of group dynamics, however, it is useful to outline the thoughts of various theoreticians about the nature of groups.

The Reality of Groups

The object of psychology as a science is to describe, explain, predict, and control behavior. A group, though, is an abstraction or theoretical construct; only its individual members are real. The presence of a theoretical construct cannot be directly observed—it can only be inferred from behavior. Therefore, it is not surprising that social scientists have historically had difficulty agreeing on the real nature of groups. Conversely, the behavior of individuals, either alone or in collective situations, can be described, explained, predicted, and/or controlled. As a consequence, Allport (1924), a prominent psychologist in the 1920s, argued that groups are not real, and that any scientist who wished to understand human behavior should focus on the individual, not the group. Allport (1924) stated

> The only psychological elements discoverable are in the behavior and consciousness of the specific persons involved. All theories that partake of the group

fallacy have the unfortunate consequence of diverting attention from the true locus of cause and effect, namely the behavioral mechanisms of the individual ... if we take care of the individuals, psychologically speaking, the groups will be found to take care of themselves. (p. 9)

This issue may seem to be simply philosophical to the coach or athlete who could argue: "Of course, we have a team. We meet and practice, travel together, compete against other teams, have a history, and so on." They would be correct, but the issue raised by Allport (1924) is not whether an organization exists, whether it is successful, or whether it is recognized as a distinct entity. When he questioned the reality of groups, Allport (1924) questioned whether groups were anything more than the sum of the individual members.

Consider the hypothetical case of two mixed doubles tennis teams in competition. Allport (1924) might have argued that if the two males were identical in their ability, experience, and so on, and the two females were also identical in every way, then the two mixed doubles teams would be identical, including their behavior and performance. In short, Allport (1924) proposed that a group is simply a sum of its parts. If the parts are identical, the groups will be identical. As an extension of this fact, if we wish to describe, explain, predict, or control the behavior and performance of the doubles tennis teams, we must describe, explain, predict, and control the behavior and performance of the individual members. Inherent in this viewpoint is the assumption that there is no special chemistry that sets off one group or team from another.

In the decades following the publication of Allport's (1924) book, psychologists, sociologists, and anthropologists debated the reality of groups. Currently, there is almost universal agreement that groups are "real," that they differ from the simple sum of member attributes, and that group behavior and performance cannot be understood by simply examining individual behavior and performance. To illustrate, it might be useful to look at one argument supporting the conclusion that groups are real.

Mills (1984), a sociologist, pointed out that group goals are quite distinct from the goals established by individuals for themselves. He used the game of chess to illustrate his point. In chess, the goal of each of the two individual participants is to win; this personal goal is identical for both contestants. But, the goal of the dyad (the two contestants when they are considered together as a unit) can't be to win. There is no opponent for the unit represented by the two chess players. So, can we assume that this unit, the two chess players as a group, has no goal? Mills (1984) argued

> On the contrary, there is an idea in the minds of the two parties that refers to a desirable state of the dyad: it is to have a high-quality contest that each party wants to win, wherein play is imaginative, in which superior play does win. The group goal, as distinct from personal goals, then, is to have a good contest. (p. 94)

The point made by Mills (1984) has often been echoed by coaches and athletes. For example, in the 1987 Canada Cup Series, Canada and the Soviet Union (USSR) played four superb games. The first ended in a tie. The next two were tied in regulation time and extended to sudden-death overtime. One of these overtime games was won by the USSR, the second by Canada. In the final game, Canada scored a goal within the final two minutes of the third period to win 6–5. Prior to the last game, Mike Keenan, the coach of the Canadian team commented

There's a synergism involved in this and it has taken the game to greater levels than ever before. The chemistry in both teams and what it has brought out in each other is incredible. Both have been challenged to the ultimate and it has brought out the very best in both. To play at this level, the best players in the world have played as well as they've ever played. They're enjoying it. You can see it in their faces. (Kernaghan, 1987, p. C1)

Novak Djokovic, one of the world's top tennis players, provides another example of the synergism between two competitors. Referring to his long-time rival Rafael Nadal, he stated, "We make each other better players. We make each other work harder on our games, especially when we play each other. It's always a huge challenge" (Herman, 2013, para. 14).

Mills, Keenan, and Djokovic were essentially discussing the same thing. There's no doubt that the two opponents in any competition have the identical goal of winning, but they also share a common goal of playing a satisfying game. The fact that they share a common goal is evidence of the reality of groups. In summarizing his discussion, Mills (1984) pointed out

Two points need emphasis. First, the group goal is not the simple sum of personal goals, nor can it be directly inferred from them. It refers to a desirable state for the group, not simply a desirable state for individuals ... the second point is that the mental construct of the group goal resides not in some mystical collective mind, but in the minds of group members ... It may be shared by most or all group members, but since many other ideas are shared, that is not its distinction. What sets the concept of a group goal apart is that in content and substance it refers to the group as a unit—specifically to a desirable state of that unit. (p. 95)

Groups are real. They have goals, aspirations, character, and a personality different from the simple sum of the goals, aspirations, character, and personality possessed by individual group members. Further, individual behavior is different within group situations. The influence of the group can lead to increased conformity, deviance, tenacity, or many other behaviors individuals might not exhibit alone. Similarly, individual performance is different within group situations. Frequently, individual athletes who cannot or do not stand out by themselves are outstanding in a group setting.

The Utility of Groups

Given that scientists have had doubts about the reality of groups, it probably shouldn't be surprising that both lay people and social scientists have had misgivings about whether groups are positive or negative, good or bad, useful or detrimental. Exhibit 1.3 contains some of the popular sayings that have been passed on to succeeding generations. It should be apparent why these old sayings are contradictory to a layperson.

The contradictions are understandable if we consider that even among scientists there are disagreements about the utility of groups. Buys (1978a), a social scientist, wrote what he described as a partly tongue-in-cheek, partly serious article entitled "Humans Would Do Better without Groups," which presented a list of 10 negative, destructive consequences associated

Exhibit 1.3. Popular Sayings About the Utility of Groups for Task Productivity

The Group as a Benefit	The Group as a Liability
Two heads are better than one.	Too many cooks in the kitchen.
The more the merrier.	Three is a crowd.
Many hands make light work.	If you want things done well, do them yourself.
There is unity in numbers.	A camel is a horse developed by committee.

with group involvement. His fundamental point was that these negative consequences clearly show that otherwise rational, logical individuals often behave quite the opposite when they are within group situations. For example, *conformity* was identified by Buys (1978a) as one negative aspect of groups. In order for any group to be effective and operate in a coherent, unified fashion, its membership must ascribe to common standards and hold similar perceptions on what is acceptable and unacceptable. When individuals accept without question a group's decision to engage in destructive or anti-social behavior, it provides an excellent example of the negative potential of group conformity.

A second, negative correlate of group involvement is *groupthink*. The choice of the term, groupthink, was influenced by George Orwell's book, *1984*. According to Janis (1972), groupthink is a mode of thinking engaged in by members of highly cohesive groups that are strongly motivated to maintain unanimity. A catalyst for Janis' work was an interest in exploring the bases for some well-known, disastrous group endeavors such as the Bay of Pigs invasion, the inadequate defense of Pearl Harbor prior to World War II, and the escalation of the Vietnam War. Janis proposed that bad decisions can be made by groups if members develop such a degree of closeness that critical thinking is suspended or rendered ineffective. A set of shared illusions emerge that are accepted by all group members without serious dissent (see Chapter 13 for a more comprehensive discussion of groupthink).

A third negative aspect of group involvement is *deindividuation*—the loss of personal identity, self-awareness, and inner restraints resulting from the individual's submersion in the group. When Festinger, Pepitone, and Newcomb (1952) first introduced the term, they characterized deindividuation as follows: "individuals are not seen or paid attention to as individuals. The members do not feel that they stand out as individuals. Others are not singling a person out for attention nor is the person singling out others" (p. 282). The individual loses his/her sense of personal identity and becomes an indistinguishable part of the group. As a result of deindividuation, members of groups may behave in ways that are atypical of them when they are alone.

A good example of deindividuation in action comes from the aftermath of Game 7 for the National Hockey League 2011 Stanley Cup finals. The Vancouver Canucks played host to the Boston Bruins in the final game of the best-of-seven series in an attempt to capture their first championship. The result was a 4–0 win for the Boston Bruins. What happened next was a set of circumstances that is unfortunately not unique to Vancouver:

> Riot police fired tear gas, pepper spray, and flash bombs in downtown Vancouver Wednesday night to try to disperse angry rioters who set cars on fire, looted stores, and taunted police officers after the Canucks' 4–0 Stanley Cup final loss to the Boston Bruins....Two police cars were set on fire in a parking lot

on Cambie Street near one of the areas where police were being confronted by a few dozen people among the hundreds present who were throwing debris at officers…. The riots shook Vancouver residents, and prompted thousands to sign up to a Facebook campaign that aimed to identify rioters and looters. There is also a campaign underway to get people to clean up the city…. Witnesses were encouraged by Facebook campaign organizers to post pictures of rioters in the act, in the hopes that they might be recognized and identified. More than 20,000 people had joined by the morning Thursday. ("Riots Erupt," 2011, para. 1, 4–6)

Unfortunately, a loss of self-regulation in a mob setting can lead to destructive behaviors, but this is consistent with what would be expected of individuals in a state of deindividuation. As is evident in the example, however, perhaps one benefit of advanced technology and social media (specifically in these circumstances) is to identify the perpetrators and cause a reduction in perceptions of deindividuation in the future!

Inevitably, Buys's (1978a) thoughts produced a number of responses, in which his conclusion was criticized and alternate perspectives offered (Anderson, 1978; Green & Mack, 1978; Kravitz et al., 1978; Shaffer, 1978). Essentially, four major points were made in these rebuttals. One was that it isn't groups that are responsible for these negative behaviors, it is individuals. Consequently, if the behavior of individuals could be improved, groups would not be a problem. A second was that some of the phenomena listed by Buys (1978a) are characteristic of the collective behavior of individuals in crowds, not groups. A third was that many of the consequences listed by Buys (1978a) can be negative or positive depending on the context. On one hand, a social movement would be negative, for example, if it contributed to fascism and led to the elimination of civil liberties; on the other hand, it would be positive if it contributed to the enhancement of human dignity. Finally, it was pointed out that Buys (1978a) ignored many of the positive functions served by groups: the pursuit of civil liberties by action groups, the charitable work done by humanitarian groups, the effectiveness of the family unit in raising children, and so on.

The debate set off by Buys's (1978a) article is informative. The rebuttals leave no doubt concerning the question of whether groups can or should be eliminated from society—a view echoed by Buys himself. As he pointed out, "clearly, many forms of groups are beneficial, if not essential to humans. Indeed, it seems nonsensical to search for alternatives to human groups" (Buys, 1978b, p. 568). Groups are a necessary, integral, generally beneficial part of society.

Definitional Issues in the Study of Groups

In the previous two sections, it was pointed out that there has been some debate about both the reality of groups and their utility. Consequently, it probably does not come as a surprise to hear that there also has been considerable divergence in how a group should be defined. Definitional clarity is essential for effective communication; it ensures that people are discussing the same phenomenon. Thus, for example, we might state that sport is a useful vehicle to teach children aggression. Different sets of readers might define aggression quite differently and take a different meaning from that statement. For one set, the terms aggression and assertiveness might be synonymous; for another set the terms aggression and violence might be synonymous. The nature, antecedents, and consequences of those contrasting interpretations of aggression are dramatically different. So, it should be obvious that for the sake of definitional clarity, it is important to ensure that there is consistency in our understanding of what we mean by the term group.

What a Group is Not

McGrath (1984) pointed out that "groups are not just any aggregate of two or more people" (p. 6). He defined groups as "social aggregates that involve mutual awareness and potential mutual interaction" (McGrath, 1984, p. 7), and then pointed out what types of social aggregations lack these criteria (and, therefore, cannot be considered a group). According to McGrath (1984), these include

- *Artificial aggregates* such as a statistical group formed on the basis of a common property such as age, sex, social class (e.g., 20-year-old Danish university students);
- *Unorganized aggregates* such as (a) an audience that is attending to a common set of stimuli (e.g., people watching a tennis match), (b) a crowd that is in physical proximity attending to a common set of stimuli (e.g., Indianapolis 500 attendees), or (c) a public that has and is attending to a common set of issues, has indirect interaction on these issues, but may not be in physical proximity (e.g., advocates for the need to do something about climate change);
- *Units with patterned relationships* such as (a) a culture where the members share common customs, language, etc. (e.g., Canadians), (b) a subculture where members share common customs, language, etc. that are in contrast in specific ways to that of the surrounding culture (e.g., French Canadians), or (c) a kinship group where members are related by birth or marriage (e.g., the extended Eys family),
- *Structured social units* such as (a) a society where members share a geographical region, political system, and relationships characterized by interdependence, or (b) a community that is a subdivision of a society,
- *Deliberately designed social units* such as (a) an organization where a large aggregate of people is recruited for specific roles (e.g., United Way), or (b) a suborganization that is a portion of a large organization (e.g., the University fundraisers for the United Way), and
- *Less deliberately designed social units* such as an *association* that are formed for specific purposes and where interaction among members is present (e.g., Rugby Union's Six Nations Championships competed among France, England, Wales, Italy, Scotland, and Ireland).

McGrath (1984) pointed out that groups may develop within these settings; the potential is present. He emphasized, though, that each of the scenarios above, on their own, do not inherently satisfy the criteria that help to constitute a group.

What a Group Is

Every group is like all other groups, like some other groups, and like no other group. A therapy group, a social group, and a sport group are similar in some ways, but they are significantly different in numerous aspects. Consequently, theoreticians studying different types of groups have focused on different characteristics. As a result, the definitions for a group fall into a number of categories or types, each of which highlights an important aspect of the nature of groups.

One general category of definitions emphasizes that groups are characterized by a common fate for their members. Individuals may contribute to the team outcome, but in basketball, cricket, netball, and field hockey, the group wins or loses. The following definition serves as an example of the common fate definition of a group: "A set of individuals who share a common fate, that is, who are interdependent in the sense that an event [that] affects one member is likely to affect all" (Fiedler, 1967, p. 6).

A second category of definitions highlights the fact that membership in groups—in contrast to being present in a crowd of people—is associated with mutual benefit for the individuals. It was pointed out above that we have a fundamental need to form interpersonal attachments. It is enjoyable and rewarding to be a member of a badminton team; those rewards and benefits are not present when the individual is a member of a crowd awaiting the arrival of a bus. An example of a definition that emphasizes the mutual benefit aspects of a group is "a collection of individuals whose existence as a collection is rewarding to the individuals" (Bass, 1960, p. 39).

Because all groups are characterized by a stable pattern of relationships among members, one of the two most common approaches has been to define a group through its social structure. Thus, for example, status differences, roles, and group norms are not relevant (or present) in a collection of individuals meeting for a class for the first time; they are relevant (and present) in a synchronized swimming team. The following definition highlights elements of social structure:

> A group is a social unit that consists of a number of individuals who stand in (more or less) definite status and role relationships to one another and that possesses a set of values or norms of its own regulating the behavior of individual members, at least in matters of consequence to the group. (Sherif & Sherif, 1956, p. 144)

Newcomb's (1951) definition further suggests that a group's "members share norms about something ... [including] norms concerning the roles of the group members ... These distinctive features—shared norms and interlocking roles—presuppose a more than transitory relationship of interaction and communication" (p. 3).

Another very common approach highlights important processes that occur in groups such as interaction and communication among members. Since interaction and communication can occur among strangers in a movie lineup, for example, definitions focusing on group processes characteristically elaborate upon the quality of the relationship among the individuals. Some examples are

- Two or more persons who are interacting with one another in such a manner that each person influences and is influenced by each other person (Shaw, 1981, p. 8);
- For a collection of individuals to be considered a group there must be some interaction (Hare, 1976, p. 4);
- A group is an aggregation of two or more people who are to some degree in dynamic interrelation with one another (McGrath, 1984, p. 8); and

- We mean by a group a number of persons who communicate with one another, often over a span of time, and who are few enough so that each person is able to communicate with all others, not at second hand, through other people, but face-to-face (Homans, 1950, p. 1).

One difficulty with definitions that are based on common fate, mutual benefit, social structure, and group processes is that all of these characteristics could be present without necessarily guaranteeing the existence of a group. For example, two strangers might independently sneak into a gymnasium to shoot baskets on a Sunday morning. If the custodian discovers them, they would suffer a common fate: eviction. The presence of a second person could be beneficial from the perspective of having company, retrieving a stray ball, sharing the blame for sneaking in, and so on. It would also be possible for interaction and communication to occur, and norms (e.g., retrieve the other person's ball if it rolls close) and role relationships (e.g., teacher and pupil) to develop. But, the two individuals would not be a group if they didn't consider themselves to be a group. Therefore, some authors have proposed that a fundamental characteristic of a group is self-categorization. Definitions that highlight the self-categorization aspect of groups include "two or more individuals [who] … perceive themselves to be members of the same social category" (Turner, 1982, p. 15), and "a group exists when two or more people define themselves as members of it and when its existence is recognized by at least one other" (Brown, 1988, pp. 2–3). All of these characteristics have relevance for the definition of a sport team or group.

A Sport Team Defined

Even a cursory examination of the above definitions shows that all have some utility. Thus, we can draw on each to produce a reasonable definition of a sport team: a collection of two or more individuals who possess a common identity, have common goals and objectives, share a common fate, exhibit structured patterns of interaction and modes of communication, hold common perceptions about group structure, are personally and instrumentally interdependent, reciprocate interpersonal attraction, and consider themselves to be a group.

A basketball team, whether it is in an organized league or competing in three-on-three competitions, serves to highlight the components of this definition of a sport team. There are, of course, at least two people involved. The common identity exists when individual team members, opponents, and nonteam members all view the group as a unit distinguishable from other units. In sport, a common identity can result from the team's name if the team is competing in an organized league. Even in informal competitions, however, self-categorization produces a sense of common identity in athletes competing against an opponent.

The very specific objective of every sport competition—winning—serves to ensure that teams have at least one shared common purpose. Also, the common fate that is universal among sport teams is winning or losing.

Numerous examples are available for the structured patterns of interaction that exist within a sport team. The most obvious example is the offensive and defensive alignments that a team adopts. Any newcomer to a team requires some time to become completely familiar with the specific system. Another example is the distinctions made implicitly or explicitly between rookies and veterans early in training camp. The locker room assignments, uniform distinctions, and initiation practices are manifestations of structured patterns of interaction.

Basketball teams provide a good example of the appearance of structured modes of communication. Both general terminology—screen, back door, power forward—and the specific manner in which it is selectively used on particular teams make sport teams unique. Also, the specific terminology conveying particular offensive and defensive assignments is another. Although members of a team can readily translate meaningless names or phrases into something meaningful, a nonteam member cannot.

The structure of any group consists of roles, norms, positions, and status. As soon as athletes forming a team begin to interact and communicate, status differences evolve, positions are assumed, and role expectations and norms begin to form. On a basketball team, positions are established almost immediately. Status differences evolve because of differences in ability or knowledge, and roles (e.g., rebounder, shooter, captain) and norms (e.g., we all rebound and play tough defense) develop from individual interactions and communications.

Personal and task interdependence are inherent within the nature of the sport itself; the rules of sport dictate the size, general structure, and organization of the sport team. For example, an individual cannot play a basketball game alone; a specific number of participants are permitted on the soccer pitch at any given time; there are general rules on how volleyball teams must be aligned prior to the serve; and in hockey, interactions with opponents in the pregame warm-up must conform to certain standards.

Interpersonal attraction generally evolves from sport team participation. Although there are documented exceptions, friendships are usually present to some degree on most teams.

The final criterion—self-categorization—is fundamental. It develops immediately when a team forms. Even in a two-on-two basketball game played on the playground with strangers, the distinction of "we" versus "they" evolves as soon as the teams are formed.

Group Dynamics Defined

The title of our book includes the term *group dynamics*, which refers to "the influential interpersonal processes that occur within and between groups; also, the scientific study of those processes" (Forsyth, 2019, p. 18). As it pertains to the latter aspect of this definition, the protocols involved in the study of groups are discussed in depth in Chapter 2. However, we acknowledge that sport teams are characterized by energy, vitality, growth, and development; they are dynamic, not static. That dynamism is manifested in the developing nature of the structure of sport teams, their cohesiveness, and their collective efficacy (as examples). It is also manifested in interaction and communication among team members, group decision-making, and team achievements. Our book represents an attempt to summarize the body of research associated with the study of sport teams and focuses on the nature, antecedents, and consequences of the dynamic group processes characteristic of sport teams.

Conceptual Frameworks for Groups

Groups are a complex phenomenon. In order to provide greater insight into the nature of groups, numerous theoreticians have advanced conceptual frameworks that focus on their properties and/or their processes. In essence, frameworks are useful because they allow for the synthesis of knowledge under the umbrella of organizing principles and help to direct research and application (Jason et al., 2016). Given that any conceptual framework (or model) is a simplified representation of reality, it has both disadvantages and advantages. It is useful to examine these prior to introducing some conceptual or organizing framework.

One disadvantage that might be obvious is that any conceptual framework, because it is a simplified representation, can never adequately portray the total phenomenon. The developers of a conceptual framework are like the fabled three blindmen who were placed at different parts of an elephant and asked to provide a description. Each was a good scientist and provided a completely reliable and objective description of the elephant, but none of the individual descriptions was adequate as a portrayal of the total elephant. In the same vein, a conceptual framework, no matter how comprehensive, cannot provide a valid portrayal of a theoretical construct.

A second disadvantage is that human behavior is dynamic while conceptual frameworks tend to present a static picture; they are a photograph rather than a video representation. A photograph freezes its objects in a particular time and place. Thus, for example, a portrait of a sport team taken today might include smiling, contented athletes. Another portrait taken tomorrow could present a different picture.

A third, somewhat related disadvantage, is that conceptual frameworks generally portray simple causal relationships. In previous editions of this book, relationships were indicated in our framework suggesting that cohesion, for example, leads to improved group processes. In some cases, researchers used the framework as a theoretical basis for their work. This is not wholly wrong, but clearly research (and common sense) shows that there are reciprocal relationships among elements of group structure (e.g., roles), emergent states (e.g., cohesion, collective efficacy), and group processes (e.g., communication, cooperation), not to mention both group and individual outcomes.

Despite these shortcomings, there are advantages to the use of a conceptual framework. One major advantage is that complex topics can be simplified and more readily explained and understood. If the group is so abstract that early psychologists even questioned its existence, how can we make any sense of it without a simplified representation?

A second advantage is that assumptions can be more readily drawn about how the individual components of the complex phenomena are related. In the case of the sport team, a conceptual framework might permit us to make assumptions about the interrelationships of role clarity, role acceptance, team cohesion, and team performance.

Finally, a conceptual framework can help clarify what is known and unknown about a phenomenon, and, consequently, provide some direction for further research. Again, if we take a sport team as an example, a conceptual framework might serve to highlight the fact that we know very little about the relationship of density and group size to athlete satisfaction in sport. A conceptual framework might serve as a catalyst for research to examine this issue and help to highlight the complexity of groups, generally, and sport teams, specifically.

A Conceptual Framework for Group Effectiveness

All groups strive to be effective, but effectiveness takes on different meanings for different groups. A police force might judge itself effective if the community has a low crime rate, while an effective sorority could be one that maintains its annual membership, and an effective investment club is likely to be one that makes money for its members.

What makes a sport team effective? This is a complex issue. In professional sport, for example, there are a number of barometers of team effectiveness (e.g., making money). For

Exhibit 1.4. Steiner's (1972) Conceptual Framework of Group Effectiveness

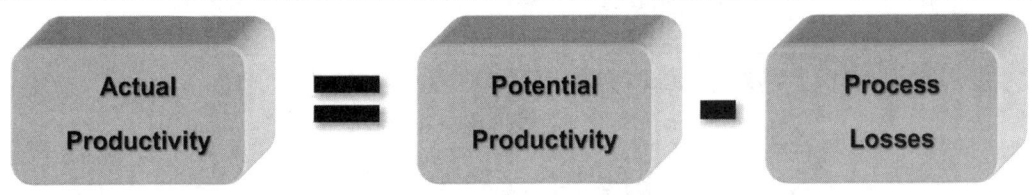

the purposes of the present discussion, it is useful to focus on team outcomes as a measure of effectiveness. In 1972, Ivan Steiner advanced a simple and popular conceptual framework of group effectiveness. A schematic representation of this conceptual framework is presented in Exhibit 1.4.

Steiner (1972) pointed out that actual productivity is the performance that is attained, whereas potential productivity is the performance that might be obtained, based upon the relevant resources in the group. The group's resources include the knowledge, ability, and skills of the individual players, their respective level of training, the adequacy of their equipment, and so on. The actual steps, actions, or behaviors taken individually or collectively by group members to carry out the group task represent the group processes. When individuals work in groups, communication, coordination, and interaction are necessary. These can be relatively ineffective and losses in efficiency occur. Steiner proposed that the two major sources of losses that occur in any group are the result of faulty coordination and reduced motivation.

Steiner's (1972) conceptual framework can be illustrated with a hypothetical example of a tug-of-war team. In the case of a two-person team, each individual might be able to pull 100 kg. Thus, the potential productivity of the group based on the group's resources is 200 kg. However, the group would likely pull less than this (possibly 180 kg) because of the inability of the two people to coordinate their efforts and/or because each person might expect the other to carry the main load. Therefore, the group would have experienced a process loss of 20 kg.

As a group increases in size, its potential productivity increases. A volleyball team that keeps 30 members throughout the season has a greater likelihood of having the necessary resources to handle almost every situation. There will always be enough players for scrimmages, replacements will be available in case of injuries, specialized lineups can be used against certain teams, and so on. But, with an increase in resources, there will also be an increase in the number of problems associated with effectively and efficiently managing the group. With 30 players, it is more difficult for the coach to run an effective practice in which all of the players are active. Frequent personal communication with each individual player is difficult. If lineups are rotated, the players will not be as familiar with each other. Also, and more importantly perhaps, with increased numbers in the group, individual team members may suffer a loss in motivation and personal accountability.

The application of Steiner's (1972) conceptual framework to the effectiveness of sport teams in general is illustrated in Exhibit 1.5. In this example, Team A will be more effective than Team B if

(a) it possesses greater relevant resources and experiences fewer process losses,
(b) it has greater relevant resources and experiences approximately equal to process losses, or
(c) it has approximately equal relevant resources and experiences fewer process losses.

Exhibit 1.5. The Application of Steiner's (1972)
Conceptual Framework of Group Effectiveness to the
Analysis of Sport Teams

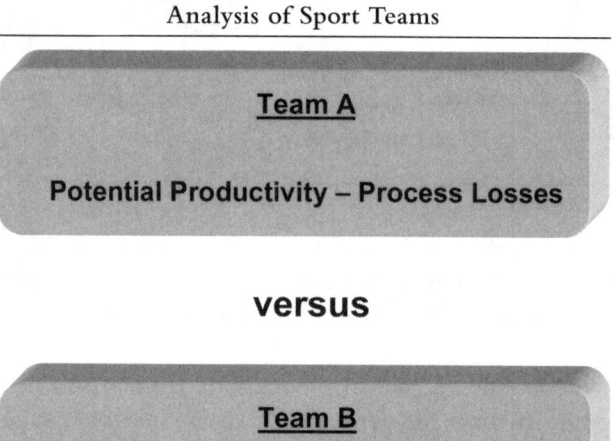

In professional sport where the desire for league parity has led to efforts to equalize team resources (e.g., the weaker teams have greater chances to draft first; soft or hard salary caps are imposed on teams in certain leagues), reducing process losses is crucial. Similarly, in amateur sport, coaches have limited control over their resources (they generally coach the talent available and have very little opportunity to supplement or change their roster during a season), thus efforts need to be made to reduce process losses. How can process losses be reduced? How can group effectiveness be increased?

Researchers in psychology, sociology, anthropology, and business have been concerned with these questions since their origin as sciences. Fortunately, information (in various chapters of the book) is available to provide the coach with some guidelines and insights.

A General Conceptual Framework for the Nature of Groups

McGrath (1984) provided a useful conceptual framework for the study of groups (see Exhibit 1.6). According to McGrath, the soul or essence of a group is *group interaction processes*: team members interacting with one another. Members of a netball team, for example, practice together regularly, interact for social and for task purposes, and come to decisions that have both personal and collective implications. In short, members are constantly interacting together in some way that is meaningful to them.

McGrath (1984) also pointed out that five general categories of factors influence group interaction processes. One of these is the *properties of the group members*. Thus, for example, members of the netball team could differ in ability, age, personality, height, weight, religion, and a host of other biological, social, and psychological attributes. These attributes have the potential to influence the interactions that occur among team members.

McGrath (1984) also identified *group structure* as another potentially important set of properties influencing group interaction processes. The properties of the group members (their ability and age for example) have an influence on the development of status differences,

Exhibit 1.6. A Conceptual Framework by McGrath (1984) for the Study of Groups

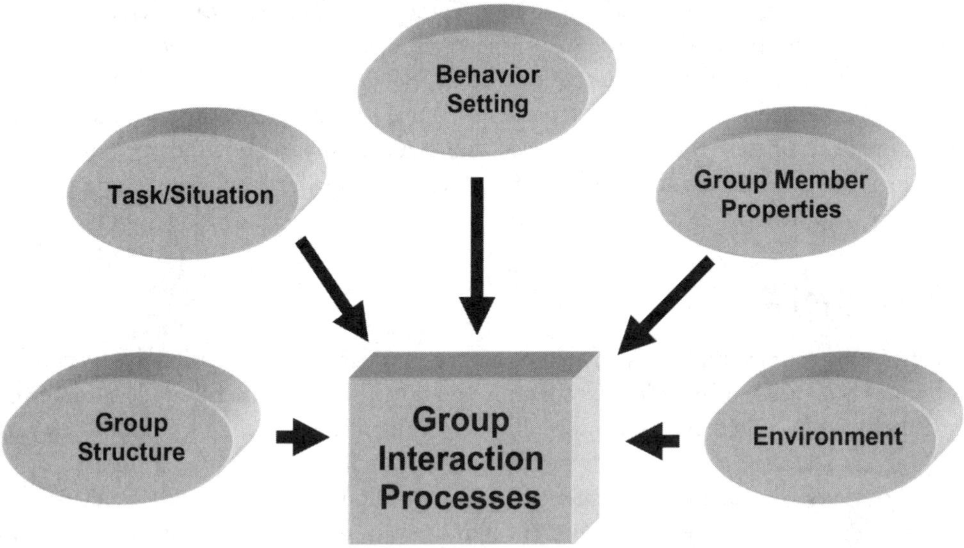

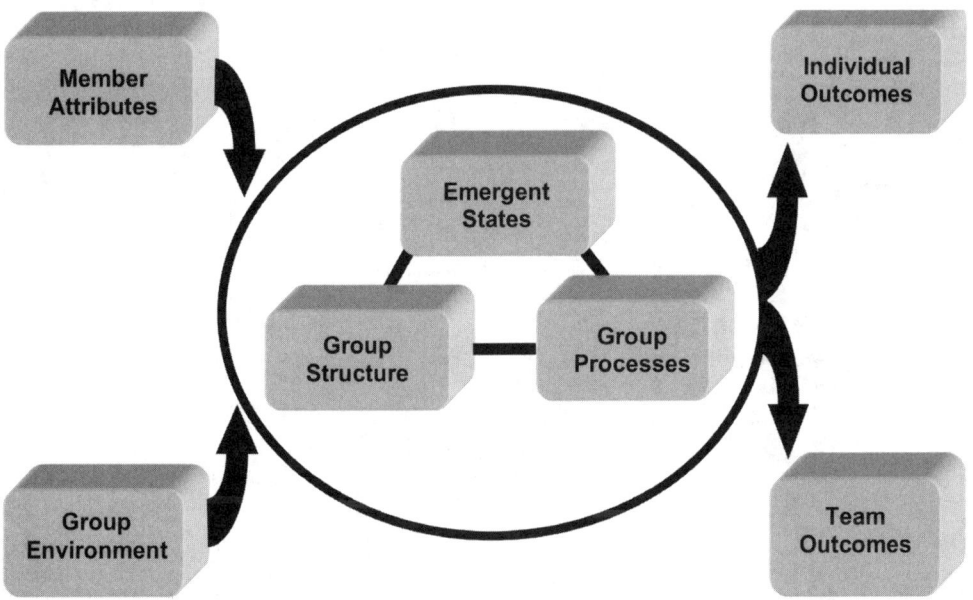

role responsibilities, player positions, and so on. In turn, group structure influences and is influenced by group interaction processes. An older, more skillful netball player, for example, is likely to have higher team status than the majority of other team members. As a consequence, in any team interactions, her opinions would likely have more impact on the collective. Further, the manner in which teammates respond to high and low status colleagues is qualitatively and quantitatively different.

Properties of the environment also influence interactions within groups. Members of a netball team might train together in the off-season. A crowded, noisy weight room would be less

Exhibit 1.7. A Conceptual Framework for the Study of Sport Teams

conducive to discussions surrounding task (e.g., weight training techniques) or social (e.g., family concerns) issues than a spacious, quiet weight room. The physical, sociocultural, and technological properties of different environments influence group interaction processes.

Finally, the *nature of the task/situation* also influences group interaction processes. The members of a netball team could be together to train, to compete against another team, to attend a banquet, or to participate in the wedding of a teammate. The fundamental nature of these tasks/situations differs and, consequently, the nature of the group interaction processes would vary accordingly.

A Conceptual Framework for Sport Teams

The conceptual framework for a sport team that was used as the organizational framework for this book is presented in Exhibit 1.7, though we do note that other useful models/frameworks exist to help understand teams (see information regarding the conceptual framework for teamwork and team effectiveness in sport outlined by McEwan and Beauchamp, 2014).

The outputs, the major consequences in groups, consist of both individual products (e.g., individual performance and adherence) and group products (e.g., team outcome and group stability). The throughputs are the group's structure, processes, and emergent states. Finally, the inputs are the attributes of individual group members, and the nature of the group's environment.

2

The Study of Groups

For thousands of years, kings, priests, politicians, educators, producers, fathers, and mothers—in fact, all individuals, have been trying day by day to influence smaller or larger groups. One might assume that this would have led to accumulated wisdom of a well integrated nature. Unfortunately, nothing is farther from the truth. (Lewin, 1947, p. 9)

The specific definition advanced by Cartwright and Zander (1968) for group dynamics is a "field of inquiry dedicated to advancing knowledge about the nature of groups, the laws of their development, and their interrelations with individuals, other groups, and larger institutions" (p. 7). The study of groups, as pointed out by Lewin (1947) in the quote used to introduce this chapter, pervades many aspects of our daily lives. Groups are elemental to being human. Despite our constant immersion in groups over the course of human history, much remains to be understood about how groups function. Certainly, we all have a viewpoint about why some groups thrive and others flounder. However, our basic intuitions about groups are not always correct. In fact, our intuitions can often lead us astray.

Commonsense versus Science

Kerlinger (1986) suggested that there are five differences between commonsense and science, and these differences illustrate why the former is a poor substitute for the latter. Essentially, all of these differences are associated with the words systematic and control. One difference is in how theories are developed and used. Whereas scientific theories evolve from systematic and controlled observations, commonsense theories often evolve from fanciful explanations of natural and human phenomena. For example, consider the wide range of theories that a person might use to account for the common cold, to justify stereotypic views of various ethnic groups, and to account for the motives of nations and their leaders. In contrast to these fanciful, often illogical explanations, scientists systematically build, test, evaluate, and modify their theories.

Another distinction between science and commonsense is that in contrast to the scientist, a person with a commonsense theory often tests it in a selective fashion. Evidence consistent with the theory is retained as a verification of the theory while exceptions are de-emphasized or ignored. For example, scouts in Major League Baseball often make assertions about players based on some justifiable reasons—pitching or batting record for example—but also some reasons that aren't logically critical, such as how someone looks when they bat or pitch. However, these evaluations now have to compete against quantified predictions of a players' success using sabermetrics. As popularized in the movie *Moneyball,* pitcher Chad Bradford had an unconventional and slow throwing style that threw many scouts off—but mathematical modelling predicted (correctly) that he would become a valuable major league player.

As pointed out above, an important feature of science that differentiates it from commonsense is the concept of control. Attempts are made when testing scientific theories to control for the influence of extraneous variables to eliminate them as possible causes for the effect being studied. Is having the opportunity to bat last an advantage for the home team in Major League Baseball? To answer this question, a layperson might simply point to the number of times home teams have won games in their last at bat. This is not a valid test of the issue. As home teams typically have more crowd support, are more familiar with their own stadium, and have not had to travel, they possess these advantages as well. Unless it is possible to account for the possible influences of the crowd, familiarity, and travel, the question cannot be validly addressed. Put simply, it is crucial to systematically rule out alternative explanations for an observed pattern.

A fourth difference is that scientists typically look for complexity in how variables might be related. In contrast, a layperson typically arrives quickly at a simple cause-effect solution. Thus, for example, a layperson who writes to an airline urging it to forbid its pilots from putting the fasten seatbelts sign on during the flight because it always caused a turbulent ride might be better advised to reexamine his or her conclusion about causality.

The final difference is that a layperson is prepared to accept a metaphysical explanation for events while a scientist is not. A metaphysical explanation is one that cannot be tested. For instance, "it is God's will," or "it's in the cards," or "it is fate" would not be explanations that a scientist would advance; they are not testable and limit further exploration of a given question. This is not to say that scientists are necessarily atheists or agnostics; only that a scientist pursues explanations that can be examined with the scientific method.

The Scientific Method

The methodology of science involves proceeding through sequential stages. This involves (1) gathering existing knowledge about a topic to generate a specific research question, (2) formulating a hypothesis, (3) testing the hypothesis through systematic observation and/or experimentation, and (4) refining explanations by ruling out alternative explanations and attempting to replicate the results. As highlighted by the latter point, a key aspect of the scientific method is that it is an ongoing and iterative process. Descriptions and explanations advanced by researchers should be considered as subject to revision, context-dependent, and reflective of an imperfect understanding.

Generating a Research Question

Anatole France, winner of the Nobel Prize for Literature in 1921, opined that "the greatest virtue of [humankind] is perhaps curiosity." Curiosity is the foundation of science. A researcher in the field of group dynamics, for example, might wonder whether the large roster size of her daughter's water polo team has an impact on team cohesion. The question might arise after the mother attends a practice and sees that not all of the athletes within the group regularly interact with one another. In fact, she notices that there seems to be sub-groups or cliques within the team.

Whereas she quickly generated a creative idea, it is unlikely that the issue of roster size and team cohesion would become a research question immediately. As Kerlinger (1986) pointed out, the "first and most important step is to get the idea out in the open, to express the problem in some reasonably manageable form … [the researcher] must struggle with it, try it out, live with it" (p. 110). Eventually, researchers pose a question to themselves. Thus, a group dynamics researcher might ask if there is a relationship between roster size and team cohesion in sport teams.

Formulating a Hypothesis

The first two processes—idea generation and hypothesis generation—are virtually linked and the transition between the two is subtle. Scientists rarely, if ever, move from an idea to a hypothesis without some hunch or intuition about the relation between the variables. As we discussed in the previous chapter, an existing theory or conceptual framework can be immensely valuable in helping researchers formulate a well-reasoned hypothesis. In the current example, the group dynamics researcher, relying on her knowledge of groups, her daughter's experiences, and/or her own experience in social and work situations might hypothesize that teams with larger rosters are more likely to have athletes who feel their team is less cohesive.

Hypothesis Testing

The next stage in the scientific process is to test the hypothesis. To do this, the scientist must operationally define the variables. An operational definition gives meaning to a variable by outlining how the researcher intends to measure it. This step is critical to ensure that we can be confident that we are studying the concepts that we truly hope to study. If the operational definition is illogical, unreliable, or not valid, the study and its conclusions are useless.

In the case of the roster size-cohesion issue, the researcher may have a relatively easy time operationally defining roster size. She would only need to go from team to team and count members. At least, this may seem straightforward at first glance. If she chose to study different sports, however, this measure may not be a good operational definition. The average football team has a much larger roster size than the average basketball team. Optimal group sizes vary from team to team and sport to sport (discussed more in Chapter 4). Thus, it would be important to consider team size in relation to the type of sport. Maybe the best operational definition of team size, if she were measuring several sports, would be roster size proportional to the average roster size in a league (roster size/average league roster size) or roster size proportional to the number of players in competition at a given time (roster size/number of players required to compete). What might seem like a simple issue often requires careful thought.

Operationally defining team cohesion might prove to be even more of a challenge. First, team cohesion is a theoretical construct; it is not something that we can directly observe or measure. It would be necessary to arrive at an answer to the following questions: What is team cohesion, and how do we properly assess it? In quantitative studies, once researchers have carefully conceptualized the nature of a theoretical construct, they then have to decide how to best measure it. In some cases, researchers may have to develop a psychometrically sound questionnaire, which is a laborious and time consuming process. Fortunately, as we will discuss throughout this book, a range of psychometrically sound questionnaires have been developed by group dynamics researchers in sport. In the case of team cohesion, for example, Carron, Widmeyer, and Brawley (1985) developed a conceptual framework in which they highlighted the distinction between social cohesion and task cohesion, as well as the distinction between an individual's attraction to the group and perceptions of group unity (see Chapter 14 for a detailed overview of cohesion and its correlates). In other cases, researchers may rely upon behavioral observation, audio-recordings, or unobtrusive measures (e.g., archival data indicating team performance).

Ruling out Alternative Explanations and Replication

Although a researcher may infrequently repeat a study exactly as it was carried out originally, replication is an essential part of the scientific method for many reasons. First, some samples of participants may be atypical of the population in general. Do 10-year old girls have the same response to a large roster size as do college males? Thus, the group dynamics researcher might obtain results that are age and gender specific. Also it is possible that the sample tested by the researcher might be idiosyncratic and unrepresentative of 10-year old female hockey players generally. Further, scientists can make errors in every stage of the process—during data collection, data entry, and data analysis. Finally, and unfortunately, cases of academic fraud have been documented. These include obfuscation (omitting unfavorable findings), fabrication (making up data), falsification (manipulation of the process to stimulate or discourage a particular result), and incorrect claims (advancing conclusions unsupported by the data). So, repeating all or part of a study is an important consideration in the scientific method.

Replication comes in various forms. At times, researchers may complete similar studies to those completed previously but with important differences. Perhaps they may utilize a different measure of cohesion or roster size, complete the study in a substantially different context, or conduct a study where they also measure a construct they expect to be responsible for the association (e.g., lack of playing time). Studies like this may help to conceptually replicate studies. However, direct replication of research using an identical design and similar context is also a critical step—especially for our most important and verifiable findings. In this case, a researcher would attempt to follow each step exactly as a previous researcher did. This is why accurate and detailed reporting is so critical to the scientific method.

Special Considerations in the Study of Sport Teams

Up to this point, we have sketched out the scientific method but glossed over several important considerations specific to researching groups. Researchers who study sport groups are interested in the individuals embedded within groups. As will become clear throughout this book, groups can powerfully shape how individuals think, feel, and act. At the same time, individuals also influence the groups to which they belong. Nonetheless, some of the most fundamental research questions in group dynamics are rooted in exploring factors that differentiate between teams. Why do some groups thrive and others implode? Although a detailed discussion of the methods and statistical intricacies are beyond the scope of this book (see Humphrey and LeBreton, 2018, for a detailed review of multilevel theory and analysis), a few key considerations need to be highlighted.

One key consideration is which level of analysis is most appropriate for the research question at hand. Understanding the dynamics of a group means understanding how multiple individuals interact with one another in the context of the group, as well as how and why these interaction patterns emerge and change across time. Group dynamics researchers are forced to grapple with questions at the individual level (e.g., what are an athlete's motives, thoughts, feelings, and behaviors?), interpersonal level (e.g., what relationship does the athlete have with their coach or closest teammate?), and the group level (e.g., how does one team differ from others?).

As an example, Benson, Šiška, Eys, Priklerová, and Slepička (2016) were interested in evaluating the performance-cohesion relationship in elite youth sport teams. To create a group-level measure of cohesion, they aggregated athletes' individual cohesion perceptions within each team—computing an average cohesion score for each team. An objective group performance measure was created by using the team's winning percentage unique to each time point. They measured group cohesion and team performance at multiple times throughout the season, demonstrating that team performance earlier in a season positively predicted task and social cohesion later in the season. In this case, the researchers were most interested in the group level association between cohesion and performance, even though they measured the cohesion perceptions of each athlete individually.

Researchers, however, are also interested in questions that span multiple levels of analysis. Staying with the example of cohesion, a researcher might want to know whether a specific personality trait (e.g., grandiose narcissism, discussed in Chapter 5) influences an athlete's confidence heading into an important game. Whereas this is an association between constructs at the individual level, a researcher might also be interested in how the relation between narcissism and athlete confidence is affected by membership in a highly cohesive group. As a hypothetical example, perhaps people higher in narcissism are typically more confident heading into an important game where they will be in the spotlight. However, perhaps being part of a cohesive team evens the playing field, so to speak, helping people lower in narcissism feel just as confident.

As alluded to in the previous example, temporal issues must also be taken into account. As the term dynamics implies, group dynamics researchers are often interested in changes across time. By collecting data from individual athletes or coaches at multiple time points, we learn a great deal from how responses can change across time. This is complicated when we also use data from the group at multiple time points. As two examples, group processes and performance are often tracked across time. In both cases, data must be collected at multiple time points. For example, a coach who implements a team-building protocol might want to know if (a) team-building activities improved the team's performance, and (b) if this increase in performance was because teammates communicated more frequently. This would require measuring baseline levels of communication within the team, as well as communication before and after the introduction of the team-building protocol. Researchers would also have to assess

Exhibit 2.1. Advantages and Disadvantages of Research Protocols in the Study of Sport Teams

Research Protocol	Advantages	Disadvantages
Nonexperimental Protocols		
Archival Studies	Access to substantial amount of data Statistical power is often not an issue No influence of collection/storage of data Accuracy of analyses can be verified easily Changes in relationship can be examined	Cannot infer causation Nature of questions is restricted
Qualitative research	Obtaining detailed information on a topic Generates additional questions/hypotheses Ability to ask diverse set of questions	Applicability to other groups/situations Researcher bias Cannot infer causation Participant reactivity to observer Social desirability
Field Studies	Spontaneous behaviors observed/recorded	Applicability to other groups/situations Cannot infer causation Participant reactivity to observer
Correlational Studies	Insights obtained without manipulating group or environment	Cannot infer causation
Experimental Protocols		
Laboratory Experiment	High degree of control Able to infer causation	Limited generalizability Experimenter demand
Field Experiment	High external validity Able to examine treatments not applicable to laboratory situations	Decreased control over external factors

performance at multiple time points to determine if teams were performing better as a function of changes in communication. Put simply, studying group dynamics can be challenging!

Research Protocols in the Study of Sport Teams

Once researchers in the area of group dynamics in sport have generated a clear research question and identified the appropriate level of analysis, it is then crucial to consider the different protocols one could adopt in the testing phase. When classifying protocols, we commonly group them into *nonexperimental* and *experimental designs* (see Exhibit 2.1). In research using nonexperimental protocols, there is no attempt by the researcher to influence the participants' responses. Conversely, in research using experimental protocols, participants are assigned randomly to two or more groups, at least one of which receives a treatment or manipulation. The specific approaches used within each of these two general types of protocols are outlined below.

Nonexperimental Protocols

Archival studies. Spanning a wide cross section of areas including medicine, economics, geography, sociology, and so on, researchers routinely access data that have been collected and stored. The archival researcher may be (but typically has not been) involved in the data collection. The data are generally available and researchers are able to access them to test a hypothesis. Research on the home advantage—a topic discussed in Chapter 4—is typically carried out using archival data. By going to the websites of various professional and amateur organizations, researchers have been able to answer a host of questions about the home advantage:

- What is the extent of the home advantage in different sports?
- Has the extent of the home advantage increased or decreased over time?
- Does size of the home crowd and/or its density have any effect on the home advantage?
- To what extent does travel—including, for example, distance covered, number of time zones crossed, mode of transportation, and days away from home—influence the home advantage?
- Is there evidence of officiating bias in the Olympics?

An example of a comprehensive archival study on the home advantage was carried out by Pollard and Pollard (2005). They were interested in examining long term trends in the home advantage in professional team sports. As a consequence, a total of over 400,000 games were analyzed from the National (1876–2002) and American Leagues (1901–2002) of baseball, the National Hockey League (1917–2003), the National Football League (1933–2002), the National Basketball Association (1946–2002), and the four levels of professional soccer, formerly called the Football League, in England (1888–2003).

The Pollard and Pollard (2005) study provides a good example of the advantages of an archival approach. First, and this is generally typical of archival research, they were able to access a substantial amount of data. In fact, most research is carried out with samples of individuals randomly selected from a population of interest. Pollard and Pollard (2005) accessed the total population of data. Also, given the amount of data accessed, concerns about statistical power (i.e., too few observations) was not an issue. Second, they had no influence on the collection and storage of the data. Also, the accuracy of their analyses and reporting can be verified readily if other researchers are interested. Third, changes in relations across time—which in their case was the nature of their research question—could be easily examined.

One disadvantage of the archival approach is that it is not possible to infer cause-effect relationships. Also, the nature of the questions that can be asked is restricted to the nature of the variables in the data base.

Qualitative research. Case studies (also known as *participant observation*) are one of two major types of qualitative research. In participant observation research, data are gathered in a natural environment where the focus is on natural behavior. Although experimental studies provide insights gained from a large number of groups on one or two variables, case studies offer insights gained from a single group on a broad spectrum of variables. As Forsyth (2019) noted, "one of the best ways to understand groups in general is to understand one group in particular" (p. 46). As was the case with archival studies, case studies have been used with a wide variety of groups including families, military units, work teams, adolescent gangs, and, of course, sport teams. Case studies often require researchers to spend a sustained period of time with a group that is of specific interest or observing groups in action at key events.

In-depth interviews represent a second major type of qualitative research. With this approach, participants are presented sequentially with a series of open-ended questions that allow them to provide rich details about the phenomenon of interest. The number of participants interviewed varies from study to study. Typically, researchers continue to interview participants until the new respondents are no longer providing novel insights related to the research question under investigation. Semi-structured interviews are valuable for understanding group dynamics in sport because they allow researchers to develop key questions ahead of time to target specific areas of interest (e.g., cohesion, conflict), while allowing researchers the flexibility to explore unexpected insights through follow-up questions.

Although participant observation and in-depth interviews represent two distinct approaches, it is possible for researchers to combine both methods. In a study of the team member selection processes that occurred within the Canadian Forces Snowbird Demonstration Team (an elite military team), the lead author spent multiple days observing and taking field notes of the pilots (Martin & Eys, 2019). This provided an opportunity to build a sense of familiarity with each pilot while also allowing insight into the day-to-day interactions within the group. After this initial observation period, one-on-one interviews were conducted with team members to understand how new members were selected for this elite unit, the norms and values endorsed by the team, and how the team ensures they select the right candidates.

The previously described study offers insight into the typical advantages and disadvantages of qualitative research. One advantage that might be obvious even from the brief description above is that it is possible to gain rich and contextualized descriptions of a phenomenon. In the study by Martin and Eys (2019), where the purpose was to gain insight into the selection processes of an elite military unit—the researchers were able to gather detailed accounts from the participants about the specific events that unfolded and how such events affected each participant and the group as a whole. Researchers are not limited to asking questions about a phenomenon that lend themselves to counting (numbers), as Einstein observed "not everything that can be counted counts, and not everything that counts can be counted." Hearing the first-hand experiences of individuals through interviews may be especially important when a phenomenon is highly sensitive or personal to participants—where personal stories can be used to construct descriptions or narratives are powerful. Finally, qualitative research typically produces additional questions in the minds of the researchers and their audience. Martin and Eys (2019) were able to use the information gathered from the military setting to propose novel future research directions for sport studies. Consequently, qualitative research helps generate new hypotheses about a phenomenon.

There are also potential disadvantages. One is that the findings from qualitative research may not be transferable to other groups. As Forsyth (2019) noted in relation to case studies, specifically, "researchers who use the case-study method must bear in mind that the group studied may be unique, and, unless they embed their work into a general theoretical conceptualization, their findings may say little about other groups' dynamics" (p. 47). Second, researcher bias is a potential limiting factor. When either observing a group or interviewing group members, the researcher is the instrument. So he or she can influence the findings through conditions such as implicit or explicit bias, incompetence, changing motivation, incompatibility with respondents, and so on. However, it might be inappropriate to label this as a disadvantage. In fact, sometimes gaining "insider status" or embedding oneself in a group's social environment is required to gain new knowledge about the phenomena under study (Van Maanen, 2011). For example, in a case study of an organizational culture of a CrossFit gym, the lead researcher spent two years with the gym to fully understand the inner workings of this particular group (Bailey, Benson, & Bruner, 2017). Third, conclusions about cause and effect are not possible. For example, interviews also often rely on retrospective accounts and thus responses may reflect biased, incomplete, and even false memories. For case studies, reactivity is a possibility; that is, the very process of observing the group from a participant perspective could change the group's dynamics. A final related point is that depending upon the topic, respondents may choose to answer in a socially desirable fashion.

Field studies. In a field study, a researcher gathers data on participants or teams in their natural environment. A videotape, audio-recorder, or checklist is used to record the number of times specific behaviors occur. Technological advances have also made it possible to capture patterns of behavior within a team through sensor data that can record the movement patterns and proximity of teammates over a period of time. In some instances, the object of scrutiny might be one person or team; in other instances, data could be gathered from multiple participants or teams and a statistical summary provided.

A good example of the former is a classic study by Tharp and Gallimore (1976). John Wooden, then basketball coach of the University of California at Los Angeles, gave Tharp and Gallimore permission to attend practice and observe his coaching behaviors. Their interest in Wooden as a teacher/coach was well founded. Between 1967 and 1975, Wooden's teams won 10 NCAA championships (including seven in a row). Over the course of the 1974–75 season, Tharp and Gallimore sat in the bleachers during practices and, using a checklist, recorded the frequency with which Wooden displayed different behaviors.

Smith, Smoll, and Curtis (1978) provide a good example of a study in which data were gathered from multiple participants. A comprehensive checklist called the *Coaching Behavior Assessment System* was developed and used to record the behaviors of 51 Little League coaches (with 542 players) over the average of approximately four complete games (See Smith, Smoll, & Curtis, 1979; Smith, Smoll, & Hunt, 1977; outlined in detail in Chapter 10).

It might be apparent that an advantage of a field study is that spontaneously occurring behaviors can be observed and recorded in a natural setting. One disadvantage is that the results might not generalize to other individuals or teams. For instance, Wooden represented a special case. Although his legendary success as a coach stands out, his behaviors might be simply characteristic of John Wooden and not college coaches in general. In addition, his coaching style might not be as effective in other contexts, such as with high school basketball players or with a team of track athletes. Further, it is not possible to establish a cause-effect relationship from field studies. That is, would any coach demonstrating the Wooden profile of behaviors be similarly successful? It is possible but not probable. Also, the presence of observers could influence the focal person leading to behavioral change.

Correlational studies. The term *correlational* is a product of the statistical procedure used in the research, the correlation coefficient (represented by the symbol r). A correlation coefficient reflects the degree of relationship or association between two variables. Values can vary from $r = -1.00$ to 1.00 with higher values (positive or negative) reflecting a stronger association. The sign reflects the direction of the relationship with a negative sign reflecting an inverse relationship and a positive sign a positive relationship. So, for example, a positive relationship might be predicted for cohesion and team success—as cohesion increases so too does team success. Conversely, an inverse or negative relationship might be predicted between role ambiguity and cohesion—as the lack of clarity about role expectations increases, cohesion perceptions decrease.

A study by Eys and Carron (2001) provides an example of a correlational study. The research question of interest was whether athlete role ambiguity (i.e., lack of clarity about personal responsibilities) was related to task cohesion and task efficacy (i.e., the belief that personal behavior will produce desired results). Female and male members of university basketball teams completed questionnaires designed to assess their perceptions of (a) four types of role ambiguity (i.e., the athlete's understanding of the scope of his/her responsibility, the behaviors required to fulfill those responsibilities, the consequences associated with a failure to carryout role responsibilities, and how role performance will be evaluated), (b) two forms of task efficacy (i.e., efficacy for frequently used offensive responsibilities and frequently used defensive responsibilities), and (c) two types of task cohesion (i.e., group integration task and individual attractions to the group task). Correlation coefficients were then computed to assess the degree of association among responses to the various variables.

Researchers have devised types of correlational studies to serve as a better test of hypotheses. For instance, researchers may adopt sophisticated analyses to integrate numerous variables when examining an association, to factor-out potential alternative explanations. Researchers may also choose to measure variables at different times, so that the predictor will precede the criterion variable in time. Although these steps may improve our confidence in the results of correlational studies, they are still hampered by challenges that emerge when we do not manipulate the experiences of participants.

An advantage of a correlational study is that it provides insight into the dynamics of groups. Also, these insights are obtained without manipulating the group or its environment. A major disadvantage is that inferences about cause and effect are not possible. A useful example that illustrates this problem is the negative correlation that exists between coaching turnover and team success. Are teams less successful because they more frequently fire and hire coaches (i.e., replacing coaches frequently is a cause for poor team performance)? Or, do unsuccessful teams frequently fire their coaches in a constant search for a remedy (i.e., poor team performance is the reason coaches are fired)? Or is it possible that neither of these causal explanations is correct? Unfortunately, even scientists sometimes forget this truism and use language to describe the magnitude of a correlation coefficient that suggests causality—so readers should beware of this limitation!

Experimental Protocols

The laboratory experiment. An infrequently used research protocol to study group dynamics in sport is the laboratory experiment. Typically, participants are recruited and then randomly assigned to a control condition and an experimental condition. Participants in both conditions carry out the protocol of the experiment except that those in the experimental group are exposed to the condition of interest—typically referred to as the *independent variable* because it is manipulated by the researcher(s). Responses (the *dependent variable*) of participants in the two conditions are then compared statistically.

Hodges and Carron (1992) studied collective efficacy in a laboratory experiment. Initially participants in the experimental condition were pretested on a hand dynamometer task. Groups of three were then provided with bogus feedback in which half were led to believe that their group was in the 75th percentile for strength (the high collective efficacy condition). The other half were led to believe that they were in the 25th percentile (the low collective efficacy group). The high and low collective efficacy triads then competed (i.e., holding a medicine ball aloft for as long as possible) against a control group. The control triad, which was composed of confederates of the experimenters, had a medicine ball that was filled with foam while the high and low collective efficacy triads used a regular medicine ball.

One advantage of a laboratory experiment is that it is possible for the researcher to exert a high degree of control over extraneous variables. Also, it is possible to make stronger causal inferences about the relation between the independent and dependent variables.

One disadvantage lies in the generalizability of results. Mullen and Copper (1994) spoke to this issue:

> Not that ad hoc, laboratory groups are, in some way, unreal groups. However, there are palpable differences between ad hoc groups of strangers created for a 20-min[ute] session in a social psychological laboratory and real groups that interact on multiple occasions and provide members with longer and deeper experiences with the group. (p. 213)

As a result of the inherent differences between real and laboratory groups, it is not uncommon to find that some psychological phenomena, seemingly robust in laboratory settings, disappear or become reduced in field studies undertaken in naturalistic settings.

Another disadvantage is referred to as *experimenter demand*. Sometimes participants, despite the best efforts of the experimenters, come to understand what the study is all about. They then strive to help the experimenters achieve their predicted or expected outcome.

Field experiments. Increasingly, researchers dissatisfied with the sterile environment of the laboratory and the lack of external validity of findings (i.e., lack of generalizability to the real world) have taken to conducting field experiments. The protocol is identical to a laboratory study in that participants are recruited, randomly assigned to a control and experimental condition and the latter is treated with the condition under investigation.

A study by Prapavessis, Carron, and Spink (1997) examining the influence of team building on cohesion provides a useful example. After securing the cooperation of the coaches in a senior men's soccer league, all teams were tested for cohesiveness. Then, the authors randomly assigned the teams to one of three conditions: control (regular participation in the league), placebo control (instructions on nutrition throughout the season), and experimental (team building interventions throughout the season). At the end of the season, all teams were retested for cohesion.

An advantage of a field experiment is that it has higher ecological validity. The participants receive the experimental treatment in a natural setting. Another advantage, one contained in the study by Prapavessis et al. (1997), is that it provides a good forum to examine treatments that might not lend themselves to a laboratory situation. Team building does not readily lend itself to manipulation in laboratory settings.

A disadvantage, however, is that it is difficult to control factors that might influence the results. In the study by Prapavessis et al. (1997), for example, there was nothing to prevent coaches in the control or placebo control conditions from introducing team building strategies throughout the season. Also, team success is a powerful correlate of team cohesion and it could override the influence of team building.

Summary

As described above, any single method entails limitations. Our best strategy to continue moving beyond Lewin's (1947) assertion that we had limited accumulated knowledge regarding the nature of groups (leading into this chapter) is to integrate insights from different methods. Just as there are likely to be situations where careful and controlled experiments are crucial to incrementally advance our understanding about an association between two variables, detailed and rich accounts of personal experiences may illuminate what it means to belong to a group.

3

Group Development

[Cappie] Poindexter will be reunited with two former Rutgers teammates, center Kia Vaughn and guard Essence Carson. She'll also be joined by two off-season acquisitions who are familiar with success ... 'These are championship-experienced veterans who will automatically change the dynamics of our team,' [said Coach Ann Donovan of the WMBA New York Liberty], 'I'm looking forward to that winning mentality.' (Anderson, 2010, p. 26)

The impetus for interest in group development processes can be traced back to Bales and Strodtbeck's (1951) analysis of problem-solving groups. In the approximately 70 years since this work, theories on how groups change and develop over time have increased at a remarkable rate. It could be asked: "how can there be so many explanations advanced for how group development occurs?" All groups are similar in some respects and they do change and develop in common ways. So, these changes and developments can be generalized across groups into distinct entities called stages. However, each group is like no other group; every group is unique and its development idiosyncratic. It is this uniqueness that has led to many different theories of group development. Prior to outlining some of these theories, it is useful to examine how group development has been defined.

Group Development Defined

All theories in group dynamics—the areas of leadership and cohesion provide two very good examples—have as their foundation the two major concerns in all groups. One of those concerns is the task; groups provide a vehicle through which some goal, objective, achievement, and/or responsibility can be achieved. A second is the social element; groups provide an opportunity for individual members to satisfy the need to belong and to have meaningful personal relationships with others.

Given the importance of task and social issues in every group, it is not surprising that group development definitions make direct or indirect reference to both. For example, Mennecke, Hoffer, and Wynne (1992) suggest group development is "the degree of maturity and cohesion that a group achieves over time as members interact, learn about one another, and structure relationships and roles within the group" (p. 526). Neither task nor social is mentioned explicitly, but both are embedded in the idea of development. As another example, Sarri and Galinsky (1974) suggest that group development refers to the "changes through time in the internal structures, processes, and cultures of the group" (p. 72), which applies equally to any type of group and can be read to refer to both social and task concerns.

Theories of Group Development

Summarizing decades of literature, Arrow, Poole, Henry, Wheelan, and Moreland (2004) highlighted five categories that encompass general theories of group development. They labeled these categories the sequential stage (linear) perspective, the repeating cycles (pendulum) perspective, the adaptive responses perspective, the robust equilibrium perspective, and the punctuated equilibrium perspective.

The Sequential Stage (Linear) Perspective

In the sequential stage perspective of group development, it is assumed that a group progressively moves through different stages of change. Critical issues arise in each successive stage and when they are successfully dealt with the group moves on. One highly cited example is Tuckman's (1965) model of forming, storming, norming, and performing. In reviewing 50 studies in search for common interpretations of how groups develop, Tuckman proposed that groups go through these four stages as they develop, prepare for, and carry out the group's task. Subsequently, Tuckman and Jensen (1977) modified this model by adding a fifth stage that they referred to as *adjourning*. The Tuckman and Jensen perspective on group development is presented in Exhibit 3.1.

In the first stage, *forming*, the group members familiarize themselves with one another and strive to identify group tasks. A fraternity group that makes the decision to enter a team in an intramural basketball league would go through this stage—even though all of the individuals belong to the same fraternity and know each other well. It would still be necessary for them to become familiar with each other's skills and abilities and to determine which offensive and defensive systems the team should use. As members begin to orient themselves as a group, issues of inclusion and dependency are a major focus.

In the second phase, tension and conflict arise in the group as interpersonal disagreements occur, resistance to the group's leader develops, and members begin to question the group's approach to the task or the task itself. In the case of the fraternity team, *storming* might be reflected in disagreements about how the offense or defense should be run, who should make substitution decisions, who should do most of the shooting, and so on. During the storming stage, group members begin to impose their preferences on the group—creating conflict and tension.

In a stage referred to as *norming*, tensions settle as the group begins to coalesce around a shared understanding of what is expected of each member. Group roles and norms are established

Exhibit 3.1. Stages of Group Development

Stage	Interpersonal Characteristics	Task Characteristics
Forming	Individuals become familiar with each other and bonds develop within the group	Members determine what the group task is and what methods are suitable to carry it out
Storming	Tension develops and conflict occurs among group members and with the leader	Resistance arises to group methods and the group task
Norming	Cohesiveness and group harmony develop and group roles are established	Task cooperation among members is prevalent
Performing	Relationships are stabilized	The group's orientation is on productivity and performance
Adjourning	Member contact decreases and emotional dependency among individual members is reduced	The task of the group is completed and the duties of members are finished

Source. "Stages of Small Group Development Revisited," by B. W. Tuckman and M. A. C. Jensen, 1977, *Group and Organization Studies*, 2, 419–427.

in terms of both social relationships and task productivity. A dominant person, an outstanding player, or even a senior member of the fraternity might emerge and become acknowledged as the leader. Other roles are also assigned or assumed: team leader, social convener, playmaker, and shooter, for example. Essentially, the norming stage is characterized by rising levels of cooperation and cohesiveness, as well as consensus on the group's goals and objectives.

In the fourth stage, *performing*, interpersonal relations are stabilized, and group energy is directed toward successful execution of the group's task(s). The fraternity team's leader, social convener, playmaker, and shooter now know and accept their roles. In the performing stage, the team is now focused on executing tasks and achieving team success.

In the *adjourning* stage, the group's task is completed, duties are terminated, group dependencies are reduced, and the group may disband. Adjourning would occur in the fraternity team—at least in terms of playing basketball—when the basketball season ends. The roles filled by the fraternity members, such as the leader, social convener, and so on would disappear with the breakup of the team. When the team members go back to just being members of the fraternity, the roles and responsibilities developed in this other context would prevail.

In summarizing the sequential stage perspectives of group development, several important points should by highlighted. First, the duration of time spent at any one stage may vary for different groups. In Tuckman and Jensen's (1977) model, for example, one group might spend considerable time in the forming stage but quickly pass through the storming stage. In fact, groups that are essentially re-forming may completely skip aspects of a stage that it has already gone through. For example, a college basketball team that is returning for another season with a majority of veterans might not have to go through some of the orientation procedures of a completely new team. However, it is possible that this group might have a storming stage that is prolonged.

A second point is that sequential models assume that groups sequentially progress through each stage. That is, when one stage is successfully completed, the group passes on to the next. A third point is that the linear models do not consider how group development can be influenced by the demands of the environment (Gersick, 1988). These two final points are the largest criticisms levied against the sequential stage models. Despite the popularity and intuitive appeal of the five-stage model, it is unlikely that all groups would follow such a linear and predictable trajectory in their development. In reality, teams go through ebbs and flows in their experiences such that storming and norming occur throughout a season (all while the team is performing). As just one example, the NHL's Dallas Stars, like many professional sport teams, experienced both highs and lows:

> The Stars were on a high when they were seemingly unbeatable … They embraced their system, and the confidence they had on the ice translated to win after win. Now, they're in the opposite situation. They lack their system's structure and their confidence is at a seemingly all-time low. However, it should simply serve as the wake-up call they need to turn things around. Dallas is, for the first time this season, able to see how they aren't invincible. They too can lose three straight after winning five in a row. They are just like any team in the league because they're all competitive. (Scott, 2017, para. 3–5)

Indeed, although Tuckman (1965) reviewed 50 studies in the process of formulating his sequential stage model, a remarkable 37 of these studies were based on therapy and laboratory-based groups. Overall, the shortcomings of sequential stage models motivated researchers to consider more dynamic models of group development.

The Repeating Cycles (Pendulum) Perspective

The repeating cycles perspective of group development emphasizes the shifts that occur in interpersonal relationships during the growth and development of the group (Worchel, 1994). A key assumption of this perspective is that a group does not move progressively through various stages in a linear fashion from the instant it forms. Instead, cycles of development repeat themselves and the resolution of issues is considered temporary.

One of the earliest models, for example, proposed that groups oscillate between focusing on task matters and social-emotional issues (Bales, 1966). Subsequently, Worchel (1994) introduced a cyclic model. The first stage, *discontent*, occurs when group members feel alienated from the group and do not consider it to be part of their identity. Initially, these feelings might exist for individuals trying out for a new sport team. Prospective members might not be included in conversations among the veteran players and, because they would not yet have been selected, they probably would not consider themselves as part of the group.

The conclusion of the discontent stage is marked by a *precipitating event*. As the tryouts come to a close and the team roster is finalized, those feelings of alienation would fade away among those individuals who have made the team and give way to a sense of belonging and purpose.

The next stage of *group identification* involves clarifying group membership boundaries by distinguishing between individuals who are members (i.e., ingroup) and non-members (i.e., outgroup). As the group solidifies its own identity and boundaries, the group identity becomes more important for individual members and group commitment increases.

The third stage—the *group productivity* stage—is marked by increased activity and energy within the group as members strive toward a common goal. Once the team begins practices and games, the focus for individual members turns to production and finding a way to contribute to the team. To allow for this in sport, it is quite common for coaches to book an exhibition schedule to get the team ready for the upcoming competitive season.

As the group begins to attain its goals during this period of the season, however, it starts to enter the *individuation* stage; here, members look for and demand recognition for their own contributions. The very early part of a season, for example, could be thought of as a honeymoon where the individual members are just happy to be part of the group. Once the honeymoon is over, however, there are desired (e.g., starter) and undesired (e.g., bench player) roles to fulfill and athletes want meaningful roles to play on a team. These roles could be fully spelled out as the exhibition season continues and athletes may or may not consider these roles as reflective of their abilities.

As this process of individuation continues, the group enters a final stage called *decay*. In this stage, the group puts less energy into achieving its goals and individual members become less interested in retaining their membership. This is where Worchel's (1994) model differs from earlier linear approaches: The group returns to the discontent (or another) stage and reenters the cycle again. To continue the example, it is possible toward the end of the exhibition portion of the schedule that athletes become weary of constant practices and the prospect of playing meaningless games. For intercollegiate athletes, concerns about school may take precedence over athletics. Regardless, personal interests in group membership may begin to decline. The beginning of the regular competitive season, however, may renew the group's energies and the cycle will repeat itself—perhaps to be renewed once again if the team makes the playoffs.

Another example of a pendulum model of group development was advanced in a model emphasizing the need for inclusion, the need for control, and the need for affection (Schutz, 1966); these are discussed in more detail in Chapter 5 (see Exhibit 5.6). Schutz proposed that all groups must sequentially and successfully handle problems in the areas of inclusion, control, and affection—from dyads to the largest groups. Essentially, different interpersonal problems predominate in different phases of the group's development. Schutz (1966) also emphasized that "these are not distinct phases…these problem areas are emphasized at certain points in a group's growth. All three problem areas are always present but not always of equal salience" (p. 171). Despite sharing similarities with a linear perspective, this model is considered to be a pendulum model because it contains the assumption that the three problem areas reappear during the life of the group. Thus, when a group has gone through the sequence of inclusion to control to affection, it begins another cycle.

Generally, problems of inclusion predominate during the initial phases of group development. These problems center around the extent to which different individuals want to communicate and interact with one another and with the group. Obviously, if the majority of individuals want little or no interaction, communication, or involvement, the chance that they will form and develop into an effective group is minimal. In contrast, if the majority of members want and emphasize inclusionary behaviors, this provides the group a solid foundation from which to proceed.

Issues related to control characterize the second problem area. Group members must resolve who will make the decisions, how the group will be led, and where the primary power and influence will lie. The control phase in Schutz's (1966) model of group development is similar to the storming stage in the Tuckman and Jensen model. Finally, as the group develops, interpersonal concerns in the area of affection arise. Concerns center around how friendly, intimate, or affectionate group members want to be with each other.

Schutz (1966) proposed that when a group disbands, it does so in a reverse sequence: affection to control to inclusion. That is, affection is the last to develop in the group; it is the first to go. After affection declines, issues relating to control, power, and influence begin to decline in importance. Eventually, group members simply don't care who's in charge. Finally, contact, communication, and involvement decline to the point where the members no longer meet as a group.

The repeating cycle models capture the ups and downs in the development of the group, reflecting what most athletes come to understand after being a member of a few sport teams. More specifically, after group members become oriented to one another, group existence is marked by instances of conflict and differentiation followed by resolution and cohesion that could be followed by additional conflict and differentiation, and so on. Exhibit 3.2 presents examples of two such case histories.

One example comes from Feinstein's (1987) book, *A Season on the Brink*. During the 1985–86 men's college basketball season, Feinstein was given complete access to coach Bobby Knight and the Indiana Hoosiers. He attended practices, team meetings, and games; he even traveled with the team and recorded what he saw and heard. That season might be considered successful by most sport team's standards, but in 1986–87, the year after Feinstein was with them, the Indiana Hoosiers won the NCAA National Championship. The bulk of Feinstein's book deals with 1985–86, but, in an epilogue, he presents an overview of the championship year. (The quotes in Exhibit 3.2 overlap both seasons.)

A second example comes from the diary maintained by Ken Dryden during the 1972 Canada-Russia hockey series, which was subsequently developed into the book, *FaceOff at the Summit* (Dryden & Mulvoy, 1973). The year 1972 marked the first opportunity for professional hockey players from North America to compete against European amateurs. From the mid-1950s, the Russians had enjoyed a clear superiority over Canadian amateur hockey teams in international exhibitions, in the Olympics, and in World Cup championships. Canadian sport fans felt that the Russians' success was achieved against inferior opposition. As such, in 1972 when an AllStar team of professionals was selected from the National Hockey League, popular consensus was that "Canada's best" would soundly beat the Russians in the eight-game series. Many Canadians considered the outcome of the first four games (which were played in Canada) a national disaster. The Russians led the series with two wins, one loss, and a tie. Team Canada eventually won the series with four wins, three losses, and one tie. The winning goal was scored in the eighth and deciding game with only 34 seconds left to play.

Feelings of cohesiveness are relatively high when a group first comes together. This is a period of orientation and general feelings of team unity arise from the common expectations, experiences, anxieties, and aspirations that all the prospective team members share. In the Team Canada and Indiana Hoosier examples, the feelings of unity might have been a result of the sacrifices that all athletes made during the summer (e.g., training). Or, it might have been the result of the common goals and aspirations that the athletes had for the upcoming competition/season. The essential point is that when a team first gets together, there is a relatively high feeling of unity.

Following the orientation period, the pendulum swings, and there is *differentiation* and *conflict*. Differentiation refers to the fact that the group physically and psychologically subdivides into smaller units and conflicts arise as athletes compete for a limited number of roles on the team. In many sports, breaking the total group into smaller units for practice is a natural consequence of the way the sport is organized; offense versus defense, forwards versus defense, setters versus spikers, and so on (Martin, Evans, & Spink, 2016; Martin, Wilson, Evans, & Spink 2015). The Team Canada quotation in Exhibit 3.2 serves to highlight the potential conflicts that can arise as a result of the competition for a starting position on the team; the Indiana Hoosier quotation highlights the drudgery, monotony, and feelings of

Exhibit 3.2. An Example of a Pendulum Model of Group Development in a Basketball Setting (the Indiana Hoosiers) and a Hockey Setting (Team Canada)

Team Canada	Indiana Hoosiers
Stage 1. Orientation: Cohesion and feelings of unity are high, the athletes share many common feelings, anxieties, and aspirations	
Practices Start: "One surprise aspect of the first week was the absolute lack of temper flare-ups—like high sticks—between people who go out of their way to knock each other down during the regular season" (Dryden & Mulvoy, 1973, p. 27).	Practices Start: "In college basketball, no date means more than October 15. On that day, basketball teams all around the country begin formal preparation for the upcoming season" (Feinstein, 1987, p. 27).
Stage 2. Differentiation and Conflict: The group physically or psychologically subdivides into smaller units; conflicts often arise as athletes compete for positions on the team	
Pre-Series Practices Continue: "All of us desperately want to play on Saturday night because it is Game 1 of a historic event. It will mean so much to be one of the best seventeen and two—that is, seventeen skaters and two goaltenders" (Dryden & Mulvoy, 1973, p. 32).	Pre-Season Practices Continue: "November is the toughest for any college basketball team. The excitement of starting practice … has worn off and practice has become drudgery … There is just day after day of practices—the same faces, the same coaches, the same drills, the same teammates" (Feinstein, 1987, p. 59).
Stage 3. Resolution and Cohesion: Cohesion increases as group members share common concerns and feelings as they prepare to face a common threat	
The First Game: "After we finished our work, Sinden names the lineup for the opening game. Red Berenson, one of the centers, told Sinden and Ferguson to get lost for a couple of minutes … 'Look,' Red said to us. 'We have thirty-five outstanding hockey players here right now but only nineteen will be dressing tomorrow night. It's no disgrace not to be playing … this is a team of thirty-five men. Let's keep it that way'" (Dryden & Mulvoy, 1973, pp. 41–42).	The First Game: "The tension in the locker room was genuine. All the reminders about Miami, all the memories of last season, not to mention the memories of forty-eight practices that had led to this afternoon combined to create a sense of dread" (Feinstein, 1987, p. 96).
Stage 4. Differentiation and Conflict: Team unity is weakened as different individuals are rewarded or punished, setting them off from the group	
During the Series: "I practiced this morning with the Black Aces and tonight I'll be in the stands with them. The Black Aces of a hockey team are the spares … As expected, the Black Aces were flat at practice. Disappointed, down, depressed, none of us is used to watching a game from the stands" (Dryden & Mulvoy, 1973, pp. 60–61).	During the Season: "The locker room would not have been much quieter if Kent State had won the game … Mentally, Knight had decided he needed Hillman and Smith in place of Robinson and Brooks. They were deep in the doghouse … After [the team] showered, he blistered them one more time. Only three players had pleased him" (Feinstein, 1987, p. 102).
Stage 5. Termination: If the season has been successful, feelings of cohesion are high. If the season has been unsuccessful, feelings of cohesion are low.	
Termination: "I just looked around the room; everyone's uniform was soaked with sweat. I felt really proud … for all of us. I didn't know more than a handful of them six weeks ago, but now I felt that I knew everyone of them in a way you rarely know anyone. We had gone from the heights to the depths—and now we were back on top again" (Dryden & Mulvoy, 1973, p. 178).	Termination: "They jumped on each other, pummeled each other, and cried … Finally, they went back to the locker room. When it was quiet Knight spoke briefly. 'What you did,' he told them, 'was refuse to lose. You've been that kind of team all year'" (Feinstein, 1987, p. 348).

boredom that arise when a team is confronted with constant early season practices and no games. Both examples help to illustrate the decline in cohesion and team unity following the orientation period.

Inevitably, the group draws together again as the pendulum swings in the opposite direction; referred to as *resolution*. In sport groups, resolution usually occurs when the team is about to meet an opponent. In response to this external threat, competition within the group decreases as the group shifts its focus toward accomplishing team goals and objectives. In the Team Canada quotation, a respected team member reminds the total group about the importance of group solidarity. In the Indiana Hoosier example, the shared aspirations for upcoming season and the memory of a failure in the previous season engender a greater sense of team unity.

As the season progresses, the sequence described above is repeated. Differentiation and conflict are followed by resolution and cohesion, which are followed by differentiation and conflict, which are followed by resolution and cohesion. The group continues to grow and develop over the course of the season but there are pendulum-like shifts until the team dissolves.

When the team is successful, the final pendulum swing is toward high cohesiveness. In fact, a meta-analysis showed that team success positively predicted subsequent cohesiveness (Carron, Colman, Wheeler, & Stevens, 2002). When teams win, feelings of cohesiveness are higher, but when they lose, declines in cohesion tend to follow. The Team Canada quotation in Exhibit 3.2 best serves to illustrate how feelings of closeness accompany team success.

Additional Models of Group Development

In their review of group development models, Arrow, Poole, Henry, Wheelan, and Moreland (2004) noted that the additional theories fall under three general categories. The first category, *adaptive response models*, emphasizes that patterns of development are idiosyncratic (i.e., unique) for all groups based on the demands and obstacles they must overcome. This category rejects the notion that all groups move through similar sequential stages.

The second category, termed *robust equilibrium models*, highlights the fact that group development is marked by early activity and change followed by a relatively stable period. As Arrow et al. (2004) noted, it is presumed that "once a group has emerged from its early period and finished settling, the structure of interest will stay relatively constant" (p. 85). This model applies to the development of structure in sport teams. For example, the early stages of a sport team's development, such as the onset of a new season, requires the delineation of roles, selection of leaders (i.e., captains), among other structural concerns. Generally, there are only slight modifications to the overall structure of teams after this process is complete.

A final category of group development models, a variation of the above, is termed *punctuated equilibrium models*. In this category, group development is viewed as consisting of stable periods of time punctuated with instances of sudden instability where the group is reorganized. This reorganization could be the result of role reassignment or changes in group membership. For example, a qualitative study explored what occurred within collegiate basketball teams following a teammate's injury (Surya, Benson, Balish, & Eys, 2015). Through a series of in-depth interviews, athletes relayed experiences in which the unexpected absence of a core player within the team led to a cascade of role adjustments within the group, as well as changes in the mood and emotional climate of the group. In some cases, interpersonal tensions flared as teammates and the coaching staff attempted to adjust to the new group.

Group Membership Changes

In all organizations, including sport, an issue that is highly consequential to group dynamics, and an oft overlooked component of group development, is the *arrival* and *departure* of team members. Sport teams frequently experience changes in the personnel as a result of graduation, resignation, retirement, promotion, transfer, and dismissal. In collegiate sports, high rates of turnover are built into the fabric of each team due to player graduation and the limited timeframe of eligibility. Benson, Eys, and Irving (2016) measured the role expectations held by intercollegiate athletes for an upcoming season (assessed during training camp) and their actual role experiences (assessed at the halfway point of the season). It was evident that both new members and returning veteran members can experience uncertainty regarding how their role might change over the course of a new season (Benson et al., 2016).

It could be argued that even the addition of one new member—coach or athlete in sport—results in the formation of a new group. That is, any membership change alters the team's dynamics—a reality discussed by Coach Donovan of the WNBA New York Liberty in the quote opening this chapter (Anderson, 2010). Even in professional sport teams, turnover in personnel is commonplace. For example, in a study of NBA teams between the 2000–2001 and 2004–2005 seasons, the average rate of athlete turnover was 36.2%—with one team experiencing 88% turnover (Morse, Shapiro, McEvoy, & Rascher, 2008). In the NFL, turnover rates are similar but have increased over the years. The average rate of athlete turnover was 32.6% between 1979 and 1992, increasing to 39.5% between 1993–2010 (Davis, Fodor, Pfahl, & Stoner, 2014). Of course, rates of turnover likely vary from team to team and sport to sport.

There also is considerable turnover in coaches and managers. In fact, only 20.6% of managers/coaches in professional sport in North America retained their position from the five-year period of 1977 to 1982; this declined to 15.3% for the five-year period from 1987 to 1992 (Dodd, 1992). A similar pattern was observed in the English Football League and Premier League (i.e., soccer) for the 28 seasons between 1972 and 2000 (Audas, Dobson, & Goddard, 2002). Over this time period, voluntary departures of managers remained relatively constant but involuntary departures (e.g., firings) showed a marked increase.

Managing the Integration of New Members

Turnover is a pervasive fact of life in all sport. In almost all instances, turnover is not one process, it is two: the departure of an existing member, and the arrival of a replacement. As the departure of existing members often coincides with introducing new members, the timeframe surrounding changes in group membership is potentially a key leverage point for reinforcing, modifying, or overhauling the dynamics of a sport team (Benson, Evans, & Eys, 2016).

Researchers who study organizations and work groups have long been interested in how new members come to learn the norms, expectations, values, and responsibilities associated with membership in a specific organization—a process termed *organizational socialization* (Van Maanen & Schein 1979). Adapting the concept of organizational socialization to sport, Benson, Evans, and Eys (2016) developed a framework to understand the ways in which athletes are integrated into collegiate sport teams. Based on interviews with both athletes and coaches, common sport team socialization processes included strategically scheduling social events, creating opportunities to facilitate knowledge transfer between more experienced members and newcomers, and coaches clarifying and establishing role expectations. Subsequent work by Benson and Eys (2017) led to the development of the Sport Team Socialization Tactics Questionnaire, a multidimensional tool to measure how athletes perceive the socialization processes that occur within their team.

Additionally, this research identified several potential benefits to integrating new teammates through processes that focus on fostering relationships between newcomers and veterans, as well as clarifying athletes' role expectations early in the season. For example, athletes reported feeling more committed to their teammates and more cohesive as a group when they perceived their group to endorse information sharing between veteran members and newcomers. Athletes also reported a greater sense of social unity among their teammates when structured social events were scheduled for new members upon their arrival to the team (Benson & Eys, 2017).

Advantages and Disadvantages of Membership Turnover

Turnover may be due to injuries, trades, the draft, or retirements and it affects some teams in some sports more than others. Player turnover is also an attempt to rebuild unsuccessful teams. In this regard, Verducci (1996) suggested that the biggest trade in baseball in 37 years occurred when the unsuccessful San Diego Padres made a 12-player trade with the Houston Astros in December of 1994. Although the fundamental purpose of member turnover in sport teams is to enhance team success, team success doesn't necessarily follow player turnover.

One disadvantage of the total turnover process is *cost*. As an example, it is estimated that the cost to replace a single worker in the United States is roughly 20% of that person's salary—a number that increases as a function of skill specialization (Boushey & Glynn, 2012). A related consideration is that it takes time, and time is money in any organization. Also, the group's effectiveness, as reflected in the group's productivity, can be compromised. In professional sport, a fourth potential cost is fan revenue. In one study, Kahane and Shmanske (1997) initially determined the amount of roster change in major league baseball (which they noted was 27% on average) and the decline in the number of spectators in attendance. The cost to the organization associated with the decline in fan support was then estimated using the average price of a ticket. Each percentage of change in a team's roster resulted in a 0.4% to 0.7% reduction in yearly attendance (i.e., from 6,000 to 12,000 spectators). At the time of the study, the loss of one average player was estimated to cost a team between $420,000 and $540,000 in lost revenue, with a star player costing a team between $540,000 and $730,000.

There are also psychological consequences associated with turnover. One is morale; the loss of a longstanding teammate is disruptive. Also, communication and established routines—both task and social—are negatively influenced.

Nonetheless, there are some advantages to personnel turnover. One of these is that fresh ideas or perspectives can be brought to the group. Another is that specific people with specific skills can be targeted so that resources missing from the group can be acquired. Finally, change is often motivating. The addition of new personnel with different skills, knowledge, and abilities may energize existing group members.

Athlete Turnover and Team Success

As Exhibit 3.3 shows, across a variety of sports, greater turnover in personnel is generally associated with lower levels of team success. For example, Davis et al. (2014) analyzed over

Exhibit 3.3. The Relationship between Professional Athlete Turnover and Team Effectiveness

Sport	Period	Results	Reference
Baseball	1960–1969	Higher athlete turnover was associated with lower team effectiveness ($r = -.51$)	Schwartz (1973)
Baseball	1951–1960	Higher athlete turnover was associated with poorer win-loss, league standing, and games behind first place.	Theberge & Loy (1976)
Basketball	1960–1969	Higher athlete turnover was associated with lower team effectiveness ($r = -.47$)	Schwartz (1973)
Basketball	1977–1981	Number of new players was associated with fewer games won ($r = -.59$)	Pfeffer & Davis-Blake (1986)
Ice Hockey	1950–1966	Athlete turnover unrelated to team success	McPherson (1976a)
Football	1979–2010	Higher athlete turnover was associated with poorer team success	Davis et al. (2014)

40 years of archival data on NFL team turnover and performance, spanning from 1979 to 2010. When focusing on games in the first half of the season, they found that teams above the 80th percentile in player turnover won 35.5% of games compared to 61.6% of games for teams below the 20th percentile in player turnover (Davis et al., 2014). Although teams with higher turnover still tended to perform worse than lower turnover teams in the second half of the season, the difference in between these two groups was less pronounced as time went on.

Five points should be emphasized about these findings. The first is that the data on player turnover and team effectiveness are correlational. They are subject to the same limitations and reservations raised about the managerial data on turnover. It is not possible with correlational data to conclude that one factor caused another.

A second point is that if player turnover is either too fast or too slow, a team's effectiveness may suffer. For example, baseball manager Billy Martin suggested that without turnover, motivation can diminish, and complacency can develop on a team.

> Longterm contracts are often harmful. I'm not saying it's true with all players, but it is with many of them. They lose incentive, their motivation, if they have a longterm contract. Subconsciously, they just don't seem to try as hard. If a guy is a fringe player and it's time to sign him to a new contract, I'd like to see baseball just let him go. Bring in somebody else, somebody who won't cost as much money and who is hungrier, who is not set in his ways with all those bad habits. I'm not talking about a Don Mattingly or a Dave Winfield or a Ricky Henderson. Keep them. But get rid of the fringe players, just keep turning them over. That will stop all that nonsense of threatening the manager and the owner. (Martin & Pepe, 1987, p. 148)

This point is well illustrated in a study examining the relationship between player turnover in professional baseball and the number of games behind first place (Loy, Theberge, Kjeldsen, & Donnelly, 1975). The operational definition for player turnover was the duration of time to *halflife*, which is the duration of time required for the team to be reduced (through player changes) to one half of its original complement. For instance, a team roster might contain 40 athletes in 2008. Through trades, retirements, injuries, and other factors, only 20 of those original 40 members might still be present on the roster in 2010. In this case, the duration of time to halflife would be two years. Loy et al. (1975) found that there is an inverted-U relationship between the duration of time to half-life and team success. That is, moderate levels of turnover can be beneficial, perhaps even necessary, but both a lack of turnover and high levels of turnover are negatively associated with team success.

The third point is that turnover in some positions is undoubtedly less disruptive than turnover in other positions. If an individual has a peripheral role on the team, his/her departure has less effect than the departure of an individual who occupies a more critical, central position. In a study using almost 40 years of data from the National Basketball Association, Fonti and Maoret (2016) found that longer-lasting relationships between pairs of athletes who both fulfilled core roles with the team were positively associated with team performance. In other words, this study showed that retaining multiple core players is associated with team success.

A fourth point is that the turnover of more skilled team members has a stronger relationship to team success. Morgan-Lopez, Fals-Stewart, and Cluff (2009) focused on turnover among the 118 players who had been on the roster of the New York Knicks of the National Basketball Association (NBA) between 1959 and 1979. Players were classified into one of five categories on the basis of ability. Morgan-Lopez et al. (2009) demonstrated that a 1% increase in players in the category labeled Perennial All-Star would have produced 1.33 more wins, and a 1% increase in players in the category labeled Major Contributors would have produced 0.60 more wins. Conversely, that same 1% increase in players labeled Contributor would have led to a decrease of 0.28 wins.

A final point is that studies of member turnover and team effectiveness in sport teams have focused almost exclusively on one measure of effectiveness: win/loss record. There are numerous indices of effectiveness that might be influenced by turnover, including team morale, or job satisfaction, along with costs associated with moving, training, and accommodating new personnel (McPherson, 1976b). It is not clear whether turnover causes organizational ineffectiveness or whether turnover occurs because the organization is ineffective. What is clear is that there are no major benefits associated with high rates of turnover but there are numerous potential problems.

The Replacement of Managers and Coaches

In amateur sport, when things don't go well, the coach usually makes changes in the athletes on the roster. However, in college and professional sport, when things don't go well, a regular occurrence is the replacement of coaches and managers. For example, Wagstaff, Gilmore, and Thelwell (2016) noted that the combination of high expectations and intense competition creates frequent turnover at the managerial level within the English Football Leagues, with an average managerial tenure of only 18.8 months (League Managers Association, 2013). Exhibit 3.4 illustrates two reasons why management turnover may occur. Although some might argue that it is not unreasonable for the more effective coach to be retained and the less effective (or ineffective) coach to be released/fired—former college basketball coach Fran Fraschilla provides another perspective:

> The line [determining] how a coach is perceived is so thin and so fluid ... I always go back to what [Houston Rockets coach] Jeff Van Gundy told me a long

Factor	Quotation
Losing as the basis for managerial turnover	Former Toronto Raptors head coach Dwane Casey claimed NBA Coach of the Year honors on Monday night, just weeks after the Raptors replaced him with assistant Nick Nurse … Casey coached the Raptors to a franchise-best 59-win season, changing their offensive game plan from iso-heavy to a pace-and-space system that took the league by storm. His accomplishments were blasted out the window—and out of Canada—after LeBron James and the Cleveland Cavaliers swept the Raptors in the second round of the playoffs. That was a damning moment for Casey, especially after the Cavs needed seven games to get by both the Pacers and the Celtics before they were swept out of the NBA Finals by the Warriors. (Winfield, 2018, para. 1–4)
Player dissatisfaction as the basis for managerial turnover	When Missouri basketball coach Norm Stewart, 64, retired last week after 32 years of guiding the Tigers, he left behind an impressive record: 731 victories (seventh-highest all time), eight conference championships, and 16 NCAA tournament appearances. Yet while Stewart is revered in his home state, storm clouds had been gathering around Stormin' Norman since midway through last season, when reports of conflicts between him and his players surfaced. Although Stewart insisted that the retirement was his decision, many close to the team believe Stewart left under pressure from athletic director Mike Alden and several players, who reportedly threatened to transfer if Stewart returned. (Mravic & O'Brien, 1999, p. 31)

Exhibit 3.4. Managerial Turnover in Sport Teams

time ago: 'Biggest game of the year. You're down one. You get a good shot. The ball is in the air. It hangs there. Good coach or bad coach? Good coach or bad coach? Good coach or bad coach?' (Wertheim, 2004, pp. 57–58)

With only rare exceptions, the principal reason that managers/coaches are terminated is because their teams are not as successful as upper management thinks they should be. A general assumption underlying turnover is that matters will improve when the new coach/manager assumes responsibility. Several researchers have attempted to test this assumption.

Manager Turnover and Team Success

The first study of the relationship between coach/manager turnover and team success used data from Major League Baseball for the periods 1920–1941 and 1951–1958, finding an inverse relationship between managerial turnover and team performance (Grusky, 1963). Put simply, the more the turnover, the poorer the performance. In other work examining the coaching turnover-team success relationship, however, the pattern of results has been mixed. For example, the same inverse relationship (higher turnover associated with poorer performance) was observed in college basketball (Eitzen & Yetman, 1972). However, other studies reported that coaching change was not related to team success in professional hockey (McPherson, 1976a) and positively related to team success in professional football (Fabianic, 1984, 1994).

Given the ambiguity in the findings, researchers sought to identify the conditions under which teams might experience more (or less) success following manager turnover.

In a study considering the coaching ability of the successor and tracking team success in the National Basketball Association for the 1977 through 1981 seasons, researchers found that replacement coaches with (a) better prior win-loss records, (b) with previous professional coaching experience, or (c) who had improved the performance of other teams were associated

Exhibit 3.5. Team Success Before, During, and After Coach Turnover

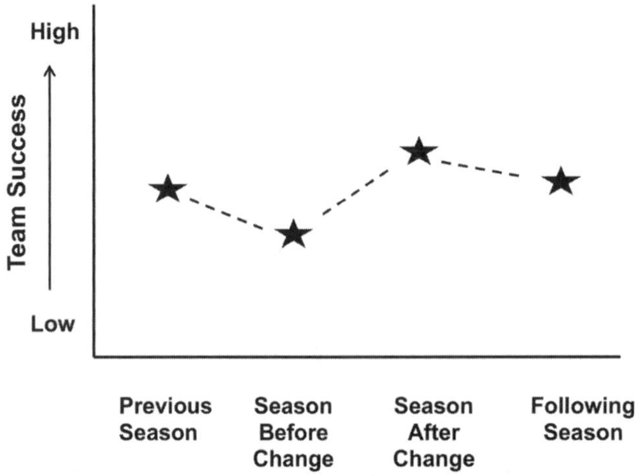

[Graph showing Team Success (Low to High) across four time points: Previous Season (moderate), Season Before Change (low), Season After Change (high), Following Season (moderately high)]

with better performance after succession (Pfeffer & Davis-Blake, 1986). This finding exemplifies the need for organizations to select new coaches with the best performance records.

The *timing of succession* and the *nature of the successor* are also important. For example, professional baseball teams that experienced a succession during the season performed worse over the year than teams with a succession between seasons (Allen, Panian, & Lotz, 1979). The same study found that internal succession was slightly less disruptive than external succession. Given that internal successors are more familiar with the players, the management, and the owners, internal succession is likely to be less disruptive to the team. Also, the successor might be able to better anticipate and avoid the difficulties of the previous manager/coach.

Several studies used research designs in which they controlled for other key variables in the analyses. In one approach, researchers tried to partial out the relative contributions of the departing and incoming coaches to team success. So for example, in analyzing the four major professional team sports in North America (football, basketball, baseball, and hockey), McTeer, White, and Persad (1995) only included cases where (a) a midseason coaching change was made, (b) the departing coach was present the full previous season, and (c) the incoming coach was retained for the next full season. The results, which are illustrated graphically in Exhibit 3.5, indicated that coaching turnover is associated with a significant short-term improvement in the latter portion of the season where the change is made but does not have an influence in the longer term.

In a study of coaching turnover in the National Football League (NFL), Brown (1982) used a research design to control for *regression to the mean*. What regression to the mean is in layperson terms is that good teams don't stay good forever and bad teams don't stay bad forever—there is a reversion to the average. Thus, a team may start the season so poorly that management fires the coach. The subsequent reversion to the mean (i.e., improved performance) is then attributed to the coaching change. The win ratios of a group of NFL teams that had experienced an early season slump and replaced their coach were compared with the win ratios of a second matched (i.e., control) group of teams that had also experienced an early season slump yet did not replace their coach. Teams that replaced their coach showed improvements in win ratios but these were virtually identical to the improvements shown in the group of control teams. Indeed, similar results were observed in studying professional football teams in the Dutch Eredivisie across 14 consecutive seasons (van Ours & van Tuijl, 2016). That is, although team performance improved following the dismissal of a coach, the performance improvements of teams were similar to teams who experienced a losing streak but did not dismiss their coach.

In another study, individual game results were taken from matches from the two top divisions of soccer in England from 1972 to 2000 (Audas et al., 2002). The researchers statistically controlled for the records of the two teams over the previous 24-month period, the record of the two teams in games immediately prior to the match, and the significance of the match for either team. On average, a change of manager during the season adversely affected the results of matches played over the remainder of the same season (Audas et al., 2002).

Cause versus Effect Interpretations

Ozzie Guillen, manager of the Chicago White Sox of the American Baseball League provided his take on manager turnover in professional baseball:

> You're not going to win the Kentucky Derby with mules ... the funny thing about it is when you win, the players are good. When they play horse---t, you're the one to get fired. When you win, the general manager gave you a great club. You just write the lineup, fall asleep, and grab the trophy. But when you lose, the GM gave you a good team, but you're really bad. (Griffin, 2010, p. S5)

Notwithstanding the difficulty of determining what's cause and what's effect, it is reasonable to assume that some permanence and stability in coaching is optimal. If a coach is going to have any effect, that effect is more likely to be felt over the long term rather than the short term. Interestingly, Eitzen and Yetman (1972) found an inverted-U relationship between coaching stability and team success in college basketball:

> Coaches who left after eight or nine years tended to leave as winners in comparison with their early years. Coaches whose tenure lasted ten, eleven, or twelve years were split evenly into those whose records were improving and those whose records were deteriorating. For those coaches whose longevity at one post exceeded twelve years ... every year but one showed a disproportionate number of coaches ending their career at a school with lasthalf records poorer than their first. (p. 115)

Another study found similar results using data from college football teams in the National Collegiate Athletic Association, spanning 1980–2004 (Humphreys, Paul, & Weinbach, 2016). In an analysis controlling for performance expectations using college football betting markets, the researchers found that the length of time coaches spent with a team initially had a positive association with performance, but then began to decline as coaches spent longer periods of time with a team. Taken together, when coaches stay at one institution for a long period of time, they have an opportunity to build a program and their record improves. Subsequently, their record tends to level off and, eventually, it declines. This decline may be due to complacency, decreasing motivation, or some other factors. Whatever its causes, there may be an optimal tenure for coaches.

Section 2

Foundations of Groups in Sport

It was a grand stage for what was likely the final World Cup match for the long-time Brazilian leaders Marta, Cristiane, and Formiga. Marta is 33. Cristiane is 34. Formiga, the oldest player in this World Cup, is 41. Formiga was replaced in the midfield in the 75th minute by Andressinha. Cristiane, who posed a consistent threat up front, had to be helped off the field and replaced in the 95th minute with an apparent injury to her left leg. That left Marta to carry the torch for Brazil's greatest generation of women's players. She played until the final whistle, running about eight miles, and then made a plea to the next generation of Brazilian soccer players watching at home. 'There won't be a Formiga forever; there won't be a Marta forever; there won't be a Cristiane,' she said. 'Women's football is relying on you for its survival. Think about this: Value it more. Cry at the beginning to smile at the end.' Marta was talking about the years of effort required to compete at this level. Despite all their sacrifice and talent, she and her teammates were never able to win the World Cup. (Clarey, 2019, pp. 23–27)

Just as the trajectory of a rocket shooting skyward can be set-off by only minute changes in positioning at the outset of its journey, the type of group that emerges depends upon its starting-point. When we consider the group dynamics of a sport team, the group that emerges will often reflect: (a) the situational needs (i.e., group environment) and, (b) the characteristics of its members (i.e., member attributes).

As an example, consider the state of the Brazilian national women's soccer team following a defeat at the 2019 Women's World Cup of Soccer. The introductory quote shows the need for the next generation of Brazilian women to step into their national soccer program. The highlighted individuals have been some of the best soccer players in the world, yet the team failed to capture a world championship during their tenure (they were runner-up in 2007 and third place in 1999). Were these results primarily due to the talent level of the other teams? Was it a failure of integrating all of the skillsets of the Brazilian players? Or perhaps it might have been the environment in which they had to compete. Brazil has never hosted the Women's World Cup, though it is also true that only one team has won as the host of the tournament (United States, 1999).

In the following two chapters, issues related to the group's environment (e.g., the size of the group and where the group competes), as well as the characteristics that members bring to the group, are considered. These issues underpin subsequent concerns of group dynamics that will be covered in later sections (i.e., group structure and processes).

4

Group Environment

Paris Saint-Germain fans amassed outside the club's stadium to cheer on the players before the Champions League last-16 game against Borussia Dortmund on Wednesday. The match at Parc des Princes was played in an empty stadium because of the coronavirus outbreak. Many sports and other events around the world have been affected by the virus, leading to sporting events being held without any fans.... PSG coach Thomas Tuchel spoke shortly before the game about the feeling of playing in an empty stadium. 'It's weird, it's horrible,' he said on BFM TV. 'I know there are more important things than football ... but the most important thing in football is the relationship between the fans and the players.' (Associated Press, 2020, paras 1, 2, 10, 11)

Groups function in a variety of situations and under countless circumstances. Within sport, some athletes have to contend with audiences exceeding 100,000 people in their direct stadium environment and greater than a billion watching on the internet and television. Others compete in the absence of spectators. Furthermore, some teams have an abundance of resources (e.g., personnel, funding) versus others who continually struggle to obtain the necessary talent to build a successful group. Clearly, there are many features that contribute to an effective group environment. In this chapter, two important variables are discussed: a group's size and its playing location (i.e., home vs. away).

Group Size

Whatever one toucan can do, is sooner done by toucans two,
And three toucans (it's very true), can do much more than two can do.
And toucans numbering two plus two can, manage more than all the zoo can.

In short, there is no toucan who can do what four or three or two can. (Prelutsky, 1983, p. 54)

Are there any exceptions you might ask? Our answer is it depends upon the task.
Two toucans adding food to a common pot will produce what a single toucan cannot.
But one toucan sufficient for a complex job will be badly hampered by a milling mob. (Carron, Widmeyer, & Brawley, 1996)

The opening poems highlight two contrasting thoughts about increases in group size. Applied to sport, increasing the number of athletes retained on the roster of a team does increase the probability that the necessary resources for team effectiveness will be available. However, for many sport teams, an excessive roster can lead to a large number of problems, such as player dissatisfaction, crowding, and lack of both adequate instruction and feedback from the coach. Thus, one pertinent question concerning group size is the optimal number of extra competitors to retain for a team.

Optimal Sport Team Size

In sport situations, all things being equal, a sufficient number of individuals should be retained to practice and compete efficiently and effectively. What this means is that the necessary resources should be available to scrimmage in team sports and provide competitive situations within training for individual sports. Consequently, a basketball team might retain 10 to 12 members, a volleyball team might retain 12 to 14 members, and a wrestling team 20 to 24 members (approximately two individuals per weight class). This would ensure that there would not be a large number of individuals inactive at any given time. Opportunities for personal instruction, reinforcement, and reward would also be available. Also, the amount of individual participation and high feelings of personal responsibility, commitment, and accountability to the group would be present. Finally, the ways in which we consider group size may differ depending on how we operationalize this concept, as illustrated in Exhibit 4.1.

It is important to keep in mind that optimal group sizes may vary from team to team and sport to sport. For example, there is evidence that very large groups usually subdivide into smaller subgroups (e.g., Baker, 1981). Sometimes this might occur because of the organizational structure adopted. American football provides a good example. Traditionally, large rosters are maintained in this sport and the total roster is generally subdivided into smaller units—each of which has its own coach. A total squad of 80 players and coaches might be subdivided into an offensive unit, a defensive unit, and in some cases a special teams unit associated with the kicking game. These units represent subgroups. Each of these subgroups can have all of the characteristics of an independent group—leadership, roles, structure, and so on. Thus, a football team of 80 may not differ substantially from a basketball team of 12 to 15 people.

Group size can also vary from one team to another within the same sport. American football again provides a good example. On one team of 80 athletes, the coaches might decide to use some of their best athletes on both offense and defense. On another team of 80 athletes, the coaches might have their personnel specialize on either offense or defense. From a social

Exhibit 4.1. Group Size can be Examined in Different Ways within Sport Teams

Index	Definition	Competitive Sport Examples
Action unit	The number of people on the playing surface at one time	*Dependent on sport Basketball = 5 Indoor Volleyball = 6 Soccer = 11 Ice Hockey = 6
Dress roster	The number of individuals in uniform during competition	*Dependent on league Basketball = 10–12 Indoor Volleyball = 12–14 Soccer = 16–23 Ice Hockey = 19–26
Team roster	The total number of athletes retained on the team	*Dependent on league and team Basketball = 12–17 Indoor Volleyball = 12–16 Soccer = 16–25 Ice Hockey = 19–26

Source. "The size of sport groups with special implications for the triad" by W.N. Widmeyer, 1971.

and a task point of view, there is considerable difference between the teams in these two contexts. In the case of the team with the roster of 80 and no subgroups, coaches might conclude that they had at least 15 players too many on the roster. These 15 would be nonparticipants who could become dissatisfied and detract from group morale. Therefore, the coaches might consider it best to release the nonparticipants. On the other hand, an entirely different conclusion might be reached in the case of the team with the roster of 80 subdivided into two units of 40 each. As a result of the specialization between offense and defense, the coaches might conclude that there were no unnecessary "extras."

Carron, Widmeyer, and Brawley (1989) attempted to determine what constitutes an ideal roster size in sport. They asked athletes from basketball, volleyball, soccer, and hockey what they felt would be ideal, too large, and too small for their sport team. As the results in Exhibit 4.2 show, athletes' perceptions of an ideal roster size were generally less than the roster size traditionally adopted by coaches (with basketball being the exception). In addition, a roster

Exhibit 4.2. Perceptions of Group Size in Sport Teams

Sport	Action Unit	Ideal Size	Too Large		Too Small	
			Size	Percent	Size	Percent
Basketball	5	11.9	15.1	127.0	8.7	74.0
Volleyball	6	9.8	12.6	125.6	7.4	75.1
Soccer	11	16.3	19.7	121.6	12.7	78.4
Hockey	6	16.1	20.5	131.5	12.9	80.1

Source. "Perceptions of ideal group size in sport teams" by A. V. Carron, W. N. Widmeyer, and L. R. Brawley, 1989, *Perceptual and Motor Skills, 69,* 1368–1379.

size that was approximately 25% greater than the perceived ideal was considered to be too large; one that was 25% smaller than the ideal was considered too small.

The athletes were also asked to list as many potential advantages and disadvantages as possible for sport teams that are too small and too large. There were three major findings. First, the athletes listed more task-related advantages and disadvantages for being on either too small or large teams than social-related advantages and disadvantages. As Carron et al. (1989) described,

> One of the task-related advantages of too small a roster was that 'there are more opportunities to participate'; a task-related disadvantage was that 'the team does not have enough depth.' One of the listed task-related advantages of too large a roster was that 'there are opportunities to rest'; a disadvantage was that 'the team's organization suffers.' (p. 1370)

A second finding was that the advantages and disadvantages listed were overwhelmingly (by a three to one ratio) game- or competition-related rather than practice-related. Opportunities to compete are the main interest of athletes. Any factors that detract from the possibility of competing are considered to be a disadvantage; any factors that contribute to the possibility of competing are considered to be an advantage.

The third result was that the athletes generated a substantially greater number of disadvantages associated with rosters that are either too large or too small than advantages. As far as athletes are concerned, there are a few perceived advantages in being a member of a team that is too large or too small; however, there are numerous disadvantages.

Outcomes Related to Group Size

Productivity and performance. One of the earliest studies on the effect of group size on group productivity was a classic unpublished study on individual and group performance in a rope-pulling task conducted by Ringelmann over 100 years ago (cited in Kravitz & Martin, 1986). Male volunteers were asked to pull on a rope as hard as they could, in a tug of war fashion in groups of varying size. The rope was connected to a strain gauge that measured the group's total effort. Ringelmann's results are summarized in Exhibit 4.3.

Using individual productivity as a baseline, Ringelmann computed group efficiency. Assuming that one person worked at 100% efficiency, then the individuals in the two-person groups worked at only 93% of their potential, the individuals in the three-person groups at only 85% of their potential, the individuals in four-person groups at only 77% of their potential, and the individuals in the eight-person groups at only 49% of their potential. The results showed that as group size increased, the group's performance (group productivity) became increasingly inferior to what might be predicted from the simple addition of individual performance. In other words, as group size increased, process losses increased.

Why did individual performance decrease (or phrased another way; why did process losses increase?) as the number of people in the group increased? Steiner (1972) proposed two possible causes for the decrease in relative individual productivity with increasing group size: (a) reduced individual motivation (it is more difficult to motivate individuals when personal accountability is reduced), and (b) coordination losses (it is more difficult to coordinate the efforts of larger groups of people). Steiner (1972) favored the latter explanation, concluding

Exhibit 4.3. A Summary of Ringelmann's Research on the Effect of Group Size on Group Productivity

No. of Individuals	No. of Coordination Links	Relative Performance per Person	Group Productivity	Process Losses
1	0	1.00	—	—
2	1	0.93	1.86	0.14
3	3	0.85	2.55	0.45
4	6	0.77	3.08	0.92
5	10	0.70	3.50	1.50
6	15	0.63	3.78	2.22
7	21	0.56	3.92	3.08
8	28	0.49	3.92	4.08

Sources. "Ringelmann Rediscovered: The Original Article" by D. A. Kravitz and B. Martin, 1986, *Journal of Personality and Social Psychology, 50,* 936–941, and *Group Processes and Group Productivity* by I. D. Steiner, 1972, New York: Academic.

that individuals may fail to synchronize their efforts in a maximally efficient manner, thus producing less productivity, but not necessarily less effort.

Steiner's (1972) preference for coordination as the explanation has intuitive appeal. A problem that arises with increasing group size is that it becomes increasingly difficult for each individual to interact with every other individual, either in a task or social context. If one person is operating alone, there is no interaction, no need to work in a coordinated fashion, no need to be concerned with the feelings of someone else. In short, there are no coordination links—where a coordination link represents the interaction between two people.

As a group increases in size, the number of coordination links increases dramatically. The number of possible two-person links in groups of varying size can be determined with the following formula:

$$\text{No. of Coordination Links} = \frac{N^2 - N}{2}$$

In a two-person group, there is one link, in three-person groups, there are three links, and in eight-person groups, there are 28 coordination links. Thus, in comparison to a two-person group, an eight-person group has four times the resources to draw upon but 28 times as many links to coordinate. As a result, one can clearly see how increases in group size have the possibility to be both advantageous and challenging to group performance and productivity.

Social loafing. Social loafing refers to the reduction in individual effort when people work in groups (Latané, Williams, & Harkins, 1979). Latané et al. (1979) suggested that social loafing is a type of social disease, having "negative consequences for individuals, social institutions, and societies" (p. 831). Certainly, as the number of group members increases, the opportunity to reduce one's efforts increase as well. This is a pervasive group challenge. Karau and Williams (1993) concluded via a meta-analysis of research studies that social loafing occurs across "a wide variety of tasks, including physical tasks (e.g., shouting, rope-pulling, and swimming), cognitive tasks (e.g., generating ideas), evaluative tasks (e.g., quality ratings of poems, editorials, and clinical therapists), and perceptual tasks (e.g., maze performance and vigilance tasks on a computer screen)" (p. 682). Further, it is evident in males and females and in different cultures—although the effect is smaller for women and from individuals who prioritize collectivism over individualism. As an example, social loafing studies are replicated when conducted with participants who value collectivism or who belong to countries/cultures where collectivism predominates, but these effects tend to be weaker.

The findings from the Karau and Williams (1993) meta-analysis also illustrated that there are a number of conditions under which the tendency to engage in social loafing is increased. These include situations where

- The individual's output cannot be evaluated independently,
- The task is perceived to be low in meaningfulness,
- The individual's personal involvement in the task is low,
- A comparison against group standards is not available or possible,
- Other individuals contributing to the collective effort are strangers,
- The individual's coworkers are expected to perform well, and
- The individual perceives that his/her contribution to the collective outcome is redundant.

At first glance, it seems possible that social loafing might not occur in sport teams. The strong commitment that individuals have made to their team, the experiences and sacrifices that they have shared, and the significant, important goals that they hold in common might help to keep motivation at a high level. However, Anshel (1995) found evidence of social loafing in elite female rowers who performed a simulated rowing task under alone and group conditions for durations of one-stroke, 1.5 minutes, and 10 minutes. Performance was measured as distance covered. Loafing was not manifested when individuals performed under the one-stroke and 1.5 minute group conditions. However, social loafing did occur under the relatively prolonged (10 minute) condition. This illustrates that social loafing can occur in tasks that are meaningful or important, have intrinsic interest, and involve competition (Hardy & Latané, 1988).

Given the negative consequences for individuals and social institutions, it is important to know how to reduce social loafing. Based on the findings in their meta-analysis, Karau and Williams (1993) suggested several ways in which social loafing might be reduced or overcome in natural settings:

- Provide individuals with specific feedback about personal performance or the group's performance,
- Monitor individual performance or make individual performance identifiable,
- Assign individuals to meaningful tasks,
- Make each person's task unique so that all individuals feel more responsibility for their work,
- Enhance the cohesiveness of the group, and
- Make each individual feel that his/her contributions to the task are important.

Exhibit 4.4. Performance Success from Groups of Varying Sizes Competing in a 3-on-3 Basketball League

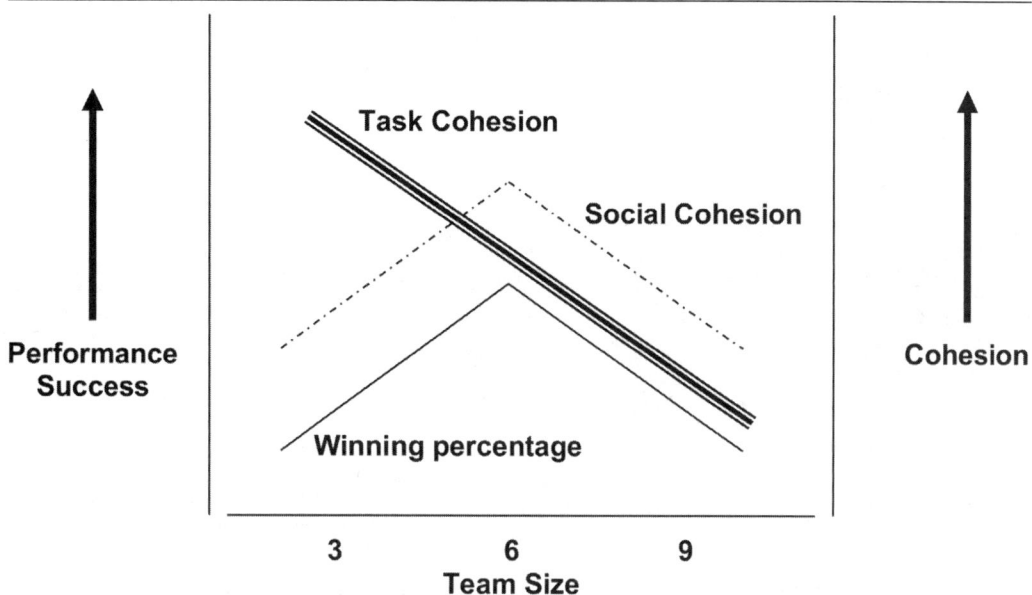

Source. "How Many Should I Carry on My Team? Consequences of Group Size" by W. N. Widmeyer, L. R. Brawley, and A. V. Carron, 1988, *Psychology of Motor Behavior and Sport: Abstracts 1988.*

Cohesion. Widmeyer, Brawley, and Carron (1990) examined the relationship of team roster size to task and social cohesion in two studies. In study one, the number of members on a basketball team was manipulated. Individuals in a three-on-three recreational basketball league were initially matched on ability and then formed into teams consisting of three, six, or nine members. After a week of practice, the teams played two games a week for eight weeks. The results revealed that task cohesion was greatest in the three-person teams and lowest in the nine-person teams. On the other hand, the six-person groups had the highest social cohesion and also were the most successful (see Exhibit 4.4).

Apparently, in the smallest teams, it was easiest to develop consensus and commitment around common group goals and objectives (i.e., task cohesion). But, with no substitutes available, there was not enough opportunity to develop social cohesiveness or to compete successfully against the six-person groups. The largest groups, on the other hand, had too many resources and this hindered the development of task cohesion, social cohesion, and the ability to compete effectively.

In their second study, Widmeyer and his colleagues (1990) examined the relationship between the size of the action unit (i.e., the number of group members actually competing at any given time) and group cohesion. College students participated in volleyball tournaments in which three different sized action units were used: three vs. three, six vs. six, and twelve vs. twelve. The level of group cohesion was greatest in the smallest unit and least in the largest.

Individual affect, cognition, and behavior. Affect, a term used to represent such emotions as satisfaction and dissatisfaction, pride and shame, enjoyment and lack of enjoyment, is influenced by group size. For example, in their study with recreational volleyball teams,

Exhibit 4.5. The Effect of Increases in Group Size on Group Member Satisfaction

Increasing Group Size…	Effect on Member Satisfaction and Group Morale…
Hinders:	
Member Participation	Decreases
Feelings of Responsibility	Decreases
Communication	Decreases
Attention, Instruction, and Reinforcement	Decreases
Leadership Opportunities	Decreases
Facilitates:	
Density and Crowding	Decreases
Feelings of Personal Threat and Inhibition	Decreases
Opportunities to Meet Other People	Increases

Source. "The Size of Sport Groups with Special Implications for the Triad" by W. N. Widmeyer, 1971.

Widmeyer et al. (1990, Study 2) found that individual enjoyment decreased as the number of individuals in the action unit increased. On the basis of a review of previous research, Widmeyer (1971) concluded that increases in group size have a major effect on individual satisfaction and group morale (see Exhibit 4.5).

Exhibit 4.5 also highlights a number of cognitions and behaviors influenced by increases in group size. Two of those are *reduced individual participation* and *feelings of responsibility*. On a volleyball team with six members, the participation of the individual athletes at practices and games would be 100%. As the size of the roster increases, the absolute participation and feeling of responsibility for the team's welfare would decrease in each athlete. Initially, increases in size might be viewed favorably since each individual would have some opportunity for a rest and the burden placed on any one person would be reduced. With further increases in group size and the resultant decrease in individual participation and responsibility, satisfaction and group morale would decrease.

Crowding and density. Widmeyer et al. (1990, Study 2) attempted to identify the factors most highly associated with individual enjoyment in action units of three, six, and twelve volleyball players. The individuals evaluated the degree to which they perceived they (1) had obtained exercise and experience fatigue, (2) were crowded, (3) were conspicuous, (4) had influence and responsibility, and (5) were on a team that possessed organization and used strategy during competitions. The results showed that all five factors contributed to enjoyment for the action units of three, six, and twelve people. In the action units of three and six, the degree to which each individual felt that he or she obtained exercise and experienced fatigue were the most important for enjoyment. In action units of 12, however, the factors that were most important for enjoyment were the degree to which the individual perceived he or she had influence and responsibility and had not been crowded. Those individuals who least enjoyed the experience of participating were those who felt that they had little responsibility or influence and were crowded while participating.

Despite the above, it is safe to say that we know very little about the effect of team roster size on perceptions of crowding/density. To better understand the nature of this relationship in sport, it is necessary to separate the three dimensions of crowding and density: (a) the group's size as represented by the number of individuals present (social density), (b) the amount of space afforded each member (spatial density), and (c) the interpersonal distance present between members (proximity) (Paulus, Annis, Seta, Schkad, & Matthews, 1976). A large soccer team of 40 members might not seem crowded if practices are held on a field large enough to insure that spatial density and proximity are not a hindrance to participation. By contrast, a smaller team of 20 members might feel very crowded if its practices are held on a field where team members cannot move freely without the risk of contact.

Communication. Another factor influenced by the size of the group is the level of communication present (see Exhibit 4.5). With increases in group size, it is more difficult to give each group member personal attention and involve them in the social activities of the group. Also, opportunities for personal instruction are reduced, as anyone who has been in large physical education classes can testify. Instruction becomes more group oriented. Not surprisingly, the amount of reinforcement and rewards provided to each individual also decreases. Each of these contributes to reduced individual satisfaction and lower group morale.

Opportunities to interact with others. One of the few positive psychosocial outcomes of an increase in group size is that there is an increase in opportunities available to meet other people who are perceived to be interesting and attractive. In pairs figure skating, for example, there is only one other person available in the "group" for friendship and communication. If the two individuals do not like each other, the group offers little in the way of social satisfaction. Conversely, when a group increases in size, the number of potential friends who are available also increases.

Leadership. Group size has four principal implications for leadership. First, with an increasing number of group members, the opportunity for any one individual to participate in the leadership of the group diminishes. Second, more demands are placed on the formal leader. Third, the formal leader has less opportunity to interact and communicate with individual members. Finally, as groups increase in size, there is an increasing tendency for group leaders to become more authoritarian and adopt a more centralized leadership style (Hare, 1981; Widmeyer, 1971). As an example, the coach of a soccer team with 25 members on its roster is more likely to be autocratic and authoritarian than the coach of a soccer team with 12 members. Individual input into decision-making is not only more difficult to coordinate in larger groups, it is less efficient to solicit it. The group can experience "paralysis of analysis" if the leader adopts an overly democratic approach.

Clearly, how many individuals to include on a team, not to mention the number of other important people surrounding the athletes (e.g., trainers, coaches, agents, medical personnel), has important practical implications toward group functioning and sustainability. These numbers are sometimes constrained by the rules of a particular league or sport, but often the absolute number are dictated by managers and coaches, who all have personal opinions on what optimal size represents. Regardless of size, however, the group eventually must compete in locations that are familiar and warm, or distant and hostile. In the next section, another important example of the group's environment is highlighted: group territory.

Group Territory

Territoriality represents a perception of proprietary rights over a physical space. Perceptions of territoriality contribute to group morale and individual satisfaction. Territoriality also provides a feeling of permanence and stability and, consequently, all groups work to establish their own territory. Team logos are placed in the stadium or rink, team mascots are very much in evidence, and special locker room areas, eating areas, and dedicated practice fields are set out.

For many sport teams, the stadium, rink, soccer pitch, grounds, or court become so intertwined with the identity of the team that it is often difficult to separate one from the other. Old Trafford in Manchester. Madison Square Garden in New York. Each of these venues brings to mind an image of its teams.

The group's territory has an influence on the members who belong within the group—athletes, coaches, and staff members—along with the array of outsiders who identify with the team as fans. For example, the presence and exuberance of a home team's fans can significantly alter the performance and preparation of the opposing team. A description of the crowd noise at Arrowhead Stadium, home of the National Football League's Kansas City Chiefs, provides a good example:

> Arrowhead Stadium gets loud, and Chiefs Kingdom has proved to be the loudest fan base in the world. In 2014, the last time [the New England Patriots] came to Arrowhead Stadium, Chiefs fans set the Guinness world record for loudest outdoor stadium. During their first practice of the week on Wednesday, the Patriots were blasting music over the Gillette Stadium speakers to simulate the crowd noise....While they are doing their best to get their offense prepared to communicate amid the noise, the Arrowhead atmosphere is impossible to replicate. (Goldman, 2019, para. 1–3, 6)

Types of Territories

Altman (1975) pointed out that a spatial location does not become part of a group's territory until the group can exert some control over it across a period of time. The nature of the control and the length of time over which the group has control have a direct influence on the development and extent of the group's sense of territoriality (see Exhibit 4.6).

Primary territories are "owned and used exclusively by individuals or groups ... [they are] clearly identified as theirs by others, are controlled on a relatively permanent basis, and

Exhibit 4.6. The Nature of Group Territory

Type of Territory	Level of Group Control	Duration of Group Control	Sport Example
Primary	High and direct. Access by others restricted. High probability territory will be defended.	Long term and permanent. Ownership may be involved.	Team locker room, stadium, or the park of professional teams.
Secondary	Moderate. Group is a habitual user and identified with territory.	Short term and temporary.	Practice fields, locker rooms, and parks shared by more than one team.
Public	Low. Group has control only when using territory.	Control does not exist or is of minimal duration.	Public tennis courts, university gyms.

Source. "The Environment and Social Behavior" by I. Altman, 1975, Monterey CA: Brooks/Cole.

Exhibit 4.7. Illustrations of Primary, Secondary, and Public Territories in Sport

Type of Territory	Quotation
Primary	Five months after US Soccer and the women's national team completed often contentious negotiations on a new collective bargaining agreement, the players and the federation have fallen out again over an old grievance: artificial turf. The dispute has an immediate cause: The women are angry that they will close their 2017 schedule with four of their final nine matches on artificial turf....The unhappiness also has resuscitated long-simmering complaints about fairness, respect, and equal treatment with the men's national team, which has played only one home match on artificial turf since the start of 2014. (Murray, 2017, para. 1, 2, 7)
Secondary	Following a foul ball, base runner [Alex] Rodriquez crossed the pitcher's mound and stepped on the rubber while returning to first base. [Pitcher Dallas] Braden twice yelled at Rodriquez, voicing his displeasure. After, in discussing the incident with the media, Braden pointed out: 'I don't care if I'm Cy Young or if I'm the 25th man on the roster…If I've got that ball in my hand and I'm out there on that mound, that's not your mound. If you want to run across the mound, go run laps in the bullpen. That's my mound.' (Carig, 2010, para. 5)
Public	If it wasn't exactly like the feudin' Hatfields and McCoys, it was pretty darn close. Although no shootin' irons came out at Monday night's Courtenay council meeting, there was plenty of racket. Members of the Comox Valley Tennis Club and the Comox Valley Pickleball Association squared off over the issue of court lines. The council chambers were so jammed with people that the overflow had to be sent into the main city hall lobby to keep an exit clear. The problem? The pickleball players want to paint their sport's court lines on some of Courtenay's existing tennis courts. The tennis players say that will ruin their sport and make it impossible to hold any sanctioned tournaments…. Dave Snider, the city's recreation director, told council that the pilot project of using tape to mark off pickleball courts at Lewis Centre 'has yielded the highest number of concerns and complaints that I've seen in my civil servant career.' (Martin, 2017, para.1–6, 29)

are central to the day-to-day lives of the occupants" (Altman, 1975, p. 112). If a sport team has the exclusive use of a locker room, practice field, stadium, dormitory, or weight lifting facility, this represents their primary territory. On many American college campuses, public use or student activity in football teams' stadiums, practice areas, or weight training rooms is prohibited. A primary territory is actively controlled by the group, while access or use by nongroup members is prohibited. Access and control over territory can be a source of contention, as illustrated by the example of the locations for competitions for the United States women's soccer team in Exhibit 4.7.

Secondary territories are those "places over which an individual or a group has some control, ownership, and regulatory power but not the same degree as over primary territory" (Altman, 1975, p. 117). In high school sport, a number of teams may share the same facility—a locker room, gymnasium, or playing field. If they do so at the same time (e.g., by splitting the area in half), certain boundary markers become demarcation lines between the groups. These boundary markers might be very actively defended and any intrusion could be met with hostility and conflict.

This hostility/conflict can occur in all manner of sports. The centerline in ice hockey is a well-accepted boundary separating the territories of the two teams during the pregame warm-up. No intrusion into an opponent's territory is permitted. If a puck goes into an opponent's territory, it must be left there to be returned (or not) at the convenience of the opponent. Any player who ventures into the other team's territory risks a confrontation. Exhibit 4.7 highlights a similar example from the sport of baseball.

The third category, *public territories*, has a "temporary quality, and almost anyone has free access and occupancy rights" (Altman, 1975, p. 118). In university gymnasia, individuals or groups may arrive to play basketball. If other individuals or groups occupy the courts, the newcomers are able to join the game. In public tennis courts, it is universally understood that players should alternate on the courts after a set number of games or fixed period of time. Also, as the quote in Exhibit 4.7 illustrates, public spaces are precious and valued, requiring management to allow for use by many interested parties.

Marking Group Territory

Signs and symbols are used either to identify or separate a home territory from the territory of other groups. In sport teams, the signs and symbols representing territoriality may consist of posters, names over lockers, ornaments, and slogans. They also may consist of trophies and flags symbolizing past successes. In their description of the Montreal Forum, the former home territory of the Canadiens, Goyens and Turowetz (1986) outlined the impact of these types of symbols:

> Unlike the teams that have made the Forum great, the building itself is squat and functional ... Inside, the Forum is just another hockey rink at first glance. If you've visited any area of size in the National Hockey League, the impression here will be one of overwhelming sameness ... it could be the Forum in Inglewood, California, or the Capital Center in the middle of nowhere between Baltimore and Washington. Second glance will uncover a series of visual clues that indicate the familiar and the fabled. The stylized CH will be the first reminder of what this building has meant to the sport. But that isn't the key to the Forum either ... Where is the real Forum? Look up. Straight above your head, in the rafters. There you'll find the real Forum. There, high above the ice, they hang silently. To call them just pieces of cloth is like describing an Arras tapestry as just another wallhanging ... Only the Forum holds twenty-three separate white panels on which these words are written in blue with red trim: 'Montreal Canadiens, Stanley Cup Champions.' (pp. 15–16)

The signs and symbols marking territoriality are quite important individually and collectively. Laboratory and field studies have shown that group morale and individual satisfaction are higher, feelings of being crowded are reduced, and a territory is considered to be more pleasant when it becomes personalized through the use of signs and symbols (e.g., Baum & Valins, 1977; Edney & Uhlig, 1977).

The Home Advantage in Sport

One aspect of territoriality that has received considerable attention in sport is what has come to be known as the *home advantage*. There seems to be little doubt that home territory is an important consideration in team success. Over 40 years ago, Schwartz and Barsky (1977) commented on the relative importance of the game location (i.e., being at home versus away) and the ability level of the two teams:

Being at home ... may be as decisive an element of play as being good. The reason for the caution with which this conclusion may be stated is that game location is a real dichotomy while team quality is not ... Therefore, the conservative inference is probably the best one: game location and team quality are equally important determinants of performance. (p. 649)

Courneya and Carron (1992) provided a formal definition of the home advantage: "the consistent finding that home teams in sport competitions win over 50% of the games played under a balanced home and away schedule" (p. 13). They also observed that the presence of a home advantage during regular season competitions is one of the most robust and replicable findings in sport psychology (home advantage in the playoffs may be another matter; this is discussed later in the chapter). A meta-analysis by Jamieson (2010; which took into account sport type, competitive level, competitive era, and length of season) found that home teams will be successful approximately 60% of the time overall. However, does this advantage exist across competitive situations? The following sections explore the findings.

Professional team sports. The extent of the home advantage varies across professional team sports and over time. In an analysis of Major League Baseball, hockey, American football, basketball, and British soccer, it was found that the home advantage (i.e., average over five years) was 53%, 55%, 58%, 61%, and 61%, respectively (see Exhibit 4.8; Pollard & Pollard, 2005). Pollard and colleagues recently followed up this study by examining whether the home advantage differed based on sex, type of team sport, and country (Pollard, Prieto, & Gómez, 2017). Several conclusions and speculative explanations were forwarded. First, for the sports in which comparisons could be made between men and women (e.g., basketball, handball, volleyball), the researchers found that the home advantage was not as strong within female sports. Pollard and colleagues (2017) suggested potential reasons including a lower number of spectators on average (i.e., reduced crowd effect) or physiological differences (i.e., less of an increase in testosterone response for women across playing locations). Second, the sports of basketball and handball were found to have a greater home advantage overall. In this case, environmental

Exhibit 4.8. Historical Trends in the Percentage Home Advantage in Selected Major Professional Sports

Sport	Initial Year	Average Home Advantage in First Five Years	Average Home Advantage in Last Five Years (1998–2002)	Difference
National Baseball League	1876	56.9	53.7	-3.2
American Baseball League	1901	58.0	52.8	-5.2
National Hockey League	1917	67.7	54.6	-13.1
National Football League	1933	53.6	58.2	4.6
National Basketball Association	1946	64.2	61.0	-3.2
British Soccer (Premier League)	1888	67.4	61.0	-6.4

Source. "Long-Term Trends in Home Advantage in Professional Team Sports in North America and England (1876–2003)" by R. Pollard and G. Pollard, 2005, *Journal of Sports Sciences, 23,* 337–350.

factors, including participation in an indoor environment (i.e., increased crowd noise/density) and crowd proximity to the athletes on the court, were suggested as explanations for this effect. Finally, Pollard and colleagues (2017) found that sports played within countries in the Balkan region (e.g., Bosnia-Herzegovina, Croatia, Macedonia), particularly for men, had a stronger home advantage and suggested: "All this pointed to territorial protection as an important contributor to [the home advantage], especially in places with a history for violent conflict, ethnic tension, changing borders, and foreign occupation" (p. 596). Although such investigations using correlational analyses and archival data preclude such a direct link to the violent past of a region, this presents an interesting anthropological or sociological explanation for territorial effects.

International competitions. Countries that host international competitions also seem to enjoy a home advantage. For example, in one of the earliest analysis of the home advantage, Leonard (1989) reported that countries win more medals when they host than they do in immediately preceding or subsequent Olympic Games.

Insight into the dynamics of the home advantage at the Olympics was provided by Balmer and his colleagues (Balmer, Nevill, & Williams, 2001, 2003). Through analysis of the Summer Olympic Games from 1896 to 1996, they found that a substantial home advantage was present in events that are subjectively judged or that rely on subjective decisions. Conversely, however, little or no home advantage was found (and there was even some support for a visitor advantage) in events that were objectively judged. Similar results were found in their analyses of the Winter Olympic Games for the period 1908 to 1998 (Balmer et al., 2001). In sports that used an objective protocol for scoring, such as short-track speed skating, no home advantage was present. In subjectively scored events such as figure skating, however, a substantial home advantage was found.

Recently, studies involving the home advantage were extended to both the winter (1976-2014; Wilson & Ramchandani, 2017a) and summer (1960–2016; Wilson & Ramchandani, 2017b) Paralympic Games. Overall, Wilson and Ramchandani (2017a; 2017b) found strong evidence for a home advantage by the host countries. Furthermore, although all sports examined were objectively judged, they noted that some sports demonstrated a stronger home advantage. In particular, participants in alpine skiing and cross-country skiing (winter sports), as well as athletics, table tennis, and wheelchair fencing (summer sports), appeared to benefit from competing in their home country.

Another international competition that demonstrates a mixed home advantage is the Fédération Internationale de Football Association's (FIFA) World Cup. Originating in the 1930s for men, the FIFA World Cup has been held 21 times (1930–2018). During this period, home nations have won six times, placed second twice, or placed third three times for a total of 11 medals—an overall 52% success rate. Given that in several of the competitions—1994 in the United States, 2002 in South Korea/Japan, 2010 in South Africa, and 2018 in Russia—the host nations were improbable possibilities for a top-three finish, the host nations' record is impressive. The same level of success for host countries in the FIFA Women's World Cup is not present. Of the eight competitions that have taken place (1991–2019), only the team from the United States has successfully defended its territory, winning once in 1999 and placing third in 2003 (a 25% success rate overall).

As a final example, Strauss and Welberg (2008) reported a clear home advantage in the 604 games played from 1910 to 2006 in continental championship soccer tournaments for men (i.e., in Europe, in Africa). Specifically, host nations won 62%, tied 19%, and lost

19% of all games played; when ties were excluded from consideration, the home advantage increased to 76.5%.

Individual sports. The evidence pertaining to the home advantage in individual sports is mixed. On one hand, some studies have found evidence of a home advantage. For example, Bray and Carron (1993) found a 17% improvement over seeding position for alpine skiers competing in their own country. As another example, McAndrew (1993) examined data from 2,086 matches within dual meets among high school wrestlers (i.e., competitions between only two teams), and found that athletes competing at home won 8.6% more matches than did visitors.

On the other hand, another study of two different sports did not find evidence of a home advantage. Because competitors in international golf and tennis have world rankings, Holder and Nevill (1997) were able to determine if athletes competing in their home countries have performances greater than would be expected (i.e., above their world ranking). Their results showed no support for a home advantage.

Finally, Jones (2013) undertook an iterative review of the home advantage in individual sports by examining (a) controlled studies in the sports of tennis, golf, and boxing, (b) Olympic sports, (c) uncontrolled studies across several sports, and (d) specific individual tasks that can be isolated within team sports (e.g., free throw shooting in basketball, shootouts in ice-hockey). The take-away message from this review: there is not strong evidence for a home advantage in individual sports overall. One exception, however, is that subjectively-judged individual sports appear to yield an advantage to those competing at home.

Understanding the Causes of the Home Advantage

What are the major causes of the home advantage? Given that competing at home typically has a small but positive association with the outcome of the competition, there is no shortage of groups willing to weigh in on this question. Coaches, athletes, spectators, the media, and sport psychology researchers have all advanced their theories. However, there is substantial scientific evidence available to explain performance differences based on location. For example, elements of geographic location (i.e., altitude), the audience (i.e., crowd size), and travel (i.e., number of time zones crossed by the visiting team) were recently implicated in a home advantage within the soccer World Cups held from 2006–2014 (Pollard & Armatas, 2017).

Courneya and Carron (1992) and Carron, Loughead, and Bray (2005), drawing on the research of Schwartz and Barsky (1977), proposed that there are four principal factors associated with the game's location that contribute to the home advantage, including the crowd (and to a certain extent, the officials), familiarity/learning, travel, and rules (see Exhibit 4.9).

As Exhibit 4.9 shows, the game location factors are assumed to affect the psychological states of coaches and athletes, which in turn are assumed to affect the behaviors of coaches and athletes.

The final component in the sequence illustrated in Exhibit 4.9 reflects the fact that game location can have an effect on performance at several levels. The primary performance measures are the foundation for team success—errors in baseball, steals in basketball, shots on net in hockey, and so on. Thus, for example, a team may have more steals or penalties at home than on the road. The secondary performance measures reflect the scoring of the competition—points scored, goals allowed, and so on. It is possible, for example, for teams to score fewer points on the road and still win. Finally, the tertiary performance measures are the traditional outcome measures, such as win/loss ratio or points obtained (i.e., two points for a

Exhibit 4.9. A Framework for Game Location Research

Game Location	Game Location Factors	Critical Psychological and Physiological States	Critical Behavioral States	Performance Outcomes
Home	Crowd	Competitors	Competitors	Primary
	Learning			Secondary
	Travel	Coaches	Coaches	
Away	Rules			Tertiary
		Officials	Officials	

Source. "The Home Advantage in Competitions: A Literature Review" by K. S. Courneya and A. V. Carron, 1992, *Journal of Sport & Exercise Psychology, 14*, 13–27.

win, one for a tie, and none for a loss). In the sections that follow, we present evidence from studies that targeted each of the components of Exhibit 4.9.

Game Location Factor: Crowd. Teams competing at home have the potential to benefit from a supportive crowd—and they do. However, what characteristics of the crowd provide for a maximum advantage? Is it the crowd's partisanship (i.e., unqualified support)? Type of behavior (i.e., cheering for the home team; booing the visiting team)? Absolute size? Density (i.e., attendance relative to venue capacity)? Intensity (i.e., noise level)?

The effect of antisocial crowd behavior—swearing, chanting obscenities, throwing objects on the floor, and fighting—is certainly a possibility. Greer (1983) examined the effect of basketball spectator booing that lasted longer than 15 seconds on points scored, turnovers, violations (fouls plus goaltending), and a composite measure of points scored minus turnovers and violations. The home team was superior on all the performance measures and the home team's superiority became greater during episodes of booing behavior.

The results relating to the influence of absolute *crowd size* have been mixed with some studies showing that larger crowds do not improve the home team's advantage while others show that they do. For example, when Dowie (1982) compared the extent of the home advantage in four divisions of English Football League (soccer), he found that the home advantage did not differ from Division 1 to Division 4, despite the average crowd size varying from 25,000 to 2,500 spectators. Also, Agnew and Carron (1994), using data from two seasons of competition in a Canadian Major Junior A ice hockey league, found that absolute crowd size was not at all useful as a predictor of game outcome.

Conversely, however, Nevill, Newell, and Gale (1996) found that absolute crowd size was positively related to the home advantage in English and Scottish soccer. Home teams had increased home winning percentages where crowd size was large, whereas the home advantage was nearly absent in two leagues (i.e., G.M. Vauxhall League, Scottish Second Division) where crowd sizes were small.

The results pertaining to *crowd density* have been relatively consistent. For example, Agnew and Carron (1994) found that crowd density was a reliable predictor of the home advantage in ice hockey. Schwartz and Barsky (1977) extended this research of density within Major League Baseball and found that when the crowd's density was low (less than 20% of capacity), the home team's winning percentage was 48%. This winning percentage increased to 55% when density was moderate (20% to 39.9%) and then to 57% when density was high (greater than 40%). It is plausible that these results reflect team quality—poor teams don't attract very many spectators so their home parks would be almost empty. Ability, not density, might be a logical explanation for the results. However, Schwartz and Barsky (1977) recognized this possibility, and replicated their results using analyses that statistically controlled for ability.

One of the challenges with isolating 'the crowd' as the factor in the home advantage (or any other factor), is the inability to control for confounding variables. For example, is it really the crowd that gives the home team the advantage, or is it the familiarity with the stadium and the lack of fatigue from travelling? Ponzo and Scoppa (2018) examined situations in soccer matches wherein the teams were playing a 'same-stadium' derby. In other words, the two teams actually share a stadium during the season and, when they play each other, one must be designated the home team. Thus, that team has control over the crowd because they admit their own season ticket holders and control the distribution of the remaining seats. This has the advantage of isolating the effect of the crowd on performance. Ponzo and Scoppa (2018) found that the crowd's encouragement afforded an advantage to the home team. Furthermore, they found evidence that the home crowd also influenced referees' decisions in terms of the awarding of penalty shots and the distribution of yellow and red cards (sanctioning actions to the offending player). Further discussion about officiating bias follows in the subsequent paragraphs.

Game Location Factor: Officiating Bias. Numerous studies have found support for the supposition that officiating bias in favor of the home team is a factor in the home advantage. For example, Sumner and Mobley (1981) found that in International Test Cricket, visiting teams were the recipients of more Leg-Before-Wicket decisions (the equivalent of a baseball strike out). Further, Mohr and Larson (1998) found that in Australian football, teams received 10% more free kick decisions when they played on their home (i.e., in-state) grounds than when they played on away (i.e., out-of-state) grounds. However, studies have also found no evidence of officiating bias (e.g., Jones, Bray, & Bolton, 2001, in English Club Cricket matches). As another example, Dennis, Carron, and Loughead (2002) analyzed videotapes of National Hockey League games to determine if incorrect officiating decisions (i.e., a penalty was called when no infraction occurred or an infraction occurred but no penalty was called) favored the home team. No evidence of officiating bias was observed; referees made an equal number of incorrect decisions toward both home and visiting teams.

Finally, Lehman and Reifman (1987) took a slightly different approach. They examined the number of fouls called on higher and lower status professional basketball players (i.e., stars and nonstars) at home and away. They reasoned that officials might feel more pressure to be lenient with a team's star player. As was predicted, fewer fouls were called on star players at home than on the road; for the nonstars, there were no differences in the number of fouls called at home and on the road.

Although this research identifies variability in officiating performance, these types of findings do not necessarily support the conclusion that there is an officiating bias that favours the home team (e.g., Sumner & Mobley, 1981; Varca, 1980). Visiting teams may deserve more negative decisions because of their style of play. To test this possibility, Nevill, Balmar, and Williams (2002) conducted a laboratory study using experimentally manipulated crowd noise. They had two groups of qualified soccer referees record their officiating decisions of a videotape-recorded match under conditions of either crowd noise or silence. Although all referees scored the same match, 2.3 fewer fouls (on average) were called against the home team by those referees experiencing crowd noise compared to those who called the match with no noise present. Nevill et al. (2002) also found that the same number of fouls was called against the visiting team regardless of noise condition, which helped substantiate their supposition that referees are more reluctant or uncertain when it comes to calling fouls against the home team.

There are several possibilities for why officiating bias can arise and/or why there are mixed results across studies. Dosseville, Edoh, and Molinaro (2016) suggested four factors that may be influential with respect to officials' responses at sport venues. First, situational factors are those that are have direct influence in the moment and could include the crowd reactions and time pressures. Second, contextual factors reflect the perceived importance of a match, stadium characteristics (e.g., sound systems), and even the anticipated reputations of particular teams and athletes that might influence decision-making. Third, officials will likely differ significantly on an individual-by-individual basis with respect to coping, emotional intelligence, and even their abilities to interact socially with players and coaches during the match. Finally, ethical and economic factors may come into play such that cultural closeness with a particular team, or competition for better assignments (as examples), may influence decision-making.

Regardless, the good news is that increased training of officials has the potential to mitigate bias favoring the home team. In a review of referee training practices in Association Football (soccer), in combination with qualitative reflections on the home advantage over time (i.e., interviews with current and former elite soccer referees in the United Kingdom), a recent study concluded that "the increase in the quality and availability of training for referees over time has been *the* significant contributory factor to a reduction in the home advantage" (Webb, Dicks, Thelwell, & Nevill, 2018, p. 1034)

Game Location Factor: Familiarity/Learning. Learning factors (see Exhibit 4.9) is an umbrella term that is used to represent environmental considerations of two types: stable and unstable. The *unstable* types consist of those elements that can be manipulated to advantage by the home team. A good example is provided in a commentary on the 2004 National League Championship Series between the Houston Astros and St. Louis Cardinals:

> For anyone who doesn't believe how much power [Roger] Clemens wields in his home ballpark, there were some subtle preparation moves in the moments prior to the game to create the perfect pitching environment for The Rocket. The ground crew hosed down the dirt in the infield for so long there were almost puddles in front of the plate. The effect, of course, is that ground balls don't scoot through quite as quickly and the Cards' swifter base runners are slowed down slightly. (Griffin, 2004, p. E4)

The *stable* types of learning factors are those idiosyncratic elements in the court, rink, or stadium with which the home team has become familiar and to which it has accommodated its play. In a close game, uncertainty and/or errors resulting from a lack of familiarity with the playing surface could prove to be decisive. Visiting teams simply do not have the same amount of experience with the home team's facility. Any research conducted pertaining to learning factors has implicitly studied the stable types.

Clarke and Norman (1995) compared the home advantage of teams competing on atypical surfaces with that of teams competing on standard surfaces for a 10-year period between 1981 and 1990. They found a trend toward a higher-than-average home advantage when team quality was controlled; in short, teams playing on larger or smaller playing surfaces than normal did have an advantage. Furthermore, Clarke and Norman (1995), as well as Barnett and Hilditch (1993), reported that teams playing on artificial turf playing surfaces had higher home advantages than teams playing on natural grass.

Another strategy that has been used to determine the role that facility familiarity plays has been to compare the extent of the home advantage prior to (and following) a move to a new facility (Loughead, Carron, Bray, & Kim, 2003; Moore & Brylinsky, 1995; Pollard, 2002).

Pollard (2002) compared the home winning percentages for the entire season before and after a facility change using 37 teams that had moved to new venues between 1987 and 2001 from the National Basketball Association (NBA), National Hockey League (NHL), and Major League Baseball (MLB). For 26 teams, there was a decrease in the home advantage following a move, 10 teams showed an increase, and one team showed no change.

Using a slightly different approach, Loughead et al. (2003) compared home team game results from three time periods: (a) the block of games (i.e., ten) immediately prior to relocating to a new venue; (b) the block of games (i.e., ten) immediately after relocating to a new venue; and (c) the block of games (i.e., the next ten) when teams were more acclimatized to their new surroundings. The overall home winning percentage prior to moving to a new venue for the 57 teams that had relocated from the National Basketball Association (1991–2000), National Hockey League (1982–2000), and the English and Scottish Professional Football Associations (1988–2000) was 55.2%. The relocation did not produce significant changes in the home advantage. In the time period immediately after relocating, the home winning percentage was reduced to 53.9% and this remained virtually unchanged (53.1%) for the next time period.

These researchers did find, however, that team quality is a moderating factor. High quality teams—teams with a home winning percentage greater than 50% prior to relocation—experienced a significant reduction in home advantage in the period immediately following relocation (from 70.6% to 59.2%). Conversely, low quality teams—teams with a home winning percentage lower than 50% prior to relocation—experienced a significant increase (from 34.1% to 46.8%).

Loughead et al. (2003) suggested three potential explanations for these findings. One was that both high- and low-quality teams might have shown a statistical regression toward the mean. Another was that high quality teams might be better able to use facility familiarity to their advantage. The third was psychological in nature—low quality teams might view a move as an opportunity for a fresh start while high quality teams might experience reduced confidence because of reduced familiarity.

Game Location Factor: Travel. As Exhibit 4.9 shows, another category of factors considered to contribute to a home team's advantage is the travel required by their opponents. Fatigue and the disruption of sleeping and/or eating routines are associated with travel. Also, distance traveled, travel in close proximity to game time, number of successive travels, and times zones crossed all have the potential to negatively influence the preparation of visiting teams (and, consequently, contribute to the home team's advantage). Referring to the schedule of National Basketball Association teams, McMahan (2018) noted

A disruption in the body's circadian rhythm, the 24-hour internal clock that tells us when to sleep and wakeup, may be at the root of the problem. This scrambling of the body clock is multiplied with the number of time zones travelled. Meaning that, for the [New York] Knicks, an away game in Los Angeles would be more difficult to win than one in Milwaukee. It's just one more home court advantage for West Coast teams, hosting sleepy teams from the East. (para. 8)

If there are disadvantages associated with travel, then the *distance traveled* might prove critical. However, the research evidence has provided mixed results. For example, in studies of professional soccer (Pollard, 1986), professional hockey (Pace & Carron, 1992), Junior-A hockey (Agnew & Carron, 1994), and high school, university, and professional basketball (Gayton & Coombs, 1995), no relationship was found between distance traveled and visitor disadvantage. In contrast, Brown, Van Raalte, Brewer, Winter, and Cornelius (2002) found that countries that had further to travel to compete in the 1998 World Cup of soccer scored fewer goals and had more goals scored against them.

Also, if there are disadvantages associated with travel, then the *duration of a road trip* could be important—the longer the trip, the greater the visitor disadvantage. Again, however, the results have been mixed. Smith, Ciacciarelli, Serzan, and Lambert (2000) undertook research with professional hockey, basketball, and baseball. The duration of the road trip failed to predict home team success in either basketball or baseball. However, insofar as professional hockey was concerned, visiting teams had less success during initial games of the road trip; as the road trip progressed, they had more success.

Another line of inquiry has been to examine the possible effects of travel across time zones. The severity of jet lag experienced by travellers and their eventual speed of recovery is a function of the number of time zones crossed and the direction of travel. Also, typically, the body readjusts faster after travel in a westward direction. Using archival data from three seasons in Major League Baseball (MLB), Recht, Lew, and Schwartz (1995) compared performance for teams based in the Eastern time zone and teams in the Pacific time zone (i.e., a three-hour time difference). The only significant finding was that home teams based in the Eastern time zone scored an average 1.24 more runs per game against visiting teams from the Pacific time zone who had just completed eastward travel. A similar finding also emerged in data gathered from the National Football League (NFL). Jehue, Street, and Huizenga (1993) found NFL teams from the Pacific time zone lost more games when visiting teams based in the Eastern and Central time zones.

Game Location Factor: Rules. The category of rule factors acknowledges that some sports involve unique rules that favor home teams (Courneya & Carron, 1992). For instance, there are norms across leagues for home teams in baseball to have the opportunity to bat last or for home hockey teams to receive the final line change. It is difficult to test the effect of the rules on the home advantage, however, because in most situations scientific control is impossible. For example, in professional baseball, the home team not only bats last, it has crowd support, is most familiar with its park, and has not had to travel—we cannot isolate only the role of the rules separate from other influences.

Courneya and Carron (1990) did have access to archival data from a situation where it was possible to assume that the only game location factor that varied for the two teams was their opportunity to bat last. They examined wins and losses in recreation slo-pitch softball leagues where the contests between the teams were double headers and home and visiting team status alternated (i.e., last bat/first bat). The games were played at neutral sites that were equally familiar to both teams, equally accessible to both teams, and equally accessible to the small numbers of fans from both teams who chose to watch. Courneya and Carron found that batting last did not provide a home advantage.

In professional hockey, there are two rules that could provide a home team with an advantage. One pertains to face-offs, the method for starting or resuming play. Athletes competing at home place their stick in the face-off circle after the visiting opponent is set, which is assumed to be advantageous. A second pertains to the shootout, the method for determining the winner when the game is still tied after an overtime period. Home teams are awarded the choice of going first or second in the shootout process. Presumably, the option selected suits the home team coach's assessment of team strength. When Liardi and Carron (2011) investigated the products of these two rules, they found some support for a home advantage. That is, home teams had better face-off success, winning 52.3%, 52.1%, and 51.4% in the offensive, defensive, and neutral zones, respectively. However, no advantage was evident in shootouts as home teams only won 47.1% of the games. This result was reinforced by Hoffman, Loughead, Dixon, and Crozier (2017), who found that "the odds of a home team winning decreased by 23% when games were determined in the shootout compared to overtime" (p. 28) in a follow-up study examining matches played between 2005 and 2014.

Psychological states of athletes and coaches. As the conceptual model presented in Exhibit 4.9 illustrates, it is assumed that the game location will have an effect on the psychological states of two groups of individuals who exert an influence on the outcome of the competition: competitors and coaches. In total, this body of research has yielded somewhat mixed results. Studies using retrospective descriptions and hypothetical scenarios have supported a conclusion that athletes' psychological states are superior at home. For example, Bray and colleagues (Bray, Culos, Gyurcsik, Widmeyer, & Brawley, 1998; Bray & Widmeyer, 1995) found that female collegiate basketball players reported their teams had higher levels of collective efficacy and that they were less anxious, more motivated, and better able to concentrate when playing at home compared to away. Athletes also believed increased self-confidence played an important role in better performance when competing at home.

Similarly, in one of the most comprehensive studies of precompetitive psychological states and home advantage, Terry, Walrond, and Carron (1998) had male university and club rugby players complete measures of mood, cognitive, and somatic state anxiety, and self-confidence prior to a pair of home and away matches. Results showed consistent game location effects across all variables. Cognitive anxiety, somatic anxiety, tension, depression, anger, fatigue, and confusion were all lower prior to the home match compared to the away match, while self-confidence and vigor were higher. However, in contrast, four studies that have directly examined athlete mood states prior to both home and away competitions have failed to observe differences (Bray & Martin, 2003; Duffy & Hinwood, 1997; Kerr & Vanschaik, 1995; Neave & Wolfson, 2003).

Neave and Wolfson (2003) noted that territoriality behaviors are prevalent among many animal species such that a protective response is stimulated when outsiders invade. Associated with that protective response are heightened levels of testosterone. Thus, Neave and Wolfson proposed that "if testosterone levels are indeed linked with assertiveness and dominance and if humans also fight harder to defend their perceived home territory, there may be alterations in testosterone levels in sport competitions when playing at home and away" (p. 270).

The psychological states of *coaches* prior to home and away competitions have received minimal research attention. Dennis (1998, Study 1) had professional hockey coaches from the

National Hockey League and Ontario Hockey League respond to questions about confidence and mood prior to home and away games. Greater confidence was reported for home games but there were no differences in various mood states (irritability, nervousness, enthusiasm, anger, sociability).

Behavioral states of athletes and coaches. As Exhibit 4.9 illustrates, the game location, specific game location factors, and psychological states of coaches and competitors are assumed to influence their behaviors. The critical behaviors of athletes that could be influenced by game location include performance, aggressiveness, persistence, effort expended, and so on.

A study by Varca (1980) provided support for the view that the differences in success at home versus away can be attributed to factors such as greater aggressiveness, hustle, and intensity. However, Varca found that aggression on offense versus defense is not as important as whether the aggression is functional or dysfunctional. On one hand, functional aggression includes behaviors such as rebounds, steals, and blocked shots—skills which facilitate effective performance. On the other hand, dysfunctional aggression includes fouls—behaviors that detract from effective performance. The college basketball teams studied by Varca were considerably more successful at home than on the road with a winning percentage of 70% at home. Also, the home teams were more functionally aggressive. They had more steals, rebounds, and blocked shots. At the same time, they committed fewer fouls—the measure of dysfunctional aggression.

In their study of game location and aggression in the National Hockey League, McGuire, Courneya, Widmeyer, and Carron (1992) pointed out that the key component of aggressive behavior—one that sets it off from assertiveness and other similar concepts—is an intention to injure. They used elite hockey players' judgments to identify 13 aggressive penalties (boarding, butt-ending, charging, cross-checking, elbowing, fighting, high-sticking, instigating, kneeing, matching, roughing, slashing, and spearing). They then examined the degree to which game location was related to aggression during the 1987–88 season. The results showed that home teams were not more aggressive than visiting teams and teams that won were not more aggressive than teams that lost.

The location of a match can also be distinguished by the nonverbal cues displayed by athletes prior to a match (Furley, Schweizer, & Memmert, 2018). Researchers showed short video clips of professional and amateur soccer players just prior to a match (e.g., waiting for the opening whistle, in a huddle) to observers who were asked to make a determination as to whether the individuals were playing at home or away. The participants were able to detect, above chance, where the athletes were playing. Furthermore, the nonverbal cues they picked up on appeared to signal assertiveness, dominance, and aggression on the part of the home players. The researchers suggested that these are evolved responses to territorial threats on display by the home players.

For coaches, the critical behaviors that could be influenced by game location include strategic and tactical decisions. For example, professional soccer teams and ice hockey teams often play cautiously and defensively initially when they are playing away from home (Pollard, 1986). Commenting on the approach taken by soccer teams on the road, Pollard (1986) noted that in European Cup competitions, visiting teams adopted ultra-defensive tactics because a 1-0 defeat was considered to be a success.

Dennis and Carron (1999) carried out two studies to determine whether hockey coaches adopt different strategies depending on the location of the game. In Study 1, when National Hockey League and Major Junior-A League coaches were interviewed, they reported using an assertive forechecking style more at home than on the road (81.1% versus 71.8% respectively).

In ice hockey, assertive forechecking has specific behavioral characteristics. In the offensive zone, constant pressure is placed on the puck carrier by at least two of the three forwards. Also, the defense plays assertively, "pinching in" along the boards. This system results in the opposition passing the puck and clearing their zone under considerable pressure. The fundamental objective of an assertive defensive strategy is to force a turnover by the opposition in its own zone in order to create a scoring opportunity.

For Study 2, Dennis and Carron (1999) conducted a video analysis of 62 National Hockey League games to assess whether the coaches stated strategies were translated into team play. It was found that the degree of assertive forechecking was even more prevalent than the coaches had suggested (i.e., 90.0% at home versus 82.2% on the road).

Can Home Territory Be a Disadvantage?

Tychkowksi (2019) made the following observation about the National Hockey League Edmonton Oilers during the 2018–2019 season:

> No offence to a very nice building and the people who fill it, but home ice has not been the advantage it's supposed to be this season. In fact, it hasn't been any kind of an advantage at all. Edmonton is below .500 at home (14-15-2) and just 3-6-1 in their last 10 games there. It's an issue (one of them, anyway) that's been giving them fits all year. It's a question they've been trying to answer for months. But with time running out on the season and a wildcard spot tantalizingly close, but still desperately far away, the time for talking about it is over. It's win or go home. Or, rather, go home and win. (para. 3–4)

Similarly, Baumeister and Steinhilber (1984) published an article that showed there are times when competing at home could be a disadvantage. In a seven-game championship series in baseball and basketball, Games 1, 2, 5, and 7 are played at the home of the team that had the superior record throughout the regular season. In the initial games, the home team won 60.2% of the time in baseball and 70.1% of the time in basketball. However, as the championship series progressed and neared completion, the home advantage seemed to reverse itself and become a disadvantage. When the final game was either Game 5, 6, or 7, the winning percentage for the home team dropped to 40.8% in baseball and 46.3% in basketball. When the championship series was tied at three games each, the home advantage virtually disappeared. The home team won only 38.5% of the time in both baseball and basketball.

To determine whether this startling reversal of the home advantage was due to the home team choking or to the visiting team excelling, Baumeister and Steinhilber (1984) analyzed individual performances in the baseline games and the seventh game. They chose errors in baseball as the measure of choking because, unlike pitching or batting, they are not directly influenced by the other team. An error, by definition, is a poor performance that, in the judgment of the official scorer, should have been handled successfully. In basketball, free throws were used. This is also an individual performance measure that is not mutually determined by the athlete and an opponent. Therefore, it is also a relatively good measure of choking.

It was expected that for all of these measures, the home team should have an advantage. In the World Series, for example, the home team is much more familiar with the playing surface and its idiosyncrasies. It has had a full season of games in the stadium whereas the visitors have only played three previous playoff games. In basketball, the home team isn't subject to the same harassment and distractions while shooting free throws. Nonetheless, despite these advantages, members of the home team performed more poorly in Game 7 than members of the visiting team. In baseball, for example, in the initial games, the home team committed less errors than the visitors (0.65 versus 1.04 per game) and had more errorless games (33 versus 18 games). But, in Game 7 situations, the home team committed more errors than the visitors (1.31 versus 0.81 per game) and had fewer errorless games (6 versus 12 games).

In basketball, the home and visiting teams were approximately equal in the initial games. The home team shot 72% from the free throw line, the visitors, 73%. In Game 7, however, while the visitors stayed about the same (74%), the home team dropped to 69%. On the basis of these results, Baumeister and Steinhilber (1984) concluded that the reversal of home advantage in Game 7 was primarily due to choking on the part of the home team, not improvement on the part of the visiting team.

According to Baumeister (1985), the underlying reason for the home team's choke is that athletes become preoccupied with self-presentation. In other words, players begin to dwell on how they will perform or how others will perceive or describe their performance. When an event increases in importance, concerns with self-presentation also increase. When there is an opportunity to claim a desired identity—"champion," "winner," "best," "smartest"—concerns with self-presentation also increase. And, when there is an opportunity to claim a desired identity in front of a sympathetic, supportive audience, concerns with self-presentation are maximal. Baumeister (1985) further suggested that relatively easy and automatic tasks soon become mechanical as individuals focus their attention inward toward self-presentational concerns. Athletes pay too much attention to what they are doing and how they are doing it. Instead of performing their skills automatically, they begin to concentrate on a step-by-step execution. Baumeister (1985) pointed out

> The pressure, the chance for self-redefinition, and the audience all encourage choking by the home team. Most pro athletes are tough and experienced enough to cope with one or two of these factors during the season. But the combination of all three—found chiefly in championship play—is psychologically different from regular season play. That may be why it is so rare for a team to win a championship the first time it qualifies for the playoffs. And, it is not surprising that even seasoned athletes become self-conscious and choke. (p. 52)

If this is the case, then is a home disadvantage also present in the playoffs in other sports? As it pertains to the general results of professional ice hockey, for example, conflicting evidence has been provided. Gayton, Matthews, and Nickless (1987) failed to find a home disadvantage. The home advantage in terms of winning percentage was 53.8% in the initial games, 52.5% when Games 5, 6, and 7 were considered as the last game, and 58.3% when the series went to a deciding seventh game. In contrast, Wright, Voyer, Wright, and Roney (1995) reported that a home disadvantage exists in National Hockey League playoff competitions using a slightly different set of comparison points (i.e., they used Games 1 and 3 as their baseline measures and compared these baseline results against the last game in the playoff series).

The home disadvantage does, however, seem to be reasonably pronounced in other ice hockey situations that might be threatening from a self-presentational perspective, both in regular season games and playoffs. For example, the earlier Hoffman et al. (2017) example highlighted that the home team's winning percentage decreased in games that went to a tie-breaking shootout. Furthermore, visiting teams have an advantage in playoff clinching situations when these games go into overtime (McEwan, 2019).

Another sport in which a home disadvantage during playoff competitions has not been found is American football. Kornspan, Lerner, Ronayne, Etzel, and Johnson (1995) found that home teams won 71% of the playoff games held in the two conferences of the National Football League—no support whatsoever for a home team choke. As a final example, Wright, Jackson, Christie, McGuire, and Wright (1991) found support for a home disadvantage in golf. They compared the scores of contending British (i.e., "home") golfers with those of contending foreign golfers from the first to final rounds of the British Open Golf Championship. It was noted that the scores of contending British golfers dropped off more during the course of the competition than those of foreign golfers who were also in contention.

Summary of research on the home disadvantage. What can we make of the above? Is it reasonable to conclude that teams choke in championship competitions played in front of home spectators? The jury seems to be out insofar as the results from sport research are concerned. That is, various authors have suggested that the conclusion that a home disadvantage is present in championship competitions should be questioned because of (a) the small number of games on which that conclusion is based, (b) the failure to find a home disadvantage in other sports (e.g., football), and (c) the failure to find a home disadvantage when perennially dominant teams are excluded from the analyses (Benjafield, Liddell, & Benjafield, 1989; Courneya & Carron, 1992; Heaton & Sigall, 1989). A fourth compelling reason why the conclusion may be tenuous is that a reanalysis of basketball and baseball by Schlenker, Phillips, Boniecki, and Schlenker (1995)—which also included playoff results in the 10 years following the work of Baumeister and Steinhilber (1984)—casts doubt about the presence of a home team choke in those sports, as well. Schlenker et al. (1995) observed that "there is no convincing evidence for a home-field championship choke that places the home team at a disadvantage in decisive contests. The home team has an advantage in all phases of a championship series" (p. 641).

Schlenker et al. (1995) suggested that the home disadvantage found by Baumeister and Steinhilber (1984) could have been due to one abnormal period in the history of baseball—between the years of 1950 and 1968. During that period, visiting teams won nine of 11 World Series that went to a seventh game. Throughout the remaining history of the World Series (and League Championship games), home teams had a consistent advantage.

However, the last word should probably go to Baumeister. In a rebuttal of the Schlenker et al. (1995) work, Baumeister (1995) pointed out that

> … despite using an imprecise, weak analysis strategy and including data that were confounded by rule changes (which they did not mention), Schlenker et al. (1995) still found results that did not differ significantly from those found by Baumeister and Steinhilber (1984). They merely found that the effect dropped below significance. This does not seem to justify a sweeping conclusion that the home-field disadvantage hypothesis is wrong. (p. 646)

5

Member Attributes

During the 1950s, the Jackie Robinson Brooklyn Dodgers were outspoken, opinionated, bigoted, tolerant, black, white, open, passionate: in short, a fascinating mix of vigorous men. (Kahn, 1972, p. xi)

During World War II, a series of conferences were attended by what was referred to as The Big Three: Franklin Roosevelt, Joseph Stalin, and Winston Churchill. The purpose of these meetings was to negotiate the terms of cooperation between the Allies in their war efforts and then, the terms for peace in Europe following the war. It is doubtful that any group could have had three more contrasting group members. They differed in personality, motives, political ideology, attitudes, and even in energy and physical health since Roosevelt's health was rapidly deteriorating by 1944. Differences were also present within The Big Three in the way in which they were able to get along with each other.

For example, Alsop (1982), Roosevelt's biographer, noted that Roosevelt and Churchill became very close personal friends and that this close friendship "was the cornerstone of the Western alliance throughout the war … a partnership of the war leaders of two great nations like no other one can think of in history" (p. 243). This type of close friendship between two group members has the potential to destroy a three-person group—particularly if the other dyadic relationships within the group are not as positive. In The Big Three, they weren't. Although Stalin and Churchill were cordial and respected each other, there was also mutual suspicion and no friendship in their relationship. Similarly, the relationship between Roosevelt and Stalin was also marked by cordiality and mutual respect but not friendship. Nikita Khrushchev (1970) pointed out in his autobiography that "Stalin was more sympathetic to Roosevelt than Churchill because Roosevelt seemed to have considerable understanding of our problems … in disputes during the working sessions in Teheran, Stalin often found Roosevelt siding with him against Churchill" (pp. 222–223).

So, here was a group composed of men of completely different personalities and political ideologies who established interpersonal relationships that varied markedly in their friendship. As a group, they were responsible for establishing and maintaining the framework for cooperation between the superpowers and their Allies. Despite their personal differences and the differences in their interpersonal relationships, they operated as a cohesive, effective group. The fact that they did testifies to the complex nature of groups.

Although the Big Three could never be described as a typical group, it did have aspects in common with every other group, including sport teams. Like every other group, it was composed of independent, dissimilar individuals. Like every other group, those individuals brought a wide range of attitudes, motives, abilities, previous experiences, and other characteristics to the group situation. The quote about Jackie Robinson's Brooklyn Dodgers used to introduce this chapter highlights this aspect of group membership. Differences among the group members—such as were present in the Big Three or the Brooklyn Dodgers—can split a group. But, in both cases, they didn't. Not surprisingly, researchers have been intrigued by the effect of group composition and member characteristics on group effectiveness. What are the conditions under which personal differences are ignored or even used as elements to build a better group? What are the conditions under which these differences destroy the fabric of the group? In short, how does group composition influence group cohesion and group effectiveness?

Group Composition

Initially, it may be helpful to look at what is meant by group composition and the approaches that have been used to study it. Group composition is defined as "the relationships among the characteristics of individuals who compose the group" (Shaw, 1981, p. 454). Teams are composed of individuals, and the skills, abilities, energies, and personal characteristics of each individual member contributes to a group's composition. As noted by Kenny and Garcia (2012), "Understanding how a group member thinks, feels, and behaves as a function of who he or she is and who the others are in the group is a central question in group research" (p. 469).

The individual attributes that the group can draw upon include physical size and body type, mental and motor abilities, attitudes, aptitudes, motives, needs, differing demographic backgrounds, and personality traits. There is no doubt that the interrelationship of group members' characteristics is complex. The difficulty in determining the relationship of individual psychosocial attributes to team effectiveness was highlighted by Steiner (1972), who noted that

> Any single individual may be regarded as a composite of many attributes. He possesses certain skills to a high degree and others in meager measure; he is well informed about some topics and ignorant of others; his personality involves a concatenation of interrelated propensities that may be patterned in myriad ways. Humans are multifaceted beings, any two of whom may resemble one another with respect to one property but may be dissimilar with respect to another. For this reason, research dealing with group composition always requires a simplification of unmanageable complexities. (pp. 106–107)

Amount of Group Resources

On the basis of common sense or intuition, two contrasting conclusions seem plausible about the relation between the amount of specific characteristics or attributes of group members and group effectiveness. On the one hand, it seems reasonable to expect that some personal qualities are beneficial to group functioning. Achievement motivation, conscientiousness, and intelligence are all potentially positive attributes for any group member. As such, having a large amount of those qualities in a large number of group members should contribute to group effectiveness. Conversely, neuroticism, excessive pride, hostility, and a lack of self-control are all potentially negative attributes. Thus, it seems plausible that if a large number of members possessed negative attributes (and in large amounts) and only a few members possessed the positive ones (and in small amounts), the team should be less effective.

On the other hand, however, the psychosocial attributes of individual team members might be unrelated to team performance. People are complex—they possess a large number of attributes in differing degrees and combinations. Kluckhohn and Murray (1949) emphasized this point when they observed that each individual is like all other people, like some other people, and like no other person. All of us are intelligent to some extent; we're like every other person in this regard. Some of us are even identical in intelligence, but our intelligence in combination with all of our other traits makes us unique; we are like no other person. We bring that uniqueness to the group.

Researchers have studied the amount of resources possessed by a group from several perspectives. One way to assess the amount of resources possessed by a group is by looking at the average level of an attribute (or several attributes) possessed by individuals in a group. A group that possesses a larger amount of a particular attribute will have a higher team mean score. For simplicity, we refer to this as the *team mean score* approach, which has been popular in the study of personality traits and team effectiveness. However, researchers have assessed group composition in other ways. A second approach is considering the maximum attribute possessed by a single person within a group (i.e., *team maximum score*). With this approach, researchers are interested in how a group member who scores extremely high on an attribute might help (or harm) group functioning. A third approach is to consider the minimum level of an attribute possessed by a single group member (i.e., *team minimum score*). In contrast to the maximum score approach, the minimum score approach focuses on how the group member who scores the lowest on a specific attribute might contribute to group functioning. The first three approaches to group composition reflect ways to assess the amount of resources possessed by a group. Although group composition can also be examined by considering the diversity and compatibility of attributes in a group, we discuss these approaches later in the chapter.

In a recent review of the literature in sport, Hardy, Benson, and Boulter (2020) discussed how Steiner's (1972) typology of group tasks might be a useful framework for understanding when different amounts of group resources (i.e., team mean score, team maximum score, team minimum score) are more relevant to team effectiveness. For example, the mean score approach might be more relevant to sport team performance for *additive tasks*, where the group outcome is based on the sum of individual products (e.g., gymnastics team). In contrast, the maximum score approach is perhaps more relevant to group functioning for *disjunctive tasks*, where the group outcome can be determined by a single individual's output (i.e., deciding who to select in the first round of the NFL). Finally, the minimum score approach might be particularly relevant to group functioning for *conjunctive tasks* (e.g., a rowing team), where performance is determined by the output of the weakest team member. An important caveat pointed out by Hardy et al. (2019), however, is minimal research has tested the utility of Steiner's typology. As noted by Bell (2007) from a meta-analytic integration of research in work and organizational groups, "results from the meta-analysis offer little support for the application of Steiner's task typology as a justification for identifying the most appropriate operationalization of the team composition variable" (p. 607). One issue with Steiner's typology is that group members interact across a range of tasks and social contexts. In addition, teammates' personalities or values might influence team dynamics beyond the field, arena, or court. Thus, it might be difficult for researchers to categorize sport teams as belonging to a single group task category, and these categories might not reflect the full range of tasks undertaken by a particular group.

As highlighted in the previous section, the amount of resources possessed by a group can be conceptualized in several ways. Another crucial question, however, is which types of member attributes are more or less beneficial for group functioning. Put another way, if the coaching staff or front office has the goal of selecting members to maximize group effectiveness, which member characteristics should they select for?

The Amount of Individual Ability

A fundamental assumption is that individual ability is the foundation for group success. Therefore, groups that possess greater numbers of members with high ability should be more successful. Researchers have consistently demonstrated that a relation exists between the amount of resources in the group (the level of ability of individual group members) and group problem solving (Heslin, 1964; Mann, 1959). In sport teams, perhaps, the most relevant attribute (resource) that group members can bring to the situation is physical skill and ability. As might be expected, there is a strong, positive relation between the average amount of individual ability present in a team and team effectiveness:

> Stylistically, it is so difficult—arguably impossible—for anyone to truly replicate what the Warriors do. Even before the addition of arguably the league's best pure scorer in Durant, Golden State possessed a point guard with the sort of 35-foot range that most players would only see in a practice setting. In the same backcourt, the Warriors had another guard who was arguably an even more accurate shooter, with a release that is the quickest in basketball—so fast that he doesn't even need to have his feet set before he shoots. Put another way, this is the best shooting team the sport has ever seen. Golden State breaks defenses regardless of how well positioned or prepared they are. The Warriors were the best jump-shooting club in the NBA when left wide open this past season. And a closer look at the numbers shows the Dubs were also the best jump-shooting team in situations where a defender was draped all over them. Because of that, there really is no surefire way to guard this team. (Herring, 2018, para. 4–5)

Several studies (Widmeyer, Loy, & Roberts, 1980; Widmeyer & Loy, 1989) were carried out to examine the member resources-group effectiveness question. In an early study of male tennis doubles teams, Widmeyer et al. (1980) found a correlation of 0.54 between the ability of the individual members and team performance. In a more comprehensive report, Widmeyer and

Loy (1989) had two independent raters judge the skill of eight female tennis players in the serve, volley, forehand, and backhand. Winloss records were assessed for the 28 teams (i.e., the eight players combined as teammates in all of the possible combinations). The results showed that the average ability of the two players was related to the team's effectiveness. The correlations for the individual components were 0.30 between the doubles team's forehand ability and team success; 0.42 for the doubles team's ability to serve and team success; 0.61 for the doubles team's ability to volley and team success; and 0.79 for the doubles team's backhand ability and team success. The correlation between overall individual tennis ability and team success was 0.77. The authors suggested that backhand ability was the best predictor of team success because of a greater variation for this stroke across all players than for any of the other abilities tested.

Jones (1974) carried out an extensive investigation of the relationship between individual ability and team success. He used individual statistics in professional tennis (singles rankings), baseball (runs batted in and earned run averages), basketball (points, assists, rebounds), and football (points for and against). These statistics were then correlated with team effectiveness as represented by rankings and win-loss records. Team effectiveness and individual skill and ability were correlated 0.70 in men's tennis, 0.80 in women's tennis, 0.91 in football, 0.94 in baseball, and 0.60 in basketball.

The fact that the highest relationship found by Jones (1974) was in baseball and the lowest was in basketball is consistent with what would be predicted from Steiner's proposition that actual productivity is a product of the potential productivity of a group minus the losses due to faulty group processes. Faulty group processes result primarily from the inability of group members to coordinate their efforts efficiently and effectively. In baseball, the amount of coordination required on offense and defense is relatively small, so the potential losses due to faulty group processes in any team would be small. Consequently, the team with the best actual productivity (win-loss record) should most frequently be the one with the best potential productivity (i.e., the best players). In the Jones study, this was the case as reflected in the very high correlation of 0.94. In basketball, greater coordinative team play is required on offense and defense. Thus, individual talent by itself (potential productivity) is not as strongly related to actual productivity. The ability to play well together (i.e., to minimize the process losses) is important. This was also reflected in the relatively lower correlation of 0.60 found by Jones. A summary of the relationships between members' ability resources and team performance outcome is presented in Exhibit 5.1.

Although the relation between individual measures of ability and team performance are not perfect (i.e., a team composed of the most highly skilled players does not always produce the best team), there is sufficiently strong evidence to support the view that coaches should always select on ability first.

The Amount of Psychosocial Attributes of Members

Much of the research examining how the amount of group member attributes relates to group performance has focused on the Big Five personality characteristics. Personality psychologists, based on empirical analyses, have organized the taxonomy of personality into five continuous dimensions that have come to be known as the Big Five. Each label attached to these five dimensions and the more specific facets considered characteristic of each are summarized in Exhibit 5.2.

Industrial and organizational psychologists have extensively examined the relations between each of the Big Five and performance in work groups. Summarizing this work, Bell

Exhibit 5.1. The Relationships between the Quantity of Members' Ability and Team Performance Outcome

Reference	Sport/Skill	Relationship to Team Performance
Jones (1974)	Women's Pro Tennis	r = .80
Jones (1974)	Men's Pro Tennis	r = .71
Jones (1974)	Pro Football	r = .91
Jones (1974)	Pro Baseball	r = .94
Jones (1974)	Pro Basketball	r = .60
Widmeyer & Gossett (1978)	Men's Intramural Basketball	r = .73
Spense (1980)	Women's Intramural Basketball	r = .78
Widmeyer et al. (1980)	Men's Club Tennis	r = .54
Widmeyer & Loy (1989)	Women's Tennis Forehand	r = .30
Widmeyer & Loy (1989)	Women's Tennis Backhand	r = .79
Widmeyer & Loy (1989)	Women's Tennis Serve	r = .42
Widmeyer & Loy (1989)	Women's Tennis Volley	r = .61
Widmeyer & Loy (1989)	Women's Tennis Overall	r = .77

Source. "Group composition in sport," by W. N. Widmeyer, 1990, *International Journal of Sport Psychology, 21*, 264–285.

(2007) conducted a meta-analysis of studies examining how personality characteristics (as well as several other group composition variables) are associated with team performance. All studies included in the meta-analysis used performance metrics that captured the general goals or objectives pursued by the team. Although studies of sport teams were not included in this meta-analysis, both laboratory (i.e., groups contrived for the duration of an experiment) and field teams (i.e., existing groups in organizations) were included.

First, personality traits were more strongly associated with team performance in field studies than laboratory studies. In field studies, conscientiousness, agreeableness, extraversion, and openness to experiences among team members positively related to team performance. In

Exhibit 5.2. The Big Five Personality Taxonomy

Trait	Specific Facets of the Trait
Extraversion	Sociability, assertiveness, energy level
Neuroticism (lower scores on this dimension, also referred to as emotional stability)	Anxiety, depression, emotional volatility
Agreeableness	Compassion, respectfulness, trust
Conscientiousness	Organizational ability, productiveness, responsibility
Openness	Intellectual curiosity, aesthetic sensitivity

Note. Specific facets are based on the BFI-2 (Soto & John, 2017).

addition, using the team mean score approach (group's average score) tended to yield slightly stronger associations than using both the maximum score (highest score possessed by a single member) and minimum score (lowest score possessed by a single member) approaches. A notable example is that emotional stability was only positively related to team performance when using the mean score approach. However, the personality trait of agreeableness did not follow this trend. For agreeableness, the minimum score was the strongest negative predictor of team performance. This means that having a single group member who is highly disagreeable might interfere with group performance.

Interestingly, Bell's (2007) meta-analysis was not limited to the Big Five personality dimensions. Several other personal attributes were examined in relation to team performance. To briefly summarize the key findings, team levels of general mental ability (i.e., a person's capacity to comprehend complex ideas, acquire new knowledge, and problem solve) were positively associated with team performance. Similarly, teams tended to perform better when they endorsed collectivism values (i.e., an orientation that prefers social harmony, cooperation, and ingroup loyalty) or had a strong preference for teamwork.

Despite much less research on the relation between personality traits and group dynamics in sport, the extant literature suggests that athletes' personality traits are important to sport team functioning. Notably, Jackson, Dimmock, Gucciardi, and Grove (2010) examined how personality traits were associated with relationship commitment in athlete-athlete dyads. They recruited athletes from a variety of dyadic sport types (e.g., badminton, beach volleyball, rowing) to complete an assessment of their own and their partner's personality traits on the Big Five—openness, conscientiousness, extraversion, agreeableness, neuroticism/emotional stability, as well as their current level of relationship commitment. Athletes were more committed to their partner when their partner scored higher in agreeableness, conscientiousness, and openness. Interestingly, athletes were also more committed to their partner when they perceived their partner to be higher in agreeableness, conscientiousness, and openness.

Beyond the Big Five, several other personality characteristics have been studied in sport contexts. Hill, Stoeber, Brown, and Appleton (2014) examined the association between team levels of perfectionism and performance in high-level rowing crews. This study looked at multiple aspects of perfectionism, including self-oriented perfectionism (i.e., holding oneself to excessively high standards and stringent self-evaluation) and team-oriented perfectionism (i.e., holding team members to high standards and stringent evaluation of others). A key strength of the study design was that the researchers tracked changes in performance over the course of a four-day regatta. They found that the level of perfectionistic standards within a team positively predicted crew performance.

Another personality trait studied in relation to sport team performance is grandiose narcissism. At the root of grandiose narcissism is a strong sense of entitlement and feelings of superiority (Krizan & Herlache, 2018). People who score highly on grandiose narcissism believe they are special and better than others. A growing area of interest for group researchers is the connection between narcissism and leadership (described in Chapter 10). However, researchers have also begun to examine how team levels of narcissism are associated with performance. Griljalva, Maynes, Badura, and Whiting (2019) tested whether narcissism helped or hindered team performance using archival data from the National Basketball Association. Although narcissism is typically assessed using a self-report questionnaire composed of self-referential statements (e.g., "I show others how special I am," from the Narcissistic Admiration and Rivalry Questionnaire; Back et al., 2013), it is understandably difficult to gain access to NBA players, let alone get them to complete personality measures. To get around this issue,

Griljalva et al. (2019) coded NBA players' Twitter account profile pictures and tweets for narcissistic content. After validating their coding system, the researchers computed narcissism scores for each team member. They assessed team performance based on wins and losses, as well as the margin of victory. The researchers also evaluated team coordination by documenting the number of assists per game. Overall, teams with higher mean and maximum levels of narcissism tended to (1) perform worse and (2) exhibited poorer team coordination over the duration of an NBA season. Interestingly, the negative effects of team narcissism were more pronounced in teams where players were more familiar with one another. This suggests that the consequences of narcissism for team effectiveness may worsen over time.

A topic that has received more attention in sport is team member motivation. Motivation is a construct that represents a person's selectivity, intensity, and persistence in behavior. For example, if one athlete chooses to train while a second does not, this choice (i.e., different selection) is considered to be a manifestation of motivation. Also, if two athletes are training and one works harder than the other, the difference in effort (i.e., greater intensity) is also a manifestation of motivation. Finally, if two athletes are training and one continues after the other has stopped, this persistence (i.e., greater duration) is also considered to be a manifestation of motivation.

Motivation accounts for both the focus (selection) and the energy (intensity and duration) for behavior. Theorists in group dynamics have assumed that it is possible to determine the nature and strength of a group's primary goals by examining the primary motivation of its individual members. Task motives are associated with the group's goals and objectives. When a group is engaged in activities that are task oriented (playing basketball, practicing with an elite team), an individual's task needs are fulfilled. Affiliation motives are associated with social needs and interpersonal relationships. Thus, when group members have an opportunity to socialize with one another before or after practice and to develop and maintain friendships through participation in sport, their social needs are fulfilled.

The influence of affiliation and task motivation on the success and satisfaction experienced by 1,200 college males participating on 144 intramural basketball teams was examined by Martens (1970). The task and affiliation motives of each athlete were assessed by a questionnaire administered prior to the season. The average response for the members of each team was then computed. Each team's win-loss record was used as the measure of success and the degree of team satisfaction was obtained by averaging the individual responses from a postseason questionnaire. The two motives were quite distinct in their effect upon performance and satisfaction. Teams higher in affiliation motivation were less successful but were more satisfied than teams lower in affiliation motivation. Thus, when members of a team are strongly concerned with developing and maintaining warm personal relationships within a group, performance effectiveness and ultimate success may suffer. Martens also found that teams higher in task motivation were more successful and more satisfied than teams lower in task motivation. So, when team members are strongly oriented toward group performance goals and effectively completing group tasks, teams are more likely to perform effectively and achieve success. Also, the individuals are more satisfied with their group experience.

A number of other authors have also examined how the personal orientation of group members relates to group effectiveness. For example, Cooper and Payne (1967) found a strong positive correlation of .72 between the task motivation of coaches/trainers and team success in soccer teams. Subsequent research found that athletes on more successful soccer teams were more task-oriented and less affiliation-oriented than athletes on less successful teams (Cooper & Payne, 1972).

Sorrentino and Sheppard (1978) examined two affiliation motives of swimmers in individual versus group competition. They discovered that approval-oriented swimmers (i.e., motive to gain approval is greater than the motive to avoid social rejection) had faster swimming speeds in group versus individual competitions, whereas rejection-threatened (i.e., motive to avoid social rejection is greater than motive to gain approval) swimmers had slower swimming speeds in group than in individual competition. Thus, teams may benefit from having athletes who are approval-oriented than rejection-threatened in order to maximize performance and minimize social loafing (see Chapter 4).

In summary, several member attributes are potentially important to team functioning. But teams are complex entities. Thus, researchers must carefully consider a range of factors (e.g., type of attribute, type of sport, how the attribute is measured at the team-level, the timing of the measurement) when examining the effect of the quantity of group resources.

Diversity of Group Resources

Early in the 2019–2020 season of the Toronto Raptors, it was clear that the team's mix of diverse personalities and skillsets was viewed as a potential strength to be harnessed:

> Sports teams can make for fascinating studies in the human condition and human interaction: a dozen or so Type-A personalities thrust together in a potentially volatile mix, a gamble that somehow interpersonal relationships will thrive… 'Everyone has their own individual personalities, but everyone on this team knows how to come outside their own box and their own bubble to be able to accept others and be in their bubbles,' says Kyle Lowry, one of the team's longest serving members and in many ways its heart. 'That's where we've got good professionals.' (Smith, 2018, para.1–8)

Indeed, several months following this news article, the Toronto Raptors went on to win their first NBA championship as a franchise.

The topic of group diversity and its implications for group functioning has been the topic of considerable research and debate for a wide variety of groups, despite considerably less research exploring the role of diversity in sport groups. However, is group diversity really beneficial, detrimental, or does it matter at all? According to researchers from sport and organizational contexts, the answer to this question depends on the nature of a group and its tasks, as well as the way in which diversity is defined (Bell, Villado, Lukasik, Belau, & Briggs, 2011; Godfrey, Kim, Eluère, & Eys, 2019; Harrison & Klein 2007). The following sections cover the different ways researchers have measured diversity when considering its implications for group functioning.

Common sense indicates that homogeneity in physical skills and attributes might not always be desirable. When World Cup or All-Star teams are selected for international competitions, for example, diversity in the skills and abilities of athletes is essential. The performance of sport teams is enhanced by the presence of different individuals who have the skills to play different roles. This variability in team resources was exemplified by former National Basketball Association coach Pat Riley when he said

> Earvin [Magic Johnson] had both style and efficiency and knew when to let one dominate over the other. He quickly established himself as a dominant player,

but he did it in a unique way. He was an avid student of all styles of basketball. Instead of crushing his teammates under his greatness, he studied their styles and figured out how he, as the man controlling the movement of the ball, could help them get the most out of their abilities. He dealt to their strengths. (Riley, 1993, p. 33)

No soccer team, field hockey team, or basketball team could hope to be successful if all team members possessed identical skills. If a basketball team was composed solely of guards, no matter how effective those guards were, the team would lack major resources when competing against teams composed of athletes capable of playing the post position, the forward position, the guard position, and so on. "The division of responsibility present on sport teams—setter and spiker in volleyball, blocking and pass receiving in football, playmaking and rebounding in basketball—requires heterogeneous skills if the team is to be successful" (Carron, 1981, p. 250).

Variety, Separation, and Disparity

When discussing how diversity might influence team effectiveness, it is first necessary to clarify how researchers measure the diversity exhibited by a particular group. Harrison and Klein (2007) advanced a useful framework for conceptualizing and measuring diversity in groups. They describe three distinct forms of diversity: *variety, separation,* and *disparity*. Teams that are completely homogeneous on an attribute would be considered to be minimally diverse across all three forms of diversity (variety, separation, and disparity). However, this is not the case in more diverse groups. As explained by Bell et al. (2011),

> …making statements that suggest diversity is 'good,' 'bad,' or unrelated to team performance without specifying the variable of interest and the ways in which diversity is conceptualized is a flawed approach (p. 730.)

Variety diversity is based on qualitative or categorical differences between members. Depending on the question under investigation, researchers might consider differences in the racial/ethnic background of players, differences in the length of time spent with the team (i.e., team tenure), or the roles that athletes are well-suited to play (i.e., skill-set diversity). When using variety to measure ethnic diversity, for example, a group consisting of players from eight different ethnic backgrounds would be considered more diverse than a group consisting of players from four different ethnic backgrounds. If researchers were using variety to measure team tenure diversity, a collegiate sport team with a mix of new recruits, second-year athletes, third-year athletes, and seniors would be more diverse than a group consisting of only new recruits and senior team members. Generally, variety in a particular variable (e.g., ethnicity, team tenure) is thought to be beneficial when it provides a team with additional perspectives, information, or skill-sets that can be collectively harnessed for the benefit of the group.

Separation diversity refers to the degree to which team members differ in their lateral position on a continuum for a particular attribute. Separation diversity is maximized when group members are polarized on a particular variable. Returning to the example of team tenure, a collegiate team composed of a 50-50 split of new recruits and seniors would be considered as maximally diverse in terms of team tenure separation. In contrast, a team composed of a mixture of new recruits, second- and third-year athletes, and seniors would only be moderately diverse. As another example, separation diversity based on national identities would be maximized when a group is composed of half Canadian athletes and half German athletes.

Disparity diversity is a final way to conceptualize differences. This dimension of diversity is best described as the concentration or inequality of a valued asset or resource within the group. Keeping with the example of team tenure, a maximally diverse sport group would be when one athlete is much more experienced than all other athletes within the group. An extreme example of maximal disparity from the professional sports realm can be illustrated in the distribution of salaries within a team. Maximal disparity diversity would occur when a single athlete is paid a very high sum of money but all other members receive the minimum contract amount for that league.

Armed with the knowledge of how diversity can be conceptualized and measured within teams, the following sections will review research on how specific types of diversity (i.e., sex differences, age/tenure, racial/ethnic differences, social psychological characteristics, ability) are linked to group dynamics. Although many of these studies were conducted prior to the advancement of Harrison and Klein's (2007) framework and thus did not explicitly state whether they measured diversity in terms of separation, variety, or disparity, we have highlighted the type of diversity used in each study based on their measurement and analytical approach.

Diversity in Sex

Is the amount of males and females within a group an important factor in sport teams? Widmeyer (1990) stated that this question has not been of great concern to researchers examining competitive sport because co-ed teams rarely compete against same-sex teams. Nonetheless, the question is important in that the answer may provide insight into the enjoyment of participants in co-ed recreational teams versus same-sex recreational teams. Further, there are some individual sport groups, particularly at the collegiate level, where both male and female athletes train together and are coached by the same person, effectively making them a mixed-sex team.

Diversity in Age and Team Tenure

The lack of research pertaining to the effect of variability in age in team dynamics is largely the result of age restrictions present in many amateur sport situations. In professional sport, no such restrictions are present. As a consequence, Timmerman (2000) used archival data from 1950 to 1997 to examine the relationship between diversity in age (measured as disparity diversity) and team performance in two professional sports, baseball and basketball. These two sports were chosen because the nature of the group task is substantially different. Basketball, for example, is characterized by high task interdependence, so high interaction and cooperation are necessary. Thus, any conflicts or difficulties emanating from diversity in age might be expected to have a detrimental influence on performance. Conversely, baseball is characterized by low task interdependence. As a result, less interaction and cooperation are necessary, and any difficulties arising from increased diversity in age might be expected to have minimal influence of team performance. Timmerman found that when controlling for team ability, disparity diversity in age was negatively associated with team success in basketball, but not in baseball.

Does diversity in age in sport and exercise groups have an effect on member satisfaction, performance, or adherence? Beauchamp, Carron, McCutcheon, and Harper (2007) examined the preferences of adults for involvement in standard exercise classes populated by participants from various categories across the age spectrum. The results showed the prospect of exercising with considerably older or younger exercisers (i.e., high amount of separation and disparity diversity), was unappealing; older and younger adults alike expressed a positive preference for exercising in standard exercise classes comprised of similarly aged participants.

Diversity in Racial Identity/Ethnicity

Research on the effect of diversity in racial identity/ethnic identity on the dynamics of groups was heavily examined in the United States in the 1960s because of the substantial increase in the number of black-white groupings resulting from school desegregation, affirmative action, and other social reforms (Davies, 1994; Shaw, 1981). Today, racially mixed groups are common in the military, the work place, the school system, and athletics.

In the sport environment, several researchers have studied the effects of racial diversity on the performance of athletic teams (Anshel & Sailes, 1990; Jones, 1974; Klein & Christiansen, 1969). For example, in the study by Timmerman (2000) described above, the association between variety diversity in race on team success in professional baseball and basketball was also examined. The findings for variety diversity in race were identical to those reported for disparity diversity in age. That is, although there was no association between racial diversity and team performance in baseball, in basketball diversity was negatively associated with team success.

Diversity in Social Psychological Characteristics

In terms of diversity of social psychological characteristics, there is no simple generalization relating group composition to group performance (cf. Widmeyer, 1990). In fact, two equally plausible possibilities present themselves. One proceeds from the supposition that similarity (birds of a feather) will lead to compatibility, increased communication and cooperation, and improved group morale and motivation (Harrison & Klein, 2007). In turn, these consequences of greater homogeneity will lead to enhanced group effectiveness. A second proceeds from the supposition that as diversity increases, a group can leverage the unique attitudes, beliefs, and perspectives of its members. In turn, these consequences of heterogeneity will lead to enhanced group effectiveness.

Fortunately, there is a rich body of literature on the association between diversity in the Big Five personality traits and performance. Bell (2007) summarized these findings in a meta-analysis that included studies evaluating how greater diversity in specific personality traits (conceptualized as separation) related to team performance. Overall, the Big Five (openness, conscientiousness, extraversion, agreeableness, neuroticism/emotional stability) were not significantly related to team performance. This suggests that when it comes to team personality composition, the amount of traits possessed by members may be more important than diversity in traits.

Nonetheless, there may be cases where diversity in psychological characteristics is important for sport team performance. There is some theoretical and empirical evidence supporting the view that variety in psychological characteristics is a valuable group composition variable

(Melnick, 1982). Given the diverse roles that can exist in task-oriented small groups, it may be helpful to have team members whose personalities differ on such traits as the need for status, affiliation motivation, achievement motivation, and preferred action style. The 'special chemistry' that is thought to exist on successful teams may be nothing more than the effective meshing of a set of personalities. Melnick (1982) stated that all things being equal, teams composed of members with very similar needs (i.e., psychological homogeneity) will find it difficult if not impossible to successfully complete the social structures of the team. Wolff (1995) provided a good instance of this scenario:

> Consider how St. John's, the school on Utopia Parkway in Queens, NY, became the most woefully misaddressed team in college basketball last year. Freshman star Felipe Lopez arrived with such ballyhoo that he had appeared on the cover of SI [*Sports Illustrated*] and was profiled in *The New Yorker* before he had ever played a college game. There was only one problem: James Scott, a senior who had come in a year earlier billed as the best juco player since Larry Johnson, believed it was his turn to shine. (p. 42)

Research within the sport environment has found inconsistent results regarding the diversity of social psychological characteristics. For example, Klein and Christiansen (1969) found that for achievement motivation, heterogeneous teams were more successful than homogeneous teams. However, in studies of men's and women's tennis doubles teams, differences in the action styles of the athletes had no effect on the performance of the team (e.g., Widmeyer, Loy, & Roberts, 1980).

Diversity in Ability

Historically, research has generally supported the notion that more diverse groups in terms of ability are more successful than homogeneous groups (e.g., Goldman, 1965; Laughlin, Branch, & Johnson, 1969). From the late 1980s onward, interest in the impact of diversity on group dynamics and group performance led to a proliferation of research. In 2007, Horwitz and Horwitz carried out a meta-analysis on a portion of that literature that focused on team task diversity and team outcomes. The results showed that both the quantity and quality of group performance were superior when work groups were composed of members with diverse task-related skills.

One possible explanation for why heterogeneous groups might outperform homogeneous groups is a phenomenon referred to as a spillover effect. The spillover effect occurs when the stronger member of a heterogeneous group has a positive influence on the subsequent performance of the weaker individual (e.g., Goldman & Goldman, 1981; Silverman & Stone, 1972). The spillover effect seems to be due to both learning and motivation. The lower ability person not only learns new strategies and techniques but the task is approached with renewed interest and energy.

A related but distinct phenomenon is the Köhler effect, which occurs when less capable team members put forth greater effort when working in a group context than as an individual. Using data from collegiate swimming and high-school-aged track-and-field athletes (which allowed comparison between individual events and relay events), Osborn, Irwin, Skogsberg, and Feltz (2012) found that weaker team members experienced greater motivation gains when competing in a team than when competing alone.

In most sport situations, the division of responsibility required ensures that diversity in the variety of skills are necessary if the team is to be successful. Volleyball involves blocking and setting, basketball involves playmaking, shooting, and rebounding, football involves blocking, tackling, passing, running, and receiving. Each of these sports profits from having a division of labor that permits different individuals to focus on developing very specific skills and abilities.

Interestingly, diversity in ability (operationalized as separation diversity) among female tennis players was negatively associated with team effectiveness (Widmeyer & Loy, 1989). Teams won more frequently when both partners were similar in ability. This finding was most noticeable when examining the ability to serve, followed by the volley, the backhand, and the forehand. The heterogeneous teams had a winning percentage of 45%; the homogeneous teams, a winning percentage of 55%. Widmeyer and Loy (1989) observed that

> …many would predict the opposite finding arguing that the heterogeneous teams should do better because they have a high ability person who can play the majority of shots. The results suggest that these female tennis players adopt a very egalitarian strategy when playing with their partners and thus their game is not marked by "poaching" or any other form of overplaying by the better players. It could also be that the homogeneous teams are directing the majority of their shots to the weaker player on heterogeneous teams. Support for these two assumptions lies in the fact that the total ability of the weakest player was more positively related to team performance outcome ($r = .74$) than was the total ability of the best player ($r = .49$). (p. 27)

Compatibility of Group Resources

The best news for [Kansas] Jayhawks fans heading into the [men's NCAA basketball] 2018–19 season is that, for the first time in three years, they actually have a roster that will fit the way that Bill Self loves to play … The problem, however, is that of the 13 scholarship players on the roster, 12 of them deserve playing time … The most difficult part of Bill Self's job next season is probably going to be the massaging of egos. (Dauster, 2018, para. 1–3.)

As this quote illustrates, collegiate coaches face the challenge of not only recruiting the most talented players available, but also striving to select group members who have complementary skillsets, personalities, and values. In 1936, Lewin published his now classic definition:

$$B = f(P,E)$$

that states that behavior is a function of the person in the environment. Compatibility, in essence, exists when there is a fit or match between the person and the environment. A person's environment can be a coach, one's teammates, the task required, the organizational demands, and so on.

Compatibility is not simply similarity, however. Individuals may be quite different and still be compatible with each other. The Los Angeles Lakers signed Anthony Davis in the 2019 offseason—a player who many hoped would elevate Lebron James's overall game and once again make the Lakers championship contenders. On their compatibility, Pina (2019) asserted,

> If LeBron James could pick any other person on Earth to be his running mate, it would be Anthony Davis. There are other superstars who'd be productive and pleasant in a winning situation, but none can accentuate James' strengths, capitalize off them, and conceal his defensive limitations. (para. 1)

In industrial and organizational psychology, there has been a longstanding interest in issues surrounding compatibility. What vocation is best suited to Fred's personality and interests? Can Marcela and Stephanie work cooperatively on this project? To make sense of the burgeoning research addressing these and similar questions, Kristof-Brown, Zimmerman, and Johnson (2005) carried out a comprehensive meta-analysis of studies examining person-job, person-organization, person-group, and person-supervisor fit. Their meta-analysis provides a good overview of the issues in compatibility in work groups and provides a basis for the sections that follow.

Under the category of person-job fit, two forms of compatibility are possible. In one, *demands-ability*, a fit is present when a person's knowledge, skills, and abilities are sufficient for what their role or job requires. In the second, *needs-supplies* or *supplies-values*, a fit is present when a person's needs, desires, and preferences are satisfied by the jobs he/she performs. The meta-analysis showed higher levels of person-job fit are linked to greater job satisfaction, organizational commitment, and a stronger intention to stay with it. Interestingly, while there is a positive relationship between person-job fit and performance, it was only modest in strength.

The second category, person-organization fit, is optimized when an organization engages in activities that are aligned with the person's values, interests, and preferences. Studies show that person-organization fit positively predicts job satisfaction, commitment, organizational satisfaction, and intent to remain. However, there was only a very small relation between person-organization fit and job performance.

Another aspect of fit examined by Kristof-Brown et al. (2005) was person-group fit. Although person-group fit might seem to be similar to cohesion, the two constructs are conceptually different. The focus with cohesion is the group as a collective (is it unified?), whereas person-group fit predominantly concerns the individual (is there interpersonal compatibility between the individual and the group as a collective?). There was a medium and positive relation between measures of person-group fit with job satisfaction, commitment, intention to stay, and job performance.

Finally, the questions associated with person-supervisor fit most closely parallel those in sport where the bulk of the research has focused on coach-athlete compatibility. When there is greater compatibility between an employee and supervisor, employees tend to express more satisfaction with the job and his/her supervisor (Kristof-Brown et al., 2005). One other interesting fact about compatibility in the workplace is that there is only a small relationship among the four types of fit. In commenting on the uniqueness of each type, Kristof et al. (2005) observed

> …these results underscore … the ability of individuals to discern among aspects of their work environment when assessing fit. In particular, the relationships

Exhibit 5.3. Fundamental Interpersonal Relations Orientation Theory

Dimension	Type	Description
Inclusion: To belong, associate, mingle, communicate, join	Wanted Inclusion	The need to be included in others' activities, to associate with others, to be considered significant.
	Expressed Inclusion	The need to include others, to actively join and associate with others, and to indicate to them that they are significant.
Control: To exert power, leadership, authority, dominance	Wanted Control	The need to have others control, dominate, lead, influence, or handle authority.
	Expressed Control	The need to control others, to lead and influence them, to take charge, exert leadership.
Affection: To love, like, affiliate with others, cohere, be affectionate.	Wanted Affection	The need to be liked, loved, friendly with others, to have others provide affection.
	Expressed Affection	The need to give others love and affection, to be friendly with others.

Source. The Interpersonal Underworld by W. C. Schutz, 1966, Palo Alto, CA: Science & Behavior Books.

between [person-supervisor fit] and the other types…[suggest] that employees do not view supervisors as isomorphic representations of the organization. (p. 316)

As a historical perspective on group member compatibility, Schutz (1958, 1966) advanced fundamental interpersonal relations orientation (FIRO) theory, which begins with the premise that *people need people*. Human beings have interpersonal (social) needs that are as important as their biological needs for sustaining health. These interpersonal needs are satisfied through the development and maintenance of compatible relationships with other people. The three principal interpersonal needs identified by Schutz (1966) are inclusion, control, and affection. Schutz also proposed that in interpersonal relationships, people not only need to express inclusion, control, and affection, they need to receive these from others. A description of the six behavior types is presented in Exhibit 5.3.

Despite its intuitive appeal, there is mixed evidence for the FIRO as a theory of compatibility. In experimental groups, researchers who have attempted to use the tenets of FIRO to predict when more compatible groups (as defined by the theory) lead to better group performance have produced findings that are inconsistent with theory (e.g., Shaw & Webb, 1982).

Compatibility of Member Abilities

There is no doubt that compatibility in ability is an important aspect of group success. If the skills and attributes of one individual mesh and complement the skills and attributes of the other, the team is more successful. What is not clear across different sports, however, is which similar skills the individuals should possess and which skills should be complementary. In some sports the answer seems intuitively obvious. On a hockey line, it is beneficial if all three of the individuals are similar in skating ability. A poor skater can't keep up with the two good skaters. But a line with three playmakers and no checker wouldn't be effective. So, complementarity in the skills of playmaking and checking is essential.

Widmeyer and colleagues (Widmeyer, Loy, & Roberts, 1980; Widmeyer, 1990) assessed the relative importance of the fit of different abilities to team success. They compared the importance of compatibility in the serve and volley versus compatibility in the forehand and backhand using men's and women's doubles tennis teams. Compatibility in the women's forehand and backhand was more important ($r = .78$) for team effectiveness than in the serve and volley ($r = .51$). In contrast, among men, serve-volley compatibility was a better predictor of performance outcome ($r = .72$) than was forehand-backhand compatibility ($r = .48$). The authors cautioned that this result could have been specific to the populations tested. The women players who were tested had a tendency to play at the baseline rather than to come to the net in a serve and volley style, whereas the men frequently engaged in a serve-volley style.

Compatibility with Group Roles

Another aspect of compatibility concerns the relation between the dispositions of individual group members and the roles they must fill in the group. A number of examples serve to illustrate this aspect. A young basketball player was told that he would have to be the "enforcer or policeman" on the team if he hoped to play regularly. He didn't want this role. Moreover, he saw himself as a potential scorer. So he left that team. As a second example, an outgoing, people-oriented athlete was asked to help two first-year athletes make the transition from high school to university. She took on this responsibility and successfully provided a complete orientation for both first year athletes. As a final example, an outstanding basketball player in her senior year was approached by her coach and asked to assume more of a leadership role because the rest of the team was very young and inexperienced. Although the athlete tried, she was always uncomfortable directing and encouraging others. Also, her own play seemed to suffer. The time and energy spent trying to fill the leader's role detracted from her concentration.

Another way of looking at person-role compatibility is to determine whether all of the individuals in a group agree regarding which role behaviors are appropriate for a position. Carron (1978) adopted this strategy when he asked participants to indicate the appropriate role behaviors for coaches and athletes. Both coaches and athletes perceived that the coaching role involves exerting a high level of control and being passive in terms of initiating interactions with athletes (inclusion) and developing warm personal friendships (affection). The athlete's role was perceived to involve very little control and also to be passive in terms of initiating interactions or establishing a friendship with the coach. These perceived role behaviors could contribute to coach-athlete incompatibility. If both the coach's and the athlete's roles involve being passive in terms of initiating interactions and developing friendships, the athletic situation would be cold and impersonal. It must be kept in mind, however, that interpersonal relationships are a product of both the personality of the individuals and the nature of the situation (See Chapter 7 for a more detailed discussion of roles).

Compatibility Between the Coach and the Athlete

The importance of coach-athlete compatibility was encapsulated by Silver (1995): "at its best, the relationship between a coach and his quarterback can elevate a team. At its worst, it can destroy an entire season" (p. 85). In one of the earliest studies of coach-athlete incompatibility (Carron & Bennett, 1977), university coaches identified the athletes with whom they were most compatible and those with whom they were most incompatible. The compatible group was comprised of athletes who satisfied a gestalt definition of most coachable and least disruptive—who were furthest removed from being problem athletes. The coaches were also asked to identify the athletes who caused the greatest problems, who were on the opposite end of the spectrum. Although control and affection were contributors to compatibility, inclusion was the most important behavior differentiating compatible and incompatible coach-athlete dyads. The relationship in the incompatible dyads was characterized by relatively detached, withdrawn, isolated behavior (i.e., a lack of inclusion) on the part of both the coach and athlete. This is consistent with the suggestion that if a coach has "an athlete who suffers from the same problem as the coach, there is a very high probability that the coach will be unable to handle the player successfully or communicate with him effectively" (Tutko & Richards, 1977, p. 74).

In a study by Horne and Carron (1985), the question of compatibility versus incompatibility was approached from the athlete's perspective. Intercollegiate athletes rated their overall relationship with their coach. None of the three behaviors (control, affection, inclusion) predicted coach-athlete incompatibility. As well, Prapavessis and Gordon (1991) examined coach-athlete compatibility with elite tennis players. Similar to Horne and Carron, none of the three behaviors differentiated compatible from incompatible dyads. Athletes in incompatible dyads were dissatisfied with their coach's authoritarian style and wanted their coaches to encourage decision-making and to value their opinions (Prapavessis and Gordon, 1991). As a consequence, problems can develop if coaches approach elite players in an authoritarian manner.

The question of who holds the perception of incompatibility—the coach or the athlete—might be quite critical to continued involvement in sport. Pease, Locke, and Burlingame (1971) studied athletes who were cut from baseball teams, finding that compatibility with coaches (in terms of inclusion, control, and affection) was not a factor. In other words, the coaches did not center out those athletes with whom they were incompatible and cut them from the team. A different picture emerged, however, when athletes who quit the team were studied. Dropouts were found to be incompatible with their coaches in control and, to a lesser extent, affection.

The 3 + 1 Cs Conceptual Model. Kelley et al. (1983) defined a dyadic relationship as a situation in which the feelings, cognitions, and behaviors of two people are mutually and causally interconnected. Jowett (2007) used this definition with its emphasis on affect (feelings), cognitions (thoughts, beliefs), and behaviors as the foundation to explore the content and quality of coach-athlete relationships through a series of qualitative and quantitative studies. Thus, her model, after some early modifications, is intended to reflect coach and athlete interdependence in terms of closeness (feelings), commitment (thoughts), complementarity (behaviors), and co-orientation (perceptual consensus). The configuration of the four constructs led to it being labeled the 3 + 1 Cs Conceptual Model.

Closeness reflects the emotional ties that coaches and athletes develop as a result of their frequent interactions in practices, competitions, and social settings. It includes trust, care, support, and concern. Commitment is a product of the desire of the coach and the athlete to maintain their relationship. Complementarity, the behavioral construct, reflects the cooperative (task-oriented) and affiliative (social-oriented) interactions between coaches and athletes during practices and competitions. Finally, co-orientation accounts for the "broader notion of coaches' and athletes' common ground or perceptual congruence as this pertains to the status of their dyadic relationship and includes actual and assumed similarity as well as empathetic understanding" (Jowett, 2007, p. 67).

The 3 + 1 Cs model focuses exclusively on the coach-athlete relationship—what in industrial psychology is referred to as the person-supervisor fit. Thus, research is concentrated on this aspect of compatibility. In one study, Jowett and Chaundy (2004) examined whether the nature of the coach athlete relationship—as assessed through the constructs in the 3 + 1 Cs model—contributed additionally to cohesion beyond what coaches account for independently. They found that this was the case for both task and social cohesion, but the relationship was stronger (as might be expected) for the former.

Two types of motivational climate can be established by a coach: a task-oriented climate, where the emphasis is on personal improvement and mastery of the task, and an ego-involving climate, where the emphasis is on winning and outcomes. Whereas athletes who felt that a task-oriented climate was emphasized experienced high levels of closeness, commitment, and complementarity in their relationship with their coach, athletes who felt that an ego-involving climate was emphasized experienced low levels of closeness, commitment, and complementarity (Olympiou, Jowett, & Duda, 2008).

On the basis of the above and other research, Jowett (2007) suggested that "coaches' dyadic relationships with their athletes become the glue that holds sport teams together" (p. 63). Parenthetically, this claim seems overstated, as the glue that typically holds sport teams together is the label given to team cohesion. When cohesion or any of its synonyms (e.g., team unity, team closeness, teamwork) are assessed, coaches are not included in the evaluation. Further, there are numerous anecdotal accounts in sport and other domains where the glue that holds the team together is its antipathy for the coach and its desire to get him/her fired (e.g., see Chapter 14). A mutiny is a cohesive group rebelling against its leadership. Having said this, however, there is still little doubt that coach and athlete compatibility has important implications for the group dynamics of sport teams.

Section 3

Group Structure

Competing at a FIFA World Cup is invariably the highlight of any footballer's career, and this week we discovered which players have moved a step closer to realizing that dream ... As always with these preliminary squad announcements, surprise inclusions and notable, often controversial, omissions dominated the headlines, even if plenty of coaches remained faithful to the tried and tested stars who had excelled during qualifying. Sadly, injuries forced the hands of many... (Fifa.com, 2010)

The first two sections of this book shed light on the nature and development of groups, as well as the importance of group member characteristics as they interact with the group's environment. The development of the group is fundamentally associated with the emergence of group structure—the focus of this section. As the term suggests, group structure represents the fact that groups establish an organization and become stable. Thus, for example, the structure of a house (e.g., its walls, floors, ceilings, and windows) provides that house with stability and permanence. The structure of a group serves the same purpose.

The structure of a group can be viewed from many different perspectives. One perspective concerns a group's physical structure. The physical structure of a group is associated with its composition and organization—the number of members, the formal reporting networks, the formal leadership hierarchy, and so on. In many instances, such as in army units or organized sport teams, individuals come into a situation where the specific organizational structure is in place. The size of the team, its organizational format, rules of conduct, the nature of its leadership structure (e.g., one captain, three cocaptains), are established through the rules or through tradition. In some other instances, such as new sport franchises, ad hoc committees, and social alliances, individuals are faced with a situation in which no preexisting physical structure is present. Consequently, one must develop.

A key aspect of the physical structure of the group is the positions of its members. *Group position* refers to the place or location of the individuals in the group. For example, in a family, members will typically sit in the same chair for meals. That location would constitute a position. As another example, in basketball, hockey, and football, the term center refers to a position occupied by one of the athletes during competition. The evolution and needs of a specific position in Canadian football (e.g., the long snapper) is exemplified in the following quote:

> Three phases: snap, protection, coverage. The importance of the kicking game and field position in Canadian football means that each of those phases must be handled effectively. The changing demands of the position have highlighted the need for long-snapping specialists, a far cry from common practice in decades past. Traditionally, a backup center could fill the position, but with the complex coverage schemes employed by today's special teams coordinators coupled with the increased size of offensive linemen, it is unlikely those players would be effective in the coverage phase. This has led to a specific body type ideal for the position: big enough to protect the kicker and quick enough to make tackles downfield. (Andrews, 2017, para. 16–17)

Different sports have different positions. Thus, the positions on a hockey team differ from those on a basketball team and both differ from those on a soccer team (though the position of 'center' features prominently for all of these sports). Anyone attempting to describe the unique characteristics or structure of these particular sport groups might begin by describing their positions.

The quote that was used to introduce this section illustrates the scenario where a broad physical structure has to be established. In the lead up to the football (soccer) World Cup tournament, teams are required to submit their rosters by a certain date indicating which players will participate. These decisions, which must take into account the current fitness of each player and past performances (among many factors), will determine the underlying structure of the teams through the tournament's duration. As such, they are viewed with great anticipation by coaching staff, players, and the nations they represent.

A group also can be viewed from the perspective of its *psychological structure*. Immediately upon group formation, individual members begin to interact and communicate. With that interaction and communication, differentiation among individuals appears and the three components that most clearly reflect the presence of a psychological structure emerge. Those three components of psychological structure are group roles, norms, and its social hierarchy.

One element that makes up the psychological structure of a group is a role. A *group role* is an expectation for the behavior of an individual who occupies a specific position. Teams (or subgroups within teams such as offense or defense in football), work groups, social groups, organizations, corporations, and societies in general establish behavioral expectations for the occupants of different positions. The following example highlights the leadership role that quickly became occupied by National Basketball Association player Danny Green when he joined the Toronto Raptors during the 2018–2019 championship season:

> No one really knew a lot about Danny Green and he's become a true voice, gifted as an athlete but also possessing quiet leadership skills that have become immediately apparent. Teammates…didn't have to accept him in that role so quickly. It's usually one that a player morphs into over time, but Green's there already because the greater group is fine with it. (Smith, 2018, p. S5)

Another element that makes up the psychological structure of the group is its norms. *Group norms* are the standards for the behavior that is expected of members of the group. Norms reflect the organization's (or group's) consensus about what is considered acceptable.

In the following example, the shared high expectations for effort and performance by two kayakers are considered instrumental for their success:

> By their own admission, [New Zealand] Olympic kayakers Erin Taylor and Lisa Carrington have a weird relationship. One minute, they're best mates, laughing at each other's jokes, finishing each other's sentences and gently teasing one another about their wildly different tastes in music. But come race day, Erin and Lisa turn into the fiercest rivals. Both want to win, and have the skill and determination to do so. It's an uneasy balance the athletes face as they switch from teammates in their K2 500 race to the individual K1 200. Competing against each other is an occupational hazard for the best friends, although they chose to see it as a positive. 'It's easier than you'd think…We have the same expectations of each other and at the end of the day, if there is criticism, it's to make the boat go faster.' (Bertrand, 2012, para. 1–2)

The final element that we will discuss in relation to the psychological structure of a group is its social hierarchy. *Group social hierarchy* has been defined as "implicit or explicit rank order of individuals or groups with respect to a valued social dimension" (Magee & Galinsky, 2008, p. 354). Status (i.e., respect and admiration) and power (i.e., control over valued group resources) constitute two distinct bases of one's rank in a group's social hierarchy. The members of any work group, army platoon, or sport team vary in terms of their social rank—their status, power, and importance to the group. The essence of social rank is illustrated in the following example in which Ben Roethlisberger, of the NFL Pittsburgh Steelers football team, discusses the degree to which quarterbacks (the central position on an American football team) are given credit for success but scrutinized following defeat:

> You know, we [quarterbacks] get too much credit when we win, too much blame when we lose. After a loss it can be tough. Living your life under a microscope. I mean every little thing. People don't treat you like a human. They don't think you eat normal food. They think you just float instead of walk. I'm a private person, so people always form a judgment when they meet me for 30 seconds or five minutes. And they never go tell 20 people when you're the greatest guy in the world. They go tell 20 people when you're the worst. (King, 2009)

Thus, social rank can be related to the location (i.e., position) that a group member occupies. Despite this quotation, it is important to bear in mind that social rank and position are not always related. The athlete with the highest status and power on one field hockey team could be the goaltender; on another, a forward. The positions that individuals occupy on a team can influence their social standing but their place in their social hierarchy is not determined by position alone. The antecedents of status are discussed more fully in Chapter 9.

The interrelationship of group positions, roles, norms, and social hierarchy to group structure can be illustrated by the example of a group of sorority members who decide to establish an intramural basketball team. Even though the individuals are all members of the same sorority, a specific structure will emerge within the basketball team. Part of that structure will be represented by the positions that the different individuals hold (e.g., center, guard, forward). The position that each person holds in the sorority is unrelated to the position held in the team.

Part of a basketball team's structure also will be represented by the roles filled by different individuals. These might include the "coordinator" who acts as liaison between the team and the central administration for intramurals, the "task specialist(s)" who introduces the offensive and defensive systems to the team, and the "social director" who serves as a catalyst for the social activities after the game.

Norms will slowly evolve for the behavioral standards group members consider appropriate. These norms may revolve around attendance at practices and games, the amount of effort expected during games, the number of shots any one person can reasonably be expected to take, and so on.

Finally, various team members will have different status, power, and importance. If the team considers task success to have the highest priority, the outstanding players and/or task specialist might be elevated to the top of the group's social hierarchy. If, on the other hand, the team considers having a good time to have the highest priority, the social director might sit atop the social hierarchy. It is also possible, of course, that during the game the outstanding players would have the highest social standing, whereas after the game the social director would have the highest social standing.

6

Group Position

The salary cap era in the CFL [Canadian Football League] has been good for Canadian offensive linemen. In the pass-happy league, starting quarterbacks have always been the most important players and therefore the highest paid. But the Canadians tasked with protecting them are also well compensated, with many earning over $200,000 annually. The reason is simple: supply and demand. "It's hard to find quality Canadian players. Period," said Jim Barker, the former Calgary Stampeders and Toronto Argonauts general manager ... CFL teams must carry at least 21 Canadians on their 46-man roster and start a minimum of seven. Playing as many Canadians as possible on the offensive line makes it easier to use Americans at other positions. (Dyck, 2018, para. 1–4, 6)

Group position refers to the place or location of the individuals in the group. As such, it represents a geographic location. The phrase "being in the right position at the right time" serves to illustrate the commonly held belief that our geographic location can be important. What about our position in groups? Sports differ in the positions occupied by various participants—catcher and outfielder in baseball, goaltender and forward in soccer, center and defenseman in ice hockey, and so on.

The physical and psychological requirements of different positions can vary dramatically within the same sport, necessitating the presence of individuals with specific abilities or characteristics to fill the positions. For example, certain positions are associated with specific anthropometric characteristics (e.g., taller individuals fill central defensive positions in soccer; Hencken & White, 2006) and physiological abilities (e.g., midfield players cover much greater distances on the soccer pitch; Di Salvo et al., 2007; Vigne, Gaudino, Rogowski, Alloatti, & Hautier, 2010). As the opening example to this chapter illustrates, to take advantage of specific rules and regulations within the Canadian Football League, even one's nationality could be considered with respect to the allocation of positional responsibilities. Further, within a given sport (e.g., baseball), over the course of different seasons, and even in different teams within the same season, the individuals who occupy the positions of catcher and outfielder vary in ability, the roles held on their teams, their team status, and so on.

The Importance of Positions in Groups

Spatial Centrality

Spatial centrality refers to the relative geographical locations of individuals in the group. Some individuals are in prominent locations that appear to be central, or of particular focus, to the majority of the group. Not surprisingly, perhaps, group researchers have dedicated a lot of brain power toward developing theories about how positions in the group may relate to individual and group processes. They have found evidence that supports the commonly-held belief that position does make a difference. As one example, Strodtbeck and Hook (1961), in a comprehensive study of jury selection, found that the jury's peer leader (termed a foreperson) was more frequently chosen from one of the two persons seated at the ends of the table. More recently, Jackson, Engstrom, and Emmers-Sommer (2007) found that their study participants, when presented with a diagram depicting a seating arrangement, identified individuals seated at the end of the table as the leaders of the group. Interestingly, when the people shown at the two ends of the table were a man and a woman, study participants were more likely to pick the same-gender person as the leader (i.e., men picked the man as the leader, women picked the woman as the leader).

Whereas the examples above relate primarily to positioning when leading to decision-making in ad hoc groups—groups that are formed over a short term—Steinzor (1955) theorized that group position also shapes a member's contribution to a group across a broader span of time. Specifically, Steinzor (1955) reported that group members on decision-making tasks will be in a better position to influence the beliefs of other members when they are in a position where they are more likely to be observed by others. This relationship between physical location and psychological impact has come to be known as the Steinzor Effect.

The cause-effect nature of group position and social impact is not clear. It may be that more dominant individuals gravitate to more dominant positions. It is also possible that more dominant positions generate more dominant impressions on the group. There is evidence to support both views. For example, Hare and Bales (1963) found that the occupants of more prominent seats had more dominant personality profiles. Also, Sommer (1969) observed that when individuals were selected to lead small group discussions, they more frequently selected seats at the head of the table. So, it is likely that certain individuals do seek out certain positions.

However, in some studies, the effect of individual differences in personal attributes has been controlled by rotating individuals among different positions while holding the content of their opinion constant. The value attached to an opinion was found to vary with the position of the speaker (e.g., Steinzor, 1955). In short, some positions have the potential to make a greater impact on the group—no matter which individuals occupy them.

Interactional Centrality

Beyond being physically central and visible, centrality may also refer to the extent that group interactions involve any one member. In this sense, a central member is the one who serves as the hub in the center of the wheel when members communicate or when the team must perform. For example, Hopkins (1964), in a discussion of how influence works in groups, argued that "centrality designates how close a member is to the 'center' of the group's interaction network and thus refers simultaneously to the frequency with which a member participates in interaction with other members and the number and range of other members with whom he interacts" (p. 28). In Hopkins's view, centrality was viewed as the center of the interaction network, not the physical center of the geographical boundaries of the group.

Hopkins's (1964) perspective makes sense. In the case of an army, the command post is the hub of activity (i.e., central) but it is not in a geographical location midway between command and the front line. In short, in a wide variety of situations, the most central location in terms of interaction, leadership, and criticality is at the extreme of the physical boundaries of the group or organization. Feld (1959), in a study of command responsibility in military organizations, stated that "the wider the responsibility, the more remote the post ... In so far as command responsibility increases, the proper station will be progressively to the rear" (pp. 17–18). Adams and Biddle (1970) also pointed out that the center-front position is the teacher's home in the classroom.

Chelladurai and Carron (1977) provided an alternative way to think about positional centrality, with a specific focus on sport. Their model contains two dimensions: propinquity and task dependence. The first dimension, *propinquity*, consists of the combined attributes of (1) observability, which is the extent to which a position provides its occupant with knowledge of ongoing events; and (2) visibility, which is the degree to which the occupant of the position is seen and watched by individuals in other positions (including opponents).

Thus, for example, catchers in baseball are in a position to observe everything that happens on the playing field—everything occurs in front of them. So the position of catcher is highly observable. Baseball catchers are also high in visibility, as they are located in a position that ensures that they are in the focus of fans and a large number of other players on the playing surface. Consequently, the position of catcher would rate high in the propinquity dimension, even though it is not geographically central. It might seem that outfielders also are in a position to observe everything that happens on the playing field, as everything occurs in front of them. However, unlike the catcher, they are not high in visibility. Consequently, they would rate much lower than catchers in the propinquity dimension.

The second dimension refers to the degree of *task interdependence* required by the position, or the extent to which the occupant of the position interacts with the occupants of other positions. A catcher in baseball would be rated high in task interdependence; an outfielder, low. Catchers control the play on the playing surface and interact continuously with other positions. When the positions of baseball are classified according to these two dimensions, a catcher would be rated high in task interdependence and propinquity, infielders moderate in both, and outfielders relatively low in both (see Exhibit 6.1).

The Importance of Positions in Sport Teams

In sport, a frequently examined question has been whether the formal structure of a team and the specific location of different positions are associated with differential status, prestige, importance, or rewards for the sport participant. One question of interest, for example, has been whether there is a greater likelihood that individuals will be nominated as the MVP of a team if they are catchers versus outfielders in baseball, goaltenders versus defensemen in hockey, forwards versus guards in basketball, and setters versus spikers in volleyball. Grusky

Exhibit 6.1. The Interaction of Propinquity and Task Interdependence

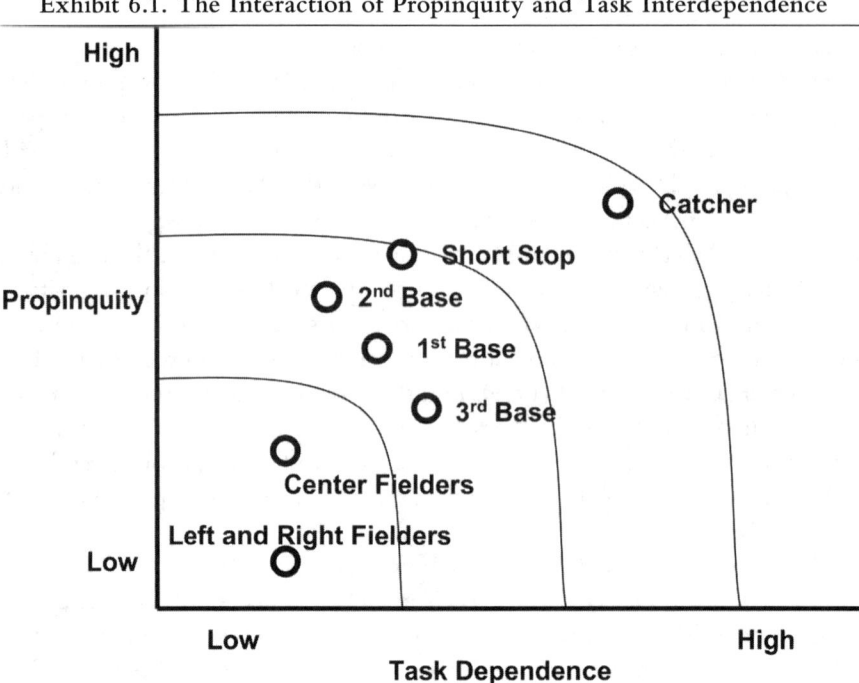

Source. "A Reanalysis of Formal Structure in Sport" by P. Chelladurai and A. V. Carron, 1977, *Journal of Applied Sport Sciences, 2,* 9–14.

(1963) carried out one of the earliest studies concerned with this question by examining the sport of baseball. He began with the following premises:

- the formal structure of an organization establishes major offices or positions and the primary responsibilities for the occupants of the positions;
- the positions in a group vary according to their spatial location, the type of task the occupant performs, and frequency of interactions with other positions; and,
- certain positions, because of their responsibilities and the behaviors required, increase the likelihood that the occupant will develop leadership skills and assume a leadership role.

According to Grusky (1963), "all else being equal, the more central one's spatial location, (1) the greater the likelihood dependent or coordinative tasks will be performed, and (2) the greater the rate of interaction with occupants of other positions" (p. 346). In short, he felt that organizational positions can be distinguished on the basis of whether they are central, high-interaction positions or peripheral, low-interaction positions. He also felt that the occupants of central, high-interaction positions would be more frequently selected as most popular, rated as more respected, and promoted to executive positions in the organization.

The prominence of specific positions in several sports has been examined with respect to task involvement. Clemente and colleagues used social network analysis in a series of studies to identify the positions that contribute most to the attacking phases in volleyball (Clemente, Martins, & Mendes, 2015), basketball (Clemente, Martins, Kalamaras, & Mendes, 2015), and soccer (Clemente, Martins, Wong, Kalamaras, & Mendes, 2015) based on the passing patterns in each sport. Perhaps unsurprisingly, volleyball players who occupied the central forward position (i.e., setters), guards in basketball, and central midfielders in soccer, were demonstrated to have the most attacking interactions in these sports, being the most central to the team's interactions during attacking.

As it pertains to leadership, Grusky (1963) proposed that in baseball, individuals in central, high-interaction positions will more likely be recruited as managers. To test his proposition, he examined the backgrounds of all of the field managers of Major League Baseball teams for the periods 1921–1941 and 1951–1958. The central, high-interaction positions were defined as catchers and infielders; the peripheral, low-interaction positions were defined as pitchers and outfielders. Grusky (1963) found that the majority of managers (76.9%) were recruited from central high-interaction positions rather than from peripheral, low-interaction (23.1%) positions. The highest percentage was former catchers (26.2%), followed by shortstops (14.0%) and third basemen (13.1%).

A number of other studies replicated or extended Grusky's (1963) work into other areas and other sports (e.g., football, basketball, field hockey, and ice hockey). Some of the areas examined included the recruitment of college coaches, the selection of team captains in high school and university, and the selection of most valuable players. Essentially, the results of these other studies were consistent with those reported by Grusky (1963) (see Exhibit 6.2).

As Exhibit 6.2 shows, Breglio (1976) found that individuals in peripheral positions in baseball were more frequently recruited to umpiring positions. Nonetheless, he considered his results to be consistent with Grusky's (1963) propositions. The task demands of umpiring require the individual to be independent and aloof. These characteristics are more likely to be developed in the peripheral positions. Therefore, if the responsibilities and behaviors acquired during competition serve to prepare the individual for other positions in the system, then umpires are more likely to come from the peripheral positions.

When Chelladurai and Carron (1977) reanalyzed the data reported in the previous studies of baseball, they found that leadership, status, and rewards were highly related to the degree of propinquity and task dependence present in a position (see Exhibit 6.3). Catchers, who are highest in these two dimensions, were also highest in team captaincy, MVP, and recruitment to management positions. Outfielders, the lowest in these two dimensions, were least frequently the recipients of these organizational rewards.

As a final point, athlete/peer leadership roles also appear to be linked to interactionally central positions. Fransen et al. (2016) examined whether task, motivational, social, and externally-focused leaders were more likely to be in centralized positions. Their results suggested that, in most sports, task and motivational leaders tended to play in central positions. However, there was a caveat. These tendencies were demonstrated more in sports where playing surface sizes were larger (e.g., soccer, field hockey, rugby). In sports with smaller surface sizes (e.g., basketball, handball, ice-hockey), Fransen et al. (2016) suggested that the dynamism involves "continual switching of positions–meaning that all players have similar communication opportunities and that a central position is not required in order to display leadership" (p. 10). Centrality may matter more in some sports than others.

An examination of the Most Valuable Player (MVP) awards in the major North American sports from 2004 to 2019 provides some additional evidence that positions (and issues of propinquity and task dependence) still seem to play a role in the distribution of rewards in some sports. For the National Basketball Association (NBA; men's basketball), those with complete

Exhibit 6.2. The Relationship between Position in Sport and Organizational Rewards

Sport	Results	Reference
Baseball		
Professional	Managerial recruitment was greatest from the high interaction positions (76.9%)	Grusky (1963)
Professional	Recruitment of umpires was greatest from the low interaction positions	Breglio (1976)
College	Selection was greatest from the high interaction positions for team captains (69%), most valuable player awards (54%), and managerial recruitment (72%)	Sage, Loy, & Ingham, (1970)
High School	Selection of team captains was greatest from the high interaction positions (93%)	Loy & Sage (1968)
Basketball		
Professional	Recruitment of coaches was greatest from the central positions (71%)	Klonsky (1975)
Football		
Professional	Recruitment of coaches was approximately equal from the central and peripheral positions	Massengale & Farrington (1977)
College	Selection of team captains was greatest from the central positions (51%)	Sage (1974)
College	Recruitment was greatest from the central positions for head coaches (65%) and from the peripheral positions for assistant coaches (51%)	Massengale & Farrington (1977)
Ice Hockey		
Professional	Recruitment was greatest from the central positions for general managers (67%), coaches (74%), captains (76%), and cocaptains (78%)	Roy (1974)

Exhibit 6.3. The Recruitment of Managers/Coaches and the Selection of Team Captains and Most Valuable Players on the Basis of Playing Position

Factor	Catchers	Infielders	Outfielders	Reference
Managers[1]	26.2%	12.2%	5.3%	Grusky (1963)
Coaches[2]	27.0%	11.0%	1.8%	Sage et al. (1970)
Team Captains[3]	27.3%	16.7%	2.2%	Loy & Sage (1968)
Team Captains[2]	15.5%	13.3%	6.4%	Sage et al. (1970)
MVP[2]	12.9%	10.4%	6.4%	Sage et al. (1970)
Average of all Studies	21.8%	12.7%	4.4%	

Note. [1] Professional, [2] College, [3] Interscholastic. *Source.* "A Reanalysis of Formal Structure in Sport" by P. Chelladurai and A. V. Carron, 1977, *Journal of Applied Sport Sciences, 2,* 9–14.

or partial point guard responsibilities received the majority of awards (eight of 15), while MVPs in the Women's National Basketball Association (WNBA) predominantly came from the forward/center positions (12 out of 15). The difference between the NBA and WNBA is worth considering further but is potentially based on differences in playing styles and tactics. For professional hockey, forwards (centers, right/left wingers) were awarded the MVP in hockey 14 out of 15 times in the National Hockey League (NHL; men's hockey), with the other time being goalie Carey Price. The same was true for women in the National Women's Hockey League (four out of four) and the Canadian Women's Hockey League (four out of four)—no players in defensive positions received accolades in any of these ice-hockey leagues. For the National Football League (NFL), only quarterbacks (12) and running backs (three) achieved this distinction (both high in propinquity and task interdependence). Finally, contrary to some of the earlier work in baseball, the distribution of awards in modern Major League Baseball is rather spread out. Across National and American leagues over the past 15 years, 11 outfielders, 13 infielders, three designated hitters, one catcher, and two pitchers were awarded this designation.

Group Position and Group Processes

The positions individuals occupy in relation to each other can also influence the nature and amount of their interaction and communication. For example, Sommer (1969) demonstrated that specific seating arrangements are closely associated with certain activities (see Exhibit 6.4). Individuals in competitive situations prefer a face-to-face or distant (i.e., across and at the opposite end of the room) arrangement. On the other hand, individuals engaged in cooperative activities prefer a side-by-side arrangement. Coacting individuals—those working on the same task but independent of one another—prefer to be seated in a distant position.

The pattern of interpersonal dynamics identified by Sommer (1969) and illustrated in Exhibit 6.4 does have implications for sport. For example, it might be useful for coaches or trainers to consider the pattern of interpersonal dynamics identified by Sommer (1969) in such decisions as locker room assignments. If teammates are in competition—for a scoring title, the same position on the team, or leadership roles—and that competition has the potential to destroy the cohesion of the team, it might be beneficial to assign them lockers in close proximity. This might not eliminate the competitiveness entirely, but it would increase their interaction and communication. Moreover, a distal arrangement only serves to contribute to or maintain the competitive orientation. Further, as the following example illustrates, strategically arranging players based on position may allow them to discuss tactics and improve performance. During a particularly difficult season, one NFL coach attempted to shake things up within the locker room:

> [Miami Dolphins coach] Dan Campbell went through his coaching Rolodex during the Dolphins' bye week, reaching out to allies for advice. The message was basically the same, regardless of the source: 'Be yourself and change it up.' Campbell listened. When players returned from their weekend off, they discovered a transformed locker room—literally. Their lockers had been moved. Instead of randomly placing the players throughout the room, they will now sit by position group (linebackers with linebackers, quarterbacks by quarterbacks, etc.). 'I went to my spot and Zach Vigil was in there,' said tight end Jordan

Exhibit 6.4. The Relation of Geographical Position to Interaction and Communication

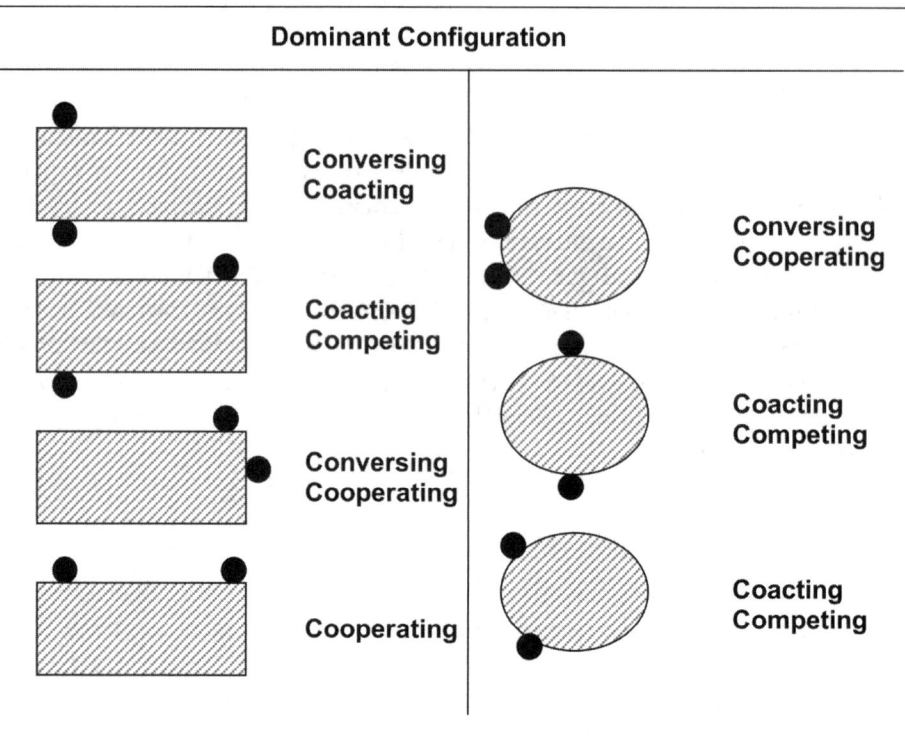

Source. Personal Space by R. Sommer, 1969, Englewood Cliffs: Prentice-Hall.

Cameron. 'I was like, 'What is this guy doing?' Campbell's rationale for the switch: players often start talking football the minute they walk in the door. They might as well sit with their own group so those talks will actually be productive. (Beasley, 2015, para. 1–4)

Positional Stacking by Race/Ethnicity

In 1970, in a classic study, Loy and McElvogue examined whether race/ethnicity is related to the likelihood an individual will occupy a geographically central or noncentral position on a sport team. Their results were unequivocal; Black individuals were most likely to be found in noncentral positions and White individuals to be found in central positions. This phenomenon came to be known as *stacking* (Loy & McElvogue, 1970) or occupational segregation (Sack, Singh, & Thiel, 2005).

Subsequent to the Loy and McElvogue (1970) publication, other authors examined whether the findings extended to other contexts (e.g., Berghorn, Yetman, & Hanna, 1988; Curtis & Loy, 1978; Jones, Leonard, Schmitt, Smith, & Tolone, 1987). As a consequence, research was undertaken with other types of sports, such as soccer and rugby; in countries other than the United States, such as Australia, New Zealand, and Great Britain; and with other ethnic groups (cf. Hallinan, 1991; Hayman, 1981; Lavoie, 1989; Maguire, 1988; Melnick, 1988; Melnick & Loy, 1996). Consistently, the pattern of results observed by Loy and McElvogue (1970) remained unchanged; White individuals were found to have a greater probability of occupying a central position, while other ethnic groups tended to occupy non-central positions.

The general consistency of the results led Hallinan (1991) to advance what he referred to as an *Anglocentric hypothesis*. The essence of this hypothesis is that in countries where stacking by race/ethnicity occurs, "there is a strong Anglo heritage as well as histories of structural inequalities resulting in discrimination for certain populations" (Hallinan, 1991, p. 76).

Much of the earliest research on stacking was undertaken with male athletes. Subsequently, a number of authors became interested in determining whether the tendency for White athletes to occupy central positions is also present in female sport teams. In college basketball teams, the findings have been mixed with some studies finding support for stacking, while others have not (Berghorn et al., 1988; Leonard, 1987; Yetman & Berghorn, 1993).

The findings across other sports have also been mixed. For example, Eitzen and Furst (1989) observed that, in college volleyball, Black athletes were statistically overrepresented in the hitter position and underrepresented in the setter position. Conversely, Melnick (1996), in a study of New Zealand netball teams, found that Maori women were not statistically underrepresented at either the center position (the most central, highest-interacting position) or goal defense (the most tactically important playing position). In discussing his results, Melnick (1996) suggested that

> Racial segregation by playing position in Anglocentric societies may be directly related to the salience of race as a categorizing variable in a particular society. Unlike the American preoccupation with race for classifying people and explaining individual differences, New Zealanders seem far less impressed with the construct. This is probably due in no small measure to the considerable amount of interracial marriage and the resulting interchange of genes that have taken place over the last century. For many New Zealanders, the establishment and reinforcement of racial boundaries is utter nonsense. (pp. 270–271)

Melnick (1996) also suggested that an important consideration for interpersonal relations and group dynamics on sport teams is the proportional representation of majority and minority members on a team. Thus, in a team composed of 90% minority players, stacking is not likely to occur, as "stacking and racial stereotyping are most likely to be present on teams where minority team members are numerically outnumbered, not where they are in the majority or in the same proportion as the majority" (Melnick, 1996, p. 267).

Given that the original research on the concept of stacking occurred five decades ago, it is useful to examine whether any strides have been made toward eliminating the over/underrepresentation of certain groups of people. With respect to athletes in the sport of baseball, Sack et al. (2005) found that "African Americans are overrepresented in the outfield over and above what can be explained by the fact that they are faster than other MLB [Major League Baseball] players" (p. 313). A decade later, Lapchick (2015a) reported on the issue of stacking and noted that the centralized positions in baseball such as pitching, infielding, and catching had small percentages of African American players (3.1 %, 7.9%, and 0%, respectively)—relative to a larger percentage occupying outfield positions (25.4%) and the overall percentage of African-Americans within the sport itself (8.2%). This is a typical distribution seen in a stacking situation.

In contrast, Woodward (2004) noted an improvement in the representation of African American quarterbacks over the past decades in the sport of football, but also highlighted that they represent 22% of all starting quarterbacks (20% when nonstarters are included) in a sport in which 67% of the athletes are African American. In recent years, Lapchick (2015b) concluded

> Most observers agree that the issue of stacking in the NFL is no longer a concern of significance … The quarterback position was the primary concern since it was so central to the game and now that African-Americans have broken down that barrier, concern about stacking has been greatly diminished. (pp. 14–15)

To complicate matters further, however, is evidence about differential treatment with respect to the behaviors required in a specific position based on race. In essence, even if a sport league attains parity in the proportion of players from ethnicities across their positions, the question remains whether athletes of different races/ethnicities are being asked to perform their positional role responsibilities differently? Bopp and Sagas (2014) termed this phenomenon 'racial tasking', and demonstrated that African American quarterbacks were being tasked with running the football almost twice the amount compared to White quarterbacks. Further, passing attempts for the latter group was 12% higher.

As noted previously, one potential benefit of having the opportunity to play in more central positions is the subsequent opportunity to contribute to sport organizations as a coach or in management following retirement. Does stacking that occurs at the athlete level then translate into the front office? An annual racial and gender report card tracks participation of various groups in important roles for the more prominent sport organizations in North America (i.e., MLB, NBA, WNBA, NFL, Major League Soccer, and the National Collegiate Athletic Association). In the most recent report, Lapchick (2018) noted some disparity across leagues regarding race and gender hiring practices:

> Are we playing fair when it comes to sports? Does everyone, regardless of race or gender, have a chance to make and run the team? While there have been some discouraging declines in 2018, I remain optimistic that our professional and college sports have leaders who are committed to diversity and inclusion and who will do what is right to provide opportunities for all people to play and work in sport. (p. 3)

The WNBA was touted as a leader in this regard, while important areas of improvement were noted for many of the other leagues.

7

Group Roles

[Brian Burke, former General Manager of the Toronto Maple Leafs of the National Hockey League] I tell the team ... you go to the symphony and in the front row is the first violin and she's elegant. She's got a beautiful long dress on, and there's a spotlight on. She's got nice earrings, and everyone came to listen to her. But there's a guy built like me in the back row blowing on a tuba. They don't start till they both sit down. Now she's going to make a lot more money than I do. She's probably going to have a longer career than I have. But if we're going to get picked up and put on a record label, they need me too. Then after we all leave, someone cleans up the hall and moves the chairs back. So there's a job for everyone. A successful organization has to have contributions at every level. (Hunter, 2010, p. S5)

A role is the pattern of behavior expected of an individual in a social situation. A role arises from the combined influence of the individual's position in the group, status in the group, and/or assigned or assumed responsibilities. In role theory, the individual who occupies a role is referred to as the *focal person*, while the other principals in the social situation are referred to as *role senders* (Kahn, Wolfe, Quinn, Snoek, & Rosenthal, 1964; King & King, 1990). In role theory terms, the team captain on a sport team, for example, could be considered as the focal person, and team members would represent one category of role sender, while management would represent another. Individuals who occupy the role of captain perceive the expectations arising from both their teammates and from management. Often the two sources (teammates and management) hold similar expectations for individuals occupying the role of captain. However, it is possible that they might not.

In the quote used to introduce this chapter, the nature of a role was highlighted. There is a direct parallel between a role on a sport team and the role in a musical production. Whatever the individual's talents—and there are good musicians and poor musicians just as there are good athletes and poor athletes—each group member must operate within a system, a production, or an overall plan, and carry out the requirements of his or her role. Some personal interpretation is always possible, but the individual's behavior must be generally consistent with what is prescribed by the role. Otherwise, group performance suffers.

Types of Group Roles

Formal vs Informal Roles

Within every group, there are two general categorizations of roles. The first is related to the degree of formalization of those roles (Mabry & Barnes, 1980). *Formal roles* are those that are directly established by the group or organization. There are a number of formal performance roles in a sport team that result from the specific offensive and defensive systems used. These roles often map directly onto one's position on the team (i.e., aspects of the physical structure). Examples include the setter and spiker in volleyball and the power forward, point guard, and small forward in basketball. However, some individuals in positions are required to contribute their efforts more than others (i.e., starters vs. nonstarters vs. practice players), and a select few may be required to incorporate and employ leadership behaviors during task performances. In other words, not everyone with the same position has the same role. Every sport team, as an organization, requires individuals to carry out these types of specific roles. The roles are so important to the success of the group that individuals are either trained or recruited to fill them.

The *informal roles* in a team evolve as a result of the interactions that take place among the group members without any formal prescription by the organization. The expectations of behavior for individuals who occupy informal roles are not as well established as formal roles, but they are present. A study by Cope, Eys, Beauchamp, Schinke, and Bosselut (2011) described the presence of 12 informal roles in an athletic environment through a content analysis of *Sports Illustrated*. These roles included the comedian, spark plug, cancer, distracter, enforcer, mentor, informal leader-verbal, informal leader-nonverbal, team player, star player, malingerer, and social convener. Their follow-up examination with athletes demonstrated that the perceived influence of these informal roles on team functioning (e.g., team performance, cohesion) varied greatly; the cancer role was viewed as most detrimental while the mentor role was viewed as most beneficial.

The suggestion that informal roles serve both positive and negative functions within sport teams concurs with previous literature devoted to understanding organizations and work groups. Researchers in these areas noted that a group's informal structure potentially serves two functions (e.g., Hare, 1994; Homans, 1950). First, informal roles can supplement the formal structure of the group. In a sport team, for example, if a captain (a formal role) is not providing the required leadership for his/her teammates, other individuals may engage in leadership behaviors informally to fill the gap. A second function of informal roles is to resist the formal group structure. In this regard, athletes may engage in behaviors that provide positive (e.g., voice alternative opinions/perspectives with the intention of helping the team function) or negative (e.g., simply be disruptive) outcomes for the group.

Overall, whether they occupy an informal team role or a formal one, athletes very quickly become aware of their role and react to its expected behaviors. The degree to which role performance is successful and/or positive helps to explain why groups are more or less effective.

Task vs Social Roles

Another general categorization of roles is related to their fundamental focus. Bales and Slater (1955) noted that roles could be considered from either a task or a social perspective. *Task roles* are those that are primarily concerned with accomplishing the group's stated purpose (e.g., performing as a team, winning the competition) while *social roles* are those that are concerned with producing greater group harmony and cohesion.

Rees and Segal (1984) carried out a study designed to assess who the task specialists and socioemotional specialists are on sport teams. The *task specialist* in a group is that individual who assumes a leadership role in the achievement of the group's goals. Task specialists influence, support, organize, and direct other group members toward the accomplishment of the group's task. This is often referred to as an instrumental role because the task specialist serves as an instrument for team success.

The *socioemotional specialist* in a group is that individual who is influential in promoting group harmony and integration. The task specialists often produce stress and tension because of their preoccupation with performance, productivity, and achievement. The socioemotional specialist helps to diffuse some of the tension by providing support, promoting team unity, and emphasizing the importance of team cohesion.

Rees and Segal (1984) found that the task leaders on the football team came almost exclusively from the first-string players while the socioemotional leaders were equally balanced between first and second string. Interestingly, considerable role integration was present—55% of the individuals who were listed among the top 10 individuals as task leaders were also listed among the top 10 socioemotional leaders. All of the athletes who occupied both roles were first-string players (see Exhibit 7.1).

When Rees and Segal (1984) looked at the effect of experience on role involvement, they found that task leaders were drawn from the total spectrum of the team: senior (33%), junior (56%), and sophomore (11%). On the other hand, the socioemotional leaders were almost exclusively the senior players on the team (90%). When individuals were listed in both roles,

Exhibit 7.1. Characteristics of Individuals in Leadership Roles in Sport Teams

Team Tenure	Task Leaders	Socioemotional Leaders	"Great People" (Both Task & Social Leaders)
Starting Status			
First String	100%	50%	100%
Second String	0%	50%	0%
Team Experience			
Senior	33%	90%	73%
Junior	56%	10%	18%
Sophomore	11%	0%	9%

Source. "Role Differentiation in Groups: The Relationship Between Instrumental and Expressive Leadership" by D. R. Reese and M. W. Segal, 1984, *Small Group Behavior, 15,* 109–123.

Exhibit 7.2. Percentage of Athletes Identifying with Sport Roles

Role Type	Rookies	Veterans	Starters	Nonstarters
Specialized Task-Oriented	82%	90%	95%	78%
Auxiliary Task-Oriented	65%	58%	46%	77%
Leadership	15%	41%	48%	13%
Social-Oriented	20%	22%	25%	18%

Note. Athletes were asked to list between two to five roles they perceived to occupy within the group, which accounts for why the column totals exceed the value of 100%. *Source.* "The Nature and Transmission of Roles in Sport Teams" by A. J. Benson, M. Surya, and M. A. Eys, 2014, *Sport, Exercise, and Performance Psychology, 3,* 228–240.

they were generally seniors (73%). It seems that ability is the most important qualification for a task leader on a sport team. Being on the first string is essential, years of experience on the team is not. On the other hand, years of experience are an essential prerequisite to be a socioemotional leader.

The findings of Rees and Segal (1984) were based on observations of two male American football teams. More recently, Benson, Surya, and Eys (2014) sought to understand how a more diverse set of athletes from a variety interdependent sport teams self-identified their roles. Based on the responses they received from basketball, football, soccer, volleyball, and hockey athletes, the role descriptions were broadly classified across four categories:

1. Specialized task-oriented roles: include task responsibilities that contribute consistently to team strategies and tactics (e.g., starting players, star players)
2. Auxiliary task-oriented roles: include task responsibilities that serve supplementary functions and support teammates in their role contributions (e.g., energy players, bench players)
3. Social-oriented roles: include responsibilities that support interpersonal relationships within the group (e.g., social organizers)
4. Leadership roles: include task and social responsibilities that direct teammates toward group goals (e.g., captains, mentors)

Similar to Rees and Segal (1964), Benson and colleagues (2014) examined the distribution of role occupancies relative to tenure on the team (rookies vs. veterans) and starting status (starters vs. nonstarters). The percentage of players who self-identified as occupying these roles can be examined in Exhibit 7.2. One clear distinction found across the percentages is that leadership roles were occupied primarily by veteran starting athletes (See Exhibit 7.2).

How Roles Develop

The emergence of roles in work groups was studied extensively by Bales (1966). He observed that certain behaviors are associated with the appearance of different group roles within

Exhibit 7.3. Behaviors Associated with
Role Development in Task-Oriented,
Problem-Solving Groups

	Behavior		
Group Role	Activity	Task Ability	Likeability
Task Specialist	High	High	Low
Social Specialist	High	Low	High
Leader	High	High	High
Underactive Deviant	Low	Low	Low
Overactive Deviant	High	Low	Low

task-oriented groups. The three general types of behaviors identified by Bales (1966) were *activity*, *task ability*, and *likability*. Behavior directed toward standing out from others is referred to as activity. On a basketball team, for example, speaking out frequently in the dressing room, encouraging others, and encouraging teammates during a game are some examples of activity behavior. Task ability is behavior that helps the group achieve its goals. As the name suggests, task ability is synonymous with expertise. Finally, likability is behavior directed toward the development and maintenance of socially satisfying relationships. Arranging group parties, coordinating social activities, and acting as a peacemaker are some examples of likability behavior.

According to Bales, the relative degree to which individuals exhibit these three behaviors has an influence on their roles within a group (Exhibit 7.3). Although group members generally fill the roles of task and socioemotional specialist, many sport teams also try to ensure that they have coaches and athlete leaders who carry out both of these roles. Usually (but not always) the head coach is the task specialist—the person most strongly oriented to the task concerns of productivity and performance. Then one of his or her assistants is the social specialist who provides the social support and diffuses the stress and tension that inevitably arise. This is an effective combination.

One anecdote that illustrates the task and socioemotional coaching roles was provided in Feinstein's (1987) account of an incident in which Bobby Knight—then head coach of the men's intercollegiate basketball team at Indiana University—criticized one of his athletes:

> Knight walked out onto the floor. He was drained. He turned to Kohn Smith. "Go talk to Daryl [Thomas]," he said. Knight knew he had gone too far with Thomas, and undoubtedly he had regretted many of the words as soon as they were out of his mouth. But he couldn't take them back. Instead he would send Smith, who was as quiet and gentle as Knight was loud and brutal, to talk to Thomas. (p. 7)

The original research on role differentiation and leadership led to the suggestion that these two roles—task specialist and socioemotional specialist—were viewed as incompatible with each other. It was felt that because the preoccupation of the task specialists with performance produced tension and stress, socioemotional specialists emerged to ensure that the group wouldn't disintegrate.

On the basis of a reanalysis and review of research concerned with group leadership and role differentiation, however, Lewis (1972) concluded that the two roles are often integrated. And, when one person fulfills both the task specialist and the socioemotional specialist roles, he or she has an overall *leadership role* in the group (see Exhibit 7.3). When this occurs, leadership within the group is more effective. Individuals who occupy both the task and social roles simultaneously are considered to be exceptional leaders.

The final two roles in Exhibit 7.3 are the *underactive deviant* and the *overactive deviant*. The underactive deviant is low on all three behaviors. It seems likely that there is a very low prevalence of this type of individual in sport teams. In contrast, individuals who are chronic complainers in the locker room, who exhibit high activity behavior but low task ability and likability behaviors, occupy the role referred to as the overactive deviant. A study by Cope, Eys, Schinke, and Bosselut (2010) examined coaches' impressions of the emergence of negative roles within sport groups. Denoted as 'cancers' or 'bad apples', individuals who occupy this type of role were perceived as manipulative and distracting to the group. The coaches also offered a number of explanations as to how these individuals emerge (e.g., aspects of their personality, external pressures, lack of group leadership).

Communicating Formal Role Responsibilities in Sport

Responsibilities associated with individual roles are often communicated formally (successfully or unsuccessfully) by people in positions of power or influence. As noted at the beginning of this chapter, those who communicate role responsibilities (typically the coach but also, in some instances, teammates, parents, fans, etc.) are referred to as *role senders* while the person who occupies the role is referred to as the *focal person* (typically the athlete).

Eys, Carron, Beauchamp, and Bray (2005) adapted a framework from Kahn et al. (1964) to illustrate how role responsibilities are communicated and which factors might influence how well this communication process takes place. As seen in Exhibit 7.4, the communication process (i.e., the role episode model) consists of a cycle of five events. Consider a typical situation in sport where a coach attempts to outline role responsibilities to an athlete; Event 1 occurs when the coach generates expectations for the responsibilities of the athlete. During Event 2 the coach, through his/her verbal or nonverbal communications, exerts pressure on the athlete to perform those responsibilities. Event 3 occurs when the athlete perceives that the coach has expectations for him or her. The response (Event 4) follows. Typically, in sport, this response is the proper execution of the role responsibilities (which is positive). However, other responses are possible. For example, if a coach's communication is unclear, an athlete's response might be dissatisfaction, frustration, and/or confusion (which are clearly negative). Finally, Event 5 highlights the fact that the coach makes judgments about how the athlete has responded to the role expectations.

Overall, there are a number of factors involved in this process that could influence how well the role is communicated, the nature of the response to role expectations, and how effectively the athlete performs his or her role. For example, in a qualitative examination of the role episode model with 11 male collegiate soccer players, Mellalieu and Juniper (2006) identified role clarity and role acceptance as vital factors that contribute to performance and should be

Exhibit 7.4. A Framework for the Communication of Role Responsibilities

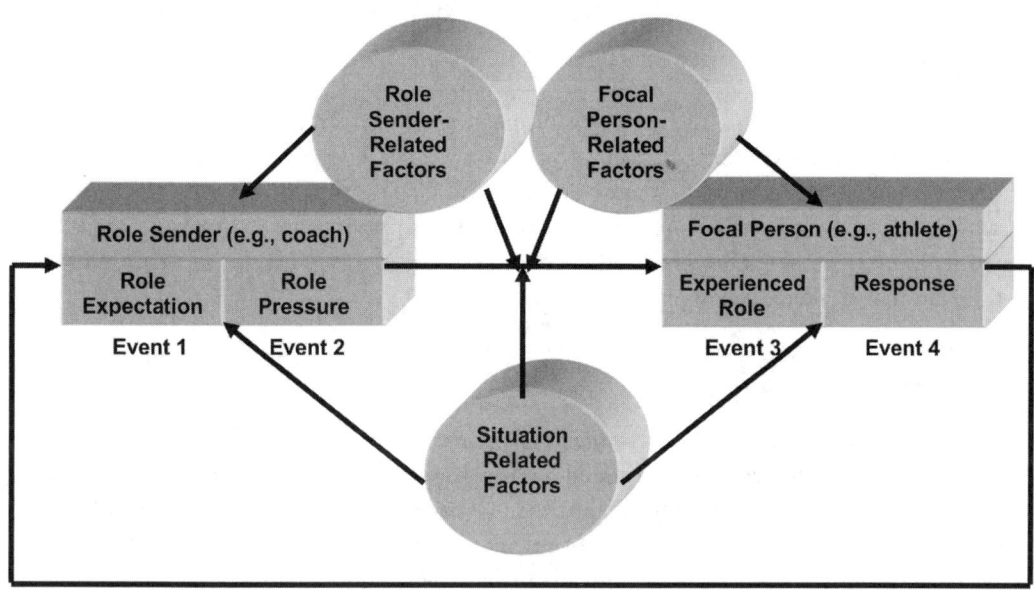

Source. *Occupational Stress: Studies in Role Conflict and Role Ambiguity* (p. 30), by R. L. Kahn, D. M. Wolfe, R. P. Quinn, J. D. Snoek, and R. A. Rosenthal, 1964, New York: Wiley.

considered in team-building interventions. These elements, and others, are highlighted in subsequent sections.

The Emergence of Informal Roles in Sport

In contrast with formal roles, which are proposed to follow a communication path experienced between role sender and focal person, informal roles tend to emerge more naturally within the group. However, what exactly drives the occupancy of informal roles? This is likely multifaceted. For example, work by Kim et al. (Kim, Gardant, Bosselut, & Eys, 2018; Kim, Godfrey, & Eys, 2019) found that athletes' personalities were associated with informal role behavior. Perhaps not surprising, for example, those athletes occupying the informal roles of the comedian or distractor were typically more extraverted. Furthermore, with respect to the latter role, those athletes also reported less conscientiousness.

In a follow-up study related to informal development, Kim, Coleman, Godfrey, Vierimaa, and Eys (2019) proposed a framework suggesting that athlete-centered factors (e.g., personality, tenure, work ethic) intersect with contextual factors (e.g., teammate influence, a role gap to fill) to promote informal role behaviors initially. Subsequently, informal role behaviors are appraised and either reinforced or rejected by other group members, leading to the continuation or termination of behaviors by the individual. For example, if one is inclined to make attempts at being funny by telling jokes or pulling pranks on teammates, the other group members could reinforce this behavior by laughing and encouraging the comedian role occupant. Alternatively, the individual could be sanctioned or ignored if the behaviors are inappropriate, with the hope that he or she will stop acting out.

The Nature and Correlates of the Elements of Role Involvement

Role Performance

Role performance represents the behavioral aspect of role involvement and is typically what role senders evaluate when expectations are communicated. On any team, there are a variety of roles that must be performed. The diversity of those roles, the difficulty (at times) of integrating individuals within specific team roles, and their importance to team success is illustrated in Exhibit 7.5 about Richard Jefferson and his experience with the San Antonio Spurs of the National Basketball Association.

Role Clarity/Ambiguity

For any team to be successful, each focal person must carry out his/her role consistent with the expectations of the role senders. As Exhibit 7.6 illustrates, the relationship between individual roles and team effectiveness is influenced by the presence of specific conditions. One of these is *role clarity*, which is one cognitive aspect of role involvement. Each athlete must clearly understand the responsibilities associated with his or her role. A quote by Great Britain's women's basketball player, Johannah Leedham-Warner, illustrates role clarity (see Exhibit 7.5).

When role clarity has been examined in both sport and work groups, it is usually under the label of *role ambiguity* that, of course, represents the flip side of role clarity. Kahn and his colleagues (1964) identified two major types of role ambiguity. One major type is referred to as *task ambiguity*, which represents uncertainty resulting "from lack of information concerning the proper definition of the job, its goals, and the permissible means of implementing them" (Kahn et al., 1964, p. 94). A second major type is referred to as *socioemotional ambiguity*. Socioemotional ambiguity represents the uncertainty that the individual possesses about the consequences to herself, to the organization, and/or to the role as a result of carrying out expected responsibilities.

Beauchamp, Bray, Eys, and Carron (2002) developed a conceptual model (see Exhibit 7.7) of role ambiguity for interactive sport teams based on the work of Kahn and colleagues. Interactive sport teams, such as hockey, basketball, and soccer, are those where athletes interact with both their own teammates and their opponents. As the model depicted in Exhibit 7.7 illustrates, on both offense and defense athletes need to understand four aspects associated with their role. One aspect pertains to the scope of their responsibilities. For example, a basketball player might have a number of general roles that he or she is required to perform, such as the point guard position and the role of captain.

The second aspect is related to the manner in which the responsibilities of a role should be carried out (i.e., the behaviors necessary to carry out role responsibilities). For example, how does a captain behave? A young inexperienced athlete just elected captain might wonder about the degree to which she should be vocal/critical/supportive with her teammates or whether she should consult with the coach about potential problem areas or athletes. A young captain may not have the answers to these questions.

A third type of role ambiguity that might be present is an uncertainty regarding how role performance is being evaluated. An individual playing a point guard role may not know whether the evaluation criteria for her position is based on statistics (e.g., points scored) or by more subjective criteria such as the leadership displayed on the court. Also, a captain may not

Exhibit 7.5. The Elements of Role Responsibilities in Sport Teams

Role Element	Illustration
Role Performance: Behavior that is consistent with role expectations	It appeared to be a perfect move: Add a high-scoring swingman with endless energy to an aging lineup in need of a small forward and presto, the Spurs' championship window would swing open again. At least that was the thinking when San Antonio acquired Richard Jefferson from the Bucks in the off-season. But as the Spurs have struggled…explanations for their slide have focused on the 29-year-old Jefferson. Part of the problem is that the role of the small forward in San Antonio's complex read-and-react offense differs significantly from the systems used by Jefferson's previous teams….Playing multiple positions hasn't helped the transition either. (Mannix, 2010, para. 1–3)
Role Clarity: The degree to which the individual understands what behavior is expected	While Britain was down 7–0 to begin the [women's EuroBasket] quarterfinal against Hungary, the team had moved the ball well during the opening few minutes. Late in the quarter they stormed back to take the lead and the offense was flowing….Leedham-Warner said: 'It's a whatever-it-takes mentality. You have to play defense, you have to play every minute, you can't rest. But the great thing about this team is that everyone understands their role. Everyone just does whatever it takes.' (Hopkins, 2019, para. 1, 3)
Role Conflict: The lack of sufficient ability, motivation, or time to achieve that goal.	The news had broken that [National Football League quarterback Andrew Luck] would shortly announce his retirement from the NFL. 'I'm in pain,' he said at the press conference. 'I'm still in pain. It's been four years of this injury-pain-rehab cycle.'….There was also the mental and emotional pain that had gone with the constant beating to his body—the costs to his family, to his self-worth. 'I haven't been able to live the life I want to live.' (Thomas, 2019, para. 1, 3)
Role Efficacy: The degree to which the individual believes that he or she has the capabilities to perform formal role functions	The occasion was a US women's national team practice as part of the World Cup victory tour…[Carli] Lloyd stroked a 55-yard field goal through the uprights and subsequently talked about giving the NFL a try. Women have played college football and arena football but never in the NFL. Besides a hefty foot, Lloyd carries brawny confidence. 'I am not afraid to step up in front of the whole world and actually do it,' she said. 'I have always been like that, from a little girl. I've never cared about going up against boys.' (Goff, 2019, para. 2, 3, 8, 9)
Role Commitment and Acceptance: A dynamic and volitional psychological bond reflected in the dedication to and responsibility for one's role	Veteran [National Hockey League] forward David Backes has fought in three of his last four games, adopting an enforcer role for the Boston Bruins. 'My wife probably does worry, but that can't be a thought in your head when you're out playing in the NHL,' Backes added. 'You know, I guess it's a calculated decision and if I'm going to stay part of this team and stay a part of a winning team, that's maybe going to be a part of my role and I'm okay with it' (TSN.ca, 2019, para. 1, 10.)
Role Satisfaction: The degree to which the individual is satisfied with his/her role responsibilities	On the basketball court, Jeremy Lin and the Toronto Raptors didn't work out. He was expected to be a key contributor of a playoff team. Instead, he barely played. Despite all of that, you can't call the addition a failure. How many players have we seen upset with their role in the past? An upcoming free-agent, who undoubtedly expected to be a part of the Raptors rotation when he signed, it would have been easy for Lin to be frustrated over a lack of minutes. However, Lin knew his frustrations wouldn't help the Raptors. So whether he was upset or not, he did the right thing. He continued to play his role and continued to be a good teammate. He helped the Raptors in the only way he could at that time. (Bossetti, 2019, para. 5–7)

Exhibit 7.6. The Complexity of Individual Roles Contributing to Team Effectiveness

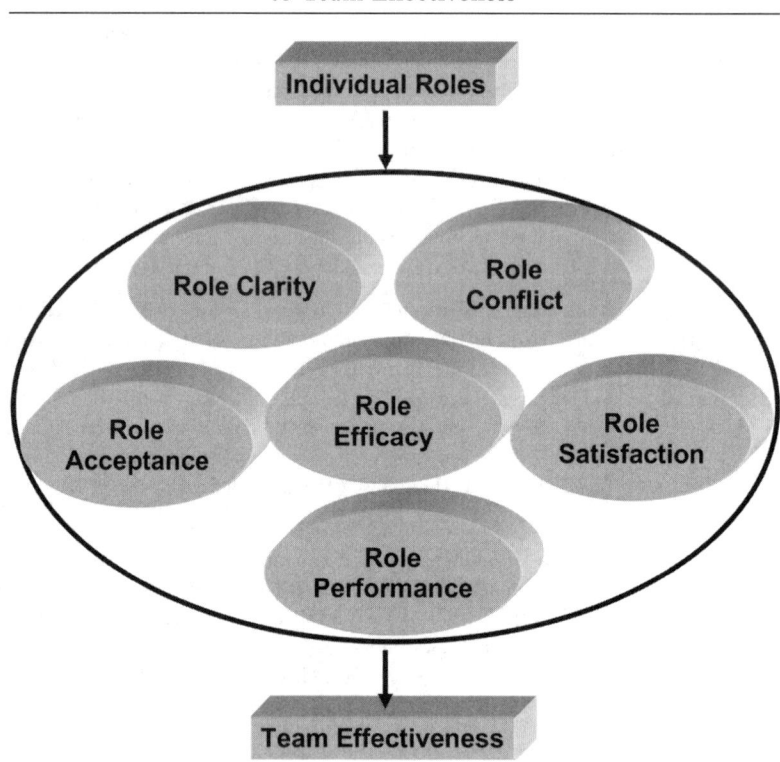

Exhibit 7.7. A Conceptual Model of Role Ambiguity for Interactive Sport Teams

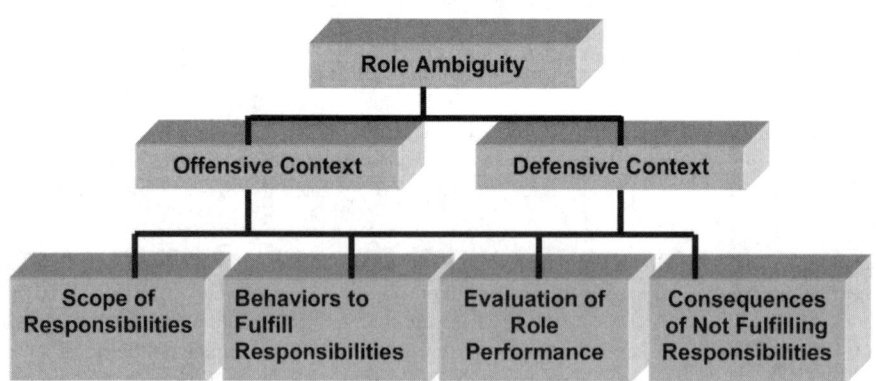

Source. "Role Ambiguity, Role Efficacy, and Role Performance: Multidimensional and Mediational Relationships Within Interdependent Sport Teams" by M. R. Beauchamp, S. R. Bray, M. A. Eys, and A. V. Carron, 2002, *Group Dynamics: Theory, Research, and Practice, 6,* 229–242.

Exhibit 7.8. Sources of Role Ambiguity in Interactive Sport Teams

Source	Potential Causes
The role sender (typically the coach)	1. The coach does not have sufficient expertise or knowledge to communicate role responsibilities 2. The coach does not communicate with his or her athletes 3. The coach communicates with athletes but communication is unclear 4. The coach communicates with athletes but sends conflicting information (e.g., be an enforcer on the ice but don't get penalties)
The focal person (typically the athlete)	1. Athlete not attending team functions or not paying attention to task instructions (e.g., in practice) 2. Athlete not informing the coach that he/she does not understand his/her role responsibilities (e.g., lack of initiative) 3. Athlete lacks expertise in sport to be able to comprehend role expectations 4. Athlete believes role responsibilities to be different from those the coach communicates.
The situation	1. Complexity of the sport (e.g., athlete moves from a high school environment to the university level) 2. Prior experiences of the athlete (e.g., athlete is new to the sport) 3. Lack of practical application for the athlete (e.g., a bench player or injured athlete)

Source. "Athletes' Perceptions of the Sources of Role Ambiguity" by M. A. Eys, A. V. Carron, M. R. Beauchamp, and S. R. Bray, 2005, *Small Group Research, 36,* 383–403.

understand whether the criteria she should be concerned about originates with the coach or teammates (i.e., who does she represent?).

Finally, the fourth type of ambiguity arises from uncertainty about the consequences of not successfully fulfilling role responsibilities. Thus, for example, the young team captain discussed above could worry that her behaviors in her role might distance her socially from teammates or possibly diminish the prestige associated with being a team captain.

It was pointed out earlier that formal roles are those established by the group or organization, whereas informal roles evolve as a result of the interactions that take place within the team. There is generally a greater probability that role clarity will be present in the case of formal roles. Nonetheless, the specific responsibilities associated with a role must be clearly spelled out. This ensures that there are no misunderstandings. However, in reality, misunderstandings exist and result in individuals not understanding their roles as well as they should.

In an effort to understand why role ambiguity exists, Eys et al. (2005) undertook a study to determine what athletes believed were potential sources of role ambiguity. The results of this study demonstrated that athletes perceived a number of different causes of role ambiguity, summarized in Exhibit 7.8. Generally, it is possible that the athlete (i.e., the focal person), the coach (i.e., the role sender), and the situation can play a part in role ambiguity being present for the role incumbent.

The importance of understanding roles in a sport environment can be demonstrated by a concise overview of research that has been conducted. Most importantly, the greater the athlete understands his or her role the more likely he or she will perform the role successfully (Beauchamp et al., 2002). In addition to better role performance, role clarity is also related to individual cognition and affect. For example, greater role clarity has been found to be related to decreased perceptions of competitive state anxiety (Beauchamp, Bray, Eys, &

Carron, 2003; Bosselut, Heuzé, Eys, & Bouthier, 2010), increased perceptions of athlete satisfaction (Beauchamp, Bray, Eys, & Carron, 2005; Eys, Carron, Bray, & Beauchamp, 2003), and greater athlete intentions to return to their team the subsequent season (Eys, Carron, Bray, & Beauchamp, 2005). Furthermore, when coaches individually tailor role information during the early socialization period for incoming athletes, this is positively associated with commitment to the coach and task cohesion perceptions (Benson & Eys, 2017).

Experiencing greater role clarity also appears to be positively related to important group processes such as intra-team communication (Cunningham & Eys, 2007) and task cohesion (Eys & Carron, 2001), which is the degree to which the group is united in the pursuit of its goals and objectives. When there is consensus on the group goals and how to achieve them, considerable pressure is placed on individual members. That is, there is greater group pressure on individual members to clearly understand their responsibilities, accept those responsibilities, and carry them out effectively.

Finally, it is important to remember that not all athletes or group members react similarly to ambiguous situations. For example, prior research has shown that role ambiguity perceptions differ for starters and nonstarters (i.e., starters experience less role ambiguity than nonstarters; Beauchamp et al., 2005) as well as veteran and rookie team members (i.e., veteran players typically experience less role ambiguity than first year players; Eys et al., 2003). Also, some individuals have a higher *need for clarity*. Bray and colleagues (2005) found that the negative relationship between role ambiguity and athlete satisfaction was more pronounced for athletes who had a higher need for their roles to be clear.

Role Conflict

Role conflict exists when, despite the presence of consensus about role responsibilities between a role sender and a role occupant, the role occupant (i.e., focal person) doesn't have sufficient ability, motivation, or time to achieve that goal. Role conflict is another *cognitive* component of role involvement. Every coach wants his or her athletes to do a good job, to help the team, to contribute to team success. This is constantly conveyed directly and indirectly to the athlete. But, an athlete may lack the necessary skills; or be confused because the behaviors considered to be associated with "doing a good job" may vary either between coaches or from one instance to the next.

Kahn et al. (1964) identified a number of different types of role conflict. One, called *intrasender conflict*, exists when the role occupant feels incongruent expectations from a single member of a role set. This is clearly illustrated in Exhibit 7.9 in the anecdote relayed by Don Cherry, a former coach of the Boston Bruins. Harry Sinden of the Boston Bruins (the only role sender) indicated that Al Secord was to be aggressive. At the same time, however, Secord was criticized for receiving penalties, a logical consequence of being aggressive. So, *from the same source*, he felt pressures to both engage and not engage in the behaviors consistent with his role.

A second type of role conflict identified by Kahn et al. (1964) is *intersender conflict*. Intersender conflict is present when the role occupant feels incongruent expectations from two or more members of a single role set. Exhibit 7.9 provides an illustration from work by Birrell and Richter (1994) in which they discussed the feminist transformation of sport using softball as a frame of reference. They pointed out that the feminist solution to low skill level is "to offer opportunities for women with little sport experience to learn the sport in a supportive environment" (Birrell & Richter, 1994, p. 235). However, the softball player quoted in Exhibit 7.9 experienced intersender conflict. On the one hand, her role as a member of the team involved

Exhibit 7.9. Examples of Role Conflict in Sport

Role Dimension	Example
Intrasender Conflict: Incongruent expectations for behavior from one member of a role set	Sinden always liked fighters, which is why I couldn't understand why Secord didn't make a hit with him. After I left the Bruins, I ran into Al one day in Boston and he was really depressed. 'I don't understand what the Bruins are doing to me,' he said. 'I'm on the bench. I asked why I wasn't playing and they told me, 'Because you're not playing your game, you're not playing aggressive and not hitting.' So naturally, I go out and be aggressive and start hitting and naturally I get a few penalties. Then they bench me again. I say, 'Why aren't I playing?' They say, 'Because you're getting too many penalties.' My head is all screwed up.' (Cherry & Fischler, 1982, p. 193)
Intersender Conflict: Incongruent expectations from different individuals from one role set	I got criticized for being too good, because if I threw a ball too hard to someone it was oppressing them. Just bullshit, absolute bullshit. And, I'll never forget this one woman, she came up to me at a party one time and she said, 'You know, you really oppress me because you're so good at softball.' It's like people were struggling with that whole feeling of how women are discouraged from sport, and how people who weren't good at it are put down in phys. ed. in grade school, and (they were) dumping all that confusion on people who are good athletes. (Softball player quoted in Birrell & Richter, 1994, p. 237)
Person-Role Conflict: Role requirements are in conflict with individual's motives or values	The news had broken that [National Football League quarterback Andrew Luck] would shortly announce his retirement from the NFL. 'I'm in pain,' he said at the press conference. 'I'm still in pain. It's been four years of this injury-pain-rehab cycle.' ... There was also the mental and emotional pain that had gone with the constant beating to his body—the costs to his family, to his self-worth. 'I haven't been able to live the life I want to live.' (Thomas, 2019, para. 1, 3)
Interrole Conflict: Incongruent expectations from two or more role sets	The whole week my son was sick, I hardly trained at all. It was hard on both of us because I wanted to go out for a run, but he felt too sick for me to leave him. I would have to wait until my husband came home from work, but sometimes he would work a double shift so I would get no running in. So not only is my training hurt, but I missed several classes because I had to stay home with him [my son]. (36-year old college distance runner quoted in Jambor & Weekes, 1996, p. 150)

playing to her capabilities. On the other hand, lesser talented individuals also sent messages that put her under pressure because her skill level was considered to be too high at times.

Person-role conflict, a third type of role conflict identified by Kahn and his colleagues, is present when a role requires certain behaviors that the person doesn't have the motivation or ability to carry out. The examples of person-role conflict in sport are numerous. The example of role conflict provided in Exhibit 7.5 about NFL quarterback Andrew Luck illustrates the incongruence between his athletic role and both his motivation to endure ongoing injury/rehab and quality of life outside of football.

It is possible to experience conflict that arises when there are incongruent expectations from two or more different role sets (e.g., being a member of a sport team *and* being a student). This is termed *interrole conflict*. A quote in Exhibit 7.9 from a nontraditional college athlete—a 36-year old married female with two children who was interviewed by Jambor and Weekes (1996)—provides a good example. There are responsibilities associated with being an athlete, a mother, a wife, and a student. As a quote in Exhibit 7.9 clearly shows, the pressures associated with these various roles can produce interrole conflict.

One generalization well supported by research is that role conflict has a bearing on an individual's commitment to the organization. When role conflict—in any of its manifestations—is high, the individual's commitment to the organization is reduced. The story of Paul Mulvey, an NHL player, is extreme but it does serve to illustrate the point. Mulvey hesitated for what he estimated to be 20 seconds when he was ordered to leave the bench and enter a fight on the ice. Between periods his coach, Don Perry

> … started screaming that Mulvey wouldn't stick up for his teammates. Mulvey got undressed—and never again put on an NHL uniform. 'Those 20 seconds,' Mulvey says, 'probably cost me a million dollars.' (Farber, 1997b, p. 72)

In addition to commitment, role conflict is negatively related to satisfaction (Jackson & Schuler, 1985), the degree to which individuals believe they have the capabilities to carry out their role functions (i.e., role efficacy; Beauchamp & Bray, 2001), and is positively related to burnout (Capel, Sisley, & Desertrain, 1987).

Role Efficacy

When role ambiguity and role conflict are minimal or absent, the role occupant is more likely to believe that he or she can successfully carry out expected responsibilities. An athlete's belief in his or her capabilities to perform role responsibilities is termed *role efficacy* and reflects a third cognitive component of role involvement. The example in Exhibit 7.5 highlights the confidence that women's soccer player Carli Lloyd has for potentially taking on a kicking role within a National Football League team, a role that would be groundbreaking within this professional sport. Strictly speaking, role efficacy is "a distinct construct representing a player's perceived capabilities to perform formal role functions in an interdependent team environment" (Bray, Brawley, & Carron, 2002, pp. 661–662). Similar to self-efficacy—the belief "in one's capabilities to organize and execute the course of action required to produce given attainments" (Bandura, 1997, p.3)—role efficacy is directly determined by the types of mastery experiences an athlete has acquired. For example, Bray et al. (2002) found that those athletes who had greater playing time and were starters on their respective teams also had higher perceptions of their ability to perform their roles. The importance of role efficacy was demonstrated in separate studies by Beauchamp et al. (2002) and Bray, Balaguer, and Duda (2004). They found positive relationships between role efficacy and role performance in British rugby and Spanish soccer players respectively.

Role Commitment and Acceptance

A final cognitive component of role involvement is role commitment, within which is housed role acceptance. Role commitment is "a dynamic and volitional psychological bond reflected in the dedication to and responsibility for one's role" (Eys et al., 2019, p. 25). In other words, how willing an athlete is to perform role responsibilities. Role acceptance is also commonly referred to in sport, and Eys et al. (2019) viewed this concept as reflecting a "decision to execute, rather than reject, the responsibilities of a role imposed by external sources, and represents the midpoint along the role commitment continuum" (p. 3). In short, role acceptance is akin to role commitment. National Hockey League player David

Backes is highlighted in Exhibit 7.5 as an individual who has modified and committed to his role as an enforcer on his team.

Furthermore, based on the general commitment literature within organizational psychology (Klein, Molloy, & Brinsfield, 2012; Meyer & Allen, 1991), Eys et al. (2019) proposed three bases of role commitment (i.e., factors leading one to commit to a role). First, an *affective* basis of role commitment reflects perceptions that one identifies and strongly attaches to a role (i.e., the athletes 'want to' be committed to their roles). Second, a *normative* basis of commitment derives from obligation and social norms to commit to a role (i.e., the athletes 'ought to' commit to their roles). Finally, *continuance* commitment perceptions are a product of perceived costs of not committing to a role (i.e., the athletes 'have to' commit to their roles). One can imagine that role commitment could be equally strong based on these foundations, though the reasoning is quite different for executing role responsibilities.

Typically, role commitment and acceptance have been confused with the degree to which an athlete is satisfied with a role. However, it is possible for an athlete to commit to role responsibilities but not be completely satisfied with them. For example, an athlete who typically does not see a lot of playing time may be dissatisfied with her position on the bench but, for a variety of reasons, agrees to occupy that role and be a contributing member of the team by trying hard in practice and encouraging other members who are in the playing unit. The example of Jeremy Lin, provided in Exhibit 7.5, illustrates a situation in which the player was frustrated and unhappy about his responsibilities on the Toronto Raptors (e.g., unsatisfied) but committed to helping the team win a championship in his limited role.

Sage (1998) provided two suggestions that would be applicable to account for the cognitions and behaviors of individuals in these situations that are less than ideal. First, athletes might accept potentially unsatisfying role responsibilities because of other benefits in the situation; for example, recognition for being a member of a popular sport group, attending team parties, and traveling to new places all might be secondary benefits. Benson, Eys, Surya, Dawson, and Schneider (2013), reporting on findings from interviews with intercollegiate athletes, highlighted several additional antecedents of role commitment and acceptance (beyond simply liking one's role), including being acknowledged and recognized for one's contributions to the team, strong group cohesion, and positive perceptions of the coach (e.g., competent and communicates role needs well).

A second suggestion that is applicable to this situation is that throughout the course of their athletic careers, athletes are conditioned to conform to the demands of the coach or other authority figures and, thus, will attempt to perform roles that may be dissatisfying. Also, in professional environments, one's contract dictates conditions of employment that may preclude other options for participation. Overall, the degree to which all athletes on a team commit and attempt to perform their role responsibilities (regardless of the prestige associated with the role) is absolutely vital to the proper functioning of the group as a whole. It is likely that this element of role involvement is the most critical in terms of how well the group performs together.

Role Satisfaction

Role satisfaction is the affective element of one's experience with a role. Locke's (1976) definition for job satisfaction is equally applicable to role satisfaction: "pleasurable emotional state resulting from the perception of one's [role] as fulfilling" (p. 1342). In an attempt to determine what aspects of a role are associated with satisfaction, Rail (1987) tested 60 administrators and coaches involved in amateur sport programs. She found that no matter what level the individuals worked at—local, provincial, or national—the same four conditions were critical for satisfaction.

One of these is the *opportunity to use specialized skills or competencies* in the role. Thus, for example, an athlete might be required to fulfill a defensive specialist role on the team and that role initially might seem unattractive; the skills required to be a defensive specialist might not appear to require high ability or competency. Consequently, satisfaction with that role might be low. If the role occupant can be led to the understanding that playing outstanding defense requires specialized skills and competencies, there is an increased likelihood that role satisfaction will be enhanced.

Another contributor to role satisfaction is *feedback and recognition*. The defensive specialist is often less visible than other members of the group. When feedback and recognition are provided to the role occupant, satisfaction is increased; when they are not, satisfaction diminishes.

A third, related factor mentioned by Rail (1987) was *role significance*. If the role is critical or perceived to be critical to team success, the occupant is more satisfied. India batsman (cricket) Cheteshwar Pujara reflected on how his teammates regarded his contributions to their team:

> With the way I have performed for the Indian team, the way I have contributed, I don't think I need to fear about anything. At the same time, the team has understood the importance of my role and my contribution for the team. I don't have to fear for anything. Obviously, when it comes to Test, I have a role to play for the team. Everyone understands that. The most important thing is to perform for the Indian team, which I have been doing. (Krishnan, 2018, para. 10)

The fourth condition identified by Rail (1987) was *autonomy*—the opportunity to work independently. It may be possible that autonomy isn't as important for role satisfaction in athletes as it was for the administrators and coaches studied by Rail (1987) but this seems unlikely. In 1980, Hackman and Oldham (1980) developed a conceptual model in an attempt to account for the motivation, satisfaction with personal growth, satisfaction with job responsibilities, and work effectiveness of individuals in achievement situations. Three critical psychological states identified by Hackman and Oldham (1980) were (1) the perceived meaningfulness of the work, (2) the perceived personal responsibility for the outcome, and (3) the knowledge of results available. Autonomy directly influences perceptions of personal responsibility for the outcome.

Enhancing Role Performance

Coach. Athletic director. Student. Counselor. Mother. Daughter. One person could play each of these roles (and others) simultaneously. Humans are social animals and, consequently, involvement in a large number of groups is inevitable. And equally inevitable is the assumption of different roles in these different groups. William Shakespeare (1896) probably expressed it best in his play *As You Like It*:

> All the world's a stage. And all the men and women merely players. They have their exits and their entrances. And one man in his time plays many parts. (Act II, Scene 7)

Unfortunately, the general behaviors considered appropriate for each of the roles listed above can be quite different. Consequently, a number of challenges are associated with performing any one role successfully. For example, the role occupant may not have sufficient ability, motivation, time, or understanding of the role to produce the behaviors expected. The last chapter of this book highlights some team building strategies that may be effective. However, some general suggestions can be found below regarding enhancing role execution.

First, an effective goal setting program at both the team and individual level can improve both role clarity and role commitment. Individual goal setting serves four important functions: it directs the individual's attention and actions toward appropriate behaviors, it motivates the individual to develop strategies to achieve the goal, it contributes to increased interest in the activity, and it leads to prolonged effort (Locke, Shaw, Saari, & Latham, 1981). All of these contribute to role clarity and role acceptance.

With regard to role conflict, some approaches suggested from other problem areas in sport have relevance. For example, Volp and Keil (1987) observed that one effective means of dealing with intrapersonal conflict is through cognitive restructuring. An underlying assumption for engaging in cognitive restructuring is the need for cognitive consistency. As Volp and Keil (1987) noted,

> All organisms prefer to live in a state of equilibrium, a state of cognitive balance. Whenever this equilibrium is threatened, cognitive inconsistency or dissonance arises, which is perceived as tension or conflict ... This is always the case when elements within a cognitive field are inconsistent with each other. The individual then takes steps to reduce conflict and restore the equilibrium. (p. 359)

In the process of cognitive restructuring, two strategies are possible. An individual can devalue one of the roles. Thus, a coach might reduce the importance (i.e., relevance) of her teaching role if the behaviors in that role are in conflict with her coaching. An individual can also bring different roles into balance (i.e., harmony) by decreasing the differences among the component parts of each role. Thus, a coach might emphasize the fact that his coaching is teaching, that elite athletes are similar to elite students (i.e., graduate students), that recruiting in athletics is like recruiting in graduate programs, and that scholarships for outstanding athletes are comparable to scholarships for outstanding students. This altered perspective would help to reduce conflict between the two roles.

When Volp and Keil (1987) compared elite athletes with medium and lesser skilled athletes, they found that elite athletes exhibited the least intrapersonal conflict. The elite athletes also made the greatest use of cognitive restructuring strategies, particularly by increasing the harmony among potentially conflicting elements. On the basis of their results, Volp and Keil (1987) suggested that

> ... competing successfully at a high level requires the athlete to cognitively restructure incoming information to reduce conflict that might otherwise be an obstacle to performance ... A successful athlete seems able to align himself or herself with the demands of the sport. The harmonization of conflicting cognitions seems to be a functional method of coping with contradictions inside the cognitive field ... that might otherwise impair motivation and performance. (p. 372)

There are other techniques in addition to cognitive restructuring that might be useful for reducing role conflict. For example, in discussing interventions related to athlete burnout, researchers (Cresswell & Eklund, 2003; Goodger, Lavallee, Gorely, & Harwood, 2010) suggested strategies such as (a) scheduling time-outs, (b) increasing participation in decision-making, and, relatedly, (c) focusing on listening to athletes. Each of these might be used to deal with role conflict.

Scheduling time-outs involves setting up periods away from the situation. A coach may feel overwhelmed by the pressures and stresses associated with teaching and coaching simultaneously, with planning and attending practices, meeting athletes, the media, parents, and other coaches. It could be beneficial to have his or her major teaching load scheduled in a term after the end of the season. Another strategy might be to timetable in a specific day, or a morning or evening, or even a period away from the concerns of the role. A time-out can vary in type, timing, and duration depending on the constraints of the situation. There are no fixed prescriptions except that time away from a role does help reduce role conflict.

Increasing the participation of others in decision-making can also help to reduce role conflict resulting from overload. Since role conflict arises because the role occupant doesn't have sufficient ability, time, motivation, or understanding, the recruitment of others to fill these gaps can alleviate some of the problem. Increased participation may be accomplished in either of two ways: by sharing responsibilities among available group members or by increasing the number of group members.

A third possibility is to attempt to offer opportunities to truly listen to the athlete as they discuss their experiences. Role expectations evolve from both the individual (the role occupant) and the group or organization (role senders). By expressing their thoughts about their role involvement, the role occupant can insure that the behavioral demands (either self-imposed or from others) are not beyond his or her capabilities. For example, an athlete could attempt to discuss with the coach the factors that are producing the greatest stress or pressure. Similarly, a coach might negotiate with the administration to reduce some responsibilities, producing role conflict.

8

Group Norms

The culture is highly interdependent and interconnected, relying on everyone doing their job. Anything less than 100% is unacceptable and once this sub-par pattern becomes evident, changes in the organization are quick to be made. As [New England Patriots] coach [Bill] Belichick always says: 'It's all about the players.' He knows that the players not only determine the fate of the team's success but also their own individual success. The expectations of winning are clear and understood. If you are not about the team and being hyper-accountable—you don't fit. The Patriot Way demands mental toughness that enables strategic focus and the ability to block out distractions. This is why the Patriots have created a dynasty of winning. Everyone on the team respects the culture and accepts the demands of what is required from the culture to win. (Llopis, 2019, para. 13–15)

The nature of group norms is clearly illustrated in the quote used to introduce this chapter. Norms are the standards for behavior that are expected of group members. Whereas the quote refers to the Patriot Way as a culture, that culture lays out what is expected of all members to fit within the group by codifying team norms. As Exhibit 8.1 shows, norms are descriptive, consensual, evaluative, informal, unobtrusive, flexible, internalized, and stable (Forsyth, 2019). Insofar as their descriptive function is concerned, norms outline the group's beliefs about the standards for behavior considered appropriate.

In terms of their evaluative function, norms put a priority on the values or standards that govern the behaviors of a wide cross section of different individuals who have membership in the group—independent of position occupied, status possessed, and/or role responsibility. As such, group norms represent the organization's or group's consensus about what is considered acceptable.

Exhibit 8.1. The Nature of Norms

Characteristic	Description
Descriptive	Norms represent the standards for behavior in a group.
Consensual	Norms are shared by group members.
Evaluative	Norms establish priorities for different behaviors, marking some as more valuable than others.
Informal	Norms are not formally adopted by the group but result from a gradual change in behavior until a consensus is reached in the group.
Unobtrusive	Norms are taken for granted and only become an important issue when they are violated.
Flexible	Minor deviations from norms are generally permitted.
Internalized	Norms are internalized by individual group members. Adherence results primarily from satisfaction produced rather than fear of sanctions.
Stable	Norms develop slowly over time and are very resistant to change.

Source. Group Dynamics (7th ed) by D. R. Forsyth, 2019, Belmont CA: Wadsworth, Cengage Learning.

Norms are also informal and unobtrusive; they are not specifically or overtly set out by the group. Gradual changes in individual behavior occur over time until a consensus is achieved about what is appropriate. Because they are not specifically set out as rules or laws, norms are most evident when they are violated. Typically, individual group members internalize norms so that adherence occurs primarily because of the satisfaction this produces rather than the fear of sanctions. Some flexibility is also present and minor deviations from a norm are acceptable. Finally, norms are stable and are resistant to change.

Because norms reflect existing group values, the group evaluates individual behavior on an ongoing basis and judges it to be acceptable or unacceptable, satisfactory or unsatisfactory. Acceptable behavior is rewarded or approved through verbal appreciation, elevated prestige, increased group acceptance, and recognition. On the other hand, unacceptable behavior is sanctioned by verbal criticism, ostracism, physical abuse, or even rejection from the group (Crosbie, 1975). The unfortunate sanctioning of perceived unacceptable behavior is illustrated in the experiences of National Football League quarterback Colin Kaepernick. Kaepernick chose not to stand during the playing of the American national anthem as a protest for the treatment of African Americans and other minorities in the United States. On the sanctioning of this non-normative behavior, Moore (2018) discussed,

> As if there were any doubt that the NFL was going to continue its blacklist against Colin Kaepernick, the former Super Bowl starting quarterback was once again denied an opportunity this week. This time, it was in Seattle, and there was none of the hemming and hawing about Kaepernick's numbers not being good enough or his playstyle not being the right fit for the offense. No, instead, an NFL source told ESPN's Adam Schefter that Seahawks officials cancelled Kaepernick's workout after he refused to commit to ending his kneeling protests during the national anthem during the 2018 season. (Sure enough, on Friday, the Seahawks went ahead and found someone else for the job.) … Kaepernick, Reid, and anybody else who would dare kneel in 2018 also threaten the league's ironclad grip on the values of obedience and discipline, and that is

a threat that cannot be brooked by such small, angry men as Bob McNair, Dan Snyder, and Jerry Jones. But Reid and Kaepernick will not submit, and for that crime, we should expect the NFL's unofficial but blatantly obvious blackballing to continue through 2018, and, in all likelihood, beyond. (para. 1, 13)

Norms emerge over time in a sport setting. Using an example of how the structure of an intramural basketball team takes shape, group norms develop around such behaviors as the average number of shots taken by any one player in a game. As norms are clarified, pressure is placed on individual members to conform to this group norm by rewarding conformity. If a team member were to violate this team's norm by taking too many shots or failing to distribute the ball, he or she will be sanctioned. The sanctions might take the form of criticism or ostracism. Other team members might begin using a derogatory nickname to try to relay their irritation or they might stop passing the ball to the norm violator. Depending on the persistence of the behavior, its seriousness, and the cohesiveness of the group, the norm violator might even be rejected from the team.

Types of Team Norms

Four general types of norms were identified by Mott (1965). These are summarized in Exhibit 8.2. A *prescribed norm* serves to specify which behaviors are considered appropriate for group members. The norm for productivity—the concept of group members expending a similar amount of effort toward group objectives—would be one example of a prescribed norm. In Exhibit 8.2, Aaron Rodgers, a quarterback for the Green Bay Packers football team, is described as encouraging this norm for productivity with his teammates.

Unwritten prescriptions are not just important for groups of athletes, but also other collections of individuals in the sport environment such as a group of coaches or officials. Hancock, Martin, Evans, and Paradis (2018) highlighted one normative expectation held by junior ice hockey officials as described by one participant in their study:

> There is also cultural stuff ... typically rookies will give away their first game fee. So a rookie comes in and works his first game, but he isn't getting paid that night because the other guys take their money. Or if you happen to be somewhere where you can go out for dinner and drinks, the rookie buys those because that's his initiation ... like, 'Congratulations! You made the league.' (p. 230)

The expectations that emerge around behaviors not considered appropriate are referred to as *proscribed norms*. Essentially, they represent the flip side of a prescribed norm. For example, the United States women's national team players adhered to the group norm of refusing to accept invitations to rejoin the team, until the goal of obtaining more equal treatment (in comparison to the men's team) was achieved (see Exhibit 8.2). As well, in many sports (e.g., ice hockey, soccer), a proscribed norm is to avoid mentioning a potential shutout (i.e., not allowing any goals during the match) for the goalie during the game. This is considered bad luck and bad etiquette.

It is important to bear in mind that norms are expectations that exist in the minds of group members. They provide guidelines about what group members should do, ought to

Exhibit 8.2. Illustrations of Various Group Norms

Type of Norm	Quotation
Prescribed Norm	It may seem hard to believe, but [quarterback] Aaron Rodgers is entering his 14th [National Football League] season. He was drafted in 2005—when Green Bay's rookie wide receivers were 9 and 10 years old. Rodgers called out those rookies for their lack of effort last week. 'He wasn't trying to call anybody out,' [reporter Wes] Hodkiewicz said of Rodgers. 'But his biggest focus was showing everybody what these drills mean to him, how competitive he takes them, and kind of the effort level he wants everybody to jump up to.' (Lawrence, 2018, para. 1, 3)
Proscribed Norm	We were a success, by any and all measures. But we were not seen as equals to the men. We grew tired of being expected to win gold without being treated as champions. In 2017, the US National Women's hockey team decided enough was enough. We threatened to boycott the world championships, in a year when they were being held on home soil…We had three main buckets to fill: we wanted increased marketing and visibility, more programming, and better funding…. Phone calls were being made to individual players, with organizers trying to field a team for the tournament. But one by one, players refused. Our group grew stronger. Every individual had their own temptations to accept an invitation to join the tournament. Players on the national team who had earned a spot on the roster, players on the outskirts of our pool, young girls looking for their first national opportunity—we stood together as one. (United States Women's Ice Hockey player Hilary Knight; Knight 2019, para. 11, 14, 15)
Permissive Norm	Soccer is different. For one thing, unlike 'turn-taking' sports like tennis and baseball, soccer is a flow sport with control of the play sweeping back and forth between the teams. The referee's main job is to ensure the flow continues within the rules by calling fouls on the fly—or not, for that matter. Soccer is close to unique in having as part of the laws of the game the idea of 'playing the advantage.' Even if a foul has been committed objectively, the referee is mandated to rule that play should continue on the grounds that the offended team retains an advantage that would be negated by the calling of the foul. This means that in soccer, the referee is largely a dispenser of justice, the strict truth be damned, which makes his or her judgment an irreducible part of the job. (Potter, 2019, para. 5–6)
Preference Norm	The game-day suit is something that has trickled down to minor hockey, adding yet another expense for parents who are already spending a lot of money on the sport. [Montreal Canadiens player] Gallagher remembers having to wear a suit and tie to games in Western Canada when he was young, but not for very long. 'We started wearing them when we were 13 or 14 years old,' Gallagher recalled. 'I remember our coaches just got rid of that idea and let us wear track suits.' (Cowan, 2018, para. 18–19)

do, and are expected to do (Homans, 1950). As was pointed out in the introduction to this chapter, they are not laws or formalized rules. Thus, if a team had a rule relating to curfew—such as anyone missing curfew will not be on the roster for the next game—it would not be considered a norm. Norms do emerge around rules and regulations, however. For example, a norm might emerge that the rule about curfew is unimportant.

As Exhibit 8.2 shows, there are also *permissive norms:* patterns of behavior that are permitted but not required. This type of norm is illustrated in Potter's (2019) description of soccer officiating and the principle of advantage. Behaviors for which a foul might be called are ignored if an advantage is retained by the attacking team, though this is at the discretion of the referee. Another place where permissive norms exist is baseball. Rainey and Larsen (1988) demonstrated empirically that baseball umpires use a strike zone that differs from what is set out in the rulebook. They had 16 high school/college level umpires describe the official rulebook definition of the strike zone. The umpires were then required to reproduce the strike zone by drawing lines across a picture of a batter's body. Finally, they were asked to draw two more lines showing the upper and lower boundaries of the strike zone they actually used.

A significant deviation was found between the top of the actual strike zone and the line umpires used. The umpires reduced the size of the strike zone by lowering the top boundary. The reasons given for not following the rule book fell into five general categories: (a) positioning problems (with a low stance behind the catcher, it is difficult to call the high pitch); (b) others' expectations (the coaches and players expect a lower strike zone); (c) major league influence (the high pitch is not called in the major leagues); (d) convenience (the letters on a player's jersey are a better reference); and (e) discretion (provide the batters with a better opportunity to hit).

The final type of norm presented in Exhibit 8.2 is the *preference norm*—behaviors preferred but not required by group members. The dress codes for minor ice hockey players tend to be determined by the organization. In some organizations, strict rules dictate that young male athletes wear a shirt and tie to competitive matches. In other organizations, a dress code is encouraged but not mandated (i.e., preferred), giving coaches some autonomy in deciding what is best for their teams.

Emergence of Team Norms

If a norm is a behavioral standard, how does it develop? One essential prerequisite is team *interactions*. The contact members have with each other helps to clarify the standards that are acceptable for behavior. It is important to remember, however, that individuals' past experiences in similar situations also play a role in the emergence and application of normative expectations. Jimerson (1999), after analyzing norms surrounding pickup basketball games, concluded that

> The preexistence of norms is clear. People come to the gym with norms in mind, but they also invoke them selectively to maximize playing time and game quality. Yet their invocation of the norms does not ensure acceptance; indeed, players often discuss whether and how to apply norms. (p. 153)

The influence of group interaction on the development of norms was further demonstrated by research conducted by Colman and Carron (2001). They examined the prevalence of norms in independent sport teams such as swimming, track and field, and wrestling. Although many of these athletes consider themselves members of a team, they compete individually and, thus, have less interaction in games and practices than their counterparts participating in sports such as basketball, hockey, or soccer. Not surprisingly, Colman and Carron (2001) found less support for the presence of norms on individual sport teams.

Finally, Crozier and Benson (2020) provided key examples that result from interactions within and between teams that may drive normative expectations. For example, higher status individuals in the team may drive team norms by making explicit statements (see Exhibit 8.2). Furthermore, specific events that occur in the lifespan of the team may cause the team to adopt norms. An unanticipated loss, for example, may force a team to alter its expectations and agree to earlier curfews and/or arrival times for warmups. Finally, observing the behavioral patterns of existing members provides additional information about what is valued within the team.

A second essential prerequisite is *reinforcement*. The behaviors that the vast majority of team members find acceptable are reinforced; unacceptable behaviors are discouraged. Consequently, each individual comes to understand the standards (norms) deemed appropriate. The role of interaction and reinforcement in the emergence of group norms is illustrated by an example. When a social media group forms (e.g., Facebook, Whatsapp), a wide range of differences is possible regarding issues such as how many times to post a comment, the acceptable lag time for responding, the type of language considered appropriate, and the permeability of allowing access to other potential members. Through interactions and reinforcement, a general understanding develops within the group; the range of behaviors considered permissible by the group decreases. The general standards that develop help the group operate smoothly. Similarly, as sport teams develop and team members interact frequently, the differences in the amount of effort they expend at practices, the type of clothing they wear on road trips, and so on, gradually decrease.

An alternative perspective regarding how norms emerge can be derived from the focus theory of normative conduct (Cialdini, Reno, & Kallgren, 1990). Cialdini et al. (1990) noted that social norms can be generated as a result of (a) observations of others' behaviors and (b) cognitions related to what we think others are expecting. Specifically, *descriptive norms* pertain to one's perceptions about the actions of others, which provide clues as to what is valued by the group. If all group members arrive to practice 15 minutes before the posted time, this suggests that the group values punctuality. Furthermore, *injunctive norms* reflect one's perceptions of what others approve of in terms of individual group member behavior. Collegiate athletes may not observe the off-season behaviors of their teammates but perceive that training and returning in better shape for the next season are expectations for everyone on the team.

The Function of Team Norms

Researchers (Jones, 2001; Wheelan, 1999) noted that norms perform important functions within the industrial/organizational domain in that they tell people what they should be doing, saying, and believing. By providing group members with general prescriptions for appropriate behavior and implicitly outlining the limits for permissible deviations from those prescriptions, norms serve two general functions within the team (Kiesler & Kiesler, 1969). One of these is *informational*. Norms help individuals gain insight into the group; they provide a standard against which new members can validate their opinions, attitudes, and behaviors. Norms also insure that individuals' opinions, attitudes, and behaviors don't deviate dramatically from other team members.

The second, related function of team norms is *integration*. The individual who understands and accepts the team norm is drawn into the group; the individual who does not is rejected or removed from the group. When team norms are accepted, team goals can be successfully pursued, and the continuation of the group is insured. The integrative function of team norms is illustrated in a story pertaining to the commitment and norm for productivity leading to the improvement of the Major League Soccer team San Jose Earthquakes:

> 'I think the team is growing a lot,' Almeyda said. 'We are trying to instill commonality within the players. For me, the way they communicate, their work ethic, and unity are fundamental. In my first meeting with them, I said I wanted a team, not individuals, in which everyone put in their own grain of sand. We are achieving that.' (Jonas, 2019, para. 11)

Partridge and Stevens (2002) outlined four specific benefits that emanate from the integrative and informational functions of norms: (a) positive norms (e.g., a strong work ethic) can facilitate performance, (b) the behavior of team members who adhere to team norms can be anticipated and others can respond accordingly, (c) embarrassing problems can be avoided through the presence of norms (e.g., being late and missing the bus), and (d) the values of the group are promoted (e.g., a disciplined and proud group of high school football players may decide to wear ties to school). Overall, conformity to team norms helps to contribute to the unity of a team. Deviance from the norms breaks down this unity.

The Stability of Norms

Once team norms are established, they are slow to change. This is demonstrated in studies designed to test the strength of norms by assessing the conformity of research participants when they are placed into social situations with incorrect, or even fraudulent, norms that have been established. In a typical study on conformity to group standards, Jacobs and Campbell (1961) had groups of four participants judge the distance a light moved. Initially, three of the four group members in each group were confederates (accomplices) of the experimenter; they all reported that the light had moved 15 to 16 inches. The naive participants in the group correctly perceived (and reported) that the light had moved approximately four inches. However, after a series of trials in which the confederates continued to endorse an incorrect standard, the naive participants also began to report that the light had moved 15 to 16 inches. When this incorrect norm was well established, the composition of the group was changed so that new naïve members replaced existing group members over a series of generations.

With each generation, the new group member (a naive participant) reported that the light had traveled about four inches. The three established group members (who were no longer confederates of the experimenter) continued to adhere to the incorrect standard and report that the light had moved approximately 15 to 16 inches. After a series of trials, the new naïve group member adopted the group norm. Although each generation showed a tendency to move closer to the correct standard, it took four to five generations before this was accomplished (see Exhibit 8.3).

What this demonstrates is the stability of group norms. There is always the question, of course, whether a laboratory study has specific application in the real world. People associated with work and sport organizations know that it does. If a team develops negative norms such as abusive behavior toward officials or other team members, a poor work ethic, or an emphasis on individual rather than team goals, these can persist over a number of seasons (i.e., generations)—long after the individuals primarily responsible for their development have left the team. Concern regarding the development of a norm for lower productivity (i.e., losing) is illustrated by comments about the Carolina Hurricanes of the National Hockey League in 2018:

> 'I like the team,' [said owner Tom Dundon]. 'I think we're improving. I think we want a culture where everybody earns their spot every day. As long as we're doing that, and we clearly have good players, then it's how do we make those players maximize their potential? How does the team maximize its potential? … But right now, and after years of missing the playoffs, the Hurricanes are at least at risk of developing the dreaded losing culture that can be much harder to get out of than simply having the draft lottery balls fall your way. (Boylen, 2018, para. 18, 21)

Exhibit 8.3. Schematic Representation of the Stability of Norms over Successive Generations within a Group

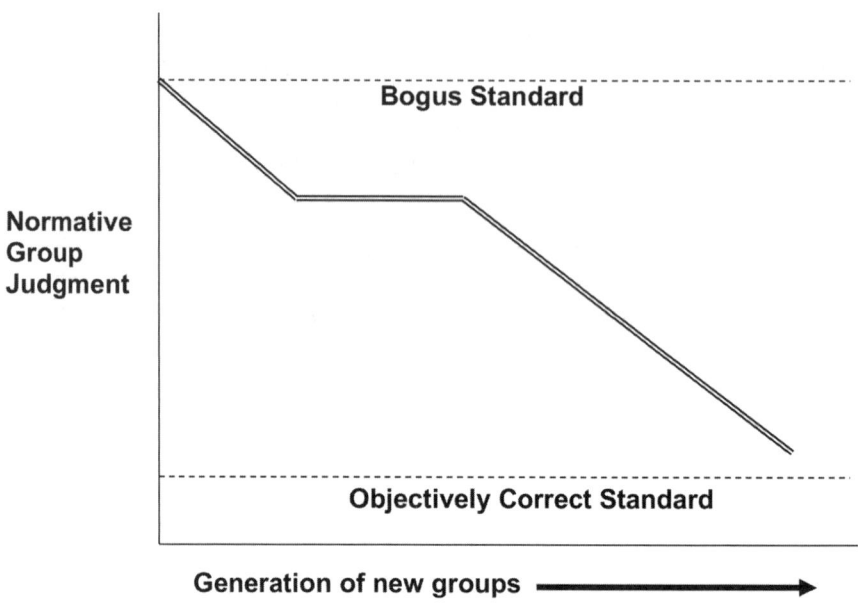

Source. "The Perpetuation of an Arbitrary Tradition Through Several Generation of a Laboratory Microculture" by R. C. Jacobs and D. T. Campbell, 1961, *The Journal of Abnormal and Social Psychology, 62,* 649–658.

Remarkably, in the following year (2018–2019) the Hurricanes competed for the conference championship during a season in which they were both celebrated and derided for their team celebrations following home victories (i.e., "the Storm Surge"), providing hope that there are ways in which to interrupt ongoing negative norms.

As another example, a common, on-going practice for a number of sport teams is to initiate new members; a practice sometimes referred to as *hazing*. Waldron (2015) found that the strongest predictor of continued hazing behaviors was the presence of team norms for this practice. In fact, "When team norms for severe and mild hazing exist, many athletes will adjust their behavior to meet this norm, even if they do not agree with it, in order to maintain and/or gain social approval" (Waldron, 2015, p. 1099).

It was pointed out previously that norms develop slowly in a team. But when they are present, they are also changed slowly. It is irrelevant whether a norm is positive or negative, correct or incorrect (as was the case in the Jacobs and Campbell [1961] study). Once it develops, it will take a number of generations before it is changed.

Factors Influencing Conformity to Group Norms

When you rise from your seat to cheer a goal during a soccer game, is this an example of conformity? After practice, when you run three miles with your teammates, are you conforming? When you and your teammates agree not to lift weights because it is believed that there are no benefits for performance, are you conforming? The answer is that it depends upon whether your behaviors and beliefs would be similar or different if you were not in a group. Would you rise to cheer the goal if you were the only fan in the stands? Would you run after practice even if the rest of the team did not?

Conformity is not just behaving as other people behave; it is being influenced by how they behave. Conformity is defined as a change in behavior or belief as a result of real or imagined group pressure (Kiesler & Kiesler, 1969). There are two distinct types of group conformity: compliance and acceptance. *Compliance* occurs when people conform without completely believing in what they are doing. Compliance is, thus, publicly acceding to social pressure while privately disagreeing, which was evidenced in the previous example about some athletes engaging in the hazing ritual for social approval despite not agreeing with the behavior.

There are times, however, when we genuinely believe in what the group has exerted pressure on us to do. You may purchase the same basketball shoes as the rest of your teammates due to a team consensus that they will help you jump higher. Caplan-Bricker (2017) highlighted the disordered eating experiences of climbers, cyclists, and runners who were influenced by those in their group environment:

> When Jesse Thomas, an elite triathlete, ran for Stanford as a college student, every guy on his team seemed to want to lose weight. He says, 'We had this joke: Oh man, I'm so hungry I'm going to go take a nap.' To a certain extent, maybe that made me feel better, like, 'It's not that big a deal. Everyone's doing it.' (para. 15)

The majority of the research that has examined the factors influencing the development of group norms has been undertaken in laboratory research on conformity. In one classic study, Sherif (1936) examined whether the emergence of a social norm could be observed in the laboratory. He used an illusion known as the autokinetic effect. With this illusion, a stationary single light is shown in a darkened room. The light appears to move (sometimes erratically) because there is no frame of reference within which to place it.

When Sherif (1936) had subjects estimate the amount of movement of the light alone and in groups, he found that the presence of others made a considerable difference in individual judgments. First, he showed individual subjects a single pinpoint of light in a dark room and asked them to judge how far the light moved. When individuals made judgments alone they established their own idiosyncratic pattern in which the estimates of movement varied erratically from one to 10 inches. However, group norms developed when the individuals were brought together as a group with one or two other naive subjects. Subjects in the group setting were asked to continue estimating the light movement and to announce their estimates so that the other group members could hear. The estimates of the group members converged so that after a period of time each person reported the same amount of movement as the other group members (see Exhibit 8.4). It was as if a funneling effect had occurred—from divergence and discrepancy to convergence and consensus.

Subjects in the autokinetic experiment were faced with an ambiguous reality, one with no obvious correct answer. Asch (1951) suspected that intelligent people would not conform in situations where they could readily see the truth for themselves. To test this hypothesis, Asch (1951), in another classic study, used confederates to influence the judgment of participants concerning the length of a line. Participants were asked to compare the length of a standard vertical line with three other lines. They were then asked to choose the line that best matched the standard line. The confederates gave their selection first and unanimously chose

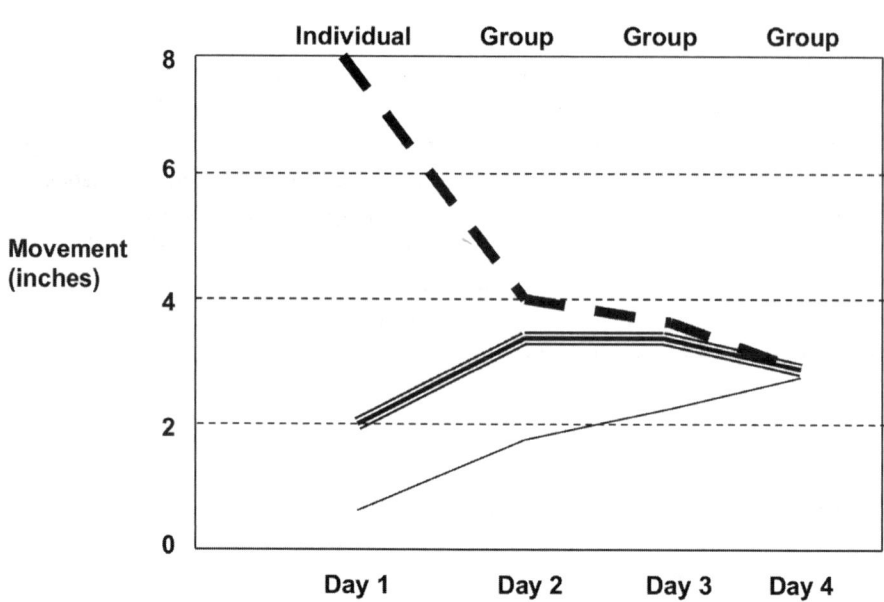

Exhibit 8.4. Norm Formation

Source. *Social Psychology* (p. 209), by M. Sherif and C. W. Sherif, 1969, New York: Harper & Row.

an incorrect line in 12 of the 18 trials. Each participant, in turn, provided a personal choice of the line that best matched the standard line in length. Thus, the naive participant was confronted with the choice of selecting either an incorrect option (thereby remaining in agreement with the group), or the correct option (thereby being in opposition to the group). Asch found that 33% of the subjects adopted the group norm (the incorrect judgment) on 50% or more of the incorrect trials. Only 25% consistently maintained an independent (correct) judgment. Interestingly, those who answered alone gave the correct response 99% of the time.

Asch's (1951) procedure became the standard for hundreds of later experiments. Bond and Smith (1996) conducted a meta-analytic review of 97 conformity studies conducted in the United States that used an Asch-type procedure. The review revealed that conformity was highest when the size of the majority was large, when the proportion of female participants was greatest, and when the majority did not consist of out-group members. As well, they found that the levels of conformity had steadily declined since Asch's original studies in the 1950s. Bond and Smith (1996) suggested that the decline in conformity might be due to the "changing cultural climate of Western societies" (p. 124). In the research that followed these early studies, the focus was on identifying the conditions that influenced conformity to social pressure and group norms. Essentially, two classes of conditions have been identified: *personal* factors and *situational* factors.

Personal Factors

Although individuals tend to be motivated to adopt the norms of their groups, not everyone is motivated to the same extent. Two of the personal factors that are associated with conformity to the group's norms are personal status and idiosyncratic credit. Individuals with greater status have a greater effect on the development of group norms. Influential team members—team leaders, the most competent athletes, individuals with the greatest status in the group—have a greater role in setting and enforcing the standards adopted by the group (Hollander, 1961). There is also less pressure on them to conform strictly to these norms.

Status and conformity to the group norms over an extended period of time contributes to the development of what has been referred to as idiosyncratic credit. High status individuals more readily build up credit and are given more latitude in the degree to which the group requires them to conform to group norms. Thus, for example, the team leaders may help to establish a norm in which the team lifts weights every day in the off-season. After this norm has been well established, the team leaders might miss a session or two. There would be less pressure exerted on them by the group if this occurred than if low status individuals missed occasionally. The following anecdote about the 2019 Golden State Warriors illustrates the concept of idiosyncratic credit as it applies to post-game expectations to meet the bus at the arena:

> 'You do have a set time, though.' [said then-Warriors player Kevin Durant]. 'After games, we usually have a time on the board when we're supposed to be on the bus, but a couple guys just don't even worry about that. They just come whenever they want.' (Wertheim, 2019, para. 8)

Another important personal factor associated with conformity to group norms is gender. Many of the earliest studies found that women were more likely to conform than men (cf. Worchel, Cooper, & Goethals, 1991). Nord (1969) summarized this early research and concluded that it has been "well established, at least in our culture, that females supply greater amounts of conformity under almost all conditions than males" (p. 198). These results were often explained by reference to sex roles in that men were expected to be independent while women were expected to be more reasonable and sensitive to others.

Although this explanation fits many of the earlier results, subsequent studies suggested that these findings might be due to the fact that the tasks used have favored the masculine sex role. Conformity is greatest in situations of high uncertainty, a situation that would exist if a female was performing a task more appropriate to the masculine sex role. When Sistrunk and McDavid (1971) included neutral, masculine-type, and feminine-type tasks, they found that conformity was greater by females in the masculine-type tasks, greater by males in the feminine-type tasks, and the same in the neutral tasks.

Within a sport environment, there is also equivocal evidence regarding whether males and females experience normative expectations similarly in their teams. Bruner, Carreau, Wilson, and Penney (2014) provided evidence suggesting that adolescent female teams collectively held stronger norms for competition, practice, and social situations than male teams. However, Colman and Carron (2001), examining norms in individual sports, generally did not find gender differences in competitive, practice, off-season, and social contexts.

Finally, one personal characteristic that appears to strongly relate to athletes' conformity to group norms is how strongly they identify with their team. Social identity is defined as "that part of an individual's self-concept which derives from his/her knowledge of his/her membership of a social group (or groups) together with the value and emotional significance attached to that membership" (Tajfel, 1981, p. 255). Essentially, from a sport group perspective, it is the degree to which the team is a part of the athlete's identity. This can be both a good thing and bad thing. Graupensperger, Benson, and Evans (2018) found that athletes exhibiting higher levels of social identity with their teams were more likely to conform with both the risky (e.g., binge drinking, concealing concussions) and pro-social (e.g., volunteering, donating) behaviors of their teammates. Furthermore, the link between antisocial behaviors and perceptions of the antisocial norms was greater for those athletes with a stronger social identity to the team (Benson, Bruner, & Eys, 2017), and the same is true for prosocial norms/behaviors (Bruner et al., 2018).

Situational Factors

Some groups or situations create contexts that impact how much a norm is valued by members, how salient a norm is, or how observable norm violations are. One important situational factor associated with conformity to group norms is group size—both the number of supportive others and the number of individuals in opposition. Insofar as the former is concerned, when the number of supportive others increases, resistance to the group norm also increases. Individuals who want to behave in a way contrary to the group norm more readily do so as the number of people supporting their position increases. In this situation the group is not able to exert as much pressure.

Similarly, when the number of people forming the opposition increases, there is a tendency for conformity to the group norm to increase. Studies on conformity behavior have shown, however, that there is a limit to the group's influence. At some critical point, further increases in the size of the opposition no longer have any social impact. This failure of increasingly larger groups to continue to exert influence on their members has been attributed to two related factors. First, a large opposition of 50 individuals could be perceived as a single unit, not 50 units. Second, a large number of opponents who are in agreement could be considered to be in collusion (Carron, 1980). Overall, however, the effect of group size (i.e., those exerting pressure on the individual) on conformity has been debated greatly. Bond (2005) provided a comprehensive overview of this issue and conducted a meta-analysis on 62 studies. In his conclusions, he noted how complex the relationship is between size of the group and conformity behaviors and encouraged future research examining this relationship in conjunction with individuals' motives to conform (e.g., to please others or avoid sanctions), specific features of the task that is undertaken, and other features of the environment.

Not surprisingly, another situational factor that influences conformity is the degree of ambiguity present in the group norm. Consider, for example, two regulations that might be established by management and eventually adopted as team norms: a curfew and an acceptable standard of dress for public appearances. If the curfew is set at midnight, a team norm could develop to adhere to the curfew. Further, there is absolutely no uncertainty about 'midnight'. Consequently, team member's deviations would be obvious.

It is more difficult to establish fixed standards concerning what is acceptable in the case of a dress code. There is the cliché that beauty is in the eye of the beholder. So too is any norm for an acceptable standard of dress—there is some ambiguity, some uncertainty about what is acceptable. A norm might develop in which a suit coat is the team standard, but considerable latitude could appear around this criterion. Thus, adherence to the team norm might not be very strong.

Cohesion also is associated with conformity to group norms. The relationship between conformity to group norms and group cohesion is reciprocal (Widmeyer, Brawley, & Carron, 1985). More cohesive groups exert greater pressure on their members to adhere to group norms. In turn, greater adherence to the group norms leads to a more cohesive group.

The leadership structure of the group also influences conformity behavior (Shaw, 1981). When group leadership is centralized (i.e., autocratic) and resides almost exclusively in the hands of one individual, there is less conformity than when it is decentralized (i.e., democratic). In short, when a number of individuals are involved in the decision-making process and have leadership responsibilities, there are more individuals to exert pressure on other members to adhere to group standards.

The Nature of Group Norms in Sport

Norms within Sport Teams

Prapavessis and Carron (1997b) conducted a study pertaining to what types of norms typically develop in sport teams. After athletes on elite cricket teams were provided with a definition of a group norm, they were asked to list the norms present in their team. The most frequently cited norms were being punctual at practices and competitions (23.4%), staying focused on the field (18%), adhering to the dress code (14.6%), providing support to teammates (11.4%), and giving maximum effort during training (10.6%).

The same issue was pursued in a more comprehensive study undertaken by Munroe, Estabrooks, Dennis, and Carron (1999). A sport team can develop expectations for individual behavior in at least four specific situations: during competitions, at practices, in social situations, and during the off-season. Munroe et al. (1999) had athletes from different sports list the important group norms for each of these four situations. Exhibit 8.5 contains an overview of four frequently cited norms for each situation.

Groups either cease to function well or cease to exist if members do not attend group functions. Consequently, it is not surprising that attendance or punctuality were frequently cited across contexts. Groups also may cease to exist or to function well if the interpersonal relationships among members are not courteous and respectful. Consequently, it also is not surprising that respect was among the most frequently cited norms in competitions, practices, and social situations. It is uncertain why respect is not a prominent team norm in the off-season. Norms only develop around matters of importance to the group. Since contact among team members is reduced in the off-season, it is possible that other matters become more critical—maintaining contact, training, and so on.

The strongest team norms are associated with work output and performance; teams put pressure on their membership to work hard. As Exhibit 8.5 shows, giving effort is a frequently

Exhibit 8.5. The Nature of the Group Norms that Develop in Sport Teams

Team Norms for Competitions	Team Norms for Practice	Team Norms for the Off-Season	Team Norms for Social Situations
Effort	Punctuality	Training	Attendance
Support for Teammates	Effort	Contact	Respect Others
Punctuality	Attendance	Skill Development	Positive Attitude
Respect	Respect	Healthy Lifestyle	Consumption of Alcohol

Source. "A Phenomenological Analysis of Group Norms in Sport Teams" by K. Munroe, P. Estabrooks, P. Dennis, and A. Carron, 1999, *The Sport Psychologist, 13,* 171–182.

mentioned norm for competitions and practices, and training was a frequently cited norm for the off-season. Further evidence of the importance of the task (performance) to sport teams is the norms that develop for the off-season. In addition to training, skill development was considered important.

The development of productivity norms is extremely prevalent in settings where the task is a major concern. Industry and sport are two good examples. A standard is established for performance and pressure is exerted on group members to adhere to this standard. A series of studies with youth sport groups demonstrates the importance of developing positive norms for productivity. Spink, Crozier, and Robinson (2013; 50 adolescent football, volleyball, and swimming athletes) and Crozier and Spink (2018; 145 female volleyball players) found that athletes' perceptions of the effort expended by their teammates (i.e., a descriptive norm) were predictive of their own self-reported effort. Furthermore, Crozier and Spink (2018) found that athletes' perceptions of their coaches' approval for exerting effort (i.e., an injunctive norm) also influenced the degree to which they exerted themselves. Clearly, the normative messaging that is received by athletes informing them about the exertions of their teammates, and the degree to which effort is valued by their coaches, is influential toward individual motivation (Crozier & Spink, 2017).

Adherence to performance norms seems to depend on various group properties. The level of cohesion present in the group is one important consideration. For example, in an often-cited study by Schachter, Ellertson, McBride, and Gregory (1951), high- and low-cohesive groups were examined in a laboratory experiment on a task that involved cutting cardboard squares. It was observed that the high-cohesive groups conformed to the norm more than the low-cohesive groups independent of whether the norm was for high or low productivity. Subsequent research has supported these findings for industrial groups (Mikalachki, 1969), military crews (Berkowitz, 1956), laboratory groups (Berkowitz, 1954), and business students (Miesing & Preble, 1985).

The implications seem clear; as Quadrant 1 of Exhibit 8.6 illustrates, if group cohesion is high and the norm for productivity is high, performance will be high. However, if cohesion is high but the norm for productivity is low, performance will be poor (Quadrant 4); a strike or a work slow-down in a business context is a good example. In the situations outlined in

Exhibit 8.6. The Interaction of Cohesion and the Group Norm for Productivity

		Group Cohesion	
		High	Low
Norm for Productivity	High	Best performance (1)	Intermediate performance (2)
	Low	Worst performance (4)	Intermediate performance (3)

Quadrants 1 and 4, the strong unity in the group would result in a great deal of pressure being exerted on members to adhere to the norm.

The two intermediate positions are represented by those situations where cohesion is low and the norm for productivity is either high (Quadrant 2) or low (Quadrant 3). The more desirable of these latter two situations would be Quadrant 2—a high norm for productivity with low cohesion. A general expectation would be present in the group to maintain a good work ethic. Because of the low cohesiveness, however, less pressure could be placed on those individuals who deviated from the norm than would be the case in Quadrant 1.

To test the above propositions, Gammage, Carron, and Estabrooks (2001) devised a laboratory experiment. They asked participants in the study to respond to one of eight written scenarios by indicating how much effort the main character in the scenario would be likely to expend training in the off-season. In the eight scenarios, the description of the group's cohesion, its norm for productivity, and the actor's potential to be observed by other group members (identifiability) were systematically varied from high to low. Gammage et al.'s (2001) results supported the general pattern of interactions illustrated in Exhibit 8.6. That is, the combination of a high norm for productivity and high cohesion was associated with the greatest amount of effort expended.

Kim (1992a, 1992b, 1995, 2001; Kim & Cho, 1996) conducted several studies examining performance norms in sport teams that have implications for both the team and the individual athlete. From an individual perspective, higher performance norms are related to higher self-monitoring (Kim & Cho, 1996) and greater satisfaction with the sport (Kim, 2001). From a group perspective, Kim (1995) found that teams that advanced to the semi-finals in a basketball tournament had higher performance norms than teams that were disqualified in the preliminaries. As well, Kim (1992a) found that teams with high performance norms at midseason also had high performance norms at post-season. In comparison, teams with low performance norms during midseason had a decline of performance norms at postseason, and, finally, Kim (1992b) found that the team leadership affected the performance norms of sport teams. Specifically, performance norms were the highest under leaders with a goal achievement and group-relations orientation.

Norms Beyond the Sport Group

Normative expectations emerge not only within sport teams but also within the sport itself; generalized expectations for behaviors of many different stakeholders. For example, formal rules proscribe specific behaviors in order to insure that the competition between teams is fair. There is considerable evidence, however, that under certain circumstances it is not only legitimate for athletes to break these rules, it is expected. The "good foul" in basketball and soccer, the "good penalty" in hockey are some examples.

Silva (1983) suggested that the norms surrounding rule violations in sport—the necessity of committing the good foul in critical situations—have "become so important that participants in many sports must learn not only the written rules, but the unwritten or normative rules of their sport in order to be successful" (p. 438). In his study, Silva presented male and female college students with seven pictures depicting rule-violating behavior in baseball, basketball, hockey, and football. The participants were required to rate the acceptability of the behavior on a fourpoint scale that varied from totally unacceptable to totally acceptable.

Silva's (1983) results showed that males perceived rule violations to be more acceptable than females. Also, the perception that rule violations are an acceptable part of the game was strongest in males who had the most sport experience, who were participating at the highest levels of competition, and who were involved in sports with the greatest amount of physical contact. These findings subsequently supported that female athletes were less accepting of aggressive acts than males and that "participants in contact and noncontact sports are less accepting than participants in collision sports" (Tucker & Parks, 2001, p. 410). Interestingly, however, Tucker and Parks (2001) did note that none of the groups examined in their study considered aggression to be legitimate in sport.

As another example, Shields, Bredemeier, Gardner, and Boston (1995) examined leadership, cohesion, and team norms regarding cheating and aggression in college and high school baseball and softball players. They asked athletes to estimate how many of their teammates would violate a rule and would deliberately hurt an opponent if it would help their team win. The athletes were also asked to indicate if their coach would want them to cheat or injure an opponent if it would help the team win. Shields et al. (1995) revealed that perceptions that cheating and aggression are acceptable were generally greater in male athletes, college level athletes, older athletes, and athletes with greater training in the sport. With regard to leadership and team norms, female athletes who had a female coach felt that teammates were less likely to cheat or aggress, and their coaches would be less accepting of such behaviors than female athletes who had a male coach. In a study examining "sportspersonship" in youth sports, Shields, LaVoi, Bredemeier, and Power (2007) highlighted the role of normative expectations toward poor sport behavior. Specifically, they found that the perceived norms of the team, coaches, and parents were related to athletes' self-reported poor sport behavior.

It also appears that spectators may be attuned to the normative behaviors present in certain sports. McNamee et al. (2007) interviewed British sports spectators about the values and norms present in a variety of individual and team sports. Their findings were generally positive (i.e., spectators believed that the general conduct of current athletes was acceptable) but that perceptions of team sports (e.g., soccer/football) were less favorable than for individual sports (e.g., tennis). Interestingly, one finding related to soccer fans was that 95% of the spectators believed that disputing referee decisions is common. However, "it does not follow…that they necessarily think this as bad" (McNamee et al., 2007, p. 43).

Finally, in the officiating of sports, norms have emerged on how to a call the game. The formal rules of basketball, for example, suggest that it is a noncontact sport, though great latitude is afforded by officials to maintain the flow of the game. Snyder and Purdy (1987) surveyed 689 high school officials in regard to enforcement of rules within basketball games. The authors found that 35% of the officials agreed with the principle of "no harm, no foul." This indicated that at least a third of the officials disregarded rule violations in game situations. As well, 77% agreed that officials try to balance up a call after they have made a bad call against a team. Finally, 73% endorsed the statement, "I believe that consistency in one's officiating is more important than the rules to the letter" (p. 398). The authors concluded that rule enforcement is elastic, and officials may adhere strictly to the rules in one segment of the game, typically in the early phase, or when the game becomes too physical, then ease up later. For example, the authors noted basketball officials frequently ignore blocks, holds, illegal picks, and rule infractions in the final minutes of a game.

The sport of soccer also formally acknowledges subjectivity in officiating decisions, and a reliance on the norms of the sport, though these decisions are recently being challenged through the use of technology. Potter (2019) provides an example from the Women's World Cup of Soccer:

The Nigerians had managed to hold France to a draw until the 72nd minute when a Nigerian player pulled down a French attacker in the box. Was it a foul? Hey, let's take a look at the video. After a couple minutes with her finger in her ear, the referee pointed to the penalty spot. The French defender Wendie Renard promptly shanked it, and the Nigerians celebrated their good fortune. But once again, video replay showed the goalkeeper had stepped forward too soon. Renard shot again, and this time scored.

This is insanity piled upon ridiculousness, smothered in injustice…the delay from the initial foul in the box until the second penalty kick was taken was almost eight minutes—an eternity on a soccer pitch, for both fans and players. But more to the point, the strict application of the stay-on-your-line rule is a violation of both the spirit and long-standing practice of the game. The penalty kick is already grossly tilted in favor of the shooter (with conversion rates between 75% and 80%). Goalkeepers have always been given a bit of leeway to help improve the odds by a small amount, and in their wisdom, referees just look the other way if a keeper creeps a few inches off the line. But there's no more of this sort of justice to be had on the pitch; it has been sacrificed in the name of technological truth-seeking. (pp. 12–13)

As the example highlights, certain behaviors that were once under the purview of on-field officials (i.e., early movement by goalkeepers during penalty shots), and often ignored, are now examined through a video assistant referee and sanctioned. This sanctioning of what was once an acceptable part of the dual between shooter and goalie has received its fair share of controversy.

Modifying Team Norms

Occasionally, an inappropriate team norm is established. For example, reconsider the previous example that expressed concern about developing a norm for poor performance of the Carolina Hurricanes hockey team. Is it possible to change this generalized expectation (i.e., this norm) concerning performance? How can it be changed? These are very real issues for coaches, managers, and/or team captains who have an interest in persuading high status individuals and/or a majority of team members to change their views on what behaviors are appropriate and/or inappropriate? Certainly, it is teams that develop expectations and, thus, teams can be used effectively to change inappropriate expectations (norms). A series of team building strategies that can be used to modify group norms is outlined in Chapter 16.

However, at its core, a norm reflects the group attitude; as such, changing group norms involves changing attitudes. A considerable amount of research has been carried out in social psychology examining the factors influencing attitude change. Penrod (1986) summarized the research results into three general categories: the source of the communication, the nature of the communication, and the nature of the target.

The Source of the Communication

What is it that makes one communicator more persuasive than another? The personal characteristics of the individuals attempting to change a team norm—the coach, team captains, team members—will have an impact on their effectiveness. Experience and competency in the group situation also are certainly important. Derek Fisher, a former member of the Los Angeles Lakers spoke to this point in a discussion with Vincent (2005) about his transition to the Golden State Warriors:

> Early on I was trying to fit in myself. We had a number of guys who had been on this team together for a few years, so it wasn't my place to come in and rearrange things … Working hard every day, playing hard in the games, as time goes on it gives me leeway to say something to a guy, challenge him, maybe get in his face a little bit. But you have to put that work in and get it on your résumé before you can start challenging guys vocally. (p. B12)

Individuals who are more credible, better liked, similar, attractive, or powerful possess greater powers of persuasion. This profile of characteristics might be expected because it is also associated with status, and, of course, individuals with high status play a significant role in norm development and maintenance.

On a team, the coaching staff or management might be interested in modifying existing norms. If a choice is available among different coaches, the best individual might not necessarily be the head coach (although he or she is certainly the most powerful). The coach who is perceived to be most credible by the athletes (in terms of trustworthiness and expertise on the specific issue), more similar, attractive, or better liked would be more effective.

Style of speech is another factor that has an effect on the degree to which a target group is influenced by a communicator. For example, the effectiveness of an argument increases if it is developed in the form of rhetorical questions—questions to which an answer is already known. For example, consider the following presentations to a team:

- We do want to become better as a team, don't we? A tired athlete doesn't play as well, right? Don't you think it would be better if we established a minimum curfew for the night before the game?; or
- If we are going to play better as a team, we have to be better rested. So a curfew has been established for the night before a game.

The first argument appears to involve a cooperative decision, while the second represents a demand. The first is more persuasive than the second.

Another element in style of speech that influences persuasion is speed. Individuals who communicate in a relatively rapid manner as opposed to a slow, more deliberate fashion are more effective. MacLachlan (1982; MacLachlan & Siegel, 1980) demonstrated the effectiveness of speed in persuasion by increasing speaker speed on radio and television commercials without altering the original pitch, inflection, and intensity of the speakers' voices. When speech speed of different speakers was increased by 25%, listeners comprehended the message just as well and also rated the speakers as more knowledgeable, intelligent, and sincere, and found the messages more interesting. In fact, normal (i.e., 140- to 150-words-per-minute) speech can be almost doubled before comprehension begins to drop abruptly (Foulke & Sticht, 1969).

The Nature of the Communication

Not surprisingly, persuasion is affected not only by who says it, but also by what that person says. According to Penrod's review, a number of elements in the communication itself can also influence reception by the target audience. One of these is the amount of discrepancy between the viewpoint being advanced and the position held by the team. For example, the members of a team might strongly believe that going out for drinks after every practice is good for team unity and morale. If the coaching staff attempted to persuade the team that complete abstinence during the season was better, the discrepancy between these two positions could produce considerable resistance.

Both the quality and quantity of the arguments advanced influence the effectiveness of the persuasion. Communications that are novel, have many points to support a particular position, and present both sides of the issue are more effective. Thus, any attempt to persuade athletes to abstain from alcohol during the season might be more successful if a physiologist was brought in to present research evidence on both sides of the issue.

Persuasion is greater when the communicator comes to a conclusion and presents it to the target group. Consider the above example in which rhetorical questions were used to advance the case for a curfew. The third question of "don't you think it would be better if we established a minimum curfew for the night before the game?" is a conclusion. It's also essential to the case. If it was left out, the total argument would not be as persuasive.

The Nature of the Target

Despite a good communicator and an effective communication, changes in norms still might not occur. The target group is the third factor in the equation. Penrod (1986) identified a number of characteristics of the target person or group that influence the degree to which a persuasive message is accepted.

The perception that there is freedom of choice is important. People who feel coerced into adopting an attitude show more resistance than those who feel that they have had a choice. One factor that increases resistance to a new perspective is ego-involvement. It is more difficult to change the attitudes of targets who are more highly ego-involvement with an issue. Also, it is possible for inoculation to occur if the initial argument is weak. This happens in much the same way that resistance to diseases develops. As a result of an inoculation with a weaker strain of bacteria, the body builds its resistance to stronger strains. Initially, if a weak argument is presented for discontinuing steroid use, for example, the target audience could develop effective counter arguments. When a better case is presented later, these counter arguments would be used to resist the persuasion.

Forewarning the target group that a new perspective will be presented is often effective. Again, however, it depends on the initial level of resistance in the target group. If resistance is high, forewarning may simply provide opportunities to prepare counter arguments against the new perspective. Freedman and Sears (1965) illustrated the difficulty of attempting to persuade individuals who have high resistance to a message. They forewarned one of two groups of high school seniors that they were going to listen to a speech titled, "Why teenagers should not be allowed to drive." Students who were forewarned were barely persuaded by the speech; however, students who were not forewarned were persuaded.

There is also evidence that people who are resistant to a new viewpoint are selective in the information they pick out of a presentation. If both sides of an argument were presented for why team members should attend practices consistently, for example, an individual who was strongly opposed would probably retain most of the negative content but little of the positive.

Dynamic Norms

One obstacle when changing norms is that individuals may feel ambivalent about change. It may even be challenging to change individuals' minds about whether modification is even possible. Using dynamic norms are one potential strategy (Sparkman & Walton, 2017). As opposed to trying to change attitudes and behaviors about what current norms are, a dynamic norm refers to what one anticipates group members to do in the future. Rather than using a descriptive norm to state 85% of students in our athletic department are highly educated on performance-enhancing substance use standards, one might rephrase to highlight that 85% of students in our athletic department intend to attend training later this year, to learn about standards for performance-enhancing substances. These aspirational norms may be one strategy to convince individuals that, even if their current group norm is not conducive to behavior change, it may be in the future.

9

Social Hierarchy in Groups

You know, those two little words, The Man, have wrecked a lot of teams—teams that couldn't decide who The Man was, teams where the wrong man became The Man. I've seen it happen, and it won't happen here. Grant Hill is The Man, and he wears it well. (Detroit Pistons' Joe Dumars, quoted by McCallum, 1996, p. 48)

When individuals come together in a group and begin to interact, it becomes evident that not all group members possess the same attributes to the same degree. As a result of these differences, some individuals begin to emerge as leaders within the group and others fall into more supportive roles. Social hierarchies emerge quickly and shape the dynamics that unfold within a group.

Scholars from the organizational domain define social hierarchy as the "implicit or explicit rank order of individuals or groups with respect to a valued social dimension" (Magee & Galinsky, 2008, p. 354). The first part of this definition (i.e., implicit or explicit) speaks to the fact that hierarchical distinctions can either be formally communicated or arise through more informal means. For instance, team captains are chosen to signify formal leadership responsibilities within the group. An informal hierarchy, however, may also develop in the group based on the status members accord to specific individuals.

A second important part of Magee and Galinsky's (2008) definition of social hierarchy is its emphasis on the rank-ordering of group members. In any given group, there are high- and low-ranking members, as well as numerous members occupying the middle of a group's hierarchy. The third aspect of the definition is that hierarchical differences reflect what is valued within a specific context. In a competitive sport context, the most competent athletes in the group are generally held in higher esteem because of their ability to contribute to team performance. In contrast, in a group that primarily gathers for social reasons, it may be the more gregarious individuals who are afforded higher status.

The Nature of Social Hierarchy

Status and Power as the Bases of Social Hierarchy

In defining the nature of social hierarchy in groups, it is important to note that there are two distinct bases of social hierarchy: Status and power. *Status* refers to the amount of respect, admiration, and influence a person wields in a specific social setting (Anderson, Hildreth, & Howland, 2015). For example, age is an attribute perceived (believed, evaluated) to be associated with higher status in some cultures. As another example, in some cultures, different occupations are accorded more status (e.g., judges, medical doctors). So in a group context, older individuals (or judges or medical doctors) may be accorded greater social status and thus occupy a more prominent role in the social hierarchy. People exert a great deal of effort to improve their social status, and higher status is linked to subjective well-being (Curhan et al., 2014). In fact, in a review of the literature on status, Anderson et al. (2015) proposed that people's desire for status is a fundamental human need.

Power refers to the amount of control or influence a person has over valued group resources and decisions (Guinote, 2014). A consistent finding is that people with higher power roles have a greater sense of control over their situation and environment, which enables them to pursue their own wants and desire (Guinote, 2014). In most sport groups, it is often the head coach who has the most power.

In a comprehensive analysis by French and Raven (1959), it was assumed that there are five sources of power in small groups (see Exhibit 9.1). *Expert* power results from knowledge, expertise, and competence at the task. Group members are influenced and will more readily

Exhibit 9.1. The French and Raven Sources of Power in Coaching Situations

Focus	Quotation
Expert Power: Results from knowledge, competence, and expertise at the task	[Coach John Wooden] used his mind and he understood the game totally. The best he could do was the best there was … our confidence in him never wavered. (Abdul-Jabbar & Knober, 1983, p. 152)
Coercive Power: Results from threats, warnings of danger, and punishment	No one would call Northwestern's Randy Walker a player's coach—not on the field, anyway. His drills are famous for their toughness and precision, and he once described practice as something akin to Pavlovian training. 'You give them positives when they run that maze the right way and find the cheese,' he said. 'You shock their asses when they don't.' (Price, 2001, p. 81)
Reference Power: Results from affection and being liked	More than anything else the assistant coach has to be respected and liked by the players in his group. The rapport is important … he's got to wear it well. If he doesn't, he'll turn off the players. They'll stop listening to him. (Madden & Anderson, 1986, p. 208)
Legitimate Power: Results from rank or position	Control was the operative word. [Coach Monte] Clark had control of the 49er operations, which meant drafting, trading, and coaching … Thomas wanted control of the first two … Monte refused to give up his power. He knew what he was doing. Thomas fired him. (Plunkett & Newhouse, 1981, pp. 144–145)
Reward Power: Results from the control of rewards and payoffs	[Coach Scotty Bowman] works them hard in practice, watching them, telling the press how hard and well they are working, making them feel they are earning their place on the team. Given a chance, usually at home, they give back an inspirational game. (Dryden, 1983, p. 41)

follow the directions of more competent group members. In a sport group, the coach is generally the most knowledgeable. In the quote in Exhibit 9.1 that is used to illustrate expert power, Kareem Abdul-Jabbar commented on the expertise of his former UCLA basketball coach, John Wooden, and the impact that this expertise had on the team's confidence. Holding expert power made it easier for Wooden to lead.

Another source of power associated with status in a group is called *coercive*. It results from threats, the possibility of reward being withheld, or punishment being applied. If a group member has the power to inflict some penalty on other group members, that power would help to produce desired outcomes. In the example presented in Exhibit 9.1, Northwestern football coach Randy Walker (cited in Price, 2001) highlights a coaching philosophy based on coercive of power.

Reference power exists when an individual is well liked and respected by other group members. In the quotation presented in Exhibit 9.1, Coach John Madden emphasized the need for assistant football coaches to have the affection and respect of the group of athletes they coach. Without it, the players would not readily respond to the coach's leadership.

When power exists because of rank or position, it is referred to as *legitimate*. Legitimate power is strongly associated with status—the greater the legitimate power, the greater the status and influence.

The fifth source of power that comes from and contributes to status is referred to as *reward*. As the name suggests, it is power that results from control over rewards and payoffs. If an individual has the power to reward other group members, he/she will have a major impact on the group. In the final quotation in Exhibit 9.1, Ken Dryden outlined how his National Hockey League coach, Scotty Bowman, used praise and public recognition as a motivator for the fringe players on the roster.

In all of the examples used above, the focus is on coaches. In any sport team, they generally have the greatest status and the greatest power. However, high status athletes on the team also may possess these same sources of power. In fact, in some instances, a high-status athlete may have more power within the group than the coach.

Overall, hierarchical differences can reflect both status-based distinctions (i.e., who has more esteem and respect within the group) and power-based distinctions (i.e., who holds a position of authority). Consider, for example, the two hierarchies illustrated in Exhibit 9.2. In the upper example, the pyramid is steeper and the head coach sits atop the social hierarchy. Similarly, among the athletes, the pyramid is also quite steep with differentiation existing between the one captain and three assistant captains. There are also potential differences between veterans and rookies. In the lower example, the pyramid is relatively flat for both the coaches and the athletes. The two co-head coaches have equal status and power. (One might be responsible for the offense, the second for the defense.) There are two assistant coaches with equal power and status. Among the athletes, three co captains share the leadership role and no hierarchical distinction is made between veterans and rookies. As we will discuss later, the congruency of these two bases of hierarchy (i.e., who has high status and who has high power) can influence group dynamics.

A Functional Perspective on Social Hierarchy

When observing high-school peer groups, workplaces, and sport teams, it is clear that differences in status and power are a natural feature of group life. But why is this the case? Several studies suggest that the reason why hierarchical differences are such a pervasive feature of

150 | Group Dynamics in Sport

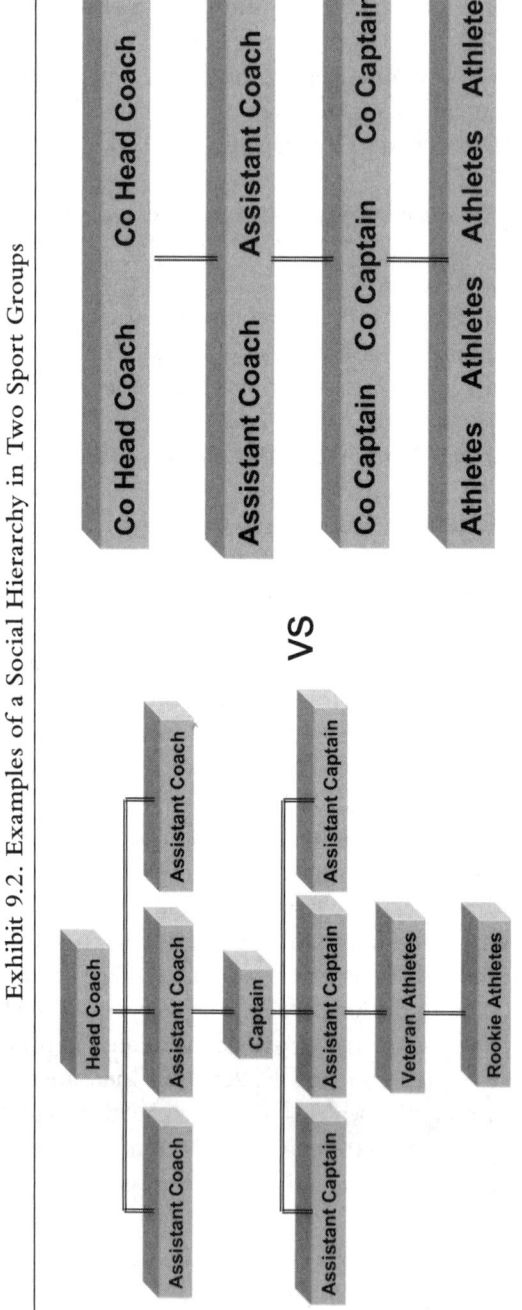

Exhibit 9.2. Examples of a Social Hierarchy in Two Sport Groups

groups is because they are generally beneficial. In a narrative review summarizing the literature on social hierarchy and group functioning, Halevy, Chou, and Galinsky (2011) identified specific reasons why hierarchy can be advantageous for groups.

One reason is that hierarchical differences can be a *source of motivation* for group members. Individuals who attain a higher position within a social hierarchy enjoy numerous benefits. For example, higher ranking group members are both the initiators and recipients of more communications within the group (Driskell & Mullen, 1990). Thus, in the case of a group where an older individual has more status, he/she likely would be the hub of the group's communication network. In addition, the value attached to viewpoints or perspectives is associated with the status of the individual who holds it; communications from group members of higher status are given greater credibility within the group. Consequently, in groups where age is associated with higher status, an opinion advanced by a younger member likely would not receive the same level of attention, respect, or acceptance as the same opinion advanced by an older member. Higher ranking members are also often given greater access to group resources and more opportunities to contribute. Put simply, it pays to be at the top. As such, a social hierarchy can incentivize individuals to demonstrate their value within the group.

A second potentially adaptive aspect of a hierarchy is that it creates a *sense of social order*. A social hierarchy helps to create a division of labor by clarifying who is responsible for which group tasks, and also who holds positions of authority. Thus, a social hierarchy coincides with greater role differentiation between members, which can facilitate higher levels of coordination between group members. As organizations become larger and more complex, the demands for greater coordination become more critical to performance. This is one of the reasons why there are so many formalized rank distinctions between members in military organizations.

A third benefit of social hierarchy is its potential to *reduce conflict and enhance cooperation*. Lower ranking group members are more likely to cooperate and abide by the instructions given by higher ranking members. Returning to the previous example, the hierarchical rank structure in military organizations clearly outlines the chain of command. In a collegiate football team, the coach is often in charge of who will play which position and the amount of playing time. As a result, athletes are likely to comply to the demands of a coach during practice or a game for the simple reason that failing to do so would be costly in terms of playing time.

A Conflict Perspective on Social Hierarchy

The previous discussion might give the impression that a social hierarchy is always beneficial for groups and their members. However, this would be a drastic oversimplification of how social hierarchy is related to the dynamics of a group. In fact, many of the advantages of social hierarchy come at a cost. For example, we previously described how the presence of social hierarchy can incentivize group members—motivating them to exert more effort and engage in desirable group behaviors in hopes of improving their social standing. In a sense, this means that hierarchies create "winners" (those who reap the benefits of higher status and power within the group) and "losers" (those who are deprived of such rewards).

Another issue created by social hierarchy is that higher ranking individuals are given more opportunities to further solidify and improve their social standing in the group. For instance, players relegated to the "bench" or practice squad might find it difficult to impress their coach due to the lack of opportunities to show their worth. As explained by Magee and Galinsky (2008), a social hierarchy can create and reinforce inequalities among group members.

The potential to create friction and conflict between members who are competing to improve their social standing within the group is another downside to social hierarchy. Although we previously covered research suggesting that social hierarchy can help to reduce conflict and improve cooperation, situations may arise in sport teams where hierarchy becomes the source of conflict and can undermine cooperation between members. In fact, a recent meta-analysis examining the link between hierarchy and team effectiveness favored this conflict-enabling perspective, showing a small net negative effect of hierarchy on team performance and team viability (Greer, de Jong, Schouten, & Dannals, 2018). None of the studies included sport teams, however, making this an area ripe for future research in the sport domain. Wolff and Spear (1995) provided commentary on the potential for interpersonal tensions to arise between new recruits and more experienced members over status within the group:

> In Al McGuire's system at Marquette, during the Warriors' heyday in the 1970s, players from Maurice Lucas to Bo Ellis to Butch Lee fell in line as underclassmen until it was their turn to shine as seniors. Then most of the shots—on the floor and in the media guide—came their way. But during the 90s, blue-chip recruits have become more and more determined to reach the NBA within two years. Thus they expect to take over their teams by the end of their freshman seasons, and that only exacerbates tensions with upperclass teammates. (p. 42)

Boroumand, Eys, and Benson (2018) conducted an experimental study to examine how the desire to protect one's own status can undermine cooperation within sport teams. Using a sample of university athletes (where playing time is a valued and contested resource), Boroumand et al. (2018) found that athletes were less willing to share task-relevant information with new team members who were highly touted for their ability and played the same position. Interestingly, this was not the case when the new members were high in ability but played a different position. These findings highlight a situation in which athletes strategically withheld information from a new team member to protect their own position and status within the group.

When Social Hierarchy is Beneficial versus Detrimental

The advantages and disadvantages of social hierarchy vary from group to group, and also between members within each group. Thus, it is important to understand when a group is more (or less) likely to benefit from greater hierarchical stratification. One important condition is the degree of interdependence between group members. Specifically, Halevy et al. (2011) suggested that groups with higher levels of interdependence between members are more likely to benefit from social hierarchy. This means that having a clear social hierarchy may not be equally beneficial across sport types. For example, a group of runners who compete individually but train together may have less to gain from establishing a clear hierarchy within their training group. In contrast, basketball and hockey teams are just two examples of groups in which there is a high degree of task and outcome interdependence between members (see Chapter 11 for a detailed discussion of the types of interdependence in sport groups), and these types of teams may benefit from having a functional social hierarchy.

The collective and personal benefits of social hierarchy also depend on the perceived legitimacy of the social rank distinctions. Group members must believe that the distribution of authority and power within the group is fair and just. An extreme example of an illegitimate social hierarchy would be a country ruled by a tyrannical dictator.

Generally, it is preferable for the two bases of hierarchy (status and power) to be aligned in a group. That is, the power hierarchy (e.g., who controls resources and decisions within the group) should be consistent with the status hierarchy (e.g., who is more respected and admired). Otherwise, group effectiveness suffers (e.g., Slusher, Van Dyke, & Rose, 1972). In the hierarchy illustrated in the top half of Exhibit 9.2, one head coach sits atop the hierarchy with greater authority than the three assistant coaches. But, if one of those assistant coaches is held in considerably higher esteem than the head coach because of their ability and contributions, there could be resistance to the head coach's decisions among the assistant coaches and the athletes. Similarly, if a veteran player who does not occupy a formal leadership role was held in much greater esteem than the captain or co captains, team effectiveness could suffer.

Agreement over the hierarchical structure within the group is another important factor. For example, researchers have found that a lack of consensus on status ranking within a group contributes to conflicting expectations, feelings of injustice, and discomfort (Bacharach, Bamberger, & Mundell, 1993; Zimmerman, 1985). Although people are generally accurate in evaluating their own status relative to others (Anderson et al., 2015), group members do not always achieve consensus on such matters.

Eys, Ritchie, Little, Slade, and Oddson (2008) investigated how status disagreements related to perceptions of cohesion within outdoor expedition groups (i.e., adventure canoe groups). Eys et al. (2008) evaluated the status ranking (both at the individual and at a group level) of four larger groups on an expedition in remote areas of Ontario, Canada. As part of academic course requirements, every member was required to lead a group of seven to nine individuals for approximately 1.5 to two days. An underlying status-based hierarchy was present (and stable)—the most competent, experienced group members were known to all. Conversely, the formal social hierarchy (i.e., the leaders of the group) changed every other day. The results demonstrated that (a) those individuals who ranked themselves higher in the group (in comparison to how the group ranked them) reported lower perceptions of social cohesion, (b) cohesion was higher when the formal and informal status hierarchies were consistent, and (c) individuals in groups with some consensus pertaining to their general status hierarchy perceived greater cohesion over those in a group with no consensus.

Taking a slightly different approach, Kilduff, Willer, and Anderson (2016) conducted two studies using laboratory groups and student project groups to evaluate both the frequency and consequences of different types of status disagreements. They focused on three distinct types of disagreements. *Upward disagreements* are instances where two group members believe they rank above one another in the group's hierarchy. *Downward disagreements* occur when two group members believe they rank below one another in the group's hierarchy. Finally, *third-party disagreements* reflect cases where two group members disagree about the position of another group member. Status disagreements were common across groups but substantially varied from group to group. Neither third-party disagreements nor downward disagreements had an effect on group performance. Upward disagreements were the most common and had a negative effect on individuals' motivation to contribute to the group, which was detrimental to group performance. Put another way, groups tended to perform worse when they had more pairs of individuals who both believed they outranked one another.

In the quote used to introduce this chapter, Joe Dumars (as quoted in McCallum, 1996) highlighted the potential problems associated with a lack of consensus on status ranking in sport teams. According to Dumars, many teams have been destroyed because of conflicts over who should be 'The Man'—who is at the top in the social hierarchy, who takes the initiative in critical situations, who is the hub of media attention, and so on. Dumars emphasized that his Detroit Pistons team would not be the site of a power struggle between Grant Hill and him to be The Man. As the following quote illustrates, such was not the case in a power struggle between Shaquille O'Neal and Kobe Bryant of the Los Angeles Lakers professional basketball team in 2003:

> This couple keeps playing 'He Said, He Said,' *Shaq* insisting he's The Man, *Kobe* suggesting that he's The Man. 'Constant one-upping can be a real issue in all relationships,' says Dr. Brenda Shoshanna, a psychologist and couples counselor based in New York City. 'It goes on with parents and children, with office workers. The Lakers need to understand that each person is a Man, working toward a common purpose. And when that happens—when a team is like five fingers on a hand—they will be unstoppable.' (Rushin, 2003, p. 21)

Personal Attributes Associated with Social Rank

Berger, Ridgeway, and Zelditch (2002) proposed that there are three elements to consider when examining an attribute/characteristic, including (a) whether it is a *discriminating* characteristic, (b) the *value* associated with various states of the characteristic, and (c) *typifications* associated with the characteristic's states. A discriminating characteristic is one that separates a population into different groups, but in and of itself has no real meaning (e.g., taller vs shorter). Depending on many factors, including culture, value can be given to various states of the discriminating characteristic (e.g., taller being valued more), and other beliefs (typifications) about those states may also be attached (e.g., leadership qualities attributed to taller individuals).

Several personal characteristics/attributes have been identified as having the potential to contribute to the social rank attainment of an individual. Jacob and Carron (1996) undertook a program of research to determine which attributes, alone or in combination, provide members of sport teams with status. They identified 17 attributes that have the potential to contribute to the social status of an individual group member in small social and work groups. These include an individual's age, experience, role (e.g., team captain), performance/skill/ability, education (both the type and amount), position (e.g., quarterback in football), social class, language, place of residence (e.g., residing in a large city versus a small town), occupation, income, marital status, ethnic background, parent's occupation, parent's income, parent's education, and religion.

In one investigation (Jacob & Carron, 1996), Canadian intercollegiate athletes were required to rate the degree of importance within their team of the 17 status attributes identified in research with social and work groups. Athletes identified experience as the most important source of status. Jacob and Carron found that following experience, one's role on the team (i.e., captain or co captain), performance/skill/ability, and then age were the major factors associated with status. Apart from age, which is undoubtedly associated with experience on sport teams, these attributes are referred to as achieved sources of status (the athletes possessed them through personal effort), not ascribed sources of status. In fact, not surprising perhaps, the athletes did not rate the ascribed sources of status (i.e., language, religion, parent's income, parent's occupation, parent's education, and so on) as at all important for status on their teams.

In an attempt to determine if the culture in which a sport team exists influences the importance of various status attributes among team members, Jacob and Carron (1996) then repeated their research with semiprofessional athletes from India. The authors felt that India was a good location to determine the impact of status because, among other factors, India:

> ... is noted for the diversity of status attributes deemed to be important ... There is an inequality in society based on gender...there are 3000 or more castes (social sections) ... 1652 languages as mother tongues and 15 of these are considered to be a major language ... [and] there has been a steady rural to urban migration over the past three decades. (Jacob & Carron, 1996, p. 375)

Three of the four primary sources of status endorsed by Canadian athletes (experience, performance/skill/ability, and age) were also singled out by the Indian athletes. The fourth status attribute rated highly by the Indian athletes was education. It was concluded that "in sport teams, culture seems less critical than the situation ... even though sport teams are considered to be microcosms of society, the sources of status prevalent in society and sport are not the same" (Jacob & Carron, 1996, p. 379).

Beyond the domain of sport, researchers identified personality characteristics and specific strategies that are associated with social rank attainment. Notably, numerous studies demonstrate that extraversion (one of the Big Five personality traits discussed in Chapter 5) is positively associated with social rank attainment (DesJardins, Srivastava, Küfner, & Back, 2015). Specifically, more extraverted individuals are more likely to emerge as a leader, achieve popularity in groups, and attain social influence (Grosz, Leckelt, & Back, 2019). Extraverts desire social status and enjoy leading others; they are also more energetic and confident in group tasks. Thus, more extraverted individuals tend to climb the social ladder in groups.

Researchers have also found that grandiose narcissism (also described in Chapter 5) is linked to higher social rank. However, the relationship between narcissism and social rank attainment is complex. A key factor underlying why narcissism is linked to higher social rank is that they aspire for status and confidently assert themselves during social interactions (Grosz et al., 2019). Consequently, narcissists tend to impress others when first meeting other group members. As demonstrated by Ong, Roberts, Arthur, Woodman, and Akehurst (2016), narcissists tend to be charismatic and well-liked during initial interactions, embodying the characteristics of a leader. However, Ong et al. (2016) found that these initially positive views of narcissists tended to sour over time due to their arrogant and exploitative tendencies. Despite an initial positive association between narcissism and social rank attainment, this relationship weakens (and sometimes even reverses) as time goes on.

Beyond personality traits, researchers have also identified specific strategies for elevating one's social rank. Cheng, Tracy, Foulsham, Kingston, and Henrich (2013) proposed that two core strategies help to propel people toward higher social rank. The first is a prestige-based strategy, which revolves around sharing expertise to gain the respect and admiration of others. The second is a dominance-based strategy, which relies on using force and intimidation to induce fear. Despite encompassing two very different strategies, research suggests that both prestige and dominance tactics help individuals attain greater influence within groups (Cheng et al., 2013).

Situational Characteristics and Social Rank

A number of characteristics within the situation are also associated with social rank, and *status* specifically. Spatial position is one. As Brown (1965) pointed out, "for Americans the spatial positions of above and in front of clearly imply superiority of status" (p. 78). In short, individuals elevated on a platform or in front of an audience usually have higher status than others in the situation. Also, in Chapter 6, it was pointed out that some team positions, such as the catcher in baseball, for example, have more status than others.

Symbols are another type of situational characteristic associated with status. Team jackets, crests, pennants, uniforms, and titles are all symbolic; and all can serve the purpose of conferring status. Goyens and Turowetz (1986) emphasized this point in their commentary on the status attached to certain team uniforms:

> Whether it be the Yankee pinstripe ... or perhaps the Kelly green with white trim of the Boston Celtics ... there is something instantly recognizable about the uniform colours of a special team in a particular sport. Few will argue that Yankee pinstripes represent baseball at its finest over the twentieth century. The same glory is attached to the Boston green and white in professional basketball. In professional hockey it is ... the red-white-and-blue of [the Montreal Canadiens]. (pp. vi–vii)

The status attached to various symbols can increase or decrease over time and according to circumstances. The more successful sport franchises at any given time are readily identifiable by the number of young children wearing replicas of their jersey. After the Toronto Raptors won their first NBA championship in franchise history, it was reported that merchandise sales had increased by 100% from last year (Ngabo & Miller, 2019).

Sport Involvement and Social Status

One approach to the study of the relationship between status and sport participation has been to examine the impact that being involved in sport has on the social status that individuals possess among their peers. It has become apparent that gender differences are present. That is, traditionally sport involvement has been a primary source of social status for males but not for females. In the case of females, Coleman (1961) reported that being a leader in activities was the most important factor associated with social status in high school. Subsequent research over the next 25 years demonstrated that the importance of leadership in high school activities is still preeminent for females (Feltz, 1978; Kane, 1988).

Even for elementary school females, sport is not the most important criterion for social status among a student's peers. When Buchanan, Blankenbaker, and Cotton (1976) examined the sources of social status among female students in Grades 4 to 6, they found that having good grades was most important. Sport involvement ranked second and was followed by being good looking and having money. Chase and Dummer (1992) replicated the findings from Buchanan et al (1976). For females in Grades 4–6, social status resulting from sport involvement had remained unchanged in relative importance. Sport ranked second with being good-looking ascending to first place. The importance attached to grades was ranked above having money.

As indicated above, sport plays a considerably different role in the achievement of social status for males. In fact, sport is one of the most important sources of peer status (Sussman, Pokhel, Ashmore, & Brown, 2007). In one of the earliest studies focusing on this question, Tannenbaum (1960) examined the attitudes of high school juniors toward different types of male students. He found that the rankings from the most to least acceptable were

1. Brilliant nonstudious athlete
2. Average nonstudious athlete
3. Average studious athlete
4. Brilliant studious athlete
5. Brilliant nonstudious nonathlete
6. Average nonstudious nonathlete
7. Average studious nonathlete
8. Brilliant studious nonathlete

Sport was the most important source of social status for high school males—followed by being in the leading crowd, being a leader in high school activities, having good grades, and coming from the right family. When this study was replicated 15 years later by Eitzen (1976), an identical pattern was still present. Sport was the most important source of status for high school males, followed by friendships, high school activities, grades, and family background.

For males, the value attached to sport starts early. In their study with boys in Grades 4–6, Buchanan et al. (1976) found that sport was ranked first followed by grades, appearance, and money. When Chase and Dummer (1992) examined this issue 16 years later, they found that sport still remained first in importance. However, grades had fallen in importance to third place while appearance increased in importance and was ranked second.

Why do differences exist in the role that sport plays in determining status for females versus males? Differences in opportunity would not seem to be the answer in the United States. As Chase and Dummer (1992) pointed out in their discussion of this issue, with the passage in the mid-1970s of the legislation referred to as Title IX, increased opportunities were made available for girls and women to participate in athletics. With these increased opportunities, changes in societal views about participation in sport could be expected. Given that this was not the case, Chase and Dummer (1992) speculated that

> …the lack of importance of sport as a social status determinant for girls may be that, in many case, Title IX still involves only one generation. The women who would have been affected by Title IX are just reaching the age at which they could be the parents of children in elementary school. As parents, these women could influence their children to have more favorable attitudes towards women's participation in athletics, and then changes may occur. (p. 422)

Research conducted in the intervening years has been equivocal with respect to Chase and Dummer's (1992) proposition that sport will be shown to have increased in importance for social status among female students.

On the one hand, a study by Holland and Andre (1999) showed that while males were slightly more likely than females to want to be remembered as a star athlete and slightly less likely to want to be remembered as a brilliant student or activity leader, these results were not statistically significant. Furthermore, the characteristics associated with those individuals who wanted to be remembered as an athlete, student, or leader, were similar for both genders. Both these results seem to support the notion that differences in perceptions of athlete status between the genders are diminishing.

On the other hand, a report by the Women's Sport Foundation (Sabo & Veliz, 2008) suggested that the stereotypical differences pertaining to sport involvement and status persist.

Sabo and Veliz (2008) asked 2,185 boys and girls between third and twelfth grades to identify the one sure thing that would make a student popular in their grade level. With respect to what would make a girl popular in school, only 4% of girls and 3% of boys stated being very good at sports. In contrast, being good looking was suggested by 44% and 57% respectively for female popularity. As for the popularity of boys, 18% of girls and 30% of boys (the highest percentage) noted that being good at sports would ensure their popularity.

Section 4

Group Processes and Emergent States

While stability and youth can help any national team program thrive, Garra Charrúa is [Uruguay men's national soccer team's coach Oscar] Tabárez's secret tactical weapon. Literally meaning 'The Claw,' this characteristic brings to the forefront the mentality where Tabárez's players believe they have greater fury and intensity compared to that of their opponents. The notion of Garra isn't new. It dates back centuries and has come to mean different things in different eras. The phrase comes from the Charrúa Indians, a group of warriors wiped out in the 19th century. Overshadowed in football terms by neighbors Brazil, Argentina, and, in recent years, Chile, La Celeste [Uruguay] have always had to fight harder to maintain par. (Lisi, 2018, para. 5–6)

Once the parameters have been set for a group, in terms of who the members are and the environments in which it will perform, and a structure begins to form, it is then necessary to move the group to action. The complexity of group work is reflected in the many processes and emergent states that arise over the lifespan of a team.

Group processes are a product of team member interactions and behaviors that have the potential to be observed (Marks, Mathieu, & Zaccaro, 2001; McEwan & Beauchamp, 2014). When members interact with one another, we might try to identify patterns in the quality of their interactions. For example, we may ask whether there is effective leadership by noting the number of times athlete leaders encourage their teammates verbally, tapping into both leadership (Chapter 10) and communication processes (Chapter 13). Also, if we wanted the group to clearly define the vision for the group, we may lead members through goal-setting processes (Chapter 12) or other teambuilding/teamwork activities (Chapter 16).

In contrast, emergent states refer to how members experience or perceive their groups. In other words, emergent states involve members' feelings and evaluations of their group and are typically in flux. Cohesion (Chapter 14) and collective efficacy (Chapter 15) represent two well-studied topics in sport psychology, which are chiefly studied by asking members to reflect upon their group. Keep in mind that a group does not "do" cohesion or collective efficacy, but rather experiences, feels, or perceives these phenomena.

Whereas group processes and emergent states are unique aspects of groups, they are each important and reciprocally influence one another (McEwan & Beauchamp, 2014). In the example above, the Uruguayan soccer players hold a collective belief (i.e., Garra) that likely reinforces collective processes and behaviors that are effortful and assertive/aggressive that, if executed, further reinforces their mentality about the team.

The following chapters explore the group processes of leadership, cooperation, goal setting, communication, and teambuilding/teamwork, while also summarizing research on two emergent states—cohesion and collective efficacy.

10

Group Leadership

The leadership of the team is vital... [said the New Zealand All Blacks coach] ... we put a lot of emphasis on that and on the alignment between the senior players and the coaches...the alignment between the captain, the vice-captain, and me as coach, and the alignment between the senior players and the other players. (Johnson, Martin, Palmer, Watson, & Ramsey, 2012, p. 61)

No discussion of group structure and processes is complete without dealing with group leadership. It is probably the group role most closely associated with group effectiveness. As the opening quote illustrates, leadership is not about a single person. Instead, researchers and practitioners have embraced a more holistic perspective wherein leadership is conceptualized as a multilevel and dynamic group process (e.g., a team captain may occupy a leadership role in relation to certain team members but is perhaps more of a follower during interactions with his coach). This process occurs at the individual level (e.g., do I self-identify as a leader or follower?), dyadic level (e.g., between a coach and an athlete) and the group-level (e.g., between a coach and her assistant coaching staff). This chapter provides an overview of historical and contemporary perspectives of leadership, including the oft-overlooked role of followership.

In Chapter 7, two types of group roles were discussed: informal and formal. Informal roles emerge as a result of the interactions and communications that take place among group members. In such cases, group members must be collectively willing to follow and recognize someone for their leadership ability. Individuals who emerge from the group to occupy leadership roles are referred to as *emergent leaders*. As discussed later in the chapter, effective leadership arising from within the team is crucial to the group environment. Formal roles, in contrast, are specifically prescribed by the organization or group. Individuals who occupy formal leadership roles are referred to as *prescribed leaders*. Coaches and managers of professional sport teams are one example of prescribed group leaders—they are the occupants of a formal group role. They possess what French and Raven (1959) referred to as legitimate power, expert power, coercive power, reward power, and sometimes, referent power.

Leaders who occupy formal group roles in sport, in education, in industry, and in the military may engage in very different behaviors. Nonetheless, there are parallels among them. A major source of that similarity lies in their fundamental responsibilities. Every formal leader in every type of group has two identical responsibilities.

The first is to ensure that the demands of the organization are satisfied; that the group is effective in terms of its goals and objectives. Typically for coaches at the professional level, the primary demand is to ensure a successful season by winning games. For the general manager of a professional sport team, effectiveness might mean increased attendance, organizational development, a positive winning percentage, or a combination of factors. As discussed in Chapter 3 on group development, if the team is unsuccessful, it is often the leader (e.g., the coach, general manager) who is held accountable.

The second responsibility of every leader is to ensure that the needs and aspirations of group members/subordinates are fulfilled. Phil Jackson, former coach of the Los Angeles Lakers of the National Basketball Association, alluded to this responsibility when he pondered what he would miss about coaching. Using a previous hiatus as a benchmark, Jackson and Arkush (2004) noted, "I missed the joy of the journey, of watching the guys I coached grow to become better players, and better men" (p. 270). When team-member aspirations are met and the team is successful, the coach or manager of a sport team is considered to be an effective leader. A leader that is ineffective or uses an approach that is inconsistent with the needs of his or her team can be a source of stress for athletes (Fletcher & Hanton, 2003). Although this seems fairly intuitive, there are still more questions than answers about leadership; a fact that continues to support the suggestion that leadership is "one of the most observed and least understood phenomena on earth" (Burns, 1978, p. 2).

Universal Approaches to Leadership

Universal Trait Approach

The universal trait approach is one of the oldest approaches to the study of leadership. It has sometimes been referred to as The Great Person Theory of Leadership because it is based on the assumption that human progress is due to the accomplishments of great people. By the mid-20th century, considerable research had been carried by organizational and industrial psychologists to determine what common personality traits helped outstanding leaders become successful. This approach was initially met with limited success. Nonetheless, researchers have found that personality traits are associated with both leadership emergence and perceived effectiveness (see Chapter 5, Exhibit 5.1 for a description of the Big Five personality traits). A meta-analysis by Judge, Bono, Ilies, and Gerhardt (2002) indicated that people who are relatively high on extraversion, openness, and conscientiousness are more likely to emerge as leaders, and are more effective when they become leaders. Neuroticism, in contrast, is negatively related to both leader emergence and leadership effectiveness. Interestingly, agreeableness is positively associated with leadership effectiveness but unrelated to leader emergence. A caveat, however, is that none of the studies in the meta-analysis included sport groups.

Universal Behavior Approach

Although personality traits represent behavioral tendencies, some researchers have zoomed in on the specific behaviors in which leaders engage rather than focusing on more abstract concepts like their personality, orientation, or motivation. For example, Tharp and Gallimore (1976), intrigued by the success of John Wooden (who coached the UCLA Bruins to 10 NCAA basketball championships in 12 years), systematically recorded his behaviors during 30 hours of practice time. Of the 2,326 behaviors charted, 50.3% were directed toward instruction (what to do and how to do it) while commands to hustle and to intensify activity made up 12.7%. The other behaviors observed included scolding and reinstructing (8%), praising and encouraging (6.9%), and simple declarations of displeasure (6.6%).

As another example of research examining universal behaviors, Laios, Theodorakis, and Gargalianos (2003) summarized what they believed were behaviors coaches should engage in to be effective leaders. These included (a) developing interpersonal skills, (b) working toward a cohesive team, (c) listening well, (d) making strong decisions and being accountable for those decisions, (e) being an active and direct problem solver, (f) creating standards for performance, (g) recognizing and rewarding generously, (h) conveying enthusiasm, (i) teaching relevant skills, and (j) using punishment as the last resort but making those punishments clear beforehand. Although this study highlights what might be thought of as desirable behaviors for coaches, these are not the only ones displayed by coaches at all levels.

Perhaps the most comprehensive program for analyzing coaching behaviors was undertaken by Smith, Smoll, and their colleagues (e.g., Smith, Smoll, & Curtis, 1978; Smith, Smoll, & Hunt, 1977). In their Coaching Behavior Assessment System (CBAS; see Exhibit 10.1), 12 behaviors (B 1 - B 12) considered to be typical of coaches in athletic situations are identified. Using the CBAS, an observer can record the ongoing behavior of a coach by assessing the frequency of various types of behaviors. The twelve behaviors included in the CBAS fall into two classes: reactive and spontaneous. Reactive behaviors are responses to something the athlete has done, such as a good or bad performance. Spontaneous behaviors are those initiated by the coach; they are not the result of prior activity by the athlete.

Reactive behaviors are further subdivided into three categories: reactions by the coach to desirable performances by the athlete, reactions by the coach to an athlete's mistakes or errors, and reactions by the coach to misbehaviors on the part of the athlete. When an athlete's performance is effective or desirable, it can be positively reinforced by the coach (B 1, or Behavior 1) or ignored through non-reinforcement (B 2). A mistake or error by the athlete can be reacted to with encouragement (B 3), with instruction about the correct technique (B 4), with punishment (B 5), with both punishment and instruction on the correct technique (B 6), or the mistake can simply be ignored (B 7). Finally, misbehaviors on the part of the athlete can lead to coaching behaviors associated with keeping control (B 8).

The spontaneous behaviors of the coach are subdivided into two categories: game-related and game-unrelated. When a coach exhibits a spontaneous behavior during the game, it either involves providing instruction on techniques (B 9), giving general encouragement (B 10), or organizing and administering the team (B 11). Finally, spontaneous behaviors that are irrelevant to the game represent general communications on the part of the coach (B 12).

Beyond the domain of sport teams, a number of studies have evaluated the relation between specific leadership behaviors and team effectiveness. Burke et al. (2006) conducted a meta-analysis to summarize this literature, distinguishing between task-focused and person-focused

Exhibit 10.1. The Coaching Behavior Assessment System

Stimulus Event	Coaching Response	Description
CLASS 1. GENERAL REACTIVE BEHAVIORS		
Desirable Performance	B 1. Positive Reinforcement	Verbal or nonverbal reaction to an athlete's behavior
	B 2. Non-reinforcement	Failure to reinforce an athlete's behavior
Mistake or error	B 3. Mistake-Contingent Encouragement	Encouragement following an athlete's mistake
	B 4. Mistake-Contingent Technical Instruction	Instruction to an athlete following a mistake
	B 5. Punishment	Verbal or nonverbal negative reactions to an athlete's mistake
	B 6. Punitive-Mistake Contingent Technical Instruction	Combination of negative reaction and instruction following a mistake
	B7. Ignoring Mistakes	Failure to respond in any way to an athlete's mistake
Misbehaviors	B 8. Keeping Control	Responses designed to maintain order and control
CLASS 2. SPONTANEOUS BEHAVIORS		
Game-related	B 9. General Technical Instruction	Communication to an athlete on technical instruction
	B 10. General Encouragement	Spontaneous encouragement to the athlete
	B 11. Organization	Communication of an administrative nature
Game irrelevant	B 12. General Communication	Interactions unrelated to the sport or game

Sources. "Coaching Behaviors in Little League Baseball" by R. E. Smith, F. L. Smoll, and B. Curtis, 1978, *Psychological Perspectives in Youth Sports* (pp. 173–201), Washington, DC: Hemisphere, and "A System for the Behavioral Assessment of Athletic Coaches" by R. E. Smith. F. L. Smoll, and E. Hunt, 1977, *Research Quarterly, 48,* 401–407.

leadership. Task-focused leadership behaviors include transactional behaviors (i.e., establishing a contingent reward structure with followers), initiating structure (i.e., providing clear directives and emphasizing goal attainment), and boundary spanning (i.e., networking and communicating with others on behalf of the group and securing additional resources/information for the group). Notably, task-focused leadership behaviors accounted for 11% variance in subjective ratings of team effectiveness but only 4% variance in objective team performance (i.e., group productivity).

Person-focused leadership behaviors contrast with those focused on the task because they are oriented toward developing individualized and meaningful connections with followers. Transformational leadership is an exemplar person-focused style aimed at inspiring and fostering positive change in followers, described in detail later in the chapter. Person-focused behaviors also include consideration (i.e., actions directed toward maintaining social cohesion), empowerment (i.e., emphasizing the personal growth of followers), and motivating behaviors (i.e., fostering sustained effort through individualized support). These leadership behaviors explained slightly more variance in team outcomes than task-focused leadership behaviors.

The meta-analytic findings revealed that person-focused leadership behaviors accounted for 13% variance in perceived team effectiveness and 8% variance in objective team performance. Overall, task-focused as well as person-focused leadership behaviors play an important role in promoting positive group dynamics.

Situational Approaches to Leadership

Contingency Theory

Situational approaches to leadership originate from the assumption that some behavioral tendencies are more effective in some situations than in others. One of the best-known situational trait approaches is the contingency theory of leadership developed by Fiedler (e.g., Fiedler, 1967; Fiedler & Chemers, 1974). According to Fiedler (1967), leadership effectiveness—defined as group performance and member satisfaction—depends equally (i.e., is contingent) upon the leader's style of interacting with the group and the favorableness of the situation.

A leader's style of interacting is considered by Fiedler (1967) to vary along a continuum from task-oriented to person-oriented, similar to the distinction used in Burke et al.'s (2006) meta-analysis of leadership behaviors. Task-oriented individuals derive their greatest satisfaction from the group's performance, productivity, and successful task completion. In contrast, person-oriented individuals derive their greatest satisfaction from social contacts, affiliation, and successful interpersonal relationships.

According to Fiedler (1967), these two interaction styles represent a hierarchy of preferences within the leader. Every leader is interested in both outcomes—people and productivity—but the importance attached to satisfying people versus being productive varies. Essentially, a task-oriented leader says, if the team can successfully carry out this task, we'll feel very good about one another and get along well. A person-oriented leader essentially says, if the team gets along well, we'll be more effective on the job. The important point about the contingency theory is the assumption that either a person-oriented or a task-oriented leader can be effective depending upon the situation.

What makes a situation favorable for a leader? One of the elements is the *power position* of a leader. If a leader is clearly in control, has authority, and possesses the support of the organization, he or she is in a powerful position to influence and direct the group. The influence wielded by Bill Belichick, who is notoriously strict and highly task-focused, is evident in NFL wide receiver Donté Stallworth's recollection of the New England Patriot's first team meeting of 2007:

> Bill [Belichick] talked about the prior AFC Championship Game, where they had a 21–6 lead at halftime, and how they blew it … He just started showing plays [from the previous season]. He showed this pass that was probably the worst pass I've ever seen [Tom] Brady throw … Bill was saying, 'What kind of throw is this? I can get Johnny Foxborough from down the street to make a better throw than this.' He had some expletives in there. Randy and I looked at each other and sat up in our seats. There was nothing said between us, but it was understood: If Brady is getting it, no one is safe. There were a lot of new guys, big-time free agents brought in that year also. Bill is this way anyway, but he was definitely trying to set the tone. I just immediately fell in line. That was all it took. (Vrentas, 2017, para. 24)

Belichick's exceptional track record, coupled with the collective support of veteran members, provided a strong basis from which he could mold the team into his vision. Conversely, if a group perceives a leader's power position to be weak, it will be more difficult to lead.

A second element that contributes to situational favorableness is *leader-member relations*. If group members have a positive interpersonal relationship with their leader, they will more readily follow a leader's directions, work harder, and make sacrifices. Favorable situations also make it easier for the leader to carry out the responsibilities of leadership. During the 2015 FIFA Women's World Cup, Team Canada players were quick to defend their captain Christine Sinclair from criticism while emphasizing the value she brought to the group—they clearly admired and respected her on and off the field:

> Despite [Christine Sinclair] being a key cog in both Canadian victories at the tournament, the 32-year-old forward from Burnaby, BC, has drawn criticism from some quarters for her play as the Canadian offence rattled and coughed like a rusty engine in the early going. In the Canadian camp, such criticism of their talisman is heresy.... Herdman said Sinclair is playing her role to perfection—'to bring other players to another level.' (Davidson, 2015, para. 5–11)

The third element in situational favorableness is the *task structure*. In some tasks, the goals and objectives are clear and the steps necessary to achieve them are readily apparent. This makes it easier for the leader because there are only a limited number of possibilities or options present. In general, sport tasks are relatively structured but there are subtle differences among different sports. For example, open team sports are those in which the athlete must continually adjust to constantly changing conditions in the situation. Hockey, basketball, and soccer are some examples. Closed individual sports are those in which the athlete is faced with a relatively fixed and unchanging environment. Track, archery, and bowling are examples. Closed sports are somewhat more structured and thus would be more favorable from a leadership perspective.

The most favorable situation for a leader is when his/her power position is strong, the task is highly structured, and leader-member relations are high. In these types of situations, a task-oriented leader is more effective than a person-oriented leader. A task-oriented leader is also more effective in the most unfavorable situations—when his/her power position is poor, the task is unstructured, and leader-member relations are poor. According to Fiedler (1967), a person-oriented leader is more effective in situations that are moderately favorable. Much of Fiedler's (1967) initial work in developing his theory was conducted with basketball teams. Subsequently, researchers used the contingency theory to examine leadership on sport teams, finding only limited support for the model (e.g., Bird, 1977).

Life Cycle Theory

The life cycle theory, proposed by Hersey and Blanchard (1969), is another contingency-based approach to leadership. The basis of the life cycle theory is the proposition that leader effectiveness is a joint product of a leader's behavior and the level of maturity of subordinates. It was pointed out above that a contingency is something that is dependent on something else; it is characterized by a qualifying statement, such as if A, then B. The contingency in the life cycle

Exhibit 10.2. The Life-Cycle Theory of Leadership

Maturity Level of Subordinates	Leader Style	Leader Behavior
Low	*Telling:* The emphasis is on directing subordinates.	High Task with Low Relationship
Low to Moderate	*Selling:* The emphasis is on persuading subordinates	High Task with High Relationship
Moderate to High	*Participating:* The emphasis is on discussion with subordinates on the approach to be taken	Low Task with High Relationship
High	*Delegating:* The emphasis is on allowing subordinates to choose	Low Task with Low Relationship

Sources. "Life Style Theory of Leadership" by P. Hersey and K. H. Blanchard, 1969, *Training and Development Journal, 23,* 26–34, and "Leadership Style: Attitudes and Behaviors" by P. Hersey and K. H. Blanchard, 1982, *Training and Development Journal, 36,* 50–52.

theory resides in the belief that as subordinates become more mature, the nature of a leader's behavior should change.

As is the case in all other leadership theories, the two leader behaviors emphasized in the life cycle model are task and relationship behaviors. For *task behavior*, the leader's focus is on performance, productivity, and task success. For *relationship behavior*, the focus is on establishing and maintaining warmth, trust, and good interpersonal relationships with subordinates. It is assumed that while they are in a leadership role, all leaders will engage in both task and relationship behaviors.

Hersey and Blanchard (1969) viewed maturity of subordinates as their ability and willingness to assume responsibility for their own behavior. This includes the capacity to set high but attainable goals, willingness and ability to take responsibility, level of education, and level of experience. Thus, for example, a young athlete being introduced to a new sport could not be expected to have the knowledge, skill level, or experience in the sport to set reasonable goals. However, an athlete competing at the professional level would. Hersey and Blanchard (1969) believe that the behaviors of a leader should reflect the fundamental differences in the maturity of subordinates.

As Exhibit 10.2 shows, when the maturity of subordinates is low, a *telling approach* is called for on the part of the leader. That is, the leader must provide considerable direction and, therefore, task behaviors are high. Also, because of the immaturity of subordinates, the relationship-oriented behaviors of the leader are reduced.

As the maturity of subordinates increases into the low to moderate range, the leader can adopt a *selling approach.* That is, the leader concentrates on persuading subordinates about the correct way of carrying out their responsibilities. As Exhibit 10.2 also shows, with subordinates who are low-to-moderate in maturity, the leader's task behaviors must be high but relationship-oriented behaviors can also be increased.

When subordinate maturity is in the moderate–to-high range, a *participating approach* is prescribed. An emphasis is placed on discussing the approach to be taken with subordinates. Consequently, the leader's task-oriented behaviors can be low and relationship-oriented behaviors can be high.

When subordinates have high maturity, they have the education, skill, and/or experience to operate independently. Consequently, a *delegating approach* can be used by the leader and both task and relationship behaviors can be reduced.

Chelladurai and Carron (1983) assessed the validity of the life cycle theory of leadership for a sport context. Maturity was operationally defined through a combination of age and basketball experience. Basketball players competing at midget high school (14 to 15 years), junior high school (15 to 16 years), senior high school (17 to 18 years), and university (19 to 23 years) levels indicated how much social support (i.e., relationship-oriented) behavior and training and instruction (i.e., task-oriented) behavior they wanted from their coaches.

The results were not consistent with the life cycle theory. Life cycle would predict that the preferences for social support would follow an Inverted-U pattern (see Exhibit 10.2): low in midget, high in both junior and senior high school, and then low in university. The results showed that there was a steady increase from midget to university basketball players in amount of social support preferred. Similarly, life cycle theory would predict high preferences for task behavior in midget and junior that would fall off in high school and university. However, a U-relationship was found; preferences for task-oriented behavior were high in midget and university but reduced in junior and senior high school.

Multidimensional Model of Leadership

Chelladurai's (1984) multidimensional model of leadership and coaching behavior outlines how antecedents such as the nature of the athlete, the nature of the coach, and situational characteristics have an effect on the coach's behavior and, in turn, the coach's behavior has consequences for athlete satisfaction and both individual and team performance (Chelladurai, 1984). A schematic summary of the model is presented in Exhibit 10.3.

Exhibit 10.3. The Multidimensional Model of Leadership

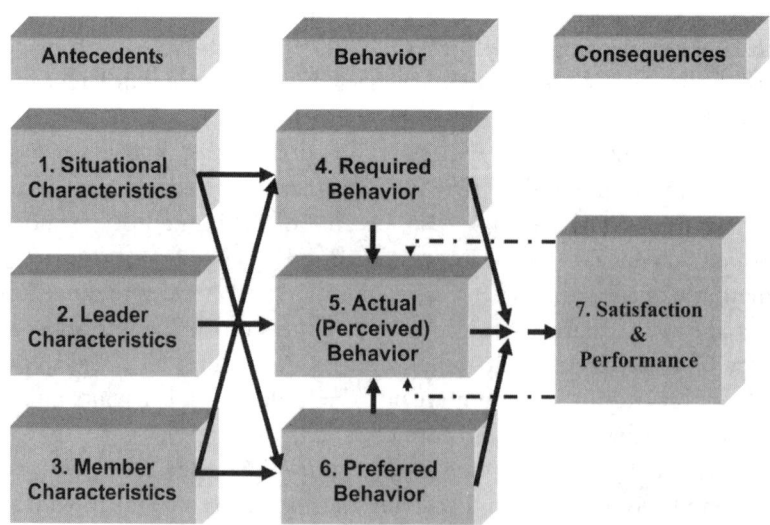

Source. "Leadership in Sports: A Review of Relevant Research," by P. Chelladurai, 1990, *Journal of Sport Psychology, 21,* pp. 328–354.

Coach behavior. As Exhibit 10.3 shows, a coach's behavior can be viewed from three perspectives: the behavior that is preferred by the athlete (Box 6), the behavior that is required (prescribed) by the situation (Box 4), and the actual behavior of the coach (Box 5). Preferred leader behavior is directly influenced by member characteristics (Box 3). It is not unreasonable to expect that athletes differing in age, experience, culture, and competence—to name but a few member characteristics—will differ in the degree to which they prefer their coaches to control training, show affection, allow for input into decision-making, and so on. A very young athlete, for example, might be much more sensitive to criticism than an older, more experienced athlete. Or, older, more experienced athletes might like more input into the development of their training programs than novices.

The behavior required of a coach (Box 4) is strongly influenced by the demands of the situation (Box 1). For example, at the beginning of a collegiate football season when 150 athletes are present, a democratic approach (where coaches and athletes jointly make decisions) would not be effective. Chaos would result. Thus, an autocratic approach by the coach is prescribed by the demands of the situation. In addition, member characteristics (Box 3) also influence the coaching behaviors required. For example, a democratic approach would be ineffective for a group of seven-year olds at the first session of a learn-to-skate program.

A coach's actual behavior (Box 5) is directly influenced by his/her personal characteristics (Box 2), including personality, age, experience, ability, and so on. Also, however, a coach's actual behavior is strongly influenced by the demands of the situation (Box 4). Two coaches of different age, ability, and experience would exhibit similar behavior in their first meeting with a group of 150 athletes. The situation requires an autocratic approach and argues against providing social support to individual athletes. A coach's actual behavior is also influenced by the preferences of athletes (Box 6).

Chelladurai (1984) proposed that athlete satisfaction and more effective performance (Box 7) result when there is congruence between a coach's actual behavior, the behavior required by the situation, and the behavior preferred by athletes. Although there are other possible consequences of participation—for example, absenteeism and adherence—performance and satisfaction are considered to be the most important. Are the athletes satisfied with their experience? Are individual performance and team performance as effective as they could be?

The Leadership Scale for Sports (LSS) was developed to assess five main behaviors considered characteristic of coaches-as-leaders (Chelladurai & Saleh, 1978). These include the degree to which a coach provides positive feedback, gives social support, trains and instructs athletes in the skills of the sport, uses a democratic approach, and is autocratic (authoritarian). Chelladurai's (1984) model has been tested in several studies and the links between the various elements in the model have been examined.

Member characteristics and coaching behavior. One link that has received attention is between member characteristics (Box 3 of Exhibit 10.3) and the type of leader behavior preferred (Box 6 of Exhibit 10.3). Two member characteristics that were shown to influence preferences for leader behavior are the sex and the experience of the athlete. Male athletes have a greater preference for autocratic behavior, training and instruction behavior, and social support behavior. Conversely, female athletes like greater input into decision-making; they have a greater preference for democratic behavior (Chelladurai & Saleh, 1978).

Athletes with more experience in a sport have a stronger preference for social support behavior from their coach (Chelladurai & Carron, 1983; Weiss & Friedrichs, 1986). As athletes have increases in ability, they must pay increasingly higher costs for additional increments in ability. These costs include the time, effort, and energy devoted to training and the sacrifice of social contacts outside of athletics. Consequently, as the athlete increases in ability, the sport environment becomes increasingly more important as a source of social support. Thus, it is perhaps not surprising that athletes of higher ability show higher preferences for more social support behavior from their coach.

Situational characteristics and coaching behavior. The situation also has an influence on the preferences that athletes have for different leader behaviors (the link between Boxes 1 and 6 in Exhibit 10.3). Other situational variables that influence an athlete's preference for leader behaviors include the type of organization and the nature of the sport. In intramural sports, where the primary emphasis is on participation and enjoyment, athletes may not want as much training and instruction, social support, or positive feedback as athletes on intercollegiate sport teams. Also, athletes in team sports such as basketball prefer more instruction than athletes in individual sports such as track and wrestling.

One conclusion that emerges from this multidimensional model of leadership is that the nature of the situation is an important consideration insofar as understanding leader effectiveness is concerned. Individual behavior is a joint product of the personality of the individual and the nature of the situational demands.

Consequences of coaching behaviors. As Exhibit 10.3 shows, the consequences of coaching behavior are satisfaction and performance. Weiss and Friedrichs (1986) tested Chelladurai's (1984) model to evaluate which coaching and situational variables were associated with athlete satisfaction. They assessed school size, percentage of the coach's workload devoted to basketball, size of the team's budget, amount of scholarship money available, and the tradition of success in the school. The only situational variable related to satisfaction was *institutional size*—athletes from larger institutions expressed greater overall satisfaction than athletes from smaller institutions. Weiss and Friedrichs (1986) also tested several coaching characteristics, including the coach's playing experience, coaching experience, age when hired, and prior win/loss record as a head coach (see Box 2 of Exhibit 10.3). Athletes evaluated their coach's perceived behavior (Box 5) and indicated their satisfaction with supervision, playing conditions, teammates, amount of work, kind of work, and school identification (Box 7). The coaches who had less playing experience, had a better prior record, and were hired at a younger age had athletes who were more satisfied. Athletes were more satisfied when coaches more frequently provided positive feedback, provided more social support, and used a more democratic style.

Transformational Leadership Theory

A popular contemporary perspective of leadership is transformational leadership theory. A full-range model of leadership encompasses both transactional and transformational leadership activities (Bass & Riggio, 2006). *Transactional leadership* is characterized by the exchange of reward (or decrease of punishment) for effort. For example, a coach who motivates athletes to work hard in practice by threatening to make them run sprints would be engaging in transactional leadership. By contrast, a coach engaging in *transformational leadership* inspires athletes to give effort for more idealized reasons such as the good of the team, the development of their skills, or the achievement of performance standards beyond their expectations. It should be noted that a contingent reward structure, which is a transactional leadership behavior, is conceptualized as providing the foundation for engaging in transformational leadership behaviours. That is, transformational leadership complements and builds upon transactional behaviors; they are not intended to wholly replace them.

Bass and Riggio (2006) highlighted that transformational leaders use a combination of four behaviors. One of these is *inspirational motivation*. This type of behavior displays confidence and assertiveness, promoting a high level of confidence in the athletes. A second is referred to as *intellectual stimulation* whereby the coach involves and stimulates athletes in decision-making. Phil Jackson was a strong proponent of encouraging personal growth among his athletes. Jackson spoke to this point, when he argued against a coach's tendency to use timeouts

> ... as a defensive weapon to halt the opponent's momentum. I don't subscribe to that philosophy and I know it's one of my unconventional tendencies that infuriates my critics to no end. They see a run by the other team and figure I'm the one who ought to stop it. I figure that my players are the ones who ought to stop it. Only by stewing in the mess that they created can they be subjected to its full embarrassing outcome, and only by discovering on their own how to extricate themselves can they be adequately prepared for the next time they lose their rhythm. (Jackson & Arkush, 2004, p. 59)

Third, *individualized consideration* involves behaviors that demonstrate a coach is considerate of the personal development of each athlete. Finally, behaviors that fall under the category of *idealized influence* are those that set good examples for followers and ultimately promote positive values and authentic pride. Adding to this perspective, Hardy et al. (2010) included specific behaviors in their examination of transformational leadership with military recruits that included providing appropriate role models, fostering group goal acceptance, and communicating high expectations for performance.

Coach transformational leadership has been linked to numerous important sport team outcomes. For example, Cronin, Arthur, Hardy, and Callow (2015) showed that coach transformational leadership is positively associated with athletes' willingness to sacrifice for the team, which in turn, is positively associated with athletes' perceptions of task cohesion. Not all athletes, however, are equally inspired by the efforts of transformational leaders. Among athletes who have a strong sense of entitlement and hubris (i.e., grandiose narcissism), coaches' transformational leadership directed toward establishing high performance expectations and fostering the acceptance of group goals were less effective at prompting extra effort (Arthur, Woodman, Ong, Hardy, & Ntoumanis, 2011). In a comprehensive overview of transformational leadership as it pertains to the sport environment, Hoption, Phelan, and Barling (2014) concluded that its promotion and adoption is less about developing great leaders and more about developing better followers.

Peer Leadership

Another important group of leaders that develops via both prescribed and emergent processes is peer/athlete leaders. Loughead and colleagues (Loughead & Hardy, 2005; Loughead, Hardy, & Eys, 2006) found that a relatively large percentage of athletes provided some form of leadership (i.e., formal or informal) on sport teams in relation to task and social functions in addition to other functions external to the team itself. Research on peer leadership indicates that formally appointed peer leaders (i.e., team captains) are rarely the only source of peer leadership within sport teams.

In fact, more often than not, athletes without a formally designated leadership role within the group are viewed by their peers as the most effective leader. For example, Fransen, Vanbeselaere, De Cuyper, Vande Broek, and Boen (2014) recruited 4,451 athletes to evaluate the frequency with which the appointed team captain was perceived as the principal leader within the team. They focused on four distinct leadership roles: task leader (i.e., directs and guides group toward collective goals and objectives), motivational leader (i.e., encourages and inspires group), social leader (i.e., promotes social harmony within the group), and external leader (i.e., the link between those within the group and those on the outside). Only close to a third of athletes identified their formal team captain as being the most prominent leader on any four of the leadership role dimensions (i.e., task, motivational, social, or external). In addition, almost half of the athletes who were identified as the task leader by a teammate were not perceived to occupy another leader role, suggesting that these leadership roles can be fulfilled by multiple team members. Nonetheless, the task leader was often identified as the most important leader within the group.

In a separate study, Fransen et al. (2015) asked athletes to rate the leadership quality exhibited by each of their teammates. Although the formally assigned team captain was perceived to be one of the top three leaders in 83% of the teams, an informal leader was perceived to be the most effective leader in more than half of the teams. Together, these studies highlight the prevalence of informal peer leadership in sport teams.

The inaugural season of the 2017–2018 Las Vegas Golden Knights of the National Hockey League provides an excellent example of how a team can thrive based on peer leadership, even in the absence of a formally appointed team captain:

> So far, the Golden Knights have had a lot going for themselves on their maiden voyage to the Stanley Cup playoffs. But the one thing they don't have—a captain—hasn't been an issue. There has been no lack of leadership in the team's locker room all season. (Carp, 2018, p. 1)

Researchers have examined interpersonal and psychological characteristics of peer leaders (Dupuis, Bloom, & Loughead, 2006; Moran & Weiss, 2006), as well as relationships between the quantity of peer leaders and other perceptions in the sport environment including athlete satisfaction (Eys, Loughead, & Hardy, 2007), communication, and cohesion (Hardy, Eys, & Loughead, 2008). Returning to the concept of transformational leadership, Price and Weiss (2013) showed that transformational leadership is not limited to coaches. Their findings indicated that coach transformational leadership was a stronger predictor of athletes' personal outcomes of perceived competence and enjoyment, compared to leadership behaviors of peers. However, peer transformational leadership played a more prominent role in relation to team outcomes. More specifically, Price and Weiss (2013) found that athletes who reported high peer transformational leadership reported feeling more cohesive as a group on task and social matters. Overall, it is evident that effective leadership arising from within the team is crucial to the group environment.

The Leadership Process Model: The Role of Followership

Although society often romanticizes great leadership, people cannot lead without followers. Indeed, a coach who is able to devise a perfect tactical strategy will struggle greatly if he or she is unable to secure the support of the group. A useful framework for understanding how leaders and followers both actively shape group dynamics is the leadership process model (Uhl-Bien, Riggio, Lowe, & Carsten, 2014). According to this model, leadership is the product of leading behaviors and following behaviors. Put another way, the leadership process is co-constructed out of a shared understanding of who will lead and who will follow in a given interaction (DeRue & Ashford, 2010).

This perspective recognizes that within a group, individuals can actively shift between roles of leading and following—and that both sets of role-related behaviors are crucial to coordinating collective efforts and pursuing group goals. Consider a team comprised of athletes with strong and bold personalities, all eager to lead. Chaos is likely to ensue if multiple group members are jockeying to show their leadership prowess at the same moment. However, if group members are able to flexibly navigate between roles of leading and following, then a team can capitalize on one another's distinct leadership strengths in different situations. Successful group efforts are thus the result of how leaders and followers jointly work together toward a shared purpose. In this sense, effective followership enables leadership.

As the leadership process model emphasizes acts of followership, Benson, Hardy, and Eys (2016) interviewed collegiate sport coaches to understand their views on effective followership. Coaches described personal qualities associated with effective followership that coalesced around four main themes: They wanted followers who internalized and adhered to team principles (i.e., a strong collective orientation). Coaches also valued group members who took ownership for their personal actions and thought critically about how to advance the team's mission. A third characteristic valued by coaches was relational transparency—coaches spoke to the benefits of having individuals who were willing to honestly and promptly engage in dialogue about group-related matters. Finally, they coveted group members who were open to others' perspectives and able to assimilate and apply new self-related information in a productive manner. As summarized by Benson et al. (2016),

> These qualities depict a follower who is proactive in his or her responsibilities, accountable, willing to challenge leader ideas and offer alternative insights, and display an overt commitment to supporting team efforts. (p. 956)

In addition to drawing attention to these generally desirable qualities, the interviewed coaches also emphasized the context-specific nature of followership. Coaches wanted followers—ranging from new team members to their most senior assistant coaches—to show initiative and challenge their ideas, but there was a time and place for such behavior. Notably, proactive followership was viewed as more appropriate during one-on-one interactions than in more public forums. Coaches were also resistant to the idea of proactive followership during performance critical situations, in which there was a lack of time to deliberate about the best way forward. A third point was that coaches were more receptive to being challenged early in the decision-making process rather than later in the decision-making process.

In addition to situational factors, coaches also spoke of how certain issues were "out of bounds" or "nonnegotiable." Although what is "nonnegotiable" varies from group to group, several of the interviewed coaches emphasized that personnel decisions related to starting status and playing time were not up for discussion. Finally, interpretations of proactive followership also varied according to the relational dynamics between a leader and follower (i.e., status of individuals interacting and interpersonal history). Overall, these findings suggest that followership is not a static position of subordination—followers are active agents within the leadership process.

Gender and Leadership

Although the number of females in leadership positions within business and industry is increasing, there is still underrepresentation (Eagly & Chin, 2010). In sport, a similar picture exists. The 2018 racial and gender report card (Lapchick, 2018) highlighted the current situation for men and women in athletics. Specifically, Lapchick (2018) pointed out:

> While the overall representation of women within college sport in all three Divisions continued to improve, it was negatively balanced by the fact that in the 47th year after the passage of Title IX, nearly 60 percent of all women's teams are still coached by men and 51 percent of all the assistant coaches on women's teams are men. (p. 24)

Questions surrounding the involvement of females and males in leadership roles have intrigued social scientists in both sport and industrial psychology. Why are males overrepresented in leadership roles? Are women as likely as men to emerge as leaders in leaderless groups? Do males and females have similar leadership styles? Does the gender of leaders have an influence on their evaluation by subordinates? In sport, there is some research that provides insight into these issues. However, in industrial psychology, a substantially larger body of research has made it possible to use meta-analysis to statistically answer these questions.

Gender and Leadership Emergence

Differences in the qualifications of male and female coaching applicants are one explanation used to account for the increased likelihood that males are hired rather than females. Murray and Mann (1993) argued, "The use of 'qualified' is, of course, prejudicial. It is often assumed in sport that males, regardless of training or experience, are more qualified than females" (p. 89). Research has shown that (a) hiring standards are lower for males coaching female teams than for males or females coaching same-sex teams, and (b) female coaches typically have a physical education degree whereas male coaches of female teams are primarily from other areas in education.

What about situations outside of sport? Eagly and Karau (1991) meta-analytically integrated research from 58 studies on the emergence of male and female leaders in initially leaderless groups. The issue of emergence of leaders is practically and theoretically significant because it can provide insight into (a) why leadership roles in natural settings are occupied considerably more often by men than women, and (b) whether men emerge into leadership roles in small groups because they exhibit certain types of behaviors more frequently than women or they carry out those behaviors differently.

The types of leadership measured in the 58 studies examined were task-oriented, socially-oriented, or general in nature (although in other studies, the type of leadership was not specified). Eagly and Karau (1991) found that both males and females tend to emerge as leaders in groups that are initially leaderless. However, men are more likely to emerge as task leaders or general leaders whereas women are more likely to emerge as social leaders. It was suggested that the fact that sex differences were equally strong for these two classes of measures suggests that men and women not only are treated differently in group settings but also behave differently ... the tendency to choose men may ... reflect a tendency to define leadership in terms of task-oriented contributions. (Eagly & Karau, 1991, p. 701)

Eagly and Karau (1991) identified several factors that might explain the tendency for men to emerge as task-oriented leaders. First, the longer the period that the group interacts before the leadership position is filled, the greater is the tendency for women to emerge as leaders. Thus, if a leader is chosen quickly, gender may play an important role in the selection process. When the opportunities to interact are increased prior to the selection of a leader, however, more information may be available on task-relevant competence. With greater exposure, there is an increased probability that gender will play less of a role.

Second, the type of task is also important. In situations where the group task requires relatively complex social interactions—negotiations and the extensive sharing of ideas, for example—there is an increased likelihood that women will emerge as group leaders. Possibly the social contributions of women to the group become more apparent (and more evident) through prolonged group discussions. Consequently, the likelihood increases that a female will emerge as the group's task leader.

As an extension to the above point regarding the type of behaviors (i.e., task vs. interpersonal) necessary to successfully complete the task, the degree to which the task is stereotypically oriented toward men or women influences leader emergence. Ridgeway (2001) summarized studies examining this phenomenon and noted that for tasks that were gender neutral or typically masculine in nature, men would initiate speech more often, spend more time talking, and use assertive gestures. When the task was more feminine in nature, women displayed these task-oriented behaviors to a greater degree.

The relative number of men and women in the group is a third factor in who will ultimately become the task leader. The tendency for men to emerge as the group's task leader is greatest when the number of men and women in a group is equal. When either women or men are the majority in the group, the chances increase that a woman will emerge as the leader. Eagly and Karau (1991) suggested that cultural changes present in society might be the explanation for these intriguing findings. That is, a greater emphasis now exists toward achieving equality of the sexes. Thus, when women are in a minority, men may refrain from expressing dominance. Conversely, when men are in a minority, women may refrain from ceding leadership.

Group size is a fourth factor in leader emergence between the genders. Males are more likely to emerge as leaders in smaller groups—especially dyads. Eagly and Karau (1991) felt that dyads are a special case and that specific social norms may shape the relations between men and women in this situation.

Finally, the tendency for males to emerge as leaders was more pronounced in earlier publications and for groups with older subjects. Eagly and Karau (1991, p. 704) wondered if "perhaps social change has created conditions more conducive to female leadership."

Gender and Leadership Behavior

As was pointed out above, two types of leadership behavior are emphasized in all theories of leadership: *task-oriented,* where the leader's focus is on organizing and directing subordinates toward productivity, performance, and task achievement; and *person-oriented*, where the leader's focus is on the development and maintenance of morale and good relationships. Are there differences between women and men in the tendency to be task-oriented versus interpersonal-oriented?

A stereotypical belief does exist in business and industry that there is a masculine mode of management, which is characterized by a task orientation, and a feminine mode of management, which is characterized by an interpersonal orientation (Eagly & Johnson, 1990). Eagly and Chin (2010) pointed out, however, that

> typical differences in the leadership styles of women and men are quite small when they occupy the same managerial role. Moreover, despite stereotype-based suspicions that women might not be effective leaders, the ways in which women differ from men in leadership style are generally associated with good managerial practices in current-day organizations. (p. 219)

As a final point, Eagly and Johnson (1990) conducted a meta-analysis on 370 comparisons from 162 studies in social psychology and industrial psychology. Consistent with their expectations, they found that in *organizational settings*, there was no evidence that men prioritized a task orientation and women prioritized an interpersonal orientation.

Gender and the Evaluation of Leadership

Earlier research on athlete preferences for coaches showed that both male and female athletes exhibited a bias toward male coaches (e.g., Parkhouse & Williams, 1986; Weinberg, Reveles, & Jackson, 1984), although subsequent work suggested this is not always the case (e.g., Fasting & Pfister, 2000). The question of how gender influences the evaluation of leadership is difficult to determine because of the relatively sparse number of studies in sport concerned with this issue. Is it because males and females coach differently? Is it because females coach in a stereotypical male way—an approach that is incongruent with gender-role expectations? Is it because of an inherent bias in favor of males in a leadership role?

Research in social and industrial psychology does offer an opportunity to gain some insight into the general issue of the evaluation of female and male leaders. Typically, the research has used one of two paradigms in laboratory settings. With the first paradigm, subjects are given a written vignette in which a manager responds to a problem. In the vignette, the gender of both the manager and the subordinates is varied systematically. For example, in half of the questionnaires, the manager is called Pat and references indicate he is male. The gender of the subordinates is changed systematically so that in a third of the questionnaires Pat supervises males, in another third, females, and in the final third, a mixed group of females and males. For the other half of the questionnaires, the manager is again called Pat but references indicate she is female. The subjects then rate the manager on various characteristics.

In the second paradigm, both a male and female confederate (i.e., research assistant, who acts 'under cover') are trained by the experimenter to lead subordinates in an identical fashion. The participants, the subordinates in the study, then evaluate the leader on a number of characteristics. Gender-related bias is evident in the extent that differences emerge in the evaluations of the two identically-trained confederates.

The advantage in these two paradigms is that tight experimental control is present. Leader characteristics are held constant and the only factor that varies is their sex. Thus, any differences that emerge are a product of bias.

Eagly, Makhijani, and Klonsky (1992) located 61 studies concerned with the evaluation of male and female leaders. When they conducted a meta-analysis on the results from these 61 studies, they found that the tendency to evaluate female leaders less favorably than male leaders is small. However, the degree of bias increases under certain circumstances. When women occupy roles that are dominated by men, and when the subordinates are men, the bias against women increases. Also, when female leaders use a stereotypical masculine leadership style that involves autocratic or directive behavior, the bias increases.

Carli (2001) pointed out that there is evidence to suggest that women who wish to use assertive and directive behaviors can reduce resistance and increase influence by tempering "their competence with displays of communality and warmth" (p. 725) such as smiling, nodding, showing support, and expressing agreement. The above points are further supported by Johnson, Murphy, Zewdie, and Reichard (2008) who conducted a series of studies on the effects of gender on leader evaluation. They concluded "for female leaders to be perceived as effective they needed to demonstrate both sensitivity and strength, although male leaders only need to demonstrate strength" (p. 39). The obvious detriment to taking this approach is that it reaffirms past stereotypes of men and women in terms of how they (should) display leadership.

Fortunately, times are changing. Elsesser and Lever (2011) conducted a large-scale study involving more than 60,000 male and female employees. In contrast to some of the earlier work we highlighted, their results showed that men rated their current female managers slightly more favorably than male managers, whereas women rated their current male managers slightly more favorably than female managers. In addition, Eagly, Johannesen-Schmidt, and Van Engen (2003) quantified the results from 45 studies, demonstrating that women engage in more transformational leadership than men—a highly positive quality that is linked to leader effectiveness. Although women continue to be underrepresented in coaching roles, there is no shortage of exceptional female leaders and coaches. As just one example, Chantal Vallée led the Windsor Lancers women's basketball teams to five straight Canadian Interuniversity Sport titles between 2011 and 2015. In 2019, she became head coach and manager of the Hamilton Honey Badgers—the first woman to hold both roles on a men's professional basketball team.

Leader Decision Styles

One important aspect of leadership is decision-making. Leaders must continually process information, weigh the alternatives, and then come to a decision. What offensive and defensive systems should be used? What training schedules are best? What athletes work best together? What time should practice start? How long should it last? Although the list of examples where decisions have to be made in sport seems endless, the process of decision-making involves four basic approaches. The major difference among them is in the relative amount of involvement or influence by the leader and his/her subordinates.

When an autocratic decision style is used, the leader makes the decision alone. Consequently, this approach involves the greatest amount of independence by the leader. A consultative decision style is similar to the autocratic approach in that the leader makes the decision alone. A difference between the two, however, is that the leader initially consults with subordinates to obtain their input. This input may or may not be used when the decision is made, but subordinates do have some involvement.

A delegative decision style is also similar to the autocratic approach in that the leader again makes the decision. But this time, however, the leader's decision involves handing over the responsibility to subordinates or to the group who then make the decision independently. Quarterback Trent Dilfer presents a fairly positive opinion of his coach, Mike Holmgren, based on the perception that he delegates a lot of decision-making to his player representatives.

> A lot of people perceive Mike [Holmgren] to be a high-ego, credit-seeking type of guy. I see a guy who delegates a lot of authority and relies a great deal on his captains. I honestly feel he'd be happier if he didn't get the credit, but maybe that's because I just played for the ultimate egomaniac. (Silver, 2001, p. 42)

The participative or democratic approach involves the greatest amount of involvement by the group in the decision-making process. The group (which could include the coach) jointly comes to a decision with the coach having no more influence than any other group member does. Greer (2002) included participative decision making as a method of creating an "environment that will stimulate motivation and help elevate a team's achievement level" (p. 40). The National Football League players' strike in 2011 was a decision arrived at through the democratic approach.

Chelladurai (1993) provided one interesting way of looking at the amount of involvement and influence by coaches and team members in the various decision styles (see Exhibit

Exhibit 10.4. Coach's and Athletes' Relative Influence in Three Decision Styles

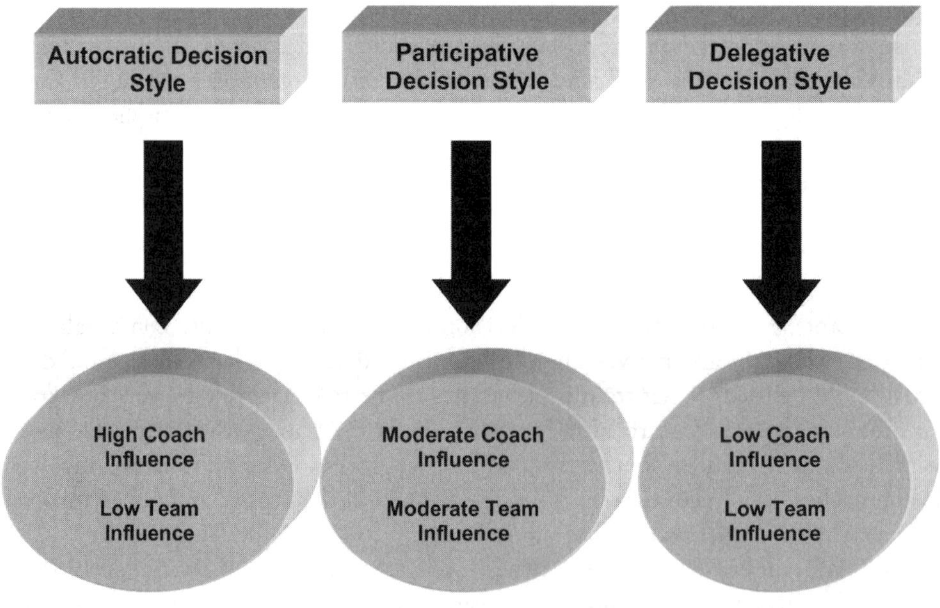

Autocratic Decision Style → High Coach Influence / Low Team Influence

Participative Decision Style → Moderate Coach Influence / Moderate Team Influence

Delegative Decision Style → Low Coach Influence / Low Team Influence

Source. "Styles of Decision Making in Coaching," by P. Chelladurai, 1993, *Applied Sport Psychology: Personal Growth to Peak Performance* (pp. 99–109), Mountain View CA: Mayfield.

10.4). He suggested that a coach's influence falls along a continuum ranging from 100% when the autocratic approach is used to 0% when the delegative approach is used. As would be expected, with the participative approach, the coach's influence at a moderate level. Chelladurai (1993) also suggested that the influence of team members is maximal when a participative approach is used.

At the management level, the delegative approach can be effective when it is clearly understood who is in command. An athletic director, general manager, or owner who hires a coach and then constantly interferes in the day-to-day leadership of the team reduces the coach's effectiveness. The sentiments expressed by Herzog and Horrigan (1987) are typical of the view held by most coaches: "The smartest people are those who hire good people and then just get the hell out of the way" (p. 12). The delegative approach is ineffective when it is unclear who is in command.

A study by Beam, Serwatka, and Wilson (2004) examined preferred leadership behaviors of athletes in the National Collegiate Athletic Association (NCAA) Divisions I and II in relation to gender, task type, and competitive level. From a gender perspective, they found that men preferred coaches to use an autocratic decision-making style to a greater degree than women. Athletes participating in individual sports also had different preferences for leader decision making than those participating in team sports. Specifically, individual sport athletes preferred a more democratic decision-making style than their team sport counterparts.

Although no explanations were put forward for this result, it is possible that those in individual sports are considerably more responsible for the outcome of their performance and likely share a closer bond with their coach than team sport athletes. Thus, individual sport athletes are more involved in the decisions that are made. Additionally, decisions in team sports may differ in nature and quantity (i.e., greater in number and affecting more people). Consequently, an authoritarian approach may be more appropriate. Finally, the authors found no differences in leadership preferences between the two competitive levels (i.e., NCAA Division I and II). Nonetheless, more diverse competitive levels may show differences in decision-making preferences (e.g., recreational vs intercollegiate sport).

Cohesion and Team Decision-Making

Brawley, Carron, and Widmeyer (1993) examined the influence of athlete involvement in team decisions on team cohesion and the athlete's understanding of and commitment to the decision. Female and male members of highly competitive, elite teams were asked to indicate the percentage of team members involved in setting team goals for practice and competition. The athletes were then asked to rate how clear the goals were and what level of influence those goals had on team behavior (i.e., effort, persistence). Athletes who were more involved in team goal setting possessed a stronger sense of task and social cohesion. Also, greater participation in setting team goals led to greater clarity (understanding) of those goals, as well as a belief that the goals had a greater influence on team behavior.

Brawley et al. (1993) suggested that the interactions that occur within a team when its members act together to arrive at a collective decision encourage common perceptions about the group. These common perceptions include beliefs about the importance of team success, the degree of task and social unity present, and the level of satisfaction present. In addition, collaboration in decision-making increases the clarity of team goals and helps to insure that those goals have a greater influence on behavior.

The Normative Model of Decision Making

Chelladurai and Haggerty (1978) took a different approach to the question of what decision style is more effective in groups. They proposed a normative model of decision-making (a contingency-based view) in which the nature of the situation is assumed to play a significant role in determining what decision style was most appropriate. In Chapter 8, we pointed out that a norm is a standard that provides the individual with guidelines for behavior in specific situations. This is what the normative model does for leaders in decision-making situations. According to Chelladurai and Haggerty (1978), seven situational factors have an influence on what type of decision style normally would be most effective. The first situational variable is *time pressure*. The amount of time available to deliberate, weigh alternatives, and consult with other people varies from one situation to another. In turn, this has a direct influence on the type of decision style that is most appropriate.

A second situational factor that has an effect on the type of decision style used is *quality requirement*. In some instances, the coach may be satisfied with any one from a number of equally good alternatives. Thus, the quality requirement in that situation is low. The decision concerning which individual to select as team captain is an example. If the coach is satisfied with all the potential candidates, the quality requirement in the situation is low. In contrast, the coach may feel that the selection of the final two or three players on the roster is important to ensure maximum flexibility. An optimal decision must be made when the quality requirement of a decision is high.

A third situational factor is *information location*. Decision-making involves the information processing and weighing alternatives. Thus, it makes good sense that those individuals who possess the best information on an issue should be involved in the decision. A coach should make the decision if he or she has the best information; if not, a consultative, delegative, or democratic approach should be taken.

Problem complexity is a fourth situational variable. Problems are complex if they involve a series of interconnected steps—where one decision has an influence on every subsequent decision. Picking the athletes for an Olympic basketball team is one example. A coach who picks her best five might be faced with the dilemma of filling out the roster with a poor defensive player who is an outstanding three-point shooter versus a versatile athlete who can play more than one position.

The fifth situational factor, *group acceptance*, is an acknowledgment that acceptance by team members may be critical for the successful implementation of a decision. A coach might autocratically decide to introduce a full-court press in basketball. If the athletes are convinced that they do not have the ability to make it work, their effort might be poor.

Another situational factor that influences the type of decision style that is most effective is the *coach's power*. Compliance by athletes with a decision is virtually assured when coaches possess the five sources of power outlined by French and Raven (1959; expert, coercive, reference, legitimate, and reward).

The final factor is *group integration*, which refers to the level of task and social cohesiveness present. Thus, for example, a participative decision style could be used effectively with a highly cohesive team. It wouldn't be as effective with a non-cohesive group.

The role that the seven situational factors play in decision-making is illustrated in Exhibit 10.5. The top branch of the decision tree is useful to illustrate the normative model in action. The first question encountered is whether there is restricted time pressure. If the answer is "no," the lower branch is taken and other situational issues become relevant. If the answer is

Exhibit 10.5. A Normative Model of Decision-Making in Sport. The Sun-Shaped Circle at the End of Each Node Identifies the Leadership Style Represented, Spanning Autocratic (A), Participative (P), and Democratic (D).

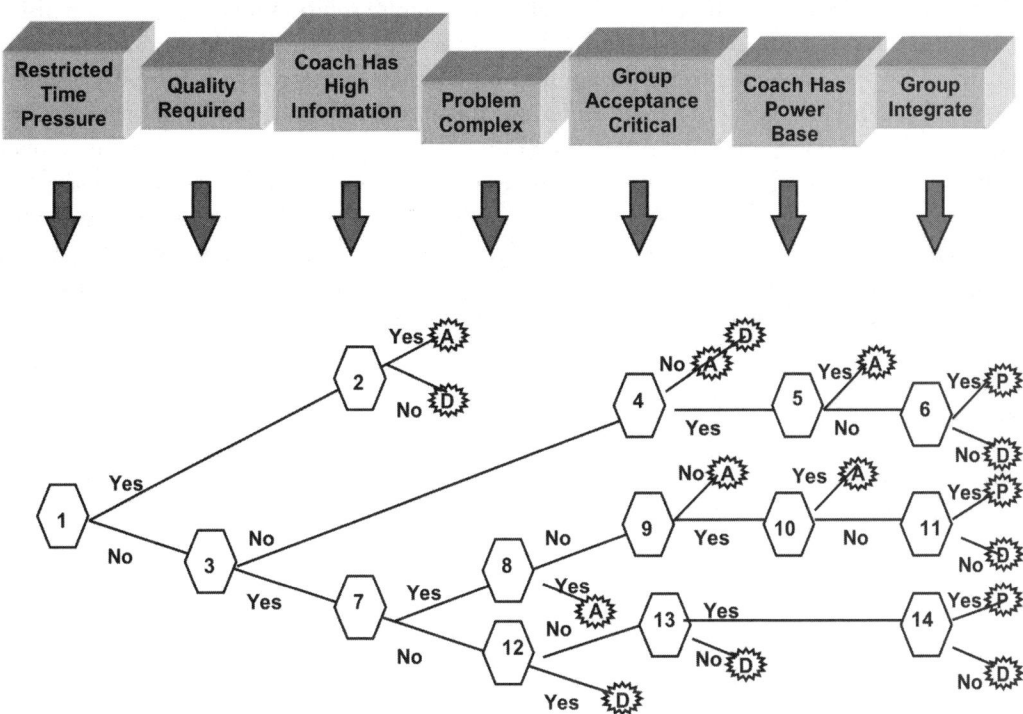

Source. "A Normative Model of Decision Styles in Coaching," by P. Chelladurai and T. R. Haggerty, 1978, *Athletic Administrator, 13*, pp. 6–9.

"yes," however, then the upper branch of the decision tree is taken and only one other question is relevant: Does the coach possess relevant information? If the answer is "yes," an autocratic decision style is prescribed. On the other hand, if the answer is "no," the coach (normally) should delegate the decision to a group member who possesses the relevant resources.

Thus, the answer to the question of what decision style is more effective is that it depends upon the situation and the circumstances. The athletic situation and the circumstances under which sport occurs seem to be primarily autocratic in nature. Coaches are highly autocratic in their approach. Whether this is due to the fact that it is simply the best approach possible or that coaches (and athletes) have come to expect this approach through a process of social learning remains unknown.

There are a number of advantages and disadvantages in providing athletes with more participation (Chelladurai, 1993). One advantage is that in discussions associated with group participation, alternative solutions and/or approaches to the problem can surface. As a result, a higher quality decision is possible. Also, when the group participates in a decision, there is a greater sense of ownership in the outcome. Consequently, there is also greater motivation to ensure that the decision is accepted and acted upon.

A third advantage of member participation in decision-making is that it contributes to the personal growth of the athlete. Fourth, group unity is positively affected. Also, as a result of the discussion that leads to the group decision, group members become better informed and more knowledgeable about what the group is trying to achieve.

One disadvantage of a participative approach is that it is more time consuming. Introducing alternatives, discussing them, and arriving at a compromise solution takes time. Competitive sport situations don't often provide enough time for full participation in decision-making. Participation also has limitations if the problem is complex—if it involves a number of interrelated alternatives. An example used earlier was the selection of an Olympic basketball team. One alternative influences a number of other interrelated alternatives. The greater the number of individuals involved, the greater the number of perspectives possible. Consequently, one highly competent individual such as a coach is as effective as a group operating democratically. Finally, a participative approach is not very effective if the team is not cohesive. Rivalry and competition between individuals or cliques could produce solutions that are not in the best interests of the group as a whole.

11

Competition and Cooperation in Groups

The competition in [Bela] Karolyi's gym was intense by design. The day after each meet, Karolyi's wife, Martha, also a coach, would stretch the girls in the order in which they placed in the competition, carefully pulling and pushing on their muscles and joints like clay sculptor's hands. Kristie Phillips and Phoebe Mills, the two hotshots, almost always finished first and second, so Martha stretched them in that order—a subtle but clear privilege in a place where privileges were doled out by the teaspoon. The message: You're worth only as much as your latest ranking. Karolyi wanted the girls to battle each other every day in the gym. "These girls are like little scorpions," he once said. "You put them all in a bottle, and one will come out alive. That scorpion will be champion." If one girl didn't perform a routine to his liking, he often made one of her teammates do extra work, building a climate of resentment among them where only the strongest would survive. (Ryan, 1995, p. 22)

Competition among group members can be a double-edged sword. Competing with teammates for status, competitive outcomes, or other rewards can be a powerful tool to promote effort. It can also be an enjoyable aspect of pursuing goals in sport. Meanwhile, competition can also leave group members feeling exhausted, demotivated, and apprehensive. This type of negative environment is described in the quote leading into this chapter regarding the intense competition among elite gymnasts and destructive practices of coaching staff (Ryan, 1995). When and how is competition adaptive, and when should we prioritize cooperation?

Understanding competition and cooperation in sport teams involves recognizing that they are a process that members 'do,' but are also a component of group structure. Just as teammates can cooperate with one another, they can also face situations that demand competition.

Exhibit 11.1. Chapter Framework for Competition and Cooperation

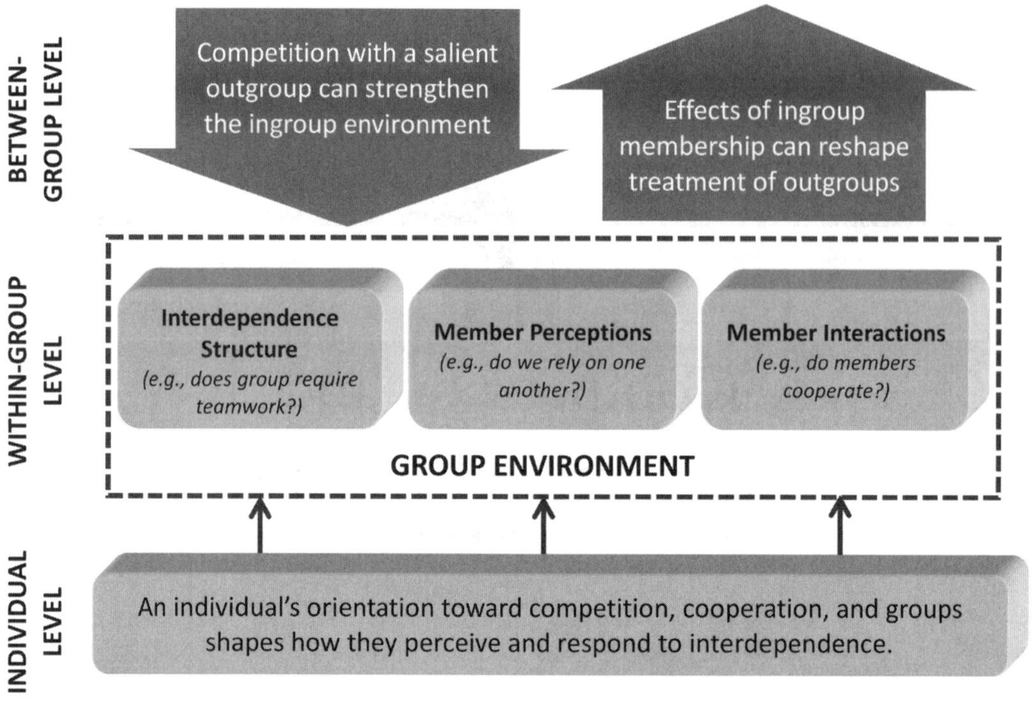

BETWEEN-GROUP LEVEL
- Competition with a salient outgroup can strengthen the ingroup environment
- Effects of ingroup membership can reshape treatment of outgroups

WITHIN-GROUP LEVEL

GROUP ENVIRONMENT
- **Interdependence Structure** (e.g., does group require teamwork?)
- **Member Perceptions** (e.g., do we rely on one another?)
- **Member Interactions** (e.g., do members cooperate?)

INDIVIDUAL LEVEL
An individual's orientation toward competition, cooperation, and groups shapes how they perceive and respond to interdependence.

Competition and cooperation are also evident at three levels: an individual level, a within-group level, and a between-group level. The individual level relates to the behavior of any given member, as well as the orientations or traits reflecting their propensity to compete or cooperate. The within-group level relates to the extent to which members engage in behaviors ranging from providing assistance to teammates, to striving to outdo one another or even actively thwarting each other's goal pursuits. Finally, competition with other groups also impacts how members of a team interact with one another and outsiders.

Beyond describing the nature of competition and cooperation, a goal of this chapter is to describe how sport teams can support cooperation while nevertheless acknowledging the potential value of competition within teams. We will focus on these processes at the within-team level but will integrate insights from the individual and between-group levels. Exhibit 11.1 specifically describes how we see these numerous levels interacting and summarizes the processes described below. This exhibit depicts the three levels, across which competition and cooperation are considered. The focus is on the ingroup, with the expectation that an interdependence structure provides the foundation for cooperation. Members in turn perceive and act upon that structure. This process is also shaped by individual differences and outgroup competition.

Studying Competition and Cooperation

Much of the original theory and evidence that is now the basis for understanding cooperation and competition in small groups emerged from research focused on how youth interact in groups. A classic research project conducted in 1954 known as the Robbers Cave Experiment was initiated by Sherif, Harvey, White, Hood, and Sherif (1961; see Exhibit 11.2). This project

Exhibit 11.2. The Robbers Cave Experiment

To examine intragroup and intergroup processes in a natural environment, Sherif and Sherif (1956) designed an experiment within a boys' camp in Robbers Cave State Park, Oklahoma. The researchers assigned the boys to one of two groups that were relatively homogeneous in age, race, religion, and socioeconomic status. In the initial phase (7 days), these two groups were kept segregated, and the two groups did not interact with one another. This strategy provided the researchers with an opportunity to chart the development of group structure and processes in the two settings. Each group created a name (i.e., the Eagles and the Rattlers).

The second phase entailed making the two groups aware of one another and hosting competitions between the groups to study the emergence of intergroup competition. Initially, there was minor intergroup tension (e.g., teasing) resulting from the competition. The boys also readily made intergroup distinctions (e.g., "we" versus "they") and engaged in practices to define their group, like creating flags. Eventually, open hostilities resulted when the Rattlers burned the Eagle's flag after losing at tug-of-war. This marked the beginning of a period of escalating intergroup hostility that eventually led the researchers to separate the two groups.

During the third and fourth phases, the researchers sought to reduce the hostility by bringing the groups together in noncompetitive situations (e.g., food hall). When this failed to reduce the hostility, researchers staged crises that required cooperative effort from both groups. The boys were asked to work together to locate the disruption to their water supply, pull a broken truck, rent movies, and prepare meals. These challenges included superordinate goals—goals that required the combined resources of the total group for success. Following these collective efforts, intergroup hostility reduced and intergroup contact and cooperation increased.

would not receive the approval of a modern-day ethical review board and lacks study design features required to consider its findings definitive. However, it produced key messages that inform the ways that we now view groups. One message is that individuals naturally orient themselves into ingroups and outgroups. A second key message is that when two groups experience competing goals, people categorize themselves more strongly within their ingroup—strengthening both outgroup hostility and ingroup identification. The third message is that we can mitigate conflicts between groups by introducing cooperative goals.

These messages are particularly innovative when considering the social climate of the United States during that time. As outlined by Johnson and Johnson (2009), the American education system of the mid-1900s included a broad orientation toward learning and behavior change as an individualistic process, which depended upon competition between students. This orientation meant that intergroup conflict and competition were tools to discern successful students. In the years that followed, researchers identified novel ways to structure youth settings and to integrate cooperation as a tool for learning (e.g., Johnson & Johnson, 2009). This research also drove our understanding of competition and cooperation.

Competition and Cooperation Within Groups

We will focus on the specific construct of interdependence to understand competition and cooperation within groups. Interdependence refers to the degree to which members of a group rely on one another (Johnson & Johnson, 1989). Deutsch (1949) theorized that individuals will act more cooperatively when they experience positive interdependence (i.e., success is possible for all members) compared to when members are independent of one another, or when they face a negatively interdependent situation (i.e., one's own success demands that others fail). The initial theorizing of Deutsch (1949) and subsequent theory development in educational psychology (e.g., Johnson & Johnson, 1989) and organizational psychology (e.g., Wageman, 1995) produced an integrated approach to understanding cooperation and competition. This approach is applied to our description of groups below.

Competition and Cooperation as a Group Structure

For a collective to represent a group, interdependence is a key feature that must be present. This interdependence emerges through how the group is structured, and the interdependence structure determines how an action by one group member will impact the outcomes of teammates.

One of the most important aspects of the interdependence structure is the group's task (Wageman, 1995). *Task interdependence* refers to the extent to which teammates must interact during the competitive task and is something that distinguishes team sport from individual sport (Evans, Eys, & Bruner, 2012). It is evident when teammates must move the ball up a field of play. It is important to remember, however, that some individual sports feature task interdependence for certain events (e.g., relays).

Sport teams nevertheless include many interdependencies that can be positive or negative. This structure is evident in the extent that members' goals align (*outcome interdependence*) and the extent that members must share resources (*resource interdependence*). Interdependence can also emerge in the psychological structure of the group, such as how some member roles are highly dependent on others. Even coaches and other leaders can shift the structure, such as how a coach may distribute rewards like playing time among athletes. These interdependencies form a complex web like the cat's cradle string game that is held in one's hands, with each athlete as a finger and each strand representing how actions of one member may influence others.

Although task, outcome, and resource interdependence could be presumed in most team sport groups, individual sport presents an interesting case where teams may entail widely varying interdependence structures—even when comparing two teams in the same sport. Evans et al. (2012) used interdependence to describe different types of individual sport teams. In addition to task interdependence, the authors distinguished teams in relation to two specific types of outcome interdependence: (a) whether teammates share collective outcomes as a team (collective outcome), and (b) whether teammates compete directly against one another during events (individual outcome). Evans et al. (2012) leveraged these distinctions in interdependence to construct a typology, illustrated in Exhibit 11.3, and revealed how sport teams can vary from independent to richly interdependent structures. Within the exhibit, we distinguish team types according to the presence of task interdependence, collective outcomes, and whether all members compete in the same event. We use exclusively task interdependence to distinguish team sport types in the exhibit, because most team sport contexts tend to involve similar collective outcomes and teammate competition patterns.

The role of the typology is evident in the two following examples of gymnastics teams. Consider first a club gymnastics team with no clear team-level outcome, where shared training facilities and coaching are the primary aspects producing interdependence. Contrast the first example with a United States collegiate gymnastics team where members compete against one another but share collective team outcomes in the form of conference and national championships. Collegiate teams are also unique because their season is comprised of dual-meet competitions between pairs of teams. Dual meets are even designed so that each team moves from one event to another as a group (e.g., one whole team completes rings routines while the other team completes floor routines). These are both gymnastics teams with similar individual outcome and resource interdependencies, but the collegiate team has a collective outcome. Furthermore, the unique design of collegiate competitions may even add to the salience of the team outcome.

Exhibit 11.3. Illustration of Different Interdependence Structures in sport Teams

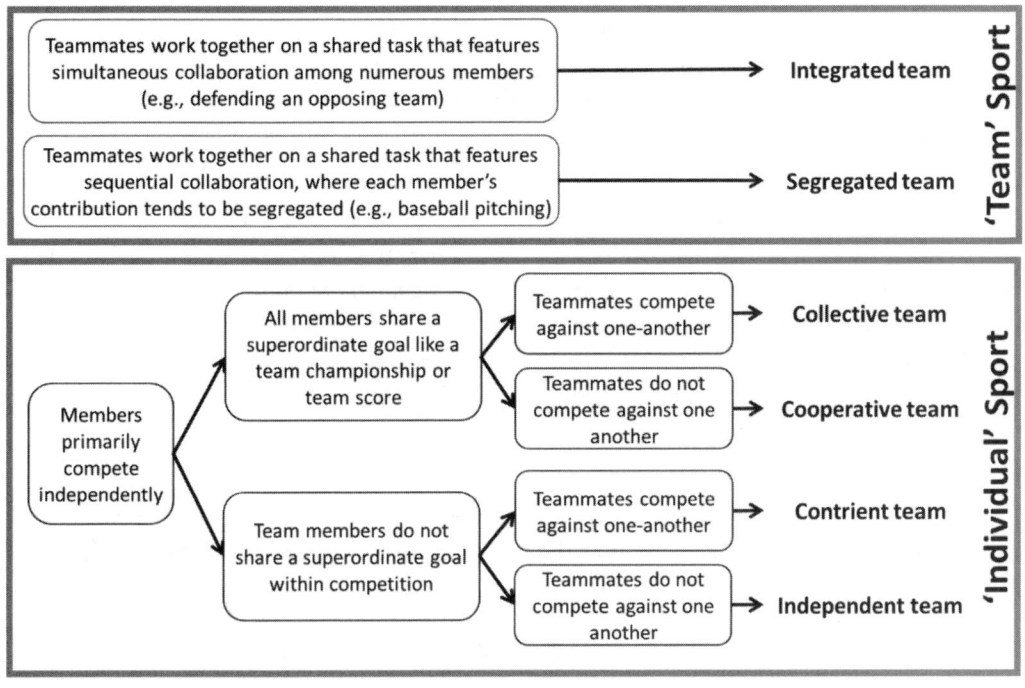

The purpose of acknowledging interdependence structures is that they determine how much a group is likely to cooperate or compete (Deutsch, 1949). Social interdependence theorists posit that members' cooperative and competitive behaviors depend on whether individuals actually perceive themselves as interdependent with others (Johnson & Johnson, 2009). This pathway was demonstrated in research by Evans and Eys (2015), who surveyed intercollegiate individual sport athletes. Across two studies, the authors demonstrated that athletes who experienced high task interdependence (e.g., relays; Study 1) or a collective outcome (e.g., team events; Study 2) were more likely to perceive that they were interdependent with teammates. They felt that they depended on teammates to perform, and that success from one team member meant that all experienced success. In turn, these teams with high interdependence reported higher group cohesion.

Competition and Cooperation as a Group Process

What does teammate cooperation and competition look like as a process in terms of how members actually interact? The social interdependence approach described above has produced a dichotomous picture of groups as either cooperative (positive) or competitive (negative) environments, depending on how they are designed. Tjosvold, West, and Smith (2003) indicated

> In cooperation, people believe their goals are positively related ... They then share information, exchange resources, and in other ways support each other to act effectively. Mutual expectations of trust and [rewards gained] through

> cooperation promote ongoing efforts to support and assist each other ... People with competitive goals conclude that they are better off when others act ineffectively ... They withhold information and ideas to increase their chances of winning the competition and may even actively obstruct the other's effective actions. These interaction patterns result in mutual hostility, restricted communication, and mutual goal independence. (p. 3)

This contrast describes cooperative group environments as those where members encourage one another, exchange resources, and trust one another. In cooperative group environments, members help one another to achieve goals whereas members of competitive group environments hinder one another's goal pursuits.

The following quote is from an elite athlete interviewed in sport psychology research, and highlights the types of goal-thwarting motives that may naturally emerge in groups with such negative competitive environments:

> [Susan—an elite gymnast] would support her teammates, as long as she clearly was better than them. As soon as their performances neared hers, Susan would begin to view them as an opponent. As she stated: 'I [was] very supportive of my teammates, only if they never beat me ... if they even came close to me, forget it. I'm not helping you.' (Krane, Greenleaf, & Snow, 1997, p. 65)

This type of process is, indeed, demonstrated in an experimental study by Boroumand et al. (2018) described in the social hierarchy chapter (Chapter 9). When athletes read a hypothetical description of an incoming athlete, they were less willing to provide support when that athlete was a high-performing athlete in their own position (i.e., competing for their position), compared to a lower-performing athlete or one in another position.

It is important to note that competition among team members need not result in a negative competitive environment within teams. At its most elemental sense, competition among teammates is a process where members work hard to be more competent than one another, as they pursue a limited individual outcome like a starting position on a team or a podium position in competition. Indeed, although elite individual sport athletes in a qualitative study by Evans, Eys, and Wolf (2013) highlighted numerous ways that teammates worked cooperatively, they also described how social comparison with teammates was a critical benchmark for success. With competition so central to sport, how do we distinguish positive forms of teammate competition?

Harenberg, Reimer, Dorsch, Karreman, and Paradis (2019) set out to examine athletes' perceptions of competition for playing positions in team sport—competition for playing time or attention with other athletes in the same position. The authors studied the extent to which positional competition induces positive processes for group members, with a focus on informational processes (e.g., learning more about one's performance) and performance-related processes (e.g., producing effort or motivation). Informational processes included aspects like making comparisons with others, gaining awareness of one's skills, and gaining recognition from the coach. Performance-related processes include pushing other teammates, feeling pushed by teammates, and expending effort to improve. Although researchers have yet to identify factors that promote or thwart these positive processes, this research helps describe positive forms of positional competition.

As another perspective on teammate competition, Grant (2019) is an organizational psychologist who focused one episode of his podcast *Work Life* on situations where teammates compete vehemently but constructively. One story involved American marathon runners Shalane Flanagan and Amy Cragg who were training partners. They garnered attention when both runners were sharing the lead during the 2016 US Olympic marathon trials. During the race, each runner had periods of struggle to maintain pace during the extreme heat. In each case, the other teammate slowed her own pace in support and to encourage the other to continue competing. When interviewing Flanagan about her experience in the marathon, Grant commented that,

> The way Shalane and Amy compete is collaborative. And it goes both ways. You heard it when Shalane slowed down to help Amy halfway through Olympic trials. But later in that same race, Amy turned around and did the same thing. (Grant, 2019)

To this, Shalane Flanagan remarked,

> With 5K to go, it got really bad. I was starting to not be able to see very well. … I felt like I wanted to stop. And I told Amy, 'You know, you can keep going, I'm not feeling good.' But she refused to leave my side. And I'm like, 'No, Amy, you can't do that. You can't sacrifice your race, you need to get going.' And part of me selfishly was like, 'Oh, thank God,' because if she was gone, I felt like I was going to literally melt into the road. (Grant, 2019)

Cragg ended up finishing first in the race, with Flanagan finishing 3rd, and both athletes qualified for the Olympics. Grant also interviewed Tore Øvrebø, a former Norwegian rower who described the orientation toward competition that they promote with youth:

> We think it's a better way to achieve the highest performance levels possible for individuals, if they don't have to compete all the time. They should share knowledge. They should share secrets. Because the point is not to beat the kid on the other side of the street or in the neighboring city or in the neighboring valley. It should be about beating those that do not speak Norwegian. (Grant, 2019)

These stories describe the orientation held by teammates who can compete while also cooperating. Social interdependence theory aligns with these descriptions. To provide the circumstances for constructive competition, Stanne, Johnson, and Johnson (1999) identified several elements: (a) winning should not be the only goal for group members, or even the most important; (b) the standards for winning should be unambiguous (e.g., clear rules of competition); and (c) all members must perceive an opportunity to experience success in the competition. Athletes must be willing to still compete but nevertheless respect teammates and possess the key features of a cooperative team environment to ensure that negative processes do not emerge.

One perspective of optimal competitive environments had come from research examining how coworkers manage conflict within organizations in competitive or cooperative ways

(DeChurch, Mesmer-Magnus, & Doty, 2013). When group members manage conflict with a cooperative orientation, their primary concern is an outcome with the greatest benefit for the group and all concerned. They are attentive to teammates and are open to others' perspectives. In contrast, a competitive conflict process occurs when members focus on coming out of the conflict with the greatest benefit for themselves. Imagine a situation where field hockey goalies face relationship conflict, where both members repeatedly say hurtful things toward one another. While a competitive approach may focus on individual gains (e.g., the starting-athlete claiming, "I will not come to practice if she is here!") a cooperative approach might entail both players arranging a group meeting with their coaching staff to discuss their issues and identify ways to prevent future conflict. DeChurch et al. (2013) aggregated findings from many studies in organizations and revealed that the cooperative conflict process is positively associated with team performance and the emotional health of the team.

Consequences of Competition and Cooperation within Groups

Competition and cooperation are both potentially beneficial within groups. Advocates of cooperation point to the social benefits of enhancing communication, trust, and shared learning. Meanwhile, competition presumably produces motives to expend increased effort to outperform others. Numerous major reviews addressed this issue by examining the outcomes of participants in studies involving tasks that were designed competitively, cooperatively, or individualistically. Johnson and Johnson (1989) included previous studies within educational settings and pointed to the benefits of cooperative tasks in relation to achievement on the task, social support among members, self-esteem, and attractions between members of the group. When you design educational interventions to promote cooperation, positive outcomes emerged for students.

Another review of cooperation and competition has particular relevance because it focused on studies that used motor performance tasks (Stanne et al., 1999). Similar to previous reviews, performance was highest on cooperative tasks relative to competitive and individualistic tasks. Nevertheless, the authors reported that competition was not always an ineffective approach. Stanne et al. (1999) specifically reported that competitive tasks had impacts on performance that were equivalent to cooperative tasks when they featured the aspects of appropriate or constructive competition described in the chapter section above (e.g., competition was with others of similar ability).

Individual Level of Competition and Cooperation

Not all people react in the same way to competitive and cooperative situations. Many aspects of individuals influence the patterns described above, with one particular point of interest being sex differences. Past research and commentary in sport research claimed that sex differences influence the propensity to compete whereby males are more competitive (e.g., Duda, 1987; Gill, 1986). A larger-scale review encompassing numerous fields paints a more detailed story (Balliet, Li, Macfarlan, & Van Vugt, 2011). In the reviewed articles, there was no significant sex difference in whether individuals cooperate or compete. However, Balliet et al. (2011) found that sex differences in competition may happen in certain circumstances. Males were more cooperative than females in same-sex tasks (i.e., male-male vs female-female), however women cooperated more within mixed-sex interactions.

Competition and cooperation can also be considered in relation to athletes' traits or orientations (i.e., a general predisposition for individuals to act in a consistent fashion across situations). When describing famous athletes, highly competitive orientations are often considered to be a critical feature of their success, whether it be Michael Jordan (basketball), Serena Williams (tennis), or Lindsey Vonn (downhill skiing).

Researchers have studied orientations toward cooperation or competition within sport. One orientation that identifies athletes likely to be more competitive in groups is an ego orientation, identifying athletes who evaluate their own success based on comparisons with others (e.g., Duda, 1995). Athletes may also be oriented to be competitive when they implicitly view sport as a competitive and war-like activity (e.g., "Competition is war"), as opposed to an orientation where athletes view competitors as partners (e.g., "I want my opponents to be at their best"; Shields, Funk, & Bredemeier, 2015).

One youth sport study focused on how athletes respond to the interdependence structures within their sport team. Donkers, Martin, and Evans (2018) asked athletes to complete surveys to describe the extent to which they were collectively oriented, with highly-collective athletes valuing the goals of the group over their own goals, caring about the well-being of the group, and seeing small groups as important. A main finding was that individual sport athletes reported higher satisfaction and intentions to return to their sport when their group included task interdependence (e.g., relays). Collectivism nevertheless moderated this effect, whereby being interdependent with teammates was especially important for athletes who reported stronger collectivist beliefs. Athletes who were more collectivist especially wanted to return to settings where they worked with teammates in competition.

Intergroup Competition

Competition between groups within sport can do great things. To illustrate, one study considered rivalries between men's basketball teams in the National Collegiate Athletics Association (Pike, Kilduff, & Galinsky, 2018). This sport context is ripe with rivalries that extend across decades, such as games featuring the North Carolina Tarheels and the Duke Blue Devils. Pike et al. (2018) tested whether the performance of a rival team increased the focal teams' performance in subsequent years. The researchers documented tournament performance in the national championships in relation to how many games each team won and compared each team's performance for a given year with their rivals from the previous season. The findings revealed that when a team's rivals performed well in the national tournament in a given year, the focal team's performance would improve in the subsequent year. The authors replicated this effect with data from professional sport leagues like the NFL and the NBA.

What the findings above mean is that rivals may become a focus of social comparison, whereby teams will intensify (or ease) their efforts to improve depending on how they compare to rivals. This social comparison effect is one of several consequences that emerge through intergroup competition.

A second way that competing with outgroups can impact the ingroup is through fostering group cohesion. This consequence was particularly evident in the Robbers Cave Experiment. Sherif et al. (1961) reported the groups became even more close knit and cohesive when between-group competition was initiated. However, success and failure also had an influence on the relative level of cohesion—a result that also has been observed in sport teams (see Chapter 14). With group success, cohesiveness was strengthened; with failure, it was weakened.

Dion (1979) suggested that there are four possible interpretations for the increases that occur in cohesiveness within the group during competition. One, based on Heider's (1958) balance theory, is founded on the premise that individuals seek out perceptual consistency. This consistency is achieved by balancing positive perceptions with negative perceptions. When ingroup membership is perceived in a positive way, the outgroup will be perceived in a negative way so that balance and consistency are achieved.

Second, the ingroup can serve as a vehicle for achieving extrinsic rewards; described as a reinforcement perspective. Competition provides an opportunity to secure rewards, and the ingroup can be a vehicle through which the individual can receive rewards. Third, competition also poses a threat to goal attainment, prestige, and self-evaluation. When groups are threatened from outside, they tend to draw closer together. Fourth is the self-enhancement hypothesis. Considering that we want to feel good about the groups to which we belong, we want to view the group positively and are attracted to settings when we are accepted.

Intergroup Processes

The groups that we belong to also produce consequences for how we treat other groups. Despite the value of competing outgroups, they also produce numerous social and psychological consequences as individuals come to categorize themselves and others as members of the ingroup and outgroup.

One of the most predominant theories used to understand consequences of intergroup competition is *social identity theory* (Tajfel & Turner, 1979). The ingroup is represented by those individuals who categorize themselves as "us" and "we"; conversely, the outgroup are the others—those individuals the ingroup categorizes as "they" and "them." People have numerous motives to make the distinction between their own groups and others. One motive is self-esteem. When our group compares well with other groups, the social identity resulting from our membership can enhance our self-esteem as well. There are other motives leading to identification beyond self-esteem, including feeling distinct from others, a sense of belonging, and gaining meaning (Vignoles, Regalia, Manzi, Golledge, & Scabini, 2006).

As Exhibit 11.4 shows, one consistent consequence of competition is a tendency of the ingroup to differentiate itself from the outgroup—a process referred to as *social categorization*. When a group forms, social categorization helps to establish a collective sense of identity and serves to distinguish between insiders and outsiders.

Exhibit 11.4 presents several additional consequences that are related to this process of self-categorization: (a) outgroup homogeneity, stereotyping, and depersonalization, (b) outgroup rejection, and (c) intergroup bias. Consider, as one example, the outgroup rejection that emerges through intergroup competition. When cooperative groups are competing with other groups, ratings of interpersonal attraction favor the ingroup and there are a greater number of friendship choices within the group (Brewer, 1979). Individuals prefer members of their ingroup. As another example, groups that are in competition also show a strong bias in favor of the ingroup. Compared to how we view outgroups, we tend to overestimate our own group's abilities, morals, and strengths—the group's product and environment are considered more favorably (e.g., Janssens & Nuttin, 1976). Similarly, members of groups experience pressure to justify wrong or immoral acts by their own members, while vilifying very similar acts from members of outgroups. One only needs to watch a few team sports to recognize how a movement that is merely an 'accidental bump' when perpetrated by a teammate becomes a 'flagrant attempt to injure' when it is an opponent.

Exhibit 11.4. Intergroup Competition, Self-Categorization, and Their Consequences

Construct	Description
Self-Categorization	We naturally sort people into groups on the basis of common attributes, so competing with an outgroup makes this process very salient. As an individual classifies themselves as a member of a group, they also categorize outgroup members into restrictive perceptual categories.
Consequences of Intergroup Competition and Self-Categorization	
1. Homogeneity, stereotyping, and depersonalization	We overestimate the differences between groups and underestimate the differences within groups, thus focusing on how members of groups are homogeneous. We also develop generalizations about how group members are expected to act.
2. Outgroup rejection	Ratings of interpersonal attraction favor ingroup members. Friendship choices are predominantly ingroup.
3. Intergroup bias	An evaluative bias develops that favors and protects the ingroup, similar to ethnocentrism in the context of one's culture.
4. Group cohesion	Group cohesion is increased by intergroup competition. Nevertheless, this depends upon success as well; winning teams show increases, losing teams show decreases.
5. Intergroup social comparison	Groups who develop rivalries or other competitions with outgroups establish a target for social comparison, where the group will judge itself relative to other salient outgroups.

Source. "An integrative theory of intergroup conflict" by H. Tajfel and J. Turner, 1979, *The Social Psychology of Intergroup Relations*, pp. 33–48.

The tradition of studying minimal groups—ad hoc categories of individuals formed on the basis of some trivial criteria—offers powerful evidence of self-categorization. For example, an instructor might tell a group of students that they all achieved the same grade in a psychology exam. With only this trivial characteristic in common, the individuals would begin the process of self-categorization (i.e., consider themselves as "we" and other individuals in the class as "they"). Minimal group studies like this comprise groups of individuals who are unfamiliar with each other, and often there is no opportunity to gain from favoring ingroup individuals. Nonetheless, a bias becomes evident almost immediately, as individuals prefer and are more willing to cooperate within their ingroup and even to harm outgroup members.

The processes related to self-categorization described above are certainly not trivial. Indeed, these processes produce many of the most intractable conflicts on the world stage. Although comparably less intergroup research is evident in sport, there is reason to expect that similar processes take place among athletes.

As an example, researchers analyzed the results of studies that included a scale that measured behaviors with teammates and opponents that were either prosocial (e.g., helping the opponent off the floor) or antisocial (e.g., deliberately fouling an opponent; Graupensperger, Jensen, & Evans, 2018). Athletes who were more prosocial (or more antisocial) tended to be so with both teammates and opponents. If an athlete was prosocial with teammates, for example, they also tended to be that way with opponents. However, an interesting finding emerged when considering how prosocial behavior towards one's teammates was associated with antisocial behavior toward opponents. For younger adolescents and children, the association was negative. Being more prosocial with one's team meant being less antisocial with opponents. Meanwhile, the association flipped with older adolescents whereby being more prosocial with one's team meant being more antisocial with opponents. At least for older adolescent athletes, ingroup love may equate to outgroup hate.

Promoting Cooperation at Within- and Between-Group Levels

Although theorists position ingroup bias as intractable, disparate lines of inquiry suggest that these biases are avoidable. Sport groups are indeed a ripe context to find ways to promote cooperation and reduce intergroup conflict. Considering that sport is a key setting for youth to develop, as one example, we should presumably pay attention to the messages that youth gain about the necessity of cooperation with other group members as well as the appropriate ways to treat outgroups. With an understanding of factors that produce competition and cooperation within and between teams as a foundation, we can structure our groups to make them more satisfying and productive.

Within-Group Cooperation

Johnson and Johnson (2009) identified several strategies for teachers to improve cooperation in the classroom, and many of these can be employed within sport. Formally, teachers who employ cooperative learning will design specific tasks to be cooperative. This entails several steps: (a) plan the cooperative task and its objectives beforehand in detail; (b) meet with students to explain the task, the types of interdependence it demands, and the social skills that students should use; (c) monitor learning and intervene as needed; and (d) evaluate learning and provide feedback.

Cooperative learning also includes a more general orientation toward learning as a cooperative activity. Within sport, group leaders can consider how they can promote the spirit of cooperation. Coaches and group leaders can thus consider ways of introducing interdependence within their group by promoting teamwork, devising collective outcomes, requiring that teammates share resources, and reframing competition between members as a way to pursue the collective outcome. As an example, a coach asking athletes to complete interval training in endurance sport may adopt cooperation by (a) using a team task like a relay, (b) creating a team goal, or (c) requiring that members collaborate to plan the training session.

Between-Group Cooperation

Many programs attempting to influence intergroup processes adopt one or more strategies used with varying success: promoting intergroup cooperation, increasing intergroup contact, utilizing group representatives, and finding a common enemy (Worchel, 1979). One of these strategies, promoting cooperation, is evident in how the Robbers Cave experiment used *superordinate* goals to unite the competing groups (e.g., requiring the boys to fix a broken water system).

Although each of these strategies carry potential benefits, the most richly studied approach is that of intergroup contact as a way to conquer conflict and prejudice (Dovidio, Love, Schellhaas, & Hewstone, 2017). The underlying idea behind intergroup contact is that exposure to an outgroup member will reduce conflict and increase harmony between outgroups.

Although Worchel (1979) pointed out the risk that intergroup contact may worsen relationships, there are several conditions that can increase the effectiveness of contact. Notably, contact seems to be more effective when it is extended in time (e.g., when cross-group friendships are formed). Contact interventions are also especially effective at targeting self-categorization when the intervention is designed to reduce how important the group categories are for people, or to help people categorize themselves in a manner such that they will actually see the outgroup member as an ingroup member (e.g., Dovidio et al., 2017).

Leveraging strategies like intergroup contact may seem challenging within sport. The way that we design sport leaves little room for contact and cooperation, beyond the handshakes that may take place before or after competition. However, sport systems and coaches may seek out opportunities for members of differing groups to interact—such as shared training camps, athlete advisory boards, or mentorship networks. Sport organizations would nevertheless be wise to heed existing research about the challenges of simply drawing outgroup members together and adopt tools from intergroup contact research to ensure that interactions are effective.

12

Team Goals

Pat [Summit, Coach of the National champion, Tennessee Lady Vols] was fed up… she told us to quit acting like babies. She also set game goals. For instance, if we made more than 15 turnovers or gave up too many rebounds, we'd have to run extra sprints. I think that really helped to turn things around. (Anderson, 1997, p. 49)

People use a range of terms to describe what they hope to achieve, from an objective, to a standard, destination, aim, or target. Encompassing many of these terms, goals refer to an end state that a group or individual envisions but has not yet attained. Formally, a goal is "the object or aim of an action, for example, to attain a specific standard of proficiency, usually within a specified time limit" (Locke & Latham, 2002, p. 705). Meanwhile, goal pursuit entails behaviors enlisted toward attaining those goals. As one example of relentlessly pursuing goals, Steve Nash was a Canadian basketball player who achieved the pinnacle of being the NBA's most valuable player in the mid 2000s. As a college-level athlete and before entering the NBA, Nash stated the following about his ambitions: "The NBA is the major dream in my life and the grail I chase every day … I am obsessed with it" (Crothers, 1995, para. 68). If this reflection seems more inspiring than the bare-bones definition of goals, it is by design: Goals should be inspiring.

In 1985, Locke and Latham (2002) suggested that sport is an ideal context to study how individuals and groups respond to goals. All individual athletes have objectives toward which their effort is directed, and these often entail components that are clearly defined. So too does the team. Teammates set goals for their group as a whole and may even develop expectations for the goals that individual teammates pursue. Even beyond a single team, goals also span organizations as broad goals or strategic aims.

This combination of individual, group, and organizational levels produces a mosaic of goals. Over 40 years ago, Zander (1971) pointed out that goal setting in groups is complex because of the interaction between personal and collective concerns. For instance, a survey

Exhibit 12.1. Examples of How Individuals Set Goals for Themselves, the Team, and Others

Illustration	Goal Holder	Goal Pursuer	Goal Outcomes
At the outset of the season, the basketball team meets to set a series of performance goals (e.g., field goal percentages) and outcome goals (e.g., making the playoffs).	Team	Team	Team
Shane is a first-year team member. He sets goals to make it to every practice and to lift weights several times a week (process goals). He plans to become a starting player by the end of the year (outcome goal).	Shane	Shane	Shane
Thomas is a senior on the team and knows how badly Shane wants to become a starter. He commits himself to drive Shane to optional early-morning shoot-arounds, to make it easier on him to attend (process goal).	Thomas	Thomas	Shane
Coach Jane wants a senior athlete named Felipe to step-up in his final year. Jane sets performance goals for him for his final year. Jane tells Felipe that she would like him to: (a) increase the number of shots that he takes and (b) become an 'energy player' this season.	Jane	Felipe	Felipe
Michael and Felipe are graduating seniors who want to signal the value of working hard to younger players. They set a process goal for one (or both) of them to be in the gym to lead group weight lifting every Tuesday. They then send an invite for all teammates to attend.	Michael & Felipe	Michael & Felipe	Team

study with 17 intercollegiate sport teams revealed that athletes perceived that several types of goals were set frequently in groups: (a) individual goals that they had formally set for themselves; (b) group goals that their team had prepared; and (c) goals that they had personally developed and held for their team to achieve (Dawson, Bray, & Widmeyer, 2002). As such, the group and its members are concurrently pursuing many goals at any moment in time. Each goal may differ with respect to (a) who set or identified the goal, (b) who is responsible for pursuing the goal, and (c) whose outcomes are likely to be impacted by pursuing the goal. Although this combination produces numerous goal types, some examples are provided within Exhibit 12.1. A group member is often responsible for pursuing his or her own goals and adopting a role within the group's goal pursuit—all while impacting other members individually as well.

Goal-Setting Effects in Organizations

Goal-Setting Effectiveness

Much of the interest in goals is attributed to the belief that individual productivity can be increased if individuals have a target or goal. Consider these two statements produced over 20 years apart. The first was by Locke et al. (1981):

> … the beneficial effect of goal setting on task performance is one of the most replicable findings in the psychological literature. Ninety percent of the studies

showed positive or partially positive effects. Furthermore, these effects are found just as reliably in field settings as in the laboratory. (p. 145)

The second was by Locke and Latham (2002):

> The effects of goal setting are very reliable. Failure to replicate them are usually due to errors [in design] … goal-setting theory is among the most valid and practical theories of employee motivation in organizational psychology. (p. 714)

There is no doubt that goal setting works to bolster task performance and motivation. When individuals develop specific measurable goals, they perform better than alternatives, such as receiving do-your-best instructions.

Goal setting doesn't just serve to improve productivity. Locke and Latham (1984) also pointed out that goals improve work quality, reduce boredom, increase clarity of expectations, increase liking for the task, increase recognition from peers and supervisors, enhance self-confidence, stimulate feelings of pride, and increase willingness to accept future challenges. Although most of these outcomes link to productivity, they also link with wellbeing. Indeed, Koestner, Lekes, Powers, and Chicoine (2002) reviewed literature on goal attainment and self-reported affect and reported that study participants report higher positive affect after attaining goals.

Performance and Group Goals

Goals are seemingly unavoidable in organizations at an anecdotal level. One need not look far to come across refrains from leaders and consultants about the value of motivating workgroups with objectives. Although researchers do not commonly study the effects of group goals, available evidence reveals that group goals are at least as effective as individual goals.

One meta-analysis combined 49 studies that reported on performance in organizational tasks after specifying a group performance goal. Studies included in the review were (a) observational, in which measures were taken before and after goals were set, or (b) experimental, in which interventions were conducted to compare groups experiencing goal-setting to control groups (Kleingeld, van Mierlo, & Arends, 2011). Group goal setting improved group performance. Furthermore, it appears that it is especially important to ensure that group goals are highly challenging and specific, when compared to effects in studies of individual goals.

Components of Effective Individual Goals

Research on goal setting for individuals in organizations has been extensive so it is possible to advance several well-supported generalizations about the components of effective goals (Latham & Locke, 2007; Locke et al., 1981). Two that are particularly critical are specificity and difficulty. First, goals should be set out in specific and measurable terms. Vague, general, imprecise ("do your best") goals do not direct the individual's attention to the important elements in the situation. Second, goals should be as hard and as challenging as possible—with the qualifier that the individual must accept them and have the ability necessary to attain or closely approximate them. Commenting on this, Locke and Latham (2002) noted

> we found a positive, linear function in that the highest or most difficult goals produced the highest levels of effort and performance ... performance leveled off or decreased only when the limits of ability were reached or when commitment to a highly difficult goal lapsed. (p. 706)

Difficult goals do set the bar higher, but they are also more satisfying. Those individuals who perceive that their goal is difficult to attain experience an increase in positive affect; these changes are not apparent when the goal achieved is perceived as easy (Wiese & Freund, 2005).

In addition to difficulty and specificity, *intermediate goals* or subgoals are essential links to long-term goals. Goal-setting programs that are set up for a long period of time (e.g., a goal for improved sales over the next 6 months) are effective. However, a goal-setting program that has short term goals (e.g., a goal for improved sales for the upcoming week) that are linked to the long term is more effective.

Fourth, *feedback* should be used for goals to have their maximum effectiveness as a source of motivation. For many tasks, progress is self-evident. However, when it is not, feedback detailing progress increases effort and persistence.

Support from the group leader is an important positive factor in the success of a goal-setting program. In organizations, having a group leader as an integral part of the goal-setting program increases its effectiveness.

Why Does Goal Setting Work?

What is it about goals that leads to such reliable improvements in performance? The answer to this question seems quite straightforward: Goals are inspiring. Goals arouse emotion, stimulate enthusiasm, and increase confidence among individuals and groups. There are four key mechanisms for how goals influence individuals' behavior: effort, persistence, direction, and task-specific strategies (Locke & Latham, 2002). Although these four mechanisms were first observed when considering individual goals, they also apply to mechanisms for goals set within groups in many respects (Weldon & Weingart, 1993).

Once a goal has been set, it has an energizing effect, and *effort* is generated by the individual to attain the goal. Moreover, challenging goals generate more effort than vague or less challenging goals—pushing people to work with greater intensity and over longer durations. As is the case for individuals, group goals also produce increased effort. The quote used to introduce this chapter speaks to how team goals can stimulate effort. Coach Pat Summit felt that at least two factors contributing to a lack of team success were turnovers and the number of rebounds given up. By setting goals in these areas, she directed her athletes' efforts toward performance elements considered important for team success.

Goals also influence *persistence*. All things being equal, individuals with a specific, challenging goal will spend more time on task than with vague, less-challenging goals or no goals. This is evident both in individuals and within groups.

Goals also *direct attention* toward salient behaviors and away from goal-irrelevant behaviors. For teams, identifying goal-relevant behaviors can provide specific indicators for members to monitor the group's performance and assess progress—being able to identify the specific behaviors that members need to complete to achieve goals.

Goals also influence behavior indirectly as a catalyst for individuals to develop and use *task-relevant strategies*. Individuals who set specific and challenging goals will inevitably experience plateaus, setbacks, and barriers. Beyond the importance of effort and persistence, it is often necessary to adopt new strategies to overcome challenges. Regarding these effects within teams, groups that set goals are more likely to demonstrate planning behaviors and may come up with novel strategies to attain goals. Team goals produce a blueprint for members when developing approaches to achieve the group's goals.

In addition to the parallels between group and individual mechanisms described above, Weldon and Weingart (1993) identified motives that only emerge when we pursue goals alongside other team members. First, individuals may experience an incentive to commit to goals when they see their actions as identifiable and indispensable. Groups provide a chance to ensure individual contributions are identifiable by all members, and that individuals feel they play an important part (see content on social loafing, Chapter 4).

When we set goals within groups, we may also benefit through morale-building communication. When members share collective goals or become aware of others' goals, they are likely to communicate in supportive ways. One example may be a running team member who cheers on a teammate who is nearing her personal-best time mid-way through a race, and whose time will help achieve a team championship.

As another mechanism attributed to groups, goals held by groups often become entrenched in members' own goal pursuits. Internalizing group goals can help individuals bask in the glory of group achievements more easily. Perhaps more important for performance, however, group-goal internalization may support extra-role behaviors. Extra-role behaviors involve going beyond one's role to support the performance of others or facilitate coordination, even if those actions aren't necessary for the individual to achieve his or her own goals. In other words, teammates may not go the extra mile unless they view group outcomes as their own.

Goal Setting Effects in Sport: Individual Goals

Alongside a rich foundation of goal-setting evidence outside of sport, considerable research interest in sport psychology has been directed toward understanding the dynamics of personal goal setting. This should not be surprising given that many athletes of different abilities and in different contexts engage in the practice. As an example at the elite sport level, Weinberg et al. (2000) conducted a study on 328 Olympic athletes to explore their use of goal setting. Their results highlighted that all the athletes had utilized goal setting to some degree and that the majority of the goals were related to improving performance followed by winning and having fun. In addition, the athletes (a) demonstrated a preference for moderately difficult goals, (b) used goal setting somewhat frequently, and (c) believed their goals were reasonably effective. These results concerning the use of individual goal setting were quite similar to those previously found by the same authors examining collegiate level athletes (i.e., NCAA Division 1; Burton, Weinberg, Yukelson, & Weigand, 1998), and apply to other types of goals beyond just increasing athletic performance. For instance, a study involving goals during injury recovery revealed that athletes who set goals adhered better to the rehabilitation regimen and held higher self-efficacy regarding rehabilitation tasks, compared to control or social support comparison groups (Evans & Hardy, 2002).

Considering key ways that goal-setting generalizations apply to sport, there are many similarities. For instance, easy goals—those perceived to be easily attainable—have a weak role in relation to performance (Kyllo & Landers, 1995). It is also evident that intermediate goals or sub goals are important links to long-term goals in sport, compared to exclusively setting long-term goals. Sport research has also supported several of the ways to support effective goal setting that are evident in organizations (Kyllo & Landers, 1995). For example, goal setting is more effective when (a) athletes either establish or are involved in establishing their personal goals, (b) coaches play a key role in the goal-setting process, and (c) goals are public (compared to goals that the individual holds privately).

In contrast, there are several key there are several key differences between goal-setting research and research in other organizations. For instance, the effect of goal-setting programs is weaker in sport compared to organizations (Kyllo & Landers, 1995). Kyllo and Landers (1995) also found that neither improbable nor difficult goals have an effect on performance. Only moderate goals—goals that athletes attribute as being plausibly achievable (i.e., 10% to 50% likelihood)—are effective in a sport setting. A third area of divergence is that poor goal setting practices seem especially prevalent in sport (e.g., vague goals with no clear stepwise path over time), and athletes report having challenges putting these principles in practice (Maitland & Gervis, 2010). For instance, athletes may struggle seeing how their short-term goals can produce long-term outcomes.

There are numerous explanations for these divergences. For instance, many sport-related tasks are complex. Goal pursuit in sport entails laying out one's goals, but also adjusting them relative to one's group and facing some uncontrollable features. As one such uncontrollable feature, perceptions of ability may be relevant for this difference. Especially considering the value that innate ability plays, sport performers who do not think they have the ability to achieve their goals may face difficulties committing to goals. Although this is only one explanation, goal setting in sport is effective but carries unique considerations.

Outcome, Performance, and Process Goals

One distinction that is especially valued within sport-based research is the distinction between *outcome*, *performance*, and *process* goals. An outcome goal represents an absolute standard; winning a gold medal for example. On the other hand, a performance goal represents a relative standard based on a previous performance; reducing the number of rebounds or turnovers, for example. Meanwhile, process goals are the tasks that one needs to complete to achieve performance goals. They are like a to-do list.

Popular wisdom holds that performance goals are superior to outcome goals for producing performance improvements. For example, Orlick (1986) advised

> day-to-day goals for training and for competition should focus on the means by which you can draw out your own potential. Daily goals should be aimed at the improvement of personal control over your performance, yourself, and the obstacles you face. (p. 10)

Kyllo and Landers (1995) found, however, that relative (performance) goals are no more effective than vague (do your best) goals; the greatest improvements in performance were achieved through absolute (outcome) goals.

However, it is not necessarily the case that an individual has to use one type of goal setting or another. Filby, Maynard, and Graydon (1999) asked 40 individuals to participate in an experiment that measured their ability to perform a soccer task. This task required the participant to continuously kick a soccer ball at a target on a wall about 8 meters away for 90 seconds; points were received on the basis of accuracy. Each participant was assigned to one of five goal setting groups: (a) outcome goal only, (b) process goal only, (c) outcome and process goals, (d) outcome, performance, and process goals, and (e) control (no goal). Their results supported the contention that integrating outcome, performance, and process goals was the most effective strategy. However, Filby et al. (1999) also cautioned that it is not just the combination of goals, but the setting of effective and properly prioritized goals that is important.

Goal-Setting and Youth Development

Sport goal setting research is also different from organizations in terms of the variety of goals that are relevant. Within youth sport, for example, personal development is one valued outcome. Goal-setting skills are actually considered to be a developmental asset that emerges through youth program experiences, and one that sport groups can help develop. As an example, adolescent athletes who experienced highly cohesive group environments were more likely to report setting challenging goals during sport (Bruner, Eys, Wilson, & Côté, 2014). One pilot intervention employed goals, followed by peer feedback, to develop skills with 10–12-year-old soccer players (Holt, Kinchin, & Clarke, 2012). Researchers asked athletes to set their own goals for practice drills, and then their teammates observed their performances and provided structured feedback. Athletes readily engaged in peer feedback and the authors argued that this was a way to implement performance monitoring while also developing peer relationships.

Goal-Setting Effects in Sport: Team Goals

Teams do establish collective goals that are critical for inspiring action. When these goals come true, they can seem like prophecy. As an example, the Toronto Raptors of the NBA prepared a video to play the evening of the first game in the season to outline the team goal. Described by Caron (2018), the video detailed the team's historical struggles to retain star players as well as tough decisions to fire a respected coach and trade loyal players in exchange for an all-star player who was only committed to the franchise for one year. Narrated by Toronto rapper Saukrates, the video ends with a clear goal: "The division isn't the goal. The conference is not the goal, … The goal is greatness. The goal is to be the last squad standing." As the eventual NBA champions that season, the Toronto Raptors objectively achieved this goal.

What types of goals do teams set for themselves for practices? For competitions? Brawley, Carron, and Widmeyer (1992) undertook a study to identify the nature of group goals in team sports. Athletes from various sports were asked to list up to five goals held by their team for both practices and for competitions. Overall, 70% of the goals listed were vague, general in nature, and not well described. The results showed that coaches and athletes do not tend to establish team goals that are specific and measurable.

Brawley et al. (1992) also found that in practices, teams have collective goals that focus on the processes needed to achieve outcomes rather than on outcomes themselves (see Exhibit 12.2). In competitions, the collective goals held by teams were relatively balanced between outcome goals and process goals. As an example within an ice hockey team setting, goals for team competitions included a balance of process (e.g., number of shots on goal) and outcome goals (e.g., winning the game), but practice goals often were constrained to process goals (e.g., working hard).

Brawley et al. (1992) found that team goals were rarely set in a way where members could actually gauge progress—they were vague and general in nature. If a goal is essentially a road map, the map will be of much better utility if it is more detailed and specific.

Exhibit 12.2. The Nature of Team Goal Setting in Sport

Situation	Type of Goal	Percent
Practices	Outcome (e.g., work hard)	10.2%
	Process (e.g., work on each of the special units)	89.8%
Competitions	Outcome (e.g., win)	53.1%
	Process (e.g., reduce penalty minutes)	46.9%

Source. "The Nature of Group Goals in Sport Teams: A Phenomenological Analysis," by L. R. Brawley, A. V. Carron, and W. N. Widmeyer, 1992, *The Sport Psychologist, 6,* 323–333.

Although the research on team goal setting is sparse, available research shows that team goal setting does improve team performance. As one example, the Kyllo and Landers (1995) meta-analysis in sport reported that goal-setting programs that included collective goals were positively associated with performance. As a second example, team building programs that focus on team goal setting within the intervention are common within sport and are at least as effective at supporting team performance as other team building activities (e.g., outdoor adventures, interpersonal relationship interventions; Martin, Carron, & Burke, 2009).

Performance is not the only indicator that we can use to understand goals within sport teams. For instance, goal setting can have an influence on unity—the social and task cohesion of the team—particularly if the athletes are actively involved in establishing the team goals (Brawley et al., 1993; Martin et al., 2009; Senécal, Loughead, & Bloom, 2008). In a study that illustrates this fact, Brawley et al. (1993) undertook research to examine the psychological consequences for team members when team goal setting is undertaken for practices and competitions. They observed that participation in team goal setting is associated with greater task and social cohesion. Brawley et al. (1993) suggested that when members interact to set shared goals as a group, they develop common perceptions about the group—not solely the group's goals, but also its unity, values, and orientation.

There is also interest in examining how decisions during goal-setting are impacted by individual differences such as personality traits, along with the social environment of the team. One question relates to how the environment surrounding a team can impact leaders, including the level of risk that they are willing to accept when setting goals. As an example, one experimental study investigated how the home field advantage influenced the goals set by football coaches. Staufenbiel, Lobinger, and Strauss (2015) asked coaches from developmental-level teams to set team goals for a hypothetical game scenario, using an online survey. What the coaches did not know, however, is that they were randomly assigned to either a home or away scenario. Coaches positioned at home fields set goals that were more challenging, and identified riskier tactics for achieving goals. Clearly, there is exciting territory to cover regarding how we set goals.

Individual Goals versus Team Goals

Our discussion of goals in this chapter has isolated team and individual goals. Individual and team goals can also conflict. In their discussion of team versus individual goals, Locke and Latham (1984) pointed out that

Exbibit 12.3. Goal Setting and Performance Alone and in a Group Situation

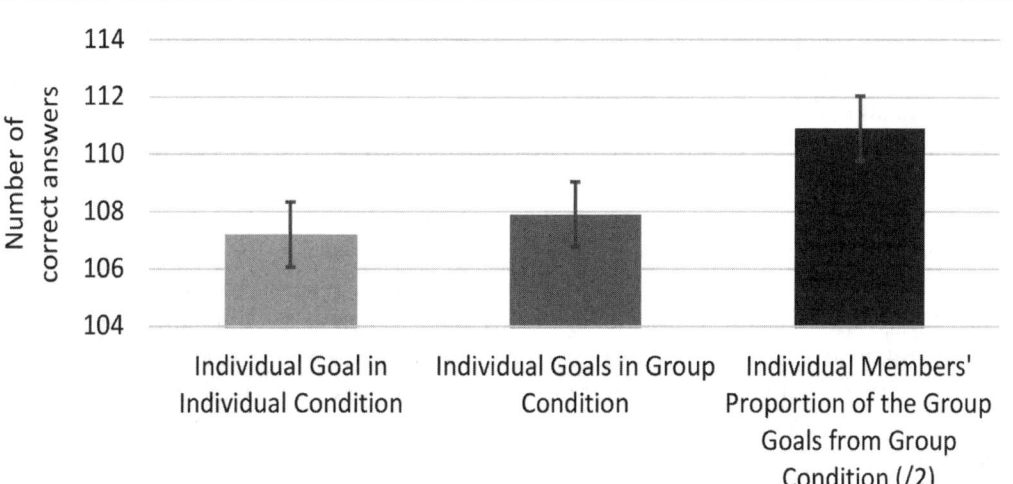

Source. "Effects of Goals and Feedback on Performance in Groups" by T. Matsui, T. Kakuyama, and M. L. Onglatco, 1987, *Journal of Applied Psychology*, 72, 407–415.

The late Rensis Likert, a psychologist at the University of Michigan, argued that group goal setting fosters a higher degree of cooperation and communication than individual goal setting, and thus is preferable ... When the tasks to be accomplished are highly interdependent, group goals are indeed appropriate. But this is unlikely to be the case where the jobs are not interdependent. (p. 37)

Applying this argument to sport, it may seem as if team goals are better than individual goals in sports such as basketball, soccer, ice hockey, field hockey—sports where a high degree of task cooperation and coordination are necessary.

There is evidence, however, that individuals set more difficult goals within groups where scores add together, such as wrestling, compared to the individual goals they would otherwise set. This was the conclusion by Matsui, Kakuyama, and Onglatco (1987), who compared performances on an additive task where participants set personal goals and then matched two sets of numbers, with participants typically matching over 100 pairings correctly per trial. Compared to an individual goal setting condition with only an individual outcome, half of the participants were assigned to pairs that involved setting a subsequent group goal. Performances were higher for the paired condition where participants averaged 114.9 correct responses, compared to 105.5 in the individual condition. Still, the authors were most interested in explaining this difference. As Exhibit 12.3 shows regarding goal difficulty, participants in both conditions set similar individual goals. Meanwhile, the authors did observe a difference when examining group goals—participants averaged collective goals of 221.8 correct responses. This means that that pairs of participants tended to set higher collective goals than what their individual goals would have combined into. Matsui et al. (1987) proposed that group tasks may lead members to set more challenging goals, and commit to those goals to a greater extent.

With this in mind, can teams combine group and individual goals in complementary ways? Within a meta-analysis of group goal setting effectiveness described earlier (Kleingeld et al.,

2011), a subset of 20 studies included interventions or designs where collective goals were set alongside individual goals for each member. This provided a natural opportunity to examine how different types of individual goals influence members' contributions to the group performance.

The researchers compared programs where individual goals were group-centric (i.e., ensuring individuals make the most substantial contribution to the group) compared with when they were individual-centric (i.e., maximizing individual development, independent from the group). When members set individual goals focused on individual development independent from the group, goal setting was negatively associated with group performance. By comparison, goal-setting interventions were beneficial when they focused on group-centric individual goals. In other words, group goal-setting interventions were only effective when individual goals were designed to build toward team goals. A core message seems to be to align group and individual goals.

Regardless of alignment between group and individual goals, a further path of social influence is that group members impact one another on the path to pursuing goals. Consider, for example, the following quote about two hall of fame professional hockey players on the same team:

> There was one time when [Bobby] Orr and Phil Esposito were running neck-and-neck for the scoring championship. Time and again Bobby would find himself in excellent scoring positions but instead of firing the puck he would look around for someone to pass to and often it was Phil. So, finally, I asked my defenseman Carol Vadnais what was going on with Bobby and why he was squandering potential points. "Don't you know?" he said. "He's trying not to get too far ahead of Phil for the scoring title." He risked the Art Ross Trophy [for the most scoring points] in order to make the team play better. (Cherry & Fischler, 1982, p. 163)

This is a picture of two athletes who chose to support one another's goal pursuit for the betterment of the group, even when in competition.

These shared goal pursuits are often overlooked. When we see an athlete crossing the finish line to mark a new world record in a running race, our narratives about this feature on the super-human physical prowess or the athletes' abilities at delaying gratification to complete another workout. We may overlook how self-regulation toward goals is inherently social. Was the athlete surrounded by teammates who completed every tough workout side-by-side? Or, did the athlete train on a team where every personal goal they met meant more tense and negative interactions with competing teammates?

The complex nature of goals within groups is challenging to observe because there are many goals pursued at any given time. This is where theory can come in: To help explain complicated processes so we can estimate how goal setting works within real life. Transactive goal dynamics theory (Fitzsimons, Finkel, & Vandellen, 2015) was designed to explain how relationships influence an individual's goal choices and pursuit. The theory focuses on how to predict the extent to which members of a group will influence one another's goal pursuit positively and negatively.

Key aspects of the theory are identified in Exhibit 12.4. *Transactive density* is an important aspect. When teammates experience a dense combination of shared goals, pursuits, and outcomes, they have an incentive to cooperate with others (Fitzsimons, Sackett, & Finkel, 2016). This is similar to the notion of interdependence, described in the cooperation chapter (Chapter 11).

Team Goals | 207

Exhibit 12.4. Core Aspects of Transactive Goal Pursuit Theory

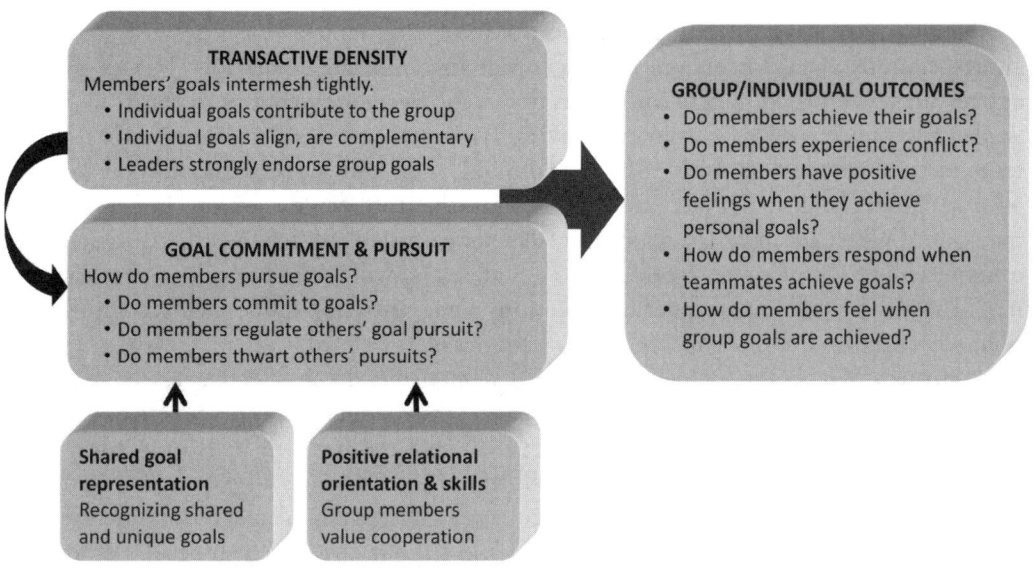

Transactive goals can help produce motivation and cooperation. However, it is also critical that members possess two antecedents that provide the foundation to commit to the group's goals and to help one another (Fitzsimons et al., 2015). First, *shared goal representations* are needed to support others' goal pursuits. Individuals often have poor representations of other group members' goals. If we do not know what our teammates hope to achieve during a season, we cannot help them pursue those goals. Second, members bring relational orientations and skills to their situation. Group members are more likely to be motivated by group goals and help others when they possess a positive personal belief about the importance of groups, and when their groups entail a culture supporting cooperation.

In sum, the key assumption of this theory is that developing many overlapping team and individual goals will link teammates' pursuits, produce positive goal pursuit behaviors, and lead to enhanced outcomes. The further key assumption is that members will be especially likely to commit to their own, and others', goals when they know and recognize the goals that their teammates are pursuing and when they possess a positive relational orientation. There is some empirical support for these propositions. Pearsall and Venkataramani (2015) conducted a small group study with students, where members had a shared team outcome, alongside conflicting individual goals. The study demonstrated that participants provided more resources to help teammates when they belonged to teams where members could accurately identify their teammate's most important objectives. The group functioned better when members were more knowledgeable about one-another's goals.

Applied Insight: Implementation Intentions

This chapter has produced numerous insights informing what a group leader may want to keep in mind when setting goals. There is information about what types of goals work well and how to align team and individual goals, alongside the value of promoting collective goals, including group members in goal-setting, and ensuring that members have shared representations of goals. A closing applied insight from this chapter involves leveraging a recent study to take the next step when goal setting.

Notably, goal setting can often fall short of producing action. This is because goals don't always indicate when, where, and how to engage in goal-related behaviors. Health psychology researchers revealed that an important next step after setting goals is to construct if-then implementation intentions (Gollwitzer, 1993). For instance, consider a team with a goal to respond to team adversity with positive communication and support. In addition to determining specific behaviors underpinning that goal, the team could create an implementation intention: "When coach calls a team timeout after a scoring run for the other team, Jill [the captain] will be the first one to call us into a huddle and will remind us of our two team values." The idea behind implementation intentions is that they help individuals recognize situations where they need to engage in specific behaviors.

Thürmer, Wieber, and Gollwitzer (2017) demonstrated the effectiveness of team and individual implementation intentions. The researchers conducted a study where participants completed physical tasks in a group setting; they held up medicine balls on a competitive task to see how long they could keep the ball in the air. Although all participants set goals, groups differed regarding whether participants set a collective implementation intention ("if our muscles hurt, then we will ignore the pain and tell ourselves: We can do it!") or an individual implementation intention.

The authors revealed that greater performances were achieved when implementation intentions were set and, furthermore, that collective implementation intentions were most effective. To explain these effects, the authors also reported that participants used more cooperative language—language focused on we or us—when they set collective implementation intentions. With these results in mind, maybe group goal setting should integrate relevant implementation intentions to identify when, where, and how goals will be pursued.

13

Communication and Coordination in Groups

"Effective teamwork begins and ends with communication." (Krzyzewski, 2020, para. 7)

With 4.7 seconds remaining in the first game of the 2018 NBA championships, George Hill of the Cleveland Cavaliers missed a free throw. The game was tied. J.R. Smith, his teammate, grabbed the rebound from the air, dribbled the ball beyond the three-point line, and attempted a last-moment pass to a teammate as time expired. Smith's decision elicited agony from teammates because it was a gaffe at an important moment. He could have attempted a shot or called his team's remaining timeout to plan a winning shot. Instead, the game went into overtime and the Cavaliers lost. Debates raged regarding what went wrong. Some individuals surmised that Smith was unaware that the game was tied or did not know the team had a timeout remaining. Smith distributed the blame across his team, saying about the moments before the time expired:

> And then I looked over at [LeBron James], and he looked like he was trying to call a timeout. So I stopped. And then the game was over." (McMenamin, 2018, para. 4)

Regardless of the account you accept, this play is a breakdown in team communication. Communication is the conduit for all efforts to work as a team. In addition to being the conduit for interdependent work on shared tasks, communication is also central for motivation and unity. As examples, goal setting could not be achieved without adequate communication,

> **Exhibit 13.1. Birds of a Feather Flock Together: Heterogeneity, Homogeneity, and Communication**
>
> Communication is shaped by variability in the personal characteristics of group members. Some characteristics rarely change such as age, sex, and religion, while other characteristics are changeable and include attitudes, knowledge, and beliefs. When members are similar on these characteristics, a group is homogeneous; heterogeneity involves diversity on such characteristics.
>
> One distinction relates to whether heterogeneity is distributed across members or is clustered into factions. Consider, for example, the difference between the two examples of heterogeneity in a professional rugby team: (a) members from varying geographical locations, so even using a common language is difficult, and (b) members from a country defined by conflict, where two clear member cliques are defined by competing belief systems. Principles described by Burgoon, Heston, and McCroskey (1974) relate to preferences for homogeneity in group communication:
>
> 1. *Communication patterns are normally homogeneous*: Individuals tend to communicate with others who are similar to them in attitudes and characteristics.
>
> 2. *Communication is more efficient among people who are homogeneous.* The more that team members are alike, the greater the likelihood that they will share common meanings in language, motives, and values.
>
> 3. *Effective communication leads to increased homogeneity.* When groups demonstrate effective communication, members adopt similar attitudes, knowledge, and beliefs.
>
> This is a cyclical relationship. Homogeneity increases the likelihood that communication will occur and that the communication will be effective. Members who communicate frequently tend to adopt similar attitudes and beliefs and share common perceptions.

and it would be challenging to develop or observe task and social cohesion without effective communication. The focus of this chapter is on understanding how communication and coordination intertwine and to identify strategies for optimizing team communication.

Describing Group Communication

Communicating entails sharing relevant information among team members. Although people often focus on verbal interactions, the giving or exchanging of information can be expressed in many different ways—verbal, nonverbal, written, and visual. As such, team communication is defined as a process that unfolds among members of a group through verbal and nonverbal interactions (Eys, Surya, & Benson, 2017).

Although this is a broad definition, others define communication using more precise aspects of interactions. For instance, researchers have defined communication more specifically as "a symbolic process by which two people, bound together in a relationship, provide each other with resources, or negotiate the exchange of resources" (Roloff, 1981, p. 30). This definition narrows the scope of communication considerably but adds a focus on its goal-oriented nature, the support and resources among team members, and inherent symbolism. In comparison, we may also focus on outcomes in terms of how communication is required to facilitate coordination as members pursue individual and team objectives.

Communication helps achieve goals in many contexts, but nevertheless follows somewhat predictable patterns across settings that are based on group characteristics. One important driver of communication patterns is group composition (see Chapter 5). Regarding the role of communication, Exhibit 13.1 focuses on how the heterogeneity and homogeneity of group member characteristics is an important consideration when considering the likelihood of effective communication.

Effective Group Communication

How do we know whether a team is communicating effectively? One subjective way is to consider whether members perceive their group's communication to be effective. Meanwhile, a contrasting and more objective way is to consider effective communication as that which supports coordination as members pursue goals.

Perceived Effectiveness

Team members provide a valuable barometer for communication effectiveness. This is because members recognize idiosyncrasies and nuances that outsiders may overlook and can draw from communication that may be difficult to observe—such as social interactions away from competition. Similarly, if we are interested in outcomes like motivation, then athletes' perceptions of the group are most relevant.

To measure athlete perceptions of communication in sport groups, Sullivan and Feltz (2003) developed the Scale for Effective Communication in Sports Teams. This questionnaire assesses four distinct components of verbal and nonverbal communication among team members. One dimension, referred to as *acceptance,* reflects communication practices that promote inclusion and support of team members such as honesty and openness in discussions. A second dimension, *distinctiveness,* refers to verbal and nonverbal communications promoting the "we" mentality of the group. Distinctiveness is most evident in the ways that groups construct verbal or physical communications that are only understood by group members, like nicknames or slang. For instance, when one coauthor of this book [Evans] conducted exercises with youth sport teams to identify their team identity, athletes used acronyms, quotes, and references from songs or movies they enjoyed. None of these phrases made sense to Evans, being an outsider, but they seemed to unite members through shared experiences and values.

The remaining two dimensions represent communication that is oriented around conflict. Communicating in a destructive fashion to deal with problems, such as shouting or name-calling, is reflective of the *negative conflict* dimension. These behaviors represent the types of tense situations commonly recognized as conflict, even by outsiders to a group. Positive conflict communications represent nonemotional and constructive attempts to rectify problems within the group. Examples might include how members express when they are upset and where they direct their communications toward compromise. Positive conflict, in some ways, is a misnomer because these behaviors manage and reduce conflict in constructive ways.

It seems intuitive that developing team members' abilities to communicate in an accepting, positive fashion, while promoting distinctiveness and reducing negative conflict will result in greater integration of athletes and better team performance. This presumption was tested with youth soccer players by McLaren and Spink (2018). Using athlete surveys, the authors reported associations between these communication dimensions and group cohesion. Task and social cohesion were both associated with conflict, in that athletes from cohesive teams reported more positive conflict and lower negative conflict. There were also differences in task and social cohesion regarding associations with acceptance and distinctiveness. Whereas higher acceptance communication was a marker of teams higher in *task* cohesion, higher distinctiveness communication was a marker of teams higher on *social* cohesion. McLaren and Spink (2018) emphasized the value of fostering positive communication to promote cohesion.

Interestingly, however, there are some (admittedly rare) instances where communication patterns that are outwardly negative or offensive might be seen as members to produce positive consequences, as the following quote illustrates:

> Even as Duke was winning its second straight NCAA title, in 1992, Christian Laettner mocked Bobby Hurley, sneered at Grant Hill, and hazed Cherokee Parks. They each responded on the court by doing something to repudiate Laettner's harsh judgment of them. 'When Laettner yelled at somebody, people said, 'Oh, they have friction,'' says Blue Devil coach Mike Krzyzewski. 'Baloney. We had communication. Friction is when no one says anything.' (Wolff, 1995, para. 35)

Beyond being a case where the conflicting forms of communication were effective, this also demonstrates how group insiders may interpret communication differently from outsiders—an example of distinctiveness.

Communication and Coordination

You only need to call to mind one brief instance of missed connections to understand how effective communication can help when coordinating efforts. For instance, imagine a volleyball play where two teammates see a serve floating down through the air, as both players exclaim "my ball"—then hesitate—before watching the ball hit the floor between them.

Experiences like this happen in everyday life. Think about the last time you walked down the street with a friend. It is likely that soon after walking together you developed a shared understanding as you navigated obstacles on the sidewalk. For example, one person may dominate regarding who steps in front of a fire hydrant or fall back to let a stranger pass through. Now, consider the last time that you walked with a group of ten people or more. It is likely there were instances where you could move as a whole but, likely, the collective fractured into subgroups before long. Some walked faster than others. Perhaps some members gambled at the crosswalk as the lights changed and continued on while others—the cautious ones—trailed and glared on as the remainder of their group walked away on the other side of the traffic stop.

These situations refer to coordination, or the integration of humans or actions to achieve a larger function. In teams, this refers to when people must integrate their actions interdependently for a limited period of time around a common function (Gorman, 2014). For the volleyball players, this was arranging their actions to defend the serve and return the ball. When specifying the processes required to coordinate in groups, Eccles and Tenenbaum (2004) distinguished communications based on whether they take place before, during, or after competition. This perspective is important because it reveals the many ways that members must coordinate, whether in the heat of action or long before a competitive season begins.

An important tenet of the framework developed by Eccles and Tanenbaum (2004) relates to the role of communication to develop *shared knowledge* among teammates, which is essential for coordination. Shared knowledge is evident in two ways. First, static attitudes and knowledge leading into performance are important for members to have a collective idea regarding how, when, and why members should work together. Second, the more dynamic form of shared knowledge about shifting environments is also contingent on communication. This form is evident in a dynamic sport like field hockey, where defending an offensive possession requires team members to develop shared knowledge of what is transpiring (e.g., where opposing team members are oriented; when an opponent will pass or shoot).

There are, however, different ways of approaching the question of how effective groups produce shared knowledge. We will consider two group phenomena that have a substantial impact on shared knowledge and, in turn, group performance.

Transactive Memory and Shared Mental Models

It is rarely efficient, or possible, for members of groups to share *all* knowledge. Instead, groups create systems where members defer to one another. Transactive memory refers to the different pockets of knowledge within a group. Specifically, a transactive memory system in a group refers to: (a) smaller pockets of information that are uniquely held by each member, and (b) each members' knowledge pertaining to who-knows-what (Ren & Argote, 2011). This distinction is evident in Exhibit 13.2.

Transactive memory systems are efficient because they represent a group mind that all members draw from. Consider, for example, how a coaching staff of a football team might specialize their preparation for a game by organizing the scouting report for the opposing team so that each coach develops knowledge about a subset of opposing players. In such a case, the

Exhibit 13.2. Depiction of Transactive Memory in a Three-Member Group

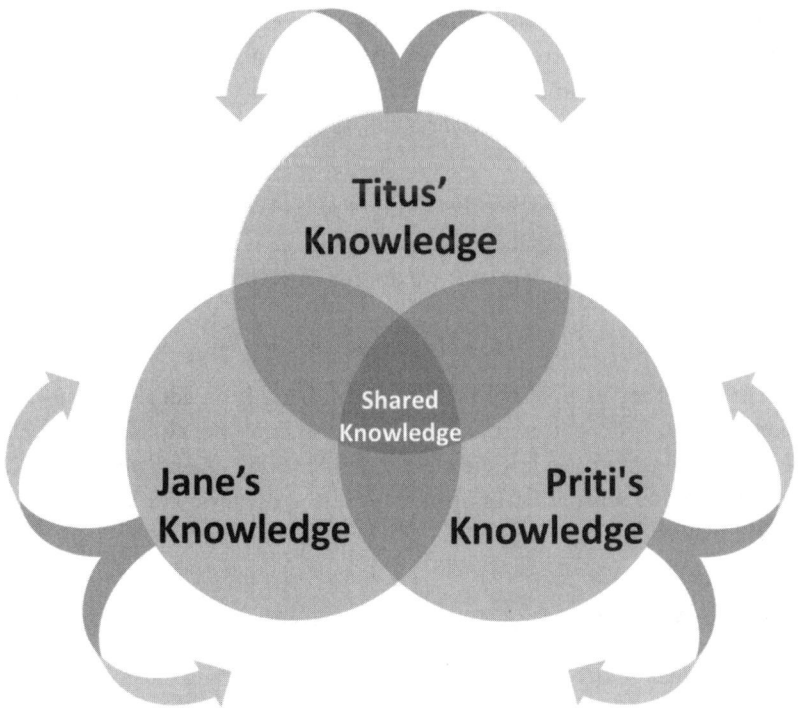

Note. Each member is within a circle that represents their personal task-specific knowledge. The dark-shaded and overlapping aspects of their circles represent knowledge shared among members. Importantly, each member also has knowledge about what other members know, termed transactive memory, reflected in the curved arrows. For example, Jane has arrows directed toward Priti and Titus to reflect her understanding of what they know.

offensive coordinator may not need to recall all information about the other team. If he or she wants to anticipate how some players from the opposing defense may respond to a specific call (e.g., defensive line), it would just entail asking the coach with knowledge about that group of opposing players (e.g., offensive line coach).

Transactive memory can also break down. Transactive memory systems fail when members' knowledge of who knows what begins to weaken, or when members communicate poorly (Ren & Argote, 2011). In the example above, perhaps the offensive coordinator forgot which coach to ask for specific insights, or some coaches presumed that important information they possessed was already known by the coordinator. In breakdowns of transactive memory systems, decisions by core individuals do not incorporate all relevant knowledge.

Another way of considering shared knowledge is in terms of *shared mental models*. A shared mental model refers to members' understanding about what the group is achieving, how it achieves these goals, and what it means to be a member (Mathieu, Heffner, Goodwin, Salas, & Cannon-Bowers, 2000). In this perspective, all athletes are likely to develop mental models regarding their actions in a team—but only some teams will have effective mental models that all members share. Teams that hold effective shared mental models communicate efficiently and anticipate their teammates' behavior.

When we watch expert teams with strong mental models, it may even seem that they can coordinate their actions without any need for communication! One example of an effective shared mental model in sport is the Tiki-Taka style of play in football. This style emerged within Spanish teams that experienced success during the 1990s and 2000s. The Tiki-Taka style of play is evident when members are focused on maintaining possession of the ball and is commonly noticeable through frequent short passes within small clusters of players. When discussing the style, players commented on the approach as a philosophy that allows them to anticipate one another, as described by player Xabi Alonso:

> We have the same idea as each other. Keep the ball, create movement around and off the ball, get in the spaces to cause danger.... We have been playing like that for the last three years. It's what we do. It seems to work. (Ladyman, 2010, para. 5)

We cannot answer whether or not the Tiki-Taka approach is an ideal playing approach. It is actually likely that it is no better than other dominant approaches. However, this is an instance where coaches and group leaders clearly defined their mental model and effectively communicated this model with athletes. This created the conditions where members understood the on-field play of their group.

Downfalls of Group Communication

Although groups produce many great performances and ideas, they create new kinds of challenges that harm communication. Communication can be used in groups to exchange information or create misunderstandings, to reduce conflicts or accelerate the growth of problems, to test new ideas or produce conformity. Most research regarding the downfalls of group communication focus on tasks where members are required to make a decision. This evidence base may not be relevant to all group tasks within sport. However, this research has identified problems that can arise in how members of groups manipulate messages during discussion.

Groupthink

Early perspectives on failures during group communication emerged through research involving *groupthink*. Janis (1972) defined groupthink as "a mode of thinking that people engage in when they are deeply involved in a cohesive in-group, when members' strivings for unanimity override their motivation to realistically appraise alternative courses of action" (p. 8). Groupthink relates to an important weakness with decision-making in groups: the tendency for group members to experience normative pressures to conform (Miranda, 1994).

Examples of groupthink abound in many contexts of group work. One tragic example is the explosion of the Challenger space shuttle, in 1985, because faulty components failed during launch. During investigations of the incident, it became evident that several engineers had noted issues with the components but, later, approved the launch. In follow-up reports, representatives of the National Space Agency (NASA) attributed many of the errors in decision-making to groupthink.

Janis' (1972, 1982; see Exhibit 13.3) eight symptoms describe the nature of groupthink. The eight symptoms can be clustered within two dimensions, focused on (a) holding views that

Exhibit 13.3. The Antecedents and Symptoms of Groupthink

Aspect of Groupthink	Description
Antecedents	
Group cohesion	High levels of cohesion could create pressures toward conformity, creating motivation against promoting a dissenting view.
Insulation	Members have very weak ties with and awareness of external groups, and may not consult with external experts.
Autocratic and impartial leadership	Groupthink may occur when leaders actively advocate adopting their favored solution, and not questioning their leadership.
Homogeneous members	Groups composed of persons similar in backgrounds and values may produce decisions with limited diversity or creativity.
Nature of group task	Some tasks may produce groupthink. Crisis or time-limited decision-making, for instance, may promote groupthink.
Symptoms	
Illusion of invulnerability	A highly optimistic picture is presented to the group.
Collective efforts to rationalize	Alternate opinions and warnings are ignored.
Belief in the group's inherent 'good'	The group is assumed to possess an inherent superiority over the opposition.
Stereotyped views of the opposition	The opposition is viewed in stereotypical terms.
Direct pressures to conform	Pressure is brought to bear against members who present alternative views.
Self-censorship	Members censor themselves to produce a unanimous group position.
Shared illusions of unanimity	Members believe that the group position is universally shared.
Emergence of self-appointed mindguards	Members protect the group from adverse information.

Source. Victims of Groupthink by I. L. Janis, 1972, Boston MA: Houghton-Mifflin.

are biased regarding the group, and (b) protecting those views against alternatives. First, groups demonstrating groupthink form a biased view that favors their group relative to others, whether that be in terms of ability, competence, morality, or other features. A historical sport example reflects this aspect within the eight-game 1972 Summit Series between Canada and the Soviet Union, described earlier in this book (See Chapter 3: Group Development, for complete description). Despite the Canadians' presumption that the series would be an easy win, Team Canada needed to win the 6th, 7th, and 8th games on USSR soil to win the series. In the book *Hockey Night in Moscow*, Ludwig (1972) described Team Canada's unchallenged assumptions about their dominance. In relation to the *illusion of invulnerability*, Ludwig described the way that mindsets leading into the competition obscured the evaluations of Soviet players' skillsets: "[Scouts] brought back only good news, nothing calculated to get Team Canada stampeding into midnight practice sessions. Only one player on the USSR could make the NHL" (p. 230).

The last four symptoms relate to how the group promotes alignment with dominant group perspectives. One *Time* magazine editorial attributed this aspect of groupthink to the tragic outcomes in the Penn State University child abuse scandal. In this scandal, an assistant coach for the Penn State football team (Jerry Sandusky) preyed upon youth through his role over a span of 15 years—before being brought to justice in 2012. Although some contested the conclusions of legal and NCAA investigations into how much information was held by the head coach and University president, the editorial focused on the responses of leaders when they were made aware of claims regarding Sandusky's behavior. Within a highly insular leadership group, at an institution that prided itself in moral behavior, the group discredited claims:

> The outsider status of Sandusky's child victims was most likely exacerbated by the fact that many were poor. The e-mails detailed in the Freeh report show that this particular insider group managed to twist logic to the point where they thought that it was more "humane" to cover up the repeated allegations of Sandusky's abuse than to report them to the police. (Cohen & DeBenedet, 2012, para. 3)

This description of the series of events highlights symptoms like *stereotyped views about the outgroup* and *self-appointed mindguards*, which led to inaction.

How do these problematic processes emerge? Janis (1972) focused on a sequence whereby antecedents produce a drive for concurrence seeking. Regarding antecedents (See Exhibit 13.3), Janis (1982) argued that the likelihood of groupthink increased in groups that were insulated from outgroups, with autocratic leadership styles, homogeneous members, and in specific types of tasks. Above all, Janis (1982) argued that cohesive teams produced groupthink at greater rates, increasing incentives to conform. Groups demonstrating this pattern were expected to demonstrate the eight symptoms of groupthink and, in turn, deficits in decision-making, often producing poor decisions. Examples of deficits include an incomplete survey of alternatives, selective bias in processing information, and failure to provide contingency plans. In other words, a group engaged in groupthink does not obtain all the information necessary or misinterprets some of the information they receive.

Decision-Making Flaws in Groups

Janis's (1982) depiction of groupthink was a critical step forward in understanding group decision-making. Many of his theoretical propositions align with subsequent findings in research, including the prevalence of such decision-making deficits as well as the symptoms of groupthink. Nevertheless, there has also been progression in understanding since the time when groupthink was initially described. First, we now recognize that Janis's (1982) antecedents were likely too narrow. It is probable that simply making decisions in a group produces pressure to conform—not only in cohesive, insular, and homogeneous groups. Second, we now recognize a wider range of deficits in decision-making that harm group decisions beyond those attributed to groupthink.

First, researchers have identified that groups exacerbate or magnify many of the heuristics and fallacies that harm individual decisions. The planning fallacy is one example. The planning fallacy refers to individuals' tendency to rely on an optimistic bias regarding how a proposed task will be completed, even though we often have contradictory knowledge and experience. People repeatedly underestimate task difficulty or the time required for completion, even when every past experience with those tasks signals they will take longer or will be more challenging. To examine the role of groups, Buehler, Messervey, and Griffin (2005) asked participants to make predictions about the time needed to complete a task and compared the estimations of participants making those predictions alone with those making them after a group discussion. They found that participants in both conditions showed the planning fallacy, but that those in groups estimated less time required to complete the task compared to the individual condition. Furthermore, this group bias was explained by the tendency for group discussions to avoid negative scenarios where the group would face challenges and, instead, a tendency to focus on positive future scenarios where everything went perfectly. Many of the issues that cloud individual decisions are worse within group communication.

There are also decision-making issues that are unique to groups, over and above groupthink. Some generalized problems with group discussions include: (a) leveling, in which a communication is reduced and simplified, (b) ordering, in which the beginning and the end of a communication are better retained than the middle portion, (c) sharpening, in which a communication is reinterpreted by emphasizing some components and deemphasizing others, and (d) assimilating, in which the meaning of a communication is shifted so that it matches a previous important message.

Although these are natural patterns of group discussion, there are additional issues that may emerge in groups. One long-studied process within group decision-making is *group polarization*, which represents the shift that occurs in the attitudes of individual members following group interaction and communication.

Group Polarization

Groups tend to adopt a more extreme position (either risky or cautious) than the sum of positions initially held by the individual members. This pattern has captivated researchers for decades because it is unexpected; holding all else constant, one might expect that members would land on the 'average' among their responses. Instead, members often shift. This means that in groups where members are already leaning toward risk, group discussions often produce a *risky shift* where the group decision is even riskier than the option favored by members before discussions. When members enter discussions with a predisposition toward caution, however, a *cautious shift* will be more likely. Risky and cautious shifts are depicted in Exhibit 13.4. Notice in the exhibit how being mildly above (or below) a neutral point of view pushed the group decision after discussion to be more risky or cautious.

Much of the early research in the area of group polarization focused on the tendency for groups to adopt riskier positions than individuals. A major contribution to this research came

Exhibit 13.4. The Group-Polarization Hypothesis

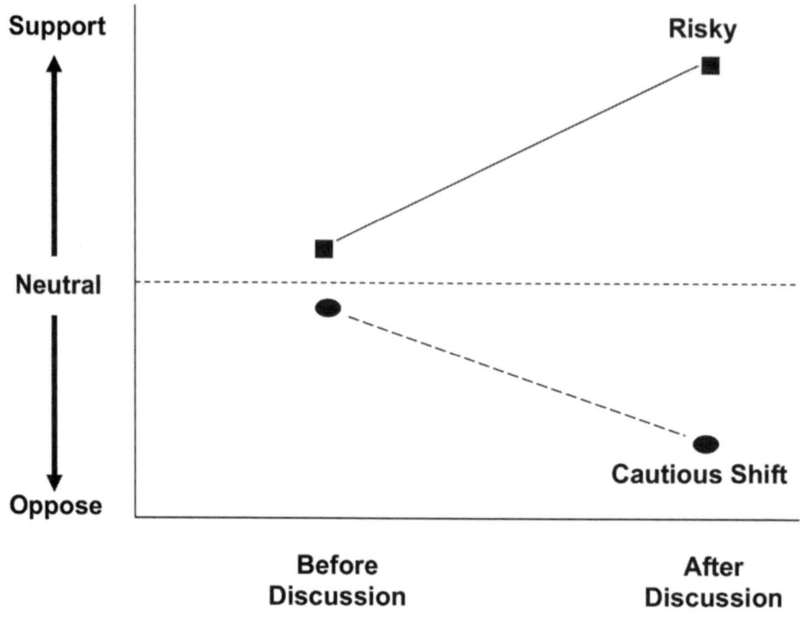

[Figure: A graph with vertical axis labeled Support (top), Neutral (middle, dashed line), Oppose (bottom), and horizontal axis showing "Before Discussion" and "After Discussion". A solid line rises from near Neutral to "Risky" (upper right). A dashed line descends from near Neutral to "Cautious Shift" (lower right).]

from the Choice Dilemma Inventory (Kogan & Wallach, 1964). This inventory consists of 12 real-life dilemmas in which a character is confronted with a choice between two alternatives. One is risky, the other more conservative. The decision that an individual (or group) must come to is what advice to give this central character. One of the dilemmas that deals with a sport situation is as follows:

> Mr. D. is the captain of College X's football team. College X is playing its traditional rival, College Y, in the final game of the season. The game is in its final seconds, and Mr. D's team, College X, is behind in the score. College X has time to run one more play. Mr. D., the captain, must decide whether it would be best to settle for a tie score with a play that would be almost certain to work or, on the other hand, should he try a more complicated and risky play that could bring victory if it succeeded, but defeat if not. Imagine that you are advising Mr. D. Listed below are several probabilities or odds that the risky play will work. Please check the lowest probability that you would consider acceptable for the risky play to be attempted. (Kogan & Wallach, 1964, p. 257)

Participants in the role of an advisor are required to select the minimum probable level for success that would lead them to advise the character to take the riskier but more attractive alternative. Options are presented on a scale varying from very unlikely chance of being successful (10% chance) to very likely of being successful (100% chance). To examine the effect of group discussion, participants initially respond to the problems independently before entering the group discussion and (finally) completing the scale again. A risky or cautious shift was identified by examining differences in responses before and after discussion.

How realistic are the dilemmas and the decisions? Interestingly, on New Year's Day in 1988, life imitated science. In the Sugar Bowl, the Auburn Tigers football team, trailing 16–13, had the ball on the Syracuse Orangemen's 13 yard-line with four seconds left in the game. Auburn's coach, Pat Dye, was faced the same dilemma as Mr. D, the Kogan and Wallach character—kick a field goal for a tie or run a play from scrimmage in an attempt to win. Dye chose to kick. And, it was successful. Sportswriter Douglas Looney described the situation following the game:

> Stoney-faced and sullen, Auburn coach Pat Dye tried to defend his nonsporting decision to play for a tie against undefeated Syracuse in the Sugar Bowl: 'My decision was not to get beat.' Not to get beat? No coach worth his whistle ought to think like this…'Our guys were not real happy,' said [Kicker Win] Lyle. 'They really didn't like it when I went out there. They were screaming that they wanted to go for the touchdown …' Afterward, the more Syracuse coach Dick MacPherson thought about what had happened, the madder he got. 'Why didn't Dye ask his players what they wanted to do?' he said, fuming. Obviously, coaches don't ask their players to make such decisions, but MacPherson was angry beyond logic. (Looney, 1988, p. 22)

From the accounts presented, it seems that the Auburn players endorsed the riskier alternative. As a group, they probably would have advocated trying for the touchdown and a win. It is possible, however, that asking the athletes individually would have led to favoring the conservative field goal decision.

Beyond understanding a tendency for polarization, review articles involving group polarization help understand when and why group polarization emerges (Isenberg, 1986). To reduce the tendency toward polarization, it is important to explain why people adopt the views of other members and, especially, why these collectives of individuals are drawn beyond the average response of all members. Burnstein and Vinokur (1977) reported that two dominant explanations focus on persuasive arguments and social comparisons, with subsequent research revealing that both arguments hold merit (Isenberg, 1986).

The *social comparison process* includes the premise that individuals are motivated to perceive themselves, and to be seen by others, in a socially desirable light. To the extent that group discussions bring out the dominant values in the group, individuals compare themselves against that standard and adopt a position that is *at least* as risky or as cautious (Burnstein & Vinokur, 1977). Meanwhile, the basis for the *persuasive arguments* approach is the belief that individuals try to process information in a logical, rational fashion. They compare their views with the views of other group members; they weigh the evidence, and then go with the best option. In a group discussion, arguments in favor of the dominant position are often stronger and more frequent.

Beyond these two approaches, there are additional tendencies that promote polarization described by Sieber and Ziegler (2019). First, diffusion of responsibility may also play a role because members feel less accountable for their decisions. Second, it is plausible that members holding riskier opinions will try to make their views heard to a greater extent. Third, there is evidence that it is *easier* to rely on the decisions made by others. Notably, when members of groups are tired or depleted, they will be even more likely to shift (Sieber & Ziegler, 2019).

Combined with the social comparison and persuasive arguments approaches, there is likely no single pathway toward group polarization. There are likely numerous mechanisms that combine in ways that ultimately create a tendency for polarization.

Enhancing Group Communication

Group communication is required but entails pitfalls. Below, we recommend evidence-based strategies to enhance communication. Our recommendations are drawn from earlier team-building descriptions (e.g., Zander, 1982; Yukelson, 1993), along with descriptions regarding enhancing communication (Eys et al., 2017). When considering these strategies, it should be kept in mind that these strategies may pertain to numerous contexts, including training, during performance tasks, and following performance (i.e., debriefing), as well as the spectrum of social interactions in-between.

Creating a Positive Environment

Enhancing the communication in groups could involve promoting a positive and team-oriented environment. Considering the value of acceptance and distinctiveness messages in sport teams, group leaders may try to speed up the emergence of these kinds of communication by developing positive nicknames and unique sayings or references to group membership. These positive approaches could be more comprehensive as well, such as providing opportunities for members to socialize and become comfortable with each other. A supportive environment can also be fostered, so that differences in opinion or values can be identified and discussed among members.

Proactive Approaches

Eys et al. (2017) emphasized the value in ensuring that members develop skills to engage in proactive communication. Focusing on providing and accepting feedback in particular, strategies include providing support for teammates, actively listening to one another, and making effort to provide feedback. Similarly, environments can be designed to enable proactive discussion by valuing diversity among members, avoiding negative cliques, and acknowledging conflict as an important and manageable component of the group (Eys et al., 2017). When groups encounter conflict, it may be useful to schedule a specific time to discuss issues that is private and free from distraction, and ensuring each member has opportunities to speak and listen. These sessions could use a trained facilitator like a sport psychologist. Such dedicated sessions to manage conflict are valuable, although constructive communication should also be embedded in the group environment.

Strategic Ways to Convey Information

Group members should use strategies to disseminate information efficiently. When a member is conveying information, Eys et al. (2017) emphasized that it may be useful to (a) use varying sensory modes (e.g., discussing team strategy verbally, followed by simulations), (b) reiterate messages numerous times and from several messengers, and (c) explain why decisions are made to provide rationale.

Double-Checking Decisions to Account for Biases

Many of the types of biases in individual and group decision-making, like groupthink, can be managed by putting checks in place that reevaluate decisions. Among these include (a) brainstorming a large number of alternatives to decisions before selecting a course of action, (b) reconsidering rejected alternatives, by recalling alternatives that were rejected earlier for any advantages that might have been overlooked, and (c) soliciting the input of experts outside the group that bring a different perspective. To work these types of processes within the fabric of group decisions, a common approach is to identify one group member to take on a role as the devil's advocate by challenging dominant views.

Training in Group Situations

Shared experiences are critical to construct shared mental models and foster transactive memory systems. Especially when groups have only a limited period of time together, group leaders should provide opportunities to ensure that the team experiences the spectrum of challenges they could face during performance. Often, this entails simulations during task-based challenges that are novel, to help team members develop a mental model to guide their interactions in situations that they had not experienced before. A related strategy may be cross-training, where members attempt performing teammates' roles. Simulations and other shared experiences like cross-training should be deliberately structured as learning experiences for members to benefit from them. One important recommendation is to include debriefing sessions for members to discuss key messages after the activity is complete.

Design Transactive Memory Systems

Group leaders can directly prompt the formation of transactive memory. Organizational charts that describe the role of each member and their requisite knowledge, as a form of reference manual, are common in organizations to prompt transactive memory. These charts could be particularly useful in large sport organizations like college sport programs, large youth sport clubs, or professional sport organizations.

14

Cohesion in Sport Groups

After Canada's basketballers thumped the Australians 90–70 in just their third exhibition game, a result many weren't expecting, head coach Nick Nurse talked at great length about the quick evolution of his team. 'Chemistry is an elusive thing,' Nurse said. "I'm happy we've been able to get some.' The coach would know. He's spent most of his coaching career (since the age of 24) trying to find the perfect recipe for creating on-court magic between the players he's guiding. More often than not, Nurse has been able to find the right ingredients. (Heroux, 2019, para. 1–3)

Across media platforms (e.g., television, internet), a variety of terms are used when commentators try to convey the idea that a team is cohesive. These include 'highly united', 'very close knit', 'sticking together', 'great teamwork', 'like a family', and 'chemistry'. All of these terms and expressions do reflect the construct of *cohesion*; the word is derived from the Latin word *cohaesus,* which means to cleave or stick together. In his comprehensive review of cohesion, Dion (2000) pointed out

> … in physics and chemistry, cohesion refers to the force(s) binding molecules of a substance together. In psychology and the social sciences, a similar metaphor applies, with the term cohesion or cohesiveness describing the process(es) keeping a small group or larger social entity (e.g., military unit, business organization, ethnic group, or society) together and united to varying degrees. (p. 7)

The sticking together of group members is not literal. Cohesion reflects the strength of the social- and task-related bonds among the members of the group. It is so fundamental to the development and maintenance of groups that it has been suggested that "there can be no such thing as a noncohesive group; it is a contradiction in terms. If a group exists it is to some extent cohesive" (Donnelly, Carron, & Chelladurai, 1978, p. 7). Obviously, however, different groups can vary in their level of cohesiveness—in the strength of social or task-related bonds that are present. Furthermore, whereas the quotes above denote a mystical nature—with coaches as alchemists—cohesion is somewhat more predictable and can be systematically fostered. To make sense out of group cohesiveness and understand its impact on team effectiveness and other important team and personal factors, it is necessary first to examine its nature.

Definitions of Cohesion in Social and Work Groups

The study of group cohesion has had a long, rich tradition in such areas as social psychology, military psychology, organizational psychology, counseling psychology, and educational psychology. It is not surprising that authors in these various disciplines define cohesion in slightly different ways. These definitional differences reflect perspectives on this complex construct and illustrate the difficulty in defining any theoretical construct—which by definition is an abstraction and, therefore, not directly observable. The variability in cohesion definitions exist, in part, because (a) there are so many vantage points from which one can consider the unitedness of a group, (b) there are several ways that unitedness can manifest, and (c) there are many goals or objectives that cohesion may contribute toward.

In what is now considered a classic definition, Festinger, Schachter, and Back (1963) defined *cohesion* as the total field of forces causing members to remain in the group. They also proposed that there are two general types of forces: the attractiveness of the group (e.g., social and affiliative aspects of a group) and means control (e.g., task, performance, and productive concerns of the group). In other words, attractiveness of the group is reflected in how the group has aspects—like close friendships or highly-engaging training sessions—that are satisfying for their own sake. Meanwhile, means control refers to the ways that the group can be a means toward achieving goals—like developing one's skillset, being paid well, or affiliating with a prestigious group. The Festinger et al. (1963) viewpoint focuses on the impetus underlying participation and involvement with the group—the primary reason why individuals join a group. This is illustrated in Exhibit 14.1a. If a large number of forces draw an individual to

Exhibit 14.1. Two Perspectives on Group Cohesiveness

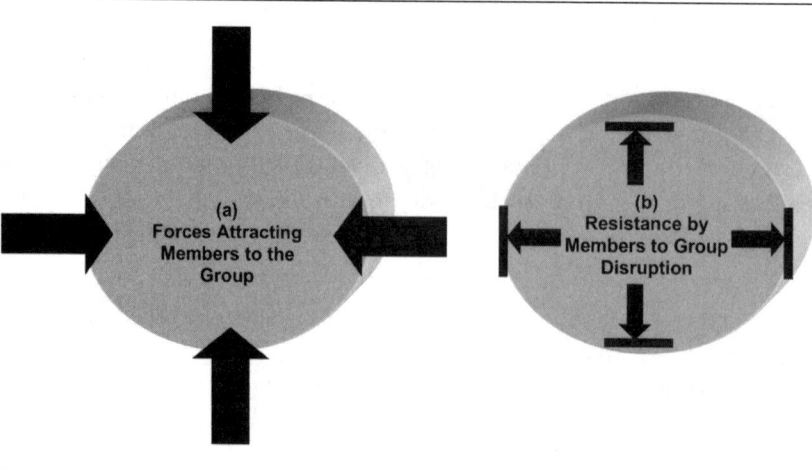

a group and each of these forces is strong, its attractiveness is high. Consequently, the level of cohesiveness would be high.

Gross and Martin (1952) felt that this definition suffered from the fact that it focuses on individual members (i.e., the forces that attract each to the group) rather than the collective itself. Thus, they suggested that it makes more sense to define cohesion as *the resistance of the group to disruptive forces*. This perspective is illustrated in Exhibit14.1b. From the perspective of the Gross and Martin (1952) definition, if a college rugby team is highly cohesive, it would be resilient. Members will be able to thrive, even when the group faces challenges arising from unfavorable events such as losing games, receiving criticism in the media, having a verbally abusive coach, or possessing poor training facilities. The cohesiveness that binds the group into an entity would help it resist pressures that can tear it apart.

Definition of Cohesion in Sport Teams

Carron, Brawley, and Widmeyer (1998) reasoned that in order to understand cohesiveness—the factors that draw members to the team and/or help the group to resist disruptive forces—it is necessary to understand the team's goals and objectives. Every group has reasons for existing and these are woven into its development and maintenance. For example, social clubs, work crews, delinquent gangs, fraternity basketball teams, counseling groups, army platoons, and professional sport teams are all different. But, they are also all similar in the sense that they exhibit cohesiveness. The members of these different groups stick together because they all endorse some underlying common purpose. An outsider who is unaware of this purpose would be unable to comprehend the bases for the cohesiveness. Similarly, an insider (a group member) who either is unaware, unappreciative, or unaccepting of the bases for cohesiveness would either choose to (or be forced to) discontinue involvement with the group.

When they advanced a definition for cohesion in sport teams, Carron et al. (1998) explicitly took the team's goals and objectives into account. As such, cohesion is defined as an emergent state that "is reflected in the tendency for a group to stick together and remain united in the pursuit of its instrumental objectives and/or for the satisfaction of member affective needs" (Carron et al., 1998, p. 213).

The value of this definition is that it serves to highlight four main characteristics of cohesion. One characteristic of cohesion that must be kept in mind in order to fully understand the construct is that it is multidimensional. What this means is that there are numerous factors that cause any group to stick together and remain united and these factors can vary from group to group.

A second important characteristic of cohesion is that it is dynamic. Cohesion in a team can change over time and the predominant factor(s) binding the team together early in its history may or may not be critical when the team is well developed. A quote from Juergen Klopp, manager of Liverpool in the English Premier League, illustrates the dynamism of group cohesion:

> Now we know so much about each other, now we like each other, now we have better times with each other in private and on the football pitch. Now we need to stay angry with the rest of the world, we need to stay aggressive … At the beginning of the season you don't have a lot of laughter in the dressing room. Now when we eat it's like "come on, please, settle." They are fantastic boys, they all like each other, a few jokes … keep this going without getting soft. (Sridhar, 2018, para. 4–5)

A third characteristic of cohesion, one that was discussed above, is that it is *instrumental* in nature. That is, all teams form for a purpose. Sport teams, work groups, and military units form for instrumental reasons. Even groups that may be considered purely social in nature have an instrumental basis for their formation. Thus, for example, acquaintances who decide to form a social club to develop or maintain better friendships are cohering for instrumental reasons.

Fourth, cohesion also has an affective dimension. Social relationships among group members may be present in a group initially and/or they might evolve over time. Even in groups like work crews, professional sport teams, or military units, social cohesion perceptions emerge—whether from the repeated experiences of working together on tasks, or when interacting in social ways that don't relate to the group's task.

The Measurement of Cohesion in Sport Teams

Another way of understanding the nature of cohesion is to examine the approaches taken to measure it—the operational definitions used. Measurement helps to give precise meaning to a phenomenon that is theoretical—that cannot be readily observed physically. When we develop measures, we also provide a common ground for people to reliably describe the phenomenon and can test our presumptions about which aspects of an operational definition are critical for its description.

Historical Perspectives

Numerous attempts have been made to measure interpersonal relations and/or cohesion in sport teams. Fiedler (1954), working with high school basketball teams, assessed interpersonal relationships within the team through measures of *assumed similarity*. That is, athletes initially indicated which statement in a block of statements was most and least characteristic of them on a personal level. Then, the process was repeated, except that each athlete used the statements to rate the person with whom he cooperated best and the person with whom he cooperated most poorly.

Both Myers (1962) and McGrath (1962) carried out research with recreational rifle teams at the University of Illinois. Myers (1962) assessed relationships within the teams by having team members indicate their esteem for teammates, their perception of their acceptance by teammates, and the degree to which they attributed failures to themselves, their teammates, or the other team.

In McGrath's (1962) study, he used one sociometric question and four behavioral items to assess interpersonal relationships. For the sociometric question, the individual indicated if any of his teammates had helped him stay calm and relaxed. For the four behavioral items, the individual rated the degree to which each teammate was warm, standoffish, disruptive, and attentive.

A slightly different approach to the study of group dynamics in sport teams during that period was taken by Stogdill (1964). During the six home games of the Ohio State football team, he had four judges sitting at different places in the stadium rate how integrated the team was on each play.

From a historical perspective, the cohesion inventory that had the most significant early effect on research in sport psychology is the Martens, Landers, and Loy (1972) Sport

Cohesiveness Questionnaire (SCQ). It was the first inventory to have a specific sport orientation and, possibly because of this, it stimulated considerable research on issues associated with cohesion in sport teams. The SCQ contains seven items asking athletes to rate friendships with teammates, personal power or influence, enjoyment, closeness, teamwork, sense of belonging, and perceived value of membership.

Whereas some researchers combined these items to create an index of group cohesion (e.g., Carron & Chelladurai, 1981), others focused on subsets of items regarding individual-to-individual attraction, individual-to-group relationships, and group-as-a-whole perceptions (Arnold & Straub, 1972). The individual-to-individual attraction subscale was comprised of friendship and power items (two items) and involved team members' perceptions of their relationships with every other group member (e.g., Arnold & Straub, 1972). Individual-to-group relationships were measured using questions that evaluated the value of membership, sense of belonging, and enjoyment, whereby the individual evaluated his or her personal relationship and involvement with the group as a totality (three items). Finally, group-as-a-whole perceptions were measured with teamwork and closeness items. Essentially, each individual team member was required to step back and answer: what are we like as a team in terms of teamwork and in terms of closeness? The assumptions of this three-level breakdown was that high cohesion would be present to the extent that (a) strong individual-to-individual relationships existed among a large number of team members, (b) members valued their membership in the group, and (c) members viewed the group as being united.

The Multidimensional Sport Cohesion Instrument (MSCI) evolved from the belief that cohesion in sport teams reflects four "factors associated with the goals and objectives the group is striving to achieve, as well as factors associated with the development and maintenance of positive interpersonal relationships" (Yukelson, Weinberg, & Jackson, 1984, p. 106). One of the factors, quality of teamwork, is a measure of how well teammates work together to achieve group success. The second factor, attraction to the group, represents the degree to which individuals are attracted to and satisfied with group membership. The third factor, unity of purpose, is composed of items that assess commitment to the group's norms, rules, and goals. The last factor, valued roles, is a measure of the degree to which there is identification with group membership.

The Group Environment Questionnaire (GEQ)

The early work on measuring cohesion offered valuable contributions to understanding this group phenomenon. However, over the past 35 years, the Group Environment Questionnaire (GEQ, Carron et al., 1985; Widmeyer et al., 1985) has been the predominant measure of sport group cohesion. This tool was developed on the basis of a conceptual model that emanated from social cognitive theories of human behavior, group dynamics theories pertaining to levels of analysis in groups, and the group dynamics perspective that groups serve both a task function and a social function. Each of these is discussed in turn.

A social cognitive basis for cohesion. Social cognitive theories are based on the premise that humans are rational beings who consistently evaluate, form judgments about, organize, and interact in and with their environment (cf. Bandura, 1986; Levine & Moreland, 1991). Using a social cognitive perspective, Carron et al. (1998) advanced five assumptions associated with the belief that cohesion can be assessed through perceptions of individual group members:

1. a group has clearly observable properties;
2. group members experience the social situation of their group, are socialized into it, and develop a set of beliefs about the group;
3. these beliefs are a product of the member's selective processing and integration of information about the group;
4. the perceptions about the group held by a member reflect the unity characteristic of the group; and
5. the social cognitions that members have about their group and its cohesiveness can be measured.

It may seem at first glance that these assumptions are relatively straightforward and not too difficult to accept. However, the theoretical perspective advanced by Carron et al. (1998) could be at odds with other theoretical perspectives advanced to understand human behavior. For example, a theoretician adopting a behaviorist approach might argue that only behavior can be measured, that cognitions are not reliable or valid indices for behavior. Thus, a behaviorist interested in studying cohesion might record the amount of time group members converse, or the degree of cooperation they exhibit.

As a second example, there are theoreticians in group dynamics who would argue that if the focus is on a group construct, then the group and not individual members should be assessed. How could you assess a team to determine its cohesiveness? The approach taken by Stogdill (1964) that was discussed above would be one example (i.e., observers in the bleachers recorded the degree to which they believed the Ohio State football team was integrated on each play).

The individual and group bases for cohesion. The importance of distinguishing between the individual and the group is a frequent theme in group dynamics. For example, Cattell (1953) pointed out that a group can be described at three different levels. At the first level, the population level, the focus is on the individual group members—their personalities, aspirations, motives, attributes, and so on. Typical questions at this level: What is the personality of team versus individual sport athletes? What are the predominant motives (orientations) of athletes on intramural basketball teams? In order to answer these questions, it is necessary to evaluate the characteristics of individual team members.

At the second or structural level, the focus is on the member-to-member interactions. For example, what are the factors contributing to coach-athlete compatibility? This question is answered by examining the specific interactions and relationship between the coach and the athlete.

With the third level, referred to by Cattell (1953) as *syntality*, the focus is on the group as a whole. What was the final ranking of nations in the 2019 FIFA Women's World Cup football (soccer) championship in France? That question can only be answered at the group level.

The task and social aspects of cohesion. It was pointed out above that the specific objectives of social groups, delinquent gangs, army platoons, and so on can vary. Also, there are differences in the specific goals and objectives of groups within a similar category. For example, not every curling team in a local club has the same reason(s) for forming and staying together. In one case, the opportunity to meet weekly and socialize may be predominant; in another, winning the club championship may be most important.

Despite this diversity, it has usually been assumed that the goals and objectives that dominate the activities of all groups can be classified into two categories. The first is represented by the activities associated with the development and maintenance of social relationships; the second, by activities associated with task accomplishment, productivity, and performance. In fact, Dion (2000) stressed that

> The conceptual distinction between task cohesion and social cohesion that has emerged independently from several models and lines of research is an important milestone in cohesion research ... and one whose importance seems to have a good deal of support, if not consensus, from cohesion researchers. (p. 21)

A conceptual model for cohesion in sport teams. Using the distinctions between task and social dimensions, as well as individual and group orientations, Carron et al. (1985) proposed a conceptual model for cohesion in sport teams (see Exhibit 14.2).

In the model, cohesion in sport teams is considered to be composed of group integration (task and social) and individual attractions to the group (task and social). The group integration scales assess a member's perceptions of the team as a totality. Thus, the focus is on these issues: How close are we as a team? Do we stick together socially? Are we unified in what we are trying to achieve? Are we united in how we are trying to achieve it?

The individual attractions to the group scales assess a member's personal attractions to the team. Thus, the focus is on these issues: Am I happy with the challenges this team provides? Is the team attractive to me personally? How well do I fit in with the team? Does the team use performance strategies that I like? Both the group integration perceptions and the individual attractions to the group perceptions help bind members to the team. In a sense, attractions to the group scales focus on the "me" aspect of the group, whereas group integration focuses more on the 'we' aspect.

As Exhibit 14.2 illustrates, members' perceptions of the team as a unit, as well as their perceptions of the attractiveness of the team personally, are centered on two concerns. One of

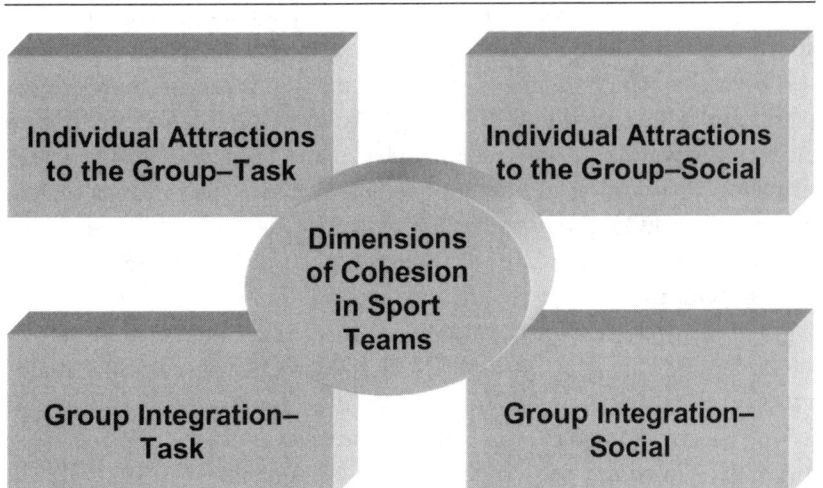

Exhibit 14.2. A Conceptual Model of Group Cohesion

Source. "The Development of an Instrument to Assess Cohesion in Sport Teams: The Group Environment Questionnaire," by A. V. Carron, W. N. Widmeyer, and L. R. Brawley, 1985, *Journal of Sport Psychology, 7,* 244–266.

Exhibit 14.3. A Sample of Statements from the Group Environment Questionnaire Used to Assess Perceptions of Cohesion in Sport Teams

Cohesion Scale	Example Statement
Interpersonal Attractions to the Group-Task	I do not like the style of play on this team
Interpersonal Attractions to the Group-Social	Some of my best friends are on this team
Group Integration-Task	Our team is united in trying to reach its goals for performance
Group Integration-Social	Members of our team would rather go out on their own than get together as a team

Source. "The Measurement of Cohesion in Sport Teams: The Group Environment Questionnaire," by W. N. Widmeyer, L. R. Brawley, and A.V. Carron, 1985, London ON: Sports Dynamics.

these is the team's task. On sport teams, members are concerned with personal performance issues and team performance issues. Concerns about the task help to bind the team together into a cohesive unit. A second element is the social aspect of the team. On sport teams, members are concerned with personal relationships as well as the togetherness, closeness, and affiliation within the team as a unit.

Some sample items for each of the four scales illustrated in Exhibit 14.2 are presented in Exhibit 14.3. Some of these items are positively worded. Consequently, if a member felt that the team was highly cohesive, he/she would strongly endorse the statement. Also, some of the items are negatively worded. In the case of these items, if a member felt that the team was highly cohesive, he/she would strongly reject the statement.

Extending the applicability of the GEQ to other populations. As noted earlier, the GEQ has been extensively used over the past three to four decades. However, as Carron and colleagues (1998) noted, one should strongly consider the applicability of a survey to their population of interest. Toward this end, and keeping in mind many of the principles and assumptions previously discussed, several researchers have developed alternatives to the original GEQ. One issue has been language, as the GEQ was developed in English. As an example, Heuzé and Fontayne (2002) developed the Questionnaire sur l'Ambiance du Groupe (QAG) for the French language. The 18 items that comprise the QAG are based on the conceptual model illustrated in Exhibit 14.2. An important departure from the original GEQ pertains to the wording of some items. Heuzé and Fontayne (2002) noted that there are cultural nuances pertaining to how individuals reference their groups that were lost in translation (from the GEQ). Specifically, they explained that cohesion questions with references toward "our group…" or "we…" were better asked as "my group…" or "my team…" within the French culture.

The length of the questionnaire has also been considered. Buton et al. (2007) developed a short version of the QAG (i.e., the QAG-a). The eight-item QAG uses a visual analog approach to measurement (i.e., ratings are made on a 10 cm line as opposed to a Likert-type structure with defined incremental points) to assess the four dimensions of cohesion outlined previously. Buton et al.'s (2007) intention was for this tool to be valuable when studying the dynamic nature of cohesion.

Finally, age of respondents was identified as an issue. Youth are not miniature adults. This has implications for a large number of issues including (but certainly not limited to) the protocol used to assess theoretical constructs such as cohesion. Eys et al. (2009a) noted that the conceptual model (and items) that form the basis for the Group Environment Questionnaire might not be applicable for youth sport athletes (ages 13 to 17 years). Can youth distinguish validly between the various dimensions of cohesion illustrated in Exhibit 14.2? Is the readability of the individual items comprehensible for youth 13–17 years? Are the negatively worded items problematic from a reading and rating perspective? Development does play a critical role in how individuals perceive their groups.

A series of projects were undertaken by Eys et al. (2009a) to develop their youth-oriented questionnaire (i.e., the Youth Sport Environment Questionnaire; YSEQ), including (a) the use of focus groups, open-ended questionnaires, and literature reviews to understand how adolescents perceive the concept of cohesion, (b) the development of potential items based on results obtained from the previous projects, (c) content analyses by group dynamics experts to create a preliminary version of the questionnaire, and (d) factor analyses to determine, and then support, the underlying factor structure. The resulting YSEQ contains 16 items. Also, in a substantial departure from the GEQ and QAG, only two manifestations of cohesion are assessed: task and social. Finally, a readability assessment of the YSEQ suggested that the measure is age-appropriate for its intended population (i.e., participants 13–17 years of age). A very similar process was conducted by Martin et al. (2012) to develop an age-appropriate survey for children (10–12 years old).

Correlations of Cohesion in Sport Teams

> The secret of football, and of team performance, is harmony. True harmony is equivalent to perfection, to beauty. Think of the movement of a champion gymnast, or the perfect synchrony of a whole symphony orchestra playing together. Harmony can be everywhere: in music, in the mind, and the body, in a football team's will to succeed; and it's the perfect understanding, this combining of forces that makes winning possible. Harmony in a team means everybody playing together and thinking as one. In the end it's all about getting the ball in the back of the net, about having the perfect touch when you have possession. This can only come from the combined efforts of all players. (Cantona & Fynn, 1996, p. 33)

One of the founders of the science of social psychology, Lewin (1935), suggested that there are two fundamental processes characteristic of all groups: maintenance and locomotion. *Maintenance* is represented by activity designed to keep the group intact, to help it maintain its unity, integrity, and stability. In the above quote, Eric Cantona, a former member of the Manchester United soccer team (and subsequently voted Manchester United's player of the 20th century), highlighted the prevalent belief about cohesiveness when he stated, "true harmony is equivalent to perfection, to beauty" (Cantona & Fynn, 1996, p. 33).

Locomotion, the second fundamental process is represented by activity designed to facilitate the promotion or achievement of the group's goals and objectives. In the previous quote by Cantona, the relationship of cohesion to locomotion is also highlighted when he pointed out that "harmony in a team means everybody playing together and thinking as one" (Cantona & Fynn, 1996, p. 33).

Thus, cohesion is a factor that directly contributes to group maintenance and, facilitates group locomotion. It plays such an important role in the dynamics of all groups, that some

Exhibit 14.4. A General Framework for Examining the Correlates of Cohesion in Sport Groups

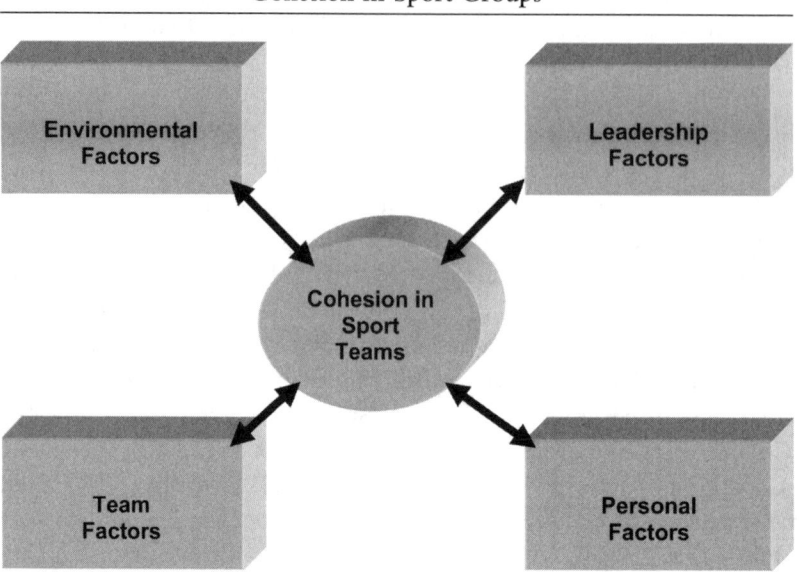

social scientists have called cohesion the most important small group variable (Golembiewski, 1962; Lott & Lott, 1965). Because cohesion is so important, gaining an understanding of the variables associated with it has been an important research objective for social scientists in sport psychology. In order to organize that research into a more coherent package, the framework illustrated in Exhibit 14.4 is used.

This framework is based on the understanding that many factors are positively related to group cohesion. Some of these factors are present in the situation, others are in the attitudes and characteristics the individual brings to the group, others are associated with aspects of leadership, and still others build within the team as a unit. There are several points to consider when examining this body of literature. First, many of the relationships between cohesion and the situational, individual, leadership, and team variables discussed are likely circular in nature. For example, cohesion influences performance success and performance success influences cohesion. Although it is often convenient to discuss the relationship between cohesion and other variables in a causal fashion (e.g., cohesion contributes to performance), it is important to bear in mind the dynamic, circular nature of most aspects of group dynamics.

It should also be pointed out that the four categories illustrated in Exhibit 14.4 should not be viewed as independent or unrelated. For example, leadership behavior and individual satisfaction are both associated with the development of group cohesion. They also have an influence on each other. A final point that must be made is that in some cases the decision to assign studies to categories is difficult. In the final analysis, we placed them where they seemed to fit best. Thus, for example, role involvement research is discussed in the section on team factors. It must be kept in mind, however, that individuals, not teams, understand, accept, and/or carry out roles. Consequently, the relationship of cohesion to role involvement also could have been introduced in the personal factors category.

Situational Factors and Cohesion

Carron et al. (1985) assumed that the resulting four manifestations illustrated in Exhibit 14.2 provide most of the differences in cohesiveness among sport teams. However, they did acknowledge that other conditions in the situation also help to keep a group together. One of these situational conditions that is a fundamental reason why members stick with teams is *contractual responsibilities*. Eligibility and/or transfer rules, geographical restrictions, and the contractual obligations that exist in professional and amateur sport can constrain the movement of athletes from one team to another. Contractual responsibilities are one major difference between a social group and a sport team. Members generally can leave social groups if they wish; they cannot do so in most professional sport situations if they want to continue participating. A contract not only makes it impossible for an athlete to leave a team, it also makes it difficult for the team to get rid of, or obtain, an athlete. The contracts of professional hockey players in the National Hockey League that bind them to their teams, for example, can make it very difficult for them to play for their country at the Olympics. The following is advice from a sports lawyer, Trevor Whiffen, to players who force the issue:

> Do so at your own peril. You are going to be putting yourself in breach of the contract you have signed with your team, which has been collectively bargained … You are putting yourself at the risk of being suspended, terminated, liable for damages to your club for the games that you miss. I would say you have a contractual obligation to play for [your] team in the NHL and don't take that lightly because if you do take that lightly and go off to play in the Olympics you are putting your entire career at risk. (Strashin, 2017, para. 15–16)

There are also *normative pressures* that contribute to cohesiveness. These are a product of our society's low regard for quitters. Quitters are considered irresponsible and undependable. Consequently, once an individual joins a group, there are pressures on him/her to continue to maintain involvement.

The *level of competition* also seems to play a role in the development of group cohesion (Granito & Rainey, 1988; Gruber & Gray, 1982). When Granito and Rainey (1988) assessed the cohesion of high school and college football teams, they found that task cohesion was greater in the high school teams. Also, Gruber and Gray found social cohesion was higher in elementary school and junior high school basketball teams than in senior high school teams. Why this might be the case, however, is a critical question. Possibly task/social unity are achieved more easily with less experienced athletes.

Geographical factors such as physical and functional proximity also contribute to group cohesiveness. When collections of strangers are brought into closer proximity, cohesiveness increases. If team members have frequent opportunities to be in close proximity (e.g., common locker room, common transportation to and from competition), they become closer. This is probably a result of the increased opportunities to interact and communicate about task and social issues (see Exhibit 14.5).

A group's *permeability*—the degree to which it is open to non-group members or members of other groups—has an influence on cohesiveness. Groups that are less permeable, possibly because they are socially or physically isolated from other groups, draw upon their own

Exhibit 14.5. An Illustration of a Situational Factor and Team Cohesion

Focus	Quotation
Geographical proximity and cohesion	[Toronto Raptors basketball players] Siakam, Delon Wright, Fred VanVleet, Norm Powell, Lucas Nogueira and Jakob Poeltl were involved in the sessions that not only built on-court cohesion but off-court relationships as well. The group basically lived together, and you can sense something special among them. 'They have an identity, they have a little pride together as a unit,' Coach Dwane Casey said. 'They play for each other, pull for each other. They work together before practice, after practice as a unit, during practice as a unit, so they've developed a chemistry that's really, really important.' (Smith, 2017, p. S4)

membership to fulfill important psychological needs. Communication and interaction occur predominantly or exclusively within the group. Also, the group becomes more cohesive.

Personal Factors and Cohesion

Demographic attributes. As Exhibit 14.4 illustrates, a second category of factors associated with the development of group cohesion is the characteristics of the group members. When there is similarity in demographic attributes of individual members—attributes such as social background, race, and gender of the group members—is cohesion enhanced? In a discussion relating to this point, Eitzen (1975) noted

> the more alike the members of a group, the more positive the bond ... This is usually explained by the assumption that internal differentiation on some salient characteristic such as religion, race, and socioeconomic status leads to greater likelihood of clique formation. (p. 41)

Exhibit 14.6 contains an example of the difficulties faced by Jackie Robinson when he broke the color barrier in Major League Baseball. Robinson's experiences notwithstanding, it is difficult to determine from available research whether similarity in personal attributes is important for team cohesiveness. Widmeyer, Silva, and Hardy (1992) identified 32 potential antecedents of cohesion and then had American and Canadian athletes rate how important each of those antecedents was for both task and social cohesion. Among the lowest ranking (i.e., rated as least important) was similarity in social background and racial similarity. What

Exhibit 14.6. An Illustration of a Personal Factor and Team Cohesion

Focus	Quotation
Similarity and cohesion	Those early days were awfully tough on Jackie. I remember times on the train when nobody would sit with him or talk with him. Pee Wee [Reese] always seemed to be the first to break the tension. He kidded Jackie before anyone else did and made him a part of the team. He was probably the first Dodger to have a meal with him off the field. Pee Wee was a real leader on our club, and when he started being friendly with Jackie everybody started being friendly. In the beginning Jackie was alone at the dining table. By the middle of the year you couldn't get a seat at the dining table with him, there were so many guys. (Allen, 1987, pp. 102–103)

isn't known from the research of Widmeyer and his colleagues, of course, is whether the behaviors of athletes are consistent with their cognitions. That is, for example, evaluating race as irrelevant for group cohesiveness is not equivalent to behaving as if race is irrelevant.

Cognitions. There are numerous cognitions that athletes and coaches hold that are related to task and social cohesion perceptions. One factor traditionally considered to be associated with greater cohesiveness is *shared perceptions,* including similarity in attitudes, beliefs, and motives. The relationship of similarity in perceptions to cohesion was emphasized by Zander (1982) who observed that "birds of feather flock together, and create a more distinct entity when they do … Persons whose beliefs do not fit together well have a hard time forming a strong group" (p. 3). In social and work groups at least, attitude similarity also seems to operate in a reciprocal fashion with group cohesiveness. That is, an initial similarity in attitude increases the likelihood that individuals will come together and develop group cohesiveness. And, over time, the group's work, experiences together, and cohesiveness increase the degree to which individual members adopt similar attitudes (Terborg, Castore, & DeNinno, 1976).

Attributions for responsibility are also cognitions athletes hold that are related to cohesion. Losing teams and their supporters try to come to grips with these questions: Why? What are the reasons we lost? What went wrong? In answering those questions, team members (and observers of the event) are more likely to identify individual members as causal agents rather than the team as a whole. Naquin and Tynan (2003) referred to this phenomenon as a *team halo effect*. Teams as a whole are given substantially more credit for their successes than for their failures. In analyzing a defeat, the actions of the individual who missed the penalty shot or the free throw, or the one who made the error at the crucial time, or the one who committed a foul that led to an opposition score, are more salient than the collective actions of the team.

An event that serves as a good illustration is Ghana's loss in the 2010 FIFA Men's World Cup of soccer. In the preliminary round when Ghana compiled a record of one win, one loss, and one tie (and advanced to the round of 16), the media's primary focus was on its excellent team play. Conversely, in the subsequent round when Asamoah Gyan missed an extra-time penalty shot and Ghana then went on to lose in the shootout, his actions were discussed extensively in the media as an important causal factor. If he had made the shot, Ghana would have won.

We have no way of knowing what Gyan's teammates considered to be the primary cause of Ghana's loss. However, available research from a wide cross section of sports contributes to a suggestion that if the team is highly cohesive it would likely have shared the blame rather than make Gyan the scapegoat (Bird, Foster, & Maruyama, 1980; Brawley, Carron, & Widmeyer, 1987; Schlenker & Miller, 1977b; Shapcott & Carron, 2010; Shapcott, Carron, Greenlees, & El Hakim, 2008). For example, Brawley et al. (1987) had athletes from several sports use their teammates as a benchmark to estimate the degree of personal responsibility for the team's win or loss. Athletes rating their team high in task cohesiveness assumed a level of personal responsibility that was equal to that of the average team member regardless of outcome (i.e., winning or losing). However, those athletes rating their team low in task cohesion showed a self-protective and self-serving pattern of attribution—they assumed less personal responsibility for the loss than they assigned to the average team member.

Overall, the relationships that exist among teammates (e.g., task and social cohesion) are proposed to be one factor contributing to the attributions teams make regarding the events they experience in terms of the degree of controllability (i.e., is the cause of the outcome under the control of the team?), stability (i.e., is the cause of the outcome stable over time), globality (i.e., is the cause of the outcome something that might affect the team across many situations?), and universality (i.e., is the cause of the outcome something experienced by many teams?) (Allen, Coffee, & Greenlees, 2012).

Perceptions of the team's cohesiveness are also related to *self-handicapping* (Carron, Prapavessis, & Grove, 1994; Hausenblas & Carron, 1996). The term self-handicapping was introduced by Jones and Berglas (1978) to represent the strategies that individuals use prior to an important achievement situation in order to protect their self-esteem. As Berglas and Jones (1978) pointed out, self-handicapping "enhances the opportunity to externalize (or excuse) failure and to internalize (reasonably accept credit for) success" (p. 406). Thus, for example, an athlete who doesn't practice prior to a championship because of a real or imagined injury can use that injury and lack of practice as reasons for a loss. Also, the athlete's self-esteem is protected because the loss occurred as a result of events outside of personal control. Conversely, if the athlete is successful, his/her self-esteem is enhanced because the victory was obtained despite the presence of an injury and lack of practice.

When research on self-handicapping with male (Carron et al., 1994) and female athletes (Hausenblas & Carron, 1996) was initially undertaken, it was uncertain how cohesion would be related to self-handicapping. Two diametrically opposite scenarios seemed possible. On the one hand, it seemed reasonable to expect that the need to use self-handicapping strategies would be reduced in cohesive groups. In cohesive groups, responsibility for failures is shared equally and the individual has a better relationship with, and greater support from, teammates. Thus, the cohesive group represents an environment in which the individual is buffered from threats to self-esteem and, consequently, the need to use self-handicapping strategies should be reduced.

On the other hand, it also seemed reasonable to predict that the need to use self-handicapping strategies would be increased in cohesive groups. In cohesive groups, members have less tendency to take advantage of others, feel greater responsibility for the group and its members, have a tendency to make more sacrifices for the group, and feel a greater responsibility to conform to group expectations. Thus, the cohesive group also represents an environment in which the individual experiences greater pressure to carry out group responsibilities and satisfy the expectations of highly valued teammates. Failure to do so would be threatening to self-esteem. As a result, the need to establish reasons for potential failure could be increased.

In both the Carron et al. (1994) study with male athletes and the Hausenblas and Carron (1996) study with female and male athletes, support was obtained for the latter possibility. That is, when task cohesion in the group was high, those athletes who had a tendency to use self-handicaps rated the severity of the self-handicaps much higher in the week prior to an important competition. Conversely, when the team was perceived to be low in task cohesion, self-handicapping also was low.

Affect. As Baumeister and Leary (1995) noted, feelings of belongingness influence our affect and emotions. If the bonds in our relationships are strong, we feel more content, more satisfied, and less anxious. What about relationships in sport teams? Is higher cohesion associated with improved mood states? A number of studies have been directed toward this issue.

One affective measure examined has been anxiety. As Baumeister and Leary (1995) suggested, it is "the extreme or prototype of negative affect ... clearly linked to damaged, lost, or threatened social bonds" (p. 506). Prapavessis and Carron (1996) reported that athletes from a variety of team sports possessing higher perceptions of the team's task cohesion also reported lower levels of cognitive anxiety.

A slightly different approach was taken by Eys, Hardy, Carron, and Beauchamp (2003). Athletes from a variety of sports not only rated their state anxiety prior to competition, they also indicated the degree to which they believed that their anxiety symptoms were either facilitative or debilitative. It is possible, for example, for an athlete to be quite nervous prior to competition but to consider that as positive (i.e., facilitative: "I'm ready") or negative (debilitative: "I'm too nervous to play well"). Eys et al. (2003) found that athletes higher in task cohesion perceived their cognitive and somatic-state anxiety symptoms as more facilitative, a result that was supported by later work by Wolf and colleagues (Wolf, Eys, & Kleinert, 2015; Wolf, Eys, Sadler, & Kleinert, 2015). Interestingly, they found that athletes who perceived their team as more cohesive appraised the importance of upcoming competitions as more important, but also appraised their prospects for coping as more positive. This is a situation that fundamentally describes a facilitative approach to a challenging environment. Overall, in their conclusions, Wolf, Eys, and Kleinert (2015) suggested that "cohesion-centered interventions might have a small relative effect [on interpretations of anxiety symptoms], but because cohesion is modifiable and affects the whole team, potentially these interventions would represent convenient and cost-effective strategies to optimize an entire team's precompetitive feeling state at once" (p. 354).

Another affective measure that has received some attention as a correlate of cohesiveness is *satisfaction*. Martens and Peterson (1971) proposed that cohesion, satisfaction, and performance are related to each other in a circular fashion. That is, the presence of cohesion contributes to team performance and, ultimately, to team success. In turn, success produces higher satisfaction in the individual athlete and this leads to the development of a greater sense of cohesion. When Williams and Hacker (1982) tested the cause-effect relationships among performance, cohesion, and satisfaction in women's intercollegiate field hockey teams, they found support for the Martens and Peterson (1971) proposal.

As a final example, cohesion has been linked with nonclinical depression and mood. Terry et al. (2000), in a study of cohesion and mood in 415 athletes from the sports of rowing, netball, and rugby, obtained results consistent with the proposition advanced by Baumeister and Leary (1995). On the basis of their results, Terry et al. (2000) concluded that different manifestations of cohesiveness are associated with different manifestations of mood and a remarkable consistency was present across the three samples. For athletes in these individual and team sports, the group integration-task dimension of cohesion was inversely related to feelings of depression.

Behavior. The perception that individual group members have of the group changes when they make investments in that group. Zander (1982) emphasized this point, writing, "a participant who is asked to give up something of value for her group becomes, because of this sacrifice, more attracted to that body" (p. 7). The role that sacrifice plays in promoting both cohesion and conformity to group norms in sport teams was examined by Prapavessis and Carron (1997b) with state-level cricket teams. The many ways that sacrifices in a team sport can be manifested were assessed—sacrifices by the self or by teammates in either the immediate situation (e.g., in practices and competitions) or in a situation removed from other team members (e.g., sacrifices in personal life or at work made in order to practice and compete). Prapavessis and Carron (1997b) found that sacrifice contributes to task and social cohesion and, in turn, task and social cohesion contribute to increased conformity to important group norms.

Cohesion is the construct representing a tendency for members to stick together. So, not surprisingly, cohesion is associated with adherence in sport teams. There are numerous aspects of adherence besides drop out behavior—including absenteeism, lateness, and early departures. Research has shown that athletes who hold the perception that their team is more cohesive are more likely to be on time for practice and to be present at practices and games (Carron, Widmeyer, & Brawley, 1988). Subsequent research examined how athlete perceptions of team cohesion might influence their sustained involvement in sport. In the two earliest studies, Spink (1995, 1998) explored the relationship between cohesion in one season and the intention to return and compete in a subsequent season. The studies had almost identical results—if cohesion was higher, stronger intentions to return were expressed. As a final example, Spink, Wilson, and Odnokon (2010) assessed cohesion of elite ice hockey players at the end of one season and tracked which members returned the team in the subsequent season, forming two groups—athletes who returned and athletes who did not. The athletes who returned had significantly higher perceptions of task cohesion during the previous season.

There is also evidence that athletes who perceive their team to be less cohesive are less likely to work hard at practice (i.e., effort). This was demonstrated by Prapavessis and Carron (1997a) in a study where the cohesion of 261 athletes from a variety of sports was assessed. Their coaches, who had agreed to cooperate in the project, were provided with a standard warm up program to use prior to practices. Also, the athletes were led to believe that they might be randomly selected to participate in a project designed to assess their fitness level. The 20 athletes who had scored at the extremes in task cohesion were targeted. The researchers arrived at practice just after the standard warm up and, using a field protocol, assessed the heart rate, blood lactate, and oxygen consumption of a targeted athlete. That athlete was subsequently brought to the lab and a maximal oxygen uptake test was administered to provide a standard for comparison against the work output measures obtained at practice. A difference in maximal work output at practice was present between the athletes who viewed their teams as high versus low in task cohesion. The athletes who held higher perceptions of their team's task cohesiveness, worked at a level that was significantly closer to their maximum.

As a final point regarding effort and cohesion, social loafing (i.e., the reduction in individual effort expended when people work in groups versus when they work alone; Latané, Williams, & Harkins, 1979) was previously identified as being linked to cohesion (see Chapter 4). Although a meta-analysis by Karau and Williams (1993) showed that social loafing is pervasive across tasks, gender, and culture, they found that it can be reduced under some circumstances. It is worth reiterating in this section that cohesive groups are likely to have a lower number of social loafers as members (Karau & Williams, 1993).

Leadership Factors and Cohesion

The interrelationship among leaders, subordinates, cohesiveness, and group performance is complex, however. For example, a group in mutiny against its leadership could be highly cohesive but would also be strongly oriented to perform poorly or contrary to the organization's goals (Schachter et al., 1951). This can occur in sport—at least in professional sport as the quote in Exhibit 14.7 illustrates. The French soccer team, reacting to the expulsion of a team member for allegedly abusing the coach, were described as having mutinied.

One general aspect of leadership that is related to the development of group cohesion is the leader's behavior. In possibly the most comprehensive examination of the relationship between coaching behaviors and team cohesion, Juntumaa, Toms, Keskivaara, and Elovainio (2007) tested 1,018 young (14 and 16 years) Finnish hockey players. They found that those athletes who perceived that their coaches provided more positive feedback behavior held higher perceptions of team cohesion. Further discussion of these links is also provided in Chapter 10.

Exhibit 14.7. An Illustration of a Leadership Factor and Team Cohesion

Focus	Quotation
A cohesive team united against team management	The French soccer team lost 2–1 to South Africa on Tuesday, ending its World Cup run. The defeat is the culmination of a chaotic few days that began when the sports daily *L'Equipe* published striker Nicolas Anelka's alleged abusive comments to coach Raymond Domenech. Since then, Anelka was expelled from the team, the team went on strike and refused to practice, team captain Patrice Evra almost fought with fitness coach Robert Duverne over the revolt, and Domenech ended up reading a letter to the press on behalf of the players. (Grégoire & Monod, 2010)

Although other studies have found similar results, typically they have reported that higher training and instruction behavior is associated with greater cohesion. For example, in their study with high school football players, Westre and Weiss (1991) found greater positive feedback behaviors as well as higher levels of training and instruction behaviors were associated with higher levels of task cohesion in athletes.

Another element in leadership that contributes to group cohesion is leader decision style. Stronger perceptions of cohesiveness are present when a more democratic (participative) approach is used to arrive at a decision; weaker perceptions when an autocratic approach is taken (Juntumaa et al., 2007; Westre & Weiss, 1991). For example, Brawley et al. (1993) found that those athletes who had had more participation in team goal setting possessed a stronger sense of task and social cohesion. It may be that any decision style that provides for greater athlete input leads to feelings of greater ownership of the decision and the group. A feeling develops that it was their decision for their group.

Not surprisingly, the nature of the coach-athlete relationship also influences cohesion. Athletes in relationships that are characterized by compatibility report greater perceptions of cohesion. In a study that serves to demonstrate this point, Jowett and Chaundy (2004) had intercollegiate athletes rate their relationship with their coach, the degree to which their coaches engaged in specific leadership behaviors (i.e., training and instruction, social support, positive feedback, autocratic behavior, and democratic behavior), and their perceptions of task and social cohesion. Consistent with the findings discussed in the previous two sections, coaching behaviors were related to task and social cohesion, with training and instruction being the most dominant behavior. When ratings of coach-athlete compatibility were included in the equation, the ability to predict both task and social cohesion was improved.

Team Factors and Cohesion

There are numerous team-related factors that are linked with group cohesion, some of which are covered in greater detail throughout this book. In brief, it is worthwhile to note some of these connections in this section. For example, it seems intuitive that the status hierarchy in a group should be linked to its unity (see Chapter 9). In a study conducted during a wilderness expedition, Eys et al. (2008) found support for this intuition. Those participants in groups that had some consensus pertaining to their general status hierarchy perceived greater cohesion over those in a group with no consensus. Also, Jacob and Carron (1998) found that the higher the athletes' perceptions of task cohesion, the smaller the degree to which they attached importance to status. Team members also hold different perceptions of the group's cohesiveness depending upon their starting status. Generally, athletes with starting status see the team as possessing more social and task cohesion (Granito & Rainey, 1988; Gruber & Gray, 1982; Jeffery-Tosoni, Eys, Schinke, & Lewko, 2011).

Role involvement is also inextricably linked to team unity (see Chapter 7). John Wooden recognized this. Commenting on the development of his great teams at UCLA, Wooden noted

> [I built teams] by defining roles for each individual and making each individual feel that their role is as important as any other role. Now there's a lead role and then there's the supporting cast, but if you don't have the good supporting cast, the thing as a whole is going to fail. (Fisher & Thomas, 1996, p. 90)

In both team and individual sports, various aspects of role involvement and cohesion are strongly related. For example, Brawley et al. (1987) reported correlations between task cohesion (i.e., group integration-task) and role clarity, role acceptance, and role performance for both team and individual sport athletes. Eys and Carron (2001) also found that task cohesion is negatively related to the four manifestations of role ambiguity (i.e., scope of responsibilities, behaviors necessary to fulfill responsibilities, evaluation of role performance, and consequences of not fulfilling role responsibilities). That is, as role ambiguity increased, task cohesion decreased. Finally, Coleman, Godfrey, Leo, Lopez-Gajardo, and Eys (2019) found that perceptions of task and social cohesion predicted affective and normative bases of role commitment. Essentially, when athletes perceived greater cohesion, they were more likely to feel that they wanted to fulfill their role responsibilities and that they ought to do so for the benefit of the team.

There is little doubt that groups exert influence on their members and more cohesive groups have greater potential influence than less cohesive groups. As discussed in Chapter 8, a positive relationship is present between group cohesion and individual conformity—when cohesion is higher, conformity to group norms is greater. In sport, this was exemplified by Shields et al. (1995), who found that team cohesion was positively related to normative expectations that peers would cheat and aggress, and that the coach would condone cheating. Also, Prapavessis and Carron (1997b) found that perceptions of task cohesion were positively related to conformity to the group norms identified as important by athletes.

The sense of competence that a group has, or its *collective efficacy* (see Chapter 15), is another important team factor related to cohesion. What causes a team to develop a sense of competence? Chow and Feltz (2014) cited a number of factors for consideration including mastery experiences (e.g., team success), vicarious experiences (e.g., seeing similar teams be successful), verbal persuasion (e.g., pep talks), physiological states (e.g., team fitness), leadership (e.g., outstanding coach), motivational climate (e.g., athletes' perceptions of the goal structures emphasized by coaches), team size (e.g., having sufficient resources); they also included cohesion.

It does seem reasonable to assume that when cohesion is higher, the sense of collective confidence also would be higher. Many studies have supported this assumption (e.g., Heuzé, Raimbault, & Fontayne, 2006; Kozub & McConnell, 2000; Spink, 1990). In fact, Leo, González-Ponce, Sánchez-Miguel, Ivarsson, and García-Calvo (2015) asked professional soccer players to respond to a series of questionnaires across three points in the season (early-, middle-, and late-season) and demonstrated that perceptions of task cohesion (Individual Attractions to the Group-Task [ATG-T] and Group Integration-Task [GI-T]) positively predicted collective efficacy perceptions. Others have also attempted to understand the interplay among these two variables and team performance. But, how are cohesion and collective efficacy related to team performance? Paskevich (1995) examined the interrelationships among cohesion, collective efficacy, and performance in 25 intercollegiate volleyball teams. He found that collective efficacy is a mediator between team task cohesion and team performance (i.e., win-loss record). That is, greater task cohesion contributes to greater collective efficacy, which, in turn, contributes to better team performance.

Sullivan and Feltz (2001) pointed out that conventional wisdom holds that teams that experience team conflict cannot be cohesive. However, they also noted that this is based on a simplistic view of conflict—that conflict can only be destructive; that it cannot be constructive. In a destructive style of conflict, the interests of one of the protagonists are enhanced at the expense of the other. On the other hand, in a constructive style of conflict, an attempt is made to reconcile the interests of both parties. With a sample of recreational hockey players, Sullivan and Feltz (2001) examined the relationship between cohesion and both constructive and destructive styles of conflict. Their results showed that constructive conflict is positively related to cohesion while destructive conflict is negatively related.

A team factor that has received recent attention pertains to the subgroups or cliques that can arise within the larger team. Martin, Wilson, Evans, and Spink (2015) defined these entities as "inevitable, variable, and identifiable subgrouping[s] of athletes within a team who exhibit particularly close task and/or social bonds" (p. 90). Is the presence of subgroups always detrimental? Youth athletes previously indicated that the lack of cliques is an indicator that the team may be cohesive (Eys, Loughead, Bray, & Carron, 2009b). However, several recent studies have been conducted by Martin et al. (2015) on this topic, and the answer may be more complex. Martin et al. (2015) found that there were both facilitative (e.g., provides a sense of belonging with a few close others, positive subgroups could serve to motivate other members) and debilitative (e.g., isolation, lack of unity) aspects of subgroup development. Coaches were also cognizant of these potential divisions in teams, though they drew a distinction between the potentially positive 'subgroups' and the more insidious 'cliques' that could develop (Martin, Evans, & Spink, 2016).

A final, very important team factor associated with cohesion that must be discussed is team performance. However, because of its importance, it is dealt with independently in the section that follows.

Team Success and Cohesion

Historical Perspective

The popular perspective on the importance of team cohesion is well illustrated in the following quote by Phil Jackson, the former coach of the Los Angeles Lakers:

> With this current group, there is one thing that worries me. I still sense a lack of cohesiveness, the oneness every team requires to win a title. There are always signs—anticipating when a teammate will be beat on defense, trusting someone will be in a designated spot, displaying the unwillingness to lose. So far, I haven't seen these, and time is running out. Achieving oneness does not guarantee success, but it greatly enhances a team's chances. Except in a rare blowout, no matter how poorly you may perform, there comes a point late in every NBA game when the margin is not substantial, maybe six or eight points. The team closest to that oneness is usually triumphant. (Jackson & Arkush, 2004, pp. 169–170)

But, what does science say about cohesion and team success? Traditionally, one of the most heavily debated issues associated with the study of group cohesion has been its relationship to team success. That debate arises largely because, over an extended period of time, research findings spanned the continuum of possibilities. Some studies suggested a positive association between cohesion and performance, others found a negative association, and yet others found no association.

Meta-Analyses of Cohesion and Performance Relationships

An effective way to resolve the inconsistencies in research is a statistical tool called meta-analysis—the empirical combination of the results from all the studies in a domain of interest. Two meta-analyses have been conducted examining the cohesion-performance link. The first was undertaken by Carron, Colman, Wheeler, and Stevens (2002) who focused on 46 studies carried out between the years 1967 and 2000. The second meta-analysis sought to reexamine this issue but with 16 studies from the years 2000–2010 (Filho, Dobersek, Gershgoren, Becker, & Tenenbaum, 2014). In both meta-analyses, results from all of the different studies (i.e., which could vary in terms of measures of performance, types of sports, gender of the athletes, and so on) were combined. Overall, with only a few discrepancies, the two meta-analyses were consistent in terms of the findings. The results showed that there is essentially a moderate and positive relationship between cohesion and performance. Moreover, both task and social cohesion are positively associated with team performance, though Filho et al. (2014) found that task cohesion was more strongly correlated with success.

Moderators of the Cohesion-Performance Relationship

A moderator is some variable that changes the basic nature of a relationship. For example, if cohesion is important for team success in youth sport but not in professional sport, level of competition would be a moderator of the cohesion-performance relationship. In their meta-analyses, both sets of researchers examined numerous possible moderator variables.

Females and males. The group dynamics literature has many examples of where the responses of males and females have been shown to differ. The cohesion-performance relationship is no exception, though the results found in the two meta-analyses differ slightly. For Carron et al. (2002) the association between cohesion and performance was significantly stronger in female teams than it was in male teams. In contrast, Filho et al. (2014) found that the relationship was strongest in mixed gender teams. Regardless, both sets of researchers encouraged future work to consider possible differences. Specifically, Filho et al. (2014) suggested "these findings illustrate the importance of considering gender idiosyncrasies ... Future researchers may focus on asking 'why' (e.g., Why do women and men differ in cohesion dynamics?)" (pp. 173–174).

Eys et al. (2015) pursued this question via interviews with coaches who had led both male and female teams in their careers. Their responses indicated that they agreed that cohesion and performance are linked for both genders, but that it is likely stronger for female teams. When asked why, the coaches provided diverse perspectives related to the nature of cohesion, what leads to cohesive male and female teams, and managing cohesion over the course of a season. As one example of a difference, the coaches noted that the direction of the relationship may be different between genders such that, in male teams, the team's performance is likely to lead to cohesion, while in female teams the direction may work the other way (cohesion leads to success). Additional research is needed to actually test this proposition.

Type of sport. A view often advanced by researchers and laypeople alike is that cohesion may be less important for outcomes like performance in individual sports like wrestling, gymnastics, and golf would be a few examples (see Carron & Chelladurai, 1981). When athletes compete alone and have limited direct influence on one another's performance, it may seem that the presence of cohesion does not contribute to the team's success. Interestingly, media commentary of the outcome of the Ryder Cup (the golf competition between European and American professionals) have not endorsed this perspective. For example, Alton (2018) described the success of the European golf team in contrast to the Americans:

> For a nation that gave us a brilliant TV show called *Band of Brothers*, the Americans find it hard to bond like brothers, or even second cousins. Gratifyingly, they seem to loathe each other. The best part of Europe winning the Ryder Cup, especially with a thrashing, is always the American meltdown afterwards. Four years ago in Scotland, [American] Phil Mickelson gave his captain, the much-loved Tom Watson, a full barrel–load post-match. 'We have strayed from a winning formula,' was the gist. Later, when asked about Mickelson's disloyalty, Watson replied with customary courtesy: 'He has a difference of opinion. That's OK. My management philosophy is different than his. It takes 12 players to win …' (para. 1–2)

Watson's view on the importance of the team in a sport such as golf is supported by research evidence. The results from both meta-analyses suggested a positive relationship between cohesion and performance for both individual and team sports. In fact, interestingly, Filho and colleagues found that relationship was actually stronger for the former. As described in Chapter 11, theorists anticipate that this association is because of the many ways that individual sport teammates may nevertheless be interdependent with one another beyond just the group's task.

Cohesion-performance versus performance-cohesion. Another important issue that sparked some interest in the group dynamics literature concerns the magnitude of the cohesion-performance relationship versus the performance-cohesion relationship. Exhibit 14.8 contains the view advanced by former professional baseball player Dirk Hayhurst. In short,

Exhibit 14.8. An Illustration of the Dynamic Relationship between Team Success and Team Cohesion

Focus	Quotation
The cohesion-performance and performance-cohesion relationships	Team chemistry. Every baseball season, you hear about it as if it's supposed to tell you something. It comes wrapped in tidy little axioms, like, 'The team is really getting along, and that's why it's winning.' Or, 'The team is toxic, and that's why it's losing.' Most journalists report it straight from the player, who in turn doesn't really understand what he's saying but assumes enough fans will accept it on the premise that happy teams should be more productive … In my experience, it's much more apt to say that prolonged winning or losing makes for good or bad team chemistry. Then, once that chemistry is in place, it can either keep a good thing going or stand in the way of getting a bad thing turned around. (Hayhurst, 2014, para 1–3, 8)

there are many opinions about whether success breeds cohesion, or whether cohesion actually precedes performance. For example, a recent study by Benson et al. (2016) examined this issue with elite youth European soccer teams and found that for this population, success bred cohesion. However, what is the message when considering the totality of research available?

Returning to the meta-analyses, both sets of researchers reported that the relationship is bidirectional: both task and social cohesion were positively related to team success, and team success was positively related to both task and social cohesion. So, the baseball opinions are partly correct. On one hand, highly successful teams are more likely to develop a sense of togetherness or family, presumably because group membership is more satisfying and team performances will feel more united. On the other hand, group leaders who adopt cohesion-promoting strategies early in a season—or when their team has a downturn in performance—may be able to enhance their team's functioning.

Negative Aspects of Cohesion

Buys (1978a) wrote an article that made the (tongue-in-cheek) case that humans would be better off without groups (Buys's commentary was discussed previously in Chapter 1). The basis for his suggestion was that group involvement serves as a catalyst for a number of negative behaviors or situations. These include conformity, groupthink, deindividuation, social loafing, and self-deception when people are in groups. Generally, with the exception of social loafing, these behaviors/situations become even more problematic when the group is more cohesive. So, although cohesion generally is assumed to be (and generally is) a positive group property, it does have the potential to be negative under some circumstances.

Could high task or social cohesion prove to be negative in sport teams? This is not a question that has generated a great deal of research attention. Paskevich, Estabrooks, Brawley, and Carron (2001) suggested that this may be a result of the fact that coaches, athletes, and even researchers consider it axiomatic that cohesion is always positive. Nonetheless, Hardy, Eys, and Carron (2005) set out to determine if intercollegiate athletes could envision situations in sport teams where cohesion might have a negative influence on the group. Fifty-six percent of athletes reported potential disadvantages to developing high social cohesion while 31% reported disadvantages to high task cohesion.

Some of the disadvantages to high social cohesion included wasting task-related time, difficulties focusing and committing to task-related goals, problematic communication between friends, and the potential for social isolation of those outside the main group. The high task cohesion related disadvantages included, for example, decreased social relations, communication problems, reduced personal enjoyment, and increased perceived pressures.

Rovio, Eskola, Kozub, Duda, and Lintunen (2009) also undertook a qualitative study with a cohesive elite level ice hockey team that showed deterioration in performance over the course of a season. One puzzling aspect for the coach and researchers was that the deterioration occurred despite the presence of consistently high team task and social cohesion.

Based on the analysis of their data, Rovio et al. concluded that the high social cohesion that was present contributed to several negative outcomes and eventually to poor team performance. One was *pressures to conform*, which manifested as an unwillingness to criticize teammates who socially loafed or failed to perform to standard. The high social cohesion in combination with a large team size, the relative youth of some of the athletes, and the unwillingness of the high status player to give critical feedback (i.e., team captain) were all major contributors to the group's unwillingness to provide constructive feedback in team meetings.

A second outcome was *groupthink*—a drive for unanimity characterized by self-censorship. Rovio et al. (2009), drawing on the work of Bernthal and Insko (1993), noted that groupthink is more likely in groups characterized by high social cohesion than high task cohesion. As a result of groupthink, the members of the team overestimated the quality of performance of the team and did not share their true feelings during team meetings scheduled to address problem issues.

The final outcome was *group polarization*—a shift in individual opinion as a result of group discussions. Rovio et al. (2009) noted,

> the development of group polarization was expected as it is assumed to be caused by normative and informational influence, as is the case of conformity ... Critical assessment of the teammates' performance decreased, whereas social cohesion, and normative pressure to conform and maintain harmony, increased. (p. 430)

What the discussion on the negative aspects of cohesion seems to exemplify, above all, is the complexity of the group. The science of group dynamics contributes strongly to a suggestion that sport teams should strive to build cohesion. However, the practitioners experienced in the art of coaching recognize that sometimes it may be necessary to disrupt the social unity that is present because it is detracting from group effectiveness. Is this paradox a cause for dismay? No. Across all of the sciences it is understood (expected) that well established protocols sometimes fail—that all procedures do not always work effectively for all people in all situations. The Hardy et al. (2005) and Rovio et al. (2009) studies do provide another perspective on cohesion. However, there seems to be little doubt that the benefits of a cohesive team far outweigh any disadvantages that may be present.

15

Collective Efficacy

I remember going to my first Olympics, where we weren't really looking at winning medals....[Later] when I got my first podium and my first win, I think that opened the door for future generations. They don't have to ever wonder whether it was possible. They know we can do it. ...We still have a ways to go to have that foundation that the powerhouse Nordic nations have. But we're getting there. We know it's possible when we put the right day together. (Blount, 2018, p. 6–10)

Kikkan Randall is quoted to lead-in this chapter and emerged as an internationally-recognized elite athlete in the early 2000s. She was the first cross country skier from the United States to win a world cup medal and was a leader of the United States team for more than a decade afterwards. During her career, the American ski team emerged as a dominant force, and several American skiers attributed their team's confidence to Kikkan's success. As described in the quote introducing this chapter, athletes no longer had to wonder about whether they could do it. Watching someone who they lived and trained with experience success, that generation of athletes experienced a shift from feeling like 'also-rans' to feeling like they could be world-leading on any given day. Appropriately, the penultimate race of Kikkan Randall's career was the 2018 Olympics team sprint with Jessie Diggins. In a race where the athletes each took three turns sprinting around a 1200m course, Diggins and Randall achieved an Olympic gold medal as a team. From the beginning of Kikkan's career to this achievement, the American ski team cultivated a strong sense of collective efficacy.

Efficacy represents the strength to which an individual believes that they can achieve an objective, or their belief that they have the capacity to carry out the responsibilities necessary to produce a desired outcome. Efficacy shares similarities with the concept of confidence; both represent positive views about the self. However, efficacy is situation-specific. Whereas individuals or groups may possess a general sense of confidence, perceptions of efficacy are developed in relation to all of the smaller things required to perform.

Most of the early research on efficacy was undertaken with individuals rather than groups. Bandura (1982), a psychologist who was the primary catalyst for efficacy research, elaborated on why self-efficacy is important:

> In their daily lives, people continuously make decisions about what courses of action to pursue and how long to continue those they have undertaken. Because acting on misjudgments of personal efficacy can produce adverse consequences, accurate appraisal of one's own capabilities has considerable functional value. Self-efficacy judgments, whether accurate or faulty, influence choice of activities and environmental settings. People avoid activities that they believe exceed their coping capabilities, but they undertake and perform assuredly those that they judge themselves capable of managing. Judgments of self-efficacy also determine how much effort people will expend and how long they will persist in the face of obstacles or aversive experiences. When beset with difficulties, people who entertain serious doubts about their capabilities slacken their efforts or give up altogether, whereas those who have a strong sense of efficacy exert greater effort to master the challenge. (p. 123)

In short, self-efficacy has a direct influence on motivation—on the activities people select, on the intensity with which they carry them out, and on the degree to which they persist in the face of adversity.

Although Bandura's (1982) original discussions centered on self (personal) efficacy, he also pointed out that people are inherently social and that many challenges that we face require collective effort. Groups vary in their perceptions of collective competency and expectations for success. Bandura referred to these perceptions and expectations as *collective efficacy*. The essence of collective efficacy was captured in a definition, advanced by Zaccaro, Blair, Peterson, and Zazanis (1995), as "a sense of collective competence shared among individuals when allocating, coordinating, and integrating their resources in a successful concerted response to specific situational demands" (p. 309). Collective efficacy is a critical perception that group members develop over time.

The Nature of Collective Efficacy

When unpacking the quote above by Zaccaro et al. (1995), several key aspects of collective efficacy are evident, including a focus on (a) shared beliefs, (b) members' coordinative capabilities, (c) resources available, and (d) being situationally specific. The first concept of shared beliefs highlights how collective efficacy should be shared among teammates, at least in part. The assumption of sharedness means that we expect members of the same team to show substantial similarity in their perceived collective efficacy. Even if we measure collective efficacy by asking individual athletes to reflect on their team's efficacy and expect members to vary, teammates will likely develop similar beliefs with time due to their shared experiences.

A second key aspect of Zaccaro et al.'s (1995) definition is its focus on members' perceptions of competence in the group's *coordinative capabilities*. When individuals work in any collective endeavor, they must carry out numerous interpersonal functions—exchange information, coordinate responses, and so on. Thus, collective efficacy in specific team tasks often requires beliefs that teammates can effectively coordinate their tasks.

A third key aspect is related to the collective resources available. For collective efficacy to be present, group members must believe that their group has sufficient skills, knowledge, and abilities within its membership for task success. In addition, as important as it is to have the necessary resources, it is equally important for members to have the collective perception that members are willing to use those skills, knowledge, and abilities for the group.

The final key aspect of the Zaccaro et al. (1995) definition relates to the *situational specificity* of collective efficacy. As described earlier in this chapter, efficacy focuses on the group's capacity for certain tasks. For example, members on a synchronized swimming team may have considerable efficacy for the group's capacity to complete all maneuvers in their program but may have little efficacy in the group's capacity to maintain coordination when it has issues with music prior to a competition or when a member falls ill. For this reason, our approaches to measure collective efficacy are often highly specific to the tasks required for a specific sport. For instance, Fletcher, Wilkinson, Bladon, and Gargiulo (2017) assessed netball athletes' collective efficacy in relation to several domains:

a. offensive performance (e.g., clearing the center pass);
b. defensive performance (e.g., controlling the opposition's possession);
c. motivation (e.g., remaining motivated after losing a game);
d. overcoming obstacles (e.g., playing at the same level even when a leader is injured);
e. communication (e.g., effectively discussing strategy during practice); and
f. general (e.g., winning).

A further observation relates to the *scope* of collective efficacy. Efficacy perceptions related to competitive performance may seem most salient in sport. However, athletes also develop efficacy regarding the wider range of demands on the groups. For instance, athletes develop meaningful efficacy perceptions related to the team's ability to manage relationships among team members (e.g., work through conflicts between members) and manage emotions within the group (e.g., provide reciprocal social support to one another; Petitta, Jiang, & Palange, 2015). Just as members may hold efficacy beliefs about their group's capacity to perform, efficacy perceptions also refer to the group's motivation, coping, and unity.

Collective Efficacy and Performance

A central focus of those studying collective efficacy is to estimate the degree to which it is associated with performance. With numerous studies conducted on this topic, Stajkovic et al. (2009) conducted a meta-analysis of 69 studies that explored the relationship between collective efficacy and performance in groups and teams within organizational settings (i.e., outside of sport). They reported a positive association, whereby groups with high collective efficacy also tended to perform better than teams with lower collective efficacy. The correlation reported between collective efficacy and performance was 0.35, which means that the association was consistent across studies and was moderate in strength. A reliable association between performance and collective efficacy has also been demonstrated in field studies in many sports (e.g., Magyar, Feltz, & Simpson, 2004; Myers, Payment, & Feltz, 2004; Paskevich, 1995; Watson, Chemers, & Preiser, 2001).

Many existing studies in sport are nevertheless cross-sectional in nature, meaning they are limited in whether they indicate which direction the association follows. In other words, does greater collective efficacy lead to better performance, or does winning and strong performances lead to stronger efficacy beliefs? Or does it work in both directions? To examine which construct drives this association, several studies have been conducted longitudinally and provide evidence that efficacy can lead to performance. For instance, early season collective efficacy among volleyball players was predictive of performance later in the season (e.g., Paskevich, 1995). Studies also reveal how efficacy perceptions are shaped by earlier performances. Feltz and Lirgg (1998), for example, obtained measures of individual and collective efficacy from intercollegiate male ice hockey players throughout their season. Hockey players' collective efficacy increased after teams won competitions and decreased after losses.

The association between collective efficacy and performance is thus likely bidirectional (Myers et al., 2004). Although it is likely that a team's belief in its capabilities to execute various functions is critical for collective performances, these perceptions are also closely bound to performance with losses or successes shaping subsequent efficacy beliefs. This bidirectional association was illustrated in a study where athletes completed collective efficacy measures before competition, at half-time, and following competition (Fransen et al., 2015). This research demonstrated that collective efficacy perceptions varied dynamically throughout competition. Furthermore, although pregame collective efficacy did not predict first half performance, (a) half-time collective efficacy was predicted by first-half team performance, and (b) half-time collective efficacy predicted team performance in the second half of competition.

Mechanisms Linking Collective Efficacy to Performance

Focusing solely on the effect of collective efficacy on performance, how can we explain the association between these two variables? Two studies by Greenlees, Graydon, and Maynard (1999, 2000) examined why collective efficacy influences performance by focusing on key constructs that are responsible for their association. Overall, their results suggested that individuals who perceived a higher degree of collective efficacy expended more effort in a task following failure (Greenless et al., 1999) and persisted in pursuing their goals to greater degree (Greenlees et al., 2000) than those with lower perceptions of collective efficacy.

Sources of Collective Efficacy

As Exhibit 15.1 shows, collective efficacy can be influenced by several factors—many of these are similar to how we develop perceptions of self-efficacy (i.e., prior performance, vicarious experiences, verbal persuasion; Bandura, 1986). Others are unique to the nature of groups and collective efforts.

Prior Performance

Prior performance is acknowledged to be the most powerful source of efficacy. When a group has been successful, a perception of efficacy develops that is accompanied by an expectation for future successes in similar situations. The quote in Exhibit 15.2 exemplifies this. Sheilagh Croxon (2003), a former head coach of the Canadian synchronized swimming team, described the preparation of the national synchro team for the 2000 Olympics; a team that

Exhibit 15.1. The Sources of Collective Efficacy

Diagram: Six boxes (Group Cohesion, Group Size, Group Leadership, Vicarious Experiences, Verbal Persuasion, Prior Performance) with arrows pointing to a central oval labeled "Collective Efficacy".

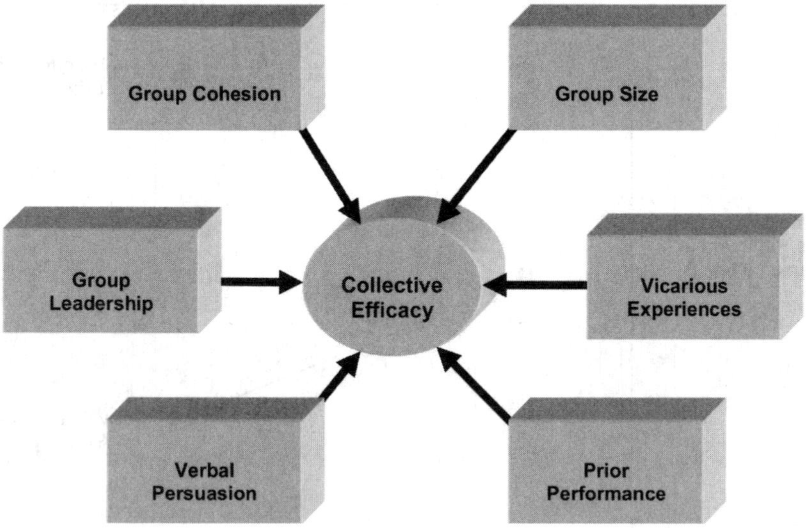

Exhibit 15.2. Examples of the Sources of Collective Efficacy

Source of Efficacy	Quotation
Prior performance	At the 1999 Pan American Games, we defeated the Americans and won gold medals in both the duet and the team event ... The team was on an incredible high for about two weeks after the Games, and then I noticed the doubts starting to creep back in. The athletes began to express sentiments like 'Do you think it was a fluke that we beat the Americans?' ... This experience emphasized to me how important it is to reflect frequently on your successes, no matter how big or small—they are so easily forgotten. (Croxon, 2003, p. 9)
Vicarious experiences	'Kikkan motivated her teammates. Like Holly had learned at Mount Marathon, if they could keep up with her in practice, and even beat her on occasion, then when it came to cross country ski racing, they would know that they too belonged on the World Cup tour—and near the top of the results. It was the associative property of success.' (Shinn, 2018, p. 172)
Verbal persuasion	Olympic athletes and coaches from other sports ... regularly came and spoke about their Olympic journeys, challenges, and experiences. Their stories provided inspiration and guidance. (Croxon, 2003, p.10)
Leadership	Knowing we were using new and different methods and working with excellent people helped to build the athletes' confidence in their abilities and improvements. (Croxon, 2003, p. 9)
Cohesion	Early in our Olympic year, we started work with the Outward Bound organization. Our first session was on a cold February day. The outdoor games and challenges were fun; however, it was obvious that this team was still in the infancy stages of problem solving. Everyone wanted to speak at once, and there were so many ideas that it took us a long time to solve simple problems. By the time we attended our second session in August, just prior to departure for Sydney, we were a highly functioning team ... The difference between February and August was simply time together, time to learn and respect what each individual brought to the group. (Croxon, 2003, p. 9)

Exhibit 15.3. The Effect of Failure on Groups High versus Low in Collective Efficacy

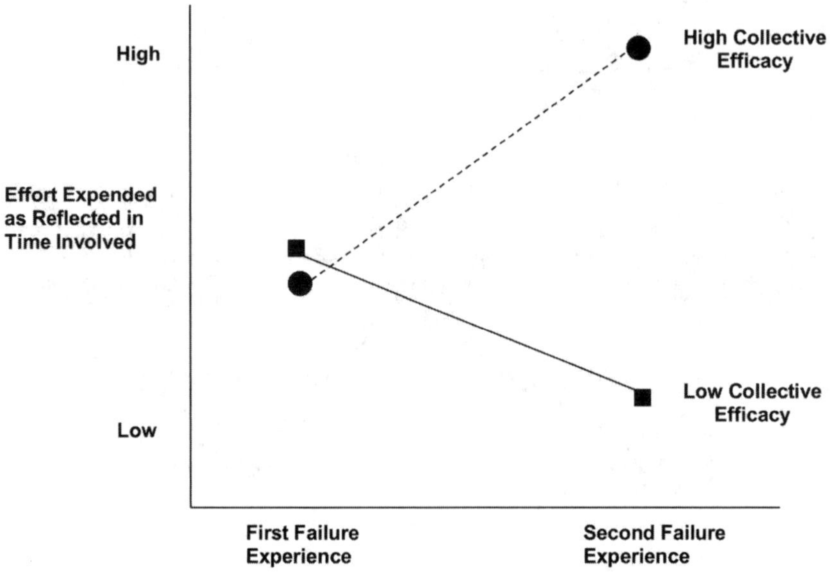

Source. "Collective Efficacy and Group Performance" by L. Hodges and A. V. Carron, 1992, *International Journal of Sport Psychology, 23,* 48–59.

had not achieved its goals on the world stage prior to attending training camp in 1998. A big issue for the team was "building belief" (p. 8) so the importance of reflecting on positive past performances was viewed as a critical element in enhancing collective efficacy.

A reliable relationship between performance and collective efficacy has been demonstrated in laboratory studies. As an example, Hodges and Carron (1992) conducted an experimental study where participants experienced manipulations to increase or decrease their group's efficacy as a means to assess how past experiences influenced collective efficacy and, in turn, effort. Participants were brought into the laboratory in groups of three and tested on a hand dynamometer—ostensibly to obtain a measure of each individual's general strength. The collective efficacy of the triad was then manipulated through bogus feedback. Triads in the high efficacy condition were informed that their group had scored at the 75th percentile on the laboratory's norms; triads in the low efficacy condition were informed that their group had scored at the 25th percentile. The triads then competed against a triad of confederates in a contest that involved holding a medicine ball aloft for as long as possible. The participants used a regular medicine ball; the medicine ball used by the confederates was filled with foam rubber.

Results from this study are illustrated in Exhibit 15.3. In Trial 1, where the confederate group was victorious, the high collective efficacy triads were slightly superior in performance to the low collective efficacy triads. In Trial 2, however, the differences became more accentuated. Triads that began with high collective efficacy and then failed on Trial 1 increased their effort considerably in Trial 2. Conversely, the triads that began with low collective efficacy and then failed in Trial 1 gave up quickly. In other words, groups who began the task with low collective efficacy reduced effort after a failed attempt, while high efficacy groups 'doubled-down'.

Vicarious Experiences

Perceptions of efficacy can also develop from vicarious experiences—seeing other groups have success or imagining scenarios where teammates perform well. If those other groups are highly similar in competence, ability, or some other important characteristic and are successful, it contributes to the development of feelings of efficacy. Conversely, expectations for success are lowered when similar others are observed to fail despite high effort. The role of vicarious experience can also apply within one's own team. The quote leading into this chapter is an example in which breakout performances from a single athlete can help the team believe that 'we' (the team) can do it.

One pathway to support vicarious experience is through imagined experiences. As one example, an intervention using motivational, mastery-oriented imagery represents one approach to enhance collective efficacy (Munroe-Chandler & Hall, 2004). In this intervention, consultants constructed an imagery script that entailed the athletes experiencing adversity (e.g., trailing in score). In turn, the script prompted athletes to imagine what their team would need to do to continue collaborating successfully, manage their emotions, and win the game.

Observing performances of one's teammates—and team as a whole—is another strategy that links to both past mastery experiences and vicarious experiences. Bruton, Shearer, and Mellalieu (2019) specifically focused on the process of observational learning, which refers to using recordings of one's team working together effectively as a means of enhancing collective efficacy and/or self-efficacy. Typically, this involves watching recordings of past performances from individual members and the entire team that are carefully chosen to support efficacy. A specific use is to combine a series of snippets from different attempts at the same task, combining the best aspects of each attempt sequentially to provide the image of a perfect performance. Correlational and experimental studies have demonstrated that observational strategies such as these can increase collective efficacy along with the self-efficacy of individual members (Bruton et al., 2019).

Verbal Persuasion

The verbal encouragement and support of others may also be effective for developing both self-efficacy and collective efficacy (Bandura, 1986). Zaccaro et al. (1995) argued that verbal persuasion in the form of "leadership actions that persuade and develop subordinate competency beliefs may be as critical a determinant … as the group's prior performance experiences, if not more so" (p. 317). There is limited evidence that persuasion can be as powerful as Zaccaro et al. (1995) claimed, and it seems unlikely that groups that lack the efficacy to successfully carry out a task can be convinced otherwise. Although it is still common for coaches or organizations to utilize inspirational speeches, and there may be value in certain pep-talks to shift collective efficacy perceptions, these efforts likely only influence collective efficacy in a fleeting and time-limited way (see Exhibit 15.4).

Group-Specific Sources of Collective Efficacy

In contrast to the initial sources of efficacy that were introduced by Bandura (1986), additional sources are unique to the efficacy developed regarding groups. Zaccaro et al. (1995) focused on three sources, which include group cohesion, leadership behaviors, and group size.

Exhibit 15.4. Precompetitive Pep-Talks and Collective Efficacy: Fact or Fiction?

Readers of this book have presumably witnessed an impassioned precompetitive speech, where leaders make elaborate pleas to motivate their team. There are many ways to debate the effectiveness of pep-talks, including their influence on competitive anxiety. Considering that confidence is one reason why leaders employ pep-talks, it is reasonable to consider whether they produce collective efficacy. The answer: Maybe. Precompetitive speeches are valued by athletes, who view them as being one way to support collective efficacy. However, not all pep-talks are equal. Vargas-Tonsing and Guan (2007) conducted research on the topic, with key findings distinguishing the *content* of speeches. The researchers compared three 'types' of messages:

a. *Informational:* Reminding athletes of important details of competition;

b. *Strategy:* Sharing critical strategic information regarding beating the opponent; and

c. *Emotional:* Sharing that opponents discount them and providing emotional pleas.

Especially when athletes perceived themselves as underdogs, athletes preferred the emotional speech and reported stronger collective efficacy. Emotional pleas are clearly a valuable component of pregame speeches. The dynamic nature of collective efficacy means that even short-lived manipulations of efficacy could be relevant for competition, so emotional speeches should be considered as an option.

Additional research has introduced several more potential sources. Below, we focus on group cohesion, team leadership, and motivational climate.

Group cohesion is one important antecedent to efficacy beliefs. Theoretically, group cohesion is a critical building block, especially when considering efficacy in collective tasks that require members to collaborate effectively. Anecdotally, Exhibit 15.2 also highlights that the development of team cohesion was another critical factor in building belief for the Canadian synchronized swimming team heading into the 2000 Olympics. Empirical research also supports these expectations. Surveys within sport demonstrate that group cohesion can predict collective efficacy (e.g., Leo, González-Ponce, García-Calvo, & Sánchez-Oliva, 2019; Paskevich, 1995). Heuzé, Raimbault, and Fontayne (2006) also examined the interrelationships among collective efficacy, cohesion, and individual performance with professional basketball players. They found a causal pattern with individual athletes' personal performances contributing to perceptions of cohesion that, in turn, contributed to perceptions of collective efficacy.

Nevertheless, the association between efficacy and cohesion is likely complex. Whereas both task and social cohesion predict collective efficacy with younger athletes, task cohesion was the sole predictor of collective efficacy in a study with professional teams (Leo et al., 2019). The efficacy-cohesion relationship is also reciprocal. Teams that have greater collective efficacy could be expected to be more cohesive and teams that are more cohesive could be expected to have greater collective efficacy (Zaccaro et al., 1995). Despite evidence that efficacy can also predict group cohesion, it is certainly the case that approaches to promote group cohesion are likely useful strategies to subsequently foster collective efficacy.

Group leadership is another source of collective efficacy. In Chelladurai's model of leadership (Chelladurai & Saleh, 1978; discussed in Chapter 10), athletes have preferences for specific leader behaviors, and, in turn, leadership has consequences for athlete performance and satisfaction. Although it is not in Chelladurai's model, efficacy is also an outcome of leadership. It is reasonable to assume, for example, that athletes who have a preference for a large amount of training and instruction from their coach will be more confident if the coach demonstrates these behaviors.

There is evidence that leaders have a direct influence on collective efficacy, regardless of athlete preferences. Hampson and Jowett (2014) surveyed developing football players and examined the extent to which collective efficacy was predicted by (a) the range of coaching behaviors outlined by Chelladurai and Selah (1978) and (b) athletes' perceptions of their relationship with their coach. Collective efficacy was highest among athletes reporting high levels of several coaching behaviors: training and instruction, democratic behavior, social support, positive feedback, and autocratic behavior. Beyond these coach behaviors, athletes also reported higher collective efficacy when they reported high closeness and commitment in their coach-athlete relationship. Behaviors from peer leaders similarly influence collective efficacy. Watson et al. (2001) assessed captains' confidence (e.g., "I am confident in my ability to influence a group I lead") along with the team's collective efficacy at the beginning and end of the season. Teams with more confident team captains had stronger collective efficacy at the beginning of the season.

Motivational climate is another potential antecedent of collective efficacy, which was not one of the originally theorized antecedents described by Zaccaro et al. (1995). Magyar et al. (2004) argued that collective efficacy may be influenced by the extent that team environments are focused toward a mastery/task orientation (e.g., learning and improvement in group processes) or an ego/outcome orientation (e.g., competition among team members, punishment for errors). Magyar et al. (2004) conducted a survey study of adolescent rowers' beliefs within 24 hours of a regatta and found that rowers reporting a mastery-oriented motivational climate also reported higher collective efficacy. As another example, Heuzé, Sarrazin, Masiero, Raimbault, and Thomas (2006) conducted a survey study with 146 basketball and handball athletes and reported that collective efficacy later in the season was greatest among athletes who reported that their team environment was high in task-oriented motivation and low in ego/outcome-oriented motivation.

Overlaps between Self-Efficacy and Collective Efficacy

By defining efficacy in a parallel way at both individual and collective levels, there are inherent links in the efficacy beliefs that we form about the self and our groups. Although the two forms of efficacy function at different levels, the nature of collective efficacy is in many ways analogous to self-efficacy.

Even though they share sources and outcomes, collective efficacy and self-efficacy are nevertheless distinct, with each involving unique perceptions. Accordingly, collective efficacy can often be a source for one's self-efficacy. There are also cases where self-efficacy may contribute to beliefs in the group. To study the interaction between self- and collective efficacy, Habeeb, Eklund, and Coffee (2019) studied cheerleading dyads as a context where members make differing contributions to the group. Whereas bases in these dyads often function as the individual supporting or throwing other members, flyers are held or supported by bases as they complete acrobatic components. This presents a natural laboratory because the flyers' performances are particularly contingent on the bases' strength and the dyads' coordination. In a setting where athletes trained alongside a range of other partners, Habeeb et al. (2019) repeatedly assessed athletes' self-, other-, and collective efficacy. Findings revealed that flyers' self-efficacy beliefs were highly dependent on their partners. For a flyer to report high self-efficacy, the flyer would need to have high efficacy in their partner and in their dyad as a whole. Meanwhile, bases' self-efficacy was less dynamic.

Group members can also enhance their teammates' self-efficacy, over-and-above the influence of collective efficacy, by directly acting in ways to support or encourage one another. This is evident in relation to the following quote regarding the 2018 Canadian Olympic Figure

Skating team's efforts to support Patrick Chan prior to his long-program performance, after a disappointing short program:

> So, in the days between his two skates, Chan's teammates set about to rebuild his confidence. ... Every time ice dancer Scott Moir saw Chan in the hallway, he hugged him and told him how good he was. "I've probably annoyed the hell out of him in the last couple of days," Moir said later. "Every time I see him I just give him a hug and I have something to say to him." Moir, who has also known Chan since they were young, had a good idea what was going through the skater's mind. "I knew he was pissed off," Moir said. "I know the competitor that Patrick is." ... as the bus wound its way to the rink, the news hit their phones: Chan had just turned in the highest score of the men's long program. ... After struggling on his landings in the short program, Chan was a different skater. It was a study in teamwork, in a sport that's not normally known for it. (Robertson, 2018, para. 5–11)

Qualitative interviews with elite athletes demonstrated a similar role of self-efficacy. When asked to describe the hallmarks of a team that is resilient in the face of adversity, athletes looked toward a sense of self-efficacy and (specifically) how teammates bolstered one another's self- and collective efficacy (Morgan, Fletcher, & Sarkar, 2013). One specific theme in their study was titled social persuasion and focused on how teammates directly provided support by feedback and encouragement when they recognized that teammates were struggling.

16

Developing Effective Sport Teams

Finding good players is easy. Getting them to play as a team is another story. (Stengel, 2010)

Positive social interactions within teams are often central to the experiences of athletes' during their careers and underpin many optimal team performances in sport. You can observe the remarkable nature of group performances in fans' fervent responses when softball players complete a swift double play, or when an American football player dives for an end zone catch. Nevertheless, members of teams naturally face inefficiencies, as well as the conflicts, that accompany social interactions (e.g., social loafing; see Chapter 4). Teams are imperfect. In response to these challenges, there are numerous effective interventions to enhance teams. It is even likely that a core motive for readers to open this book relates to getting their own groups to be a little bit better.

It is common for leaders to use interventions to develop groups in numerous settings including religious groups, airline cockpit teams, medical teams, corporate headquarters, rehabilitation programs, and fitness classes. Accordingly, team development strategies are critical for sport groups. Perhaps the most identifiable example is when coaches introduce a social event or new group activity to draw the team closer together. However, these social activities only represent a segment of the broader realm of team development. Researchers and practitioners have produced numerous insights for developing sport groups.

The Nature of Developing Effective Teams

When considering the challenge of developing a team, Bill Walsh highlighted this process in its most elemental form in terms of finding the right people. Walsh (1990), then coach of the San Francisco 49ers, said,

> Running a football franchise is not unlike running any other business: You start with a structural format and basic philosophy and then find the people who can implement it ... There were certain qualities I was seeking in those we brought into the organization:
>
> - I needed to feel comfortable with them ...
> - I wanted functional intelligence, because I knew that one person who is not very bright but very aggressive in pushing his ideas can destroy an organization ...
> - We needed knowledge and experience in the business dynamics of the National Football League ...
> - I wanted people who could be enthusiastic and inquisitive, and who would thrive on work. (pp. 123–132)

Walsh rebuilt what was considered 'the laughingstock of the NFL' from losers into champions—which has been referred to as the team of the 80s. The 49ers management selected personnel with qualities to build an organization that continued to thrive for years after Walsh left the team.

Unfortunately, acquiring the 'right people' is no guarantee that a good team will result. Developing effective teams is a demanding process. Coaches and other group leaders must pay continual attention toward how the group is functioning, and quickly respond to member conflict and other potential forms of adversity. Before considering the role of interventions to enhance groups, we cannot understate the value of setting the conditions for group effectiveness.

This book provides insights about how conditions, including member attributes, group environments, and team structures (See Exhibit 1.7) shape perceptions of group cohesion and numerous other important group processes and emergent states. One example based on the influence of group size is the Widmeyer, Brawley, and Carron (1990) study with intramural teams ranging from three to nine members, described in Chapter 4. This study demonstrated that the highest cohesion and enjoyment emerged among members belonging to groups of the smallest size. What do these findings say about team development? They indicate that leaders focused on developing group cohesion may consider designing groups so they are not much larger than the number of members needed to compete or train.

Based on decades of research with teams and consulting in organizations, Hackman (2012) summarized optimal conditions as the following: (a) the team entails the core components of a true 'group' (see Chapter 1), (b) the team is drawn together by a compelling purpose or goal (see Chapter 12), (c) the team is composed of members with complementary skills and personal orientations (see Chapter 5), (d) established norms exist to guide member conduct (see Chapter 8), and (e) the team is guided by a leader with task competencies, but also skills to draw members together (see Chapter 10).

Leaders should keep in mind that any decision related to selecting members, designing group tasks, or forming rules about how members interact will inherently shape a group's effectiveness. However, even when we set the conditions for team effectiveness, we still must engage members in activities that further enhance the group environment.

Defining Team Development

Team development interventions refer to activities conducted within small groups to improve the group's effectiveness, particularly by enhancing emergent states and group processes. These strategies are systematic and designed by a practitioner who is outside of the group's boundaries (e.g., sport psychologist) or an existing group leader like a coach.

Team building is one of the most enduring themes within this domain of literature and has been defined in many ways (cf. Hardy & Crace, 1997). The most encompassing definition describes team building as "a method of helping the group to (a) increase effectiveness, (b) satisfy the needs of its members, or (c) improve work conditions" (Brawley & Paskevich, 1997; p. 13).

Team building focuses on enhancing group effectiveness by improving members' interactions with one another and, particularly, perceptions of group cohesion. The presumption underlying this approach is that stronger cohesion perceptions will induce cooperation and maximal effort in service of team goals, while producing positive and meaningful group interactions. Although this reasoning clearly integrates group performance as an outcome, team building is particularly well suited for promoting group cohesion and positive affective experiences.

Although sport researchers tend to focus exclusively on team building interventions, this approach is only one category within a broader set of team development intervention types identified within organizational research. The four predominant types of team development interventions identified by Lacerenza, Marlow, Tannenbaum, and Salas (2018) include team building, teamwork training (or team training), leadership training, and team debriefing. In other words, team development includes formalized programs to help members *feel* like a team (i.e., team building), as well as those designed to ensure that (a) members are trained to coordinate actions like a team, (b) leaders have the skills to integrate members as a team, and (c) members adapt to challenges through effective group discussion.

Team building has the most established foundation in sport research and is featured in this chapter. However, there is increasing recognition for the value of the remaining three types of team development interventions in sport. One example relates to teamwork training, where a consultant prompts members to work together more efficiently. One example of a teamwork intervention approach in sport was reported by McEwan and Beauchamp (2018), who developed an intervention that trained team members in goal setting (a common team building strategy) alongside efforts to improve skills and knowledge needed to work well together. These sessions targeted different elements of teamwork, including how to provide effective feedback and successfully debrief after competition, and even included simulated scenarios. Over a ten-week intervention study comparing six teams experiencing the intervention to six no-intervention controls, McEwan and Beauchamp (2018) provided evidence for the efficacy of this intervention in terms of increasing members' beliefs about their capacity to work well together. The example of a teamwork intervention provides a sense for how a spectrum of approaches may support group effectiveness.

Benefits of Team Development

Team development interventions can make groups more effective. Effectiveness nevertheless depends on the context and the goals of the specific group. Outcomes may span the cognitive

> **Exhibit 16.1. Leveraging Team Development for Health-Related Outcomes**
>
> The group-related principles and strategies designed for team development have potential use in interventions designed to support the individual-level health of athletes. These outcomes differ from those of team development but are important to consider. Notably, youth and emerging adults who participate in sport are often more likely than their peers to experience numerous negative behaviors or situations, ranging from abuse and peer victimization to the use of substances like performance-enhancing drugs or alcohol (Johnson, & McRee, 2015). How can we ensure that teammates exert a positive influence on these behaviors, rather than pressuring one another or perpetrating harmful behaviors themselves?
>
> Concussions in sport provide one current example. Athletes tend to hold inaccurate beliefs about concussion reporting norms. They often anticipate that teammates hold more supportive norms toward concussion non-reporting than what their peers believe in reality (Kroshus, Kubzansky, Goldman, & Austin, 2014). In other words, athletes feel pressure to play with concussions because they think that their teammates expect them to—even if that is not actually the case.
>
> In response to these findings, Kroshus et al. (2014) recommended that team-based interventions are needed to change athletes' beliefs about their teammates' norms for concussion reporting. In such an approach, concussion specialists could help teams to set norms for concussion reporting, along with norms to identify and report cases where teammates seem to demonstrate concussion symptoms. Activities related to structuring norms, assigning roles, and personal disclosure are of use in such an intervention. Nevertheless, there are few reports of the systematic use of such approaches in sport research, so this is an area to explore in the future.

domain (e.g., do we share an understanding of our team 'system'?), affective domain (e.g., do we enjoy the team?), team process domain (e.g., do we communicate efficiently?), and the team outcome domain (e.g., do we win?). Team development can also be used to help enhance individual outcomes that may not directly link to the sport group (See Exhibit 16.1). Depending on which of these outcomes one hopes to address, differing team development strategies can be used.

Regardless of the domain of these outcomes, successful team development produces a close and effective work group that often encompasses the six work characteristics outlined by Woodcock and Francis (1994). In Exhibit 16.2, these six characteristics are illustrated by using Pat Riley's (1993) experiences when he was hired by the New York Knicks to produce a contender for the NBA championship.

The first benefit is that team leadership becomes coherent, visionary, and acceptable (Woodcock & Francis, 1994). As a result of Riley's (1993) efforts with individuals and the team as a collective, the Knicks were focused as a group and knew who they were and where they were going when they went into the season.

A second benefit is that team members understand and accept their roles and responsibilities (Woodcock & Francis, 1994). In his first step in developing a better team, Pat Riley directed his attention toward the core of the team, Patrick Ewing. Although the quote does not explicitly highlight it, Riley was anxious to ensure that Ewing understood and accepted not only the projections for the team but his own role.

Following a successful intervention, members of the team emotionally "sign up" and dedicate their efforts to collective achievement (Woodcock & Francis, 1994). When team unity on the Knicks broke down, Riley (1993) had members of various cliques on the team (e.g., the core players, the rebels, a social isolate, the complainers) take their chairs into various places in the room "to define reality … [to hold] up a mirror so they could see what they were making of themselves: human isolates in a hostile sea, linked only by their gripes" (p. 240). As the quote in Exhibit 16.2 illustrates, following this session, the clique members rededicated their efforts to the team's collective interests.

Exhibit 16.2. Illustrations of the Desired Benefits of Team Building Interventions

Area	Illustration
Leadership is coherent, visionary, and acceptable	The Knicks had started the season with a single goal: to become the hardest-working, best-conditioned, toughest, most professional, unselfish, and disliked team in the NBA. (Riley, 1993, p. 235)
Roles and functions are understood	I also told [Patrick Ewing] that . . . the pressure on him would be unmatched because he'd be expected to stand as the core of a championship team. (Riley, 1993, p. 238)
Members emotionally sign up and dedicate their efforts to collective achievements	We had an hours-long discussion about tolerance, openness, and the spirit of understanding. About how losing brings out insecurities, blaming. About sharing the weight. Things got better after that. The core became stronger, the rebels became more cooperative, the stand-aparts began to take a stake in the team's morale. (Riley, 1993, pp. 240–242)
A positive, energetic, and empowering climate is present in the group	Whenever a Chicago Bull went to the basket, intending to throw down a dunk that would rock the stadium, we [the Knicks] would come to stop him—just as hard as he had come to score. Whenever he showed us how much he wanted to win, we had to show him that we wanted the same thing, just as much. We simply didn't want to defer. Without that attitude we'd be handing the Bulls a license to tear our hearts out for the next several years. (Riley, 1993, p. 248)
Meetings are efficient in terms of time and resources	We brought on . . . probably the best weight and strength coach in the league. We spent a lot of time before and after each practice warding off potential [injuries] through weight and flexibility training, cardiovascular fitness, diet and nutrition counseling . . . All year long, no big-time injuries hit us. We were the healthiest team in the league. (Riley, 1993, p. 235)
Weaknesses in team capability diagnosed and reduced or eliminated	A tremendous share of credit for the Knicks' reemergence goes to team president Dave Checketts, who renegotiated contracts to get the team under the salary cap and made our team building trades possible. (Riley, 1993, p. 237)

A fourth consequence of team building is that the group develops a positive, energetic, and empowering climate. The attitude symbolized by the quote in Exhibit 16.2 is intended to highlight this characteristic. A collective attitude developed around defense that helped produce a sense of team identity.

When team building has been successful, group meetings are efficient and make good use of time and available resources. If the team building has helped to clearly define or clarify the group's goals, produce role clarity and acceptance, improve interpersonal relationships, and so on, then team meetings can be more focused and efficient.

Finally, if a team building program is successful, weaknesses in the team will have been diagnosed and their negative effects reduced or eliminated. In Exhibit 16.2, Riley (1993) gives credit to team president Dave Checketts for freeing up money under the NBA salary cap so players critical to team success could be hired.

Team Building Programs in Sport

The sport-specific team building literature base includes empirical research studies, case reports, and practical or theoretical reviews extending back over 30 years. Several sport team-building interventions are depicted within Exhibit 16.3. These interventions are drawn together by their focus on developing group cohesion. Furthermore, formal team

Exhibit 16.3. Example Team-Building and Teamwork Interventions in Sport

Authors and Context	Approach, Type, Theory, and Description
Newin, Bloom, and Loughead (2008): Adolescent ice hockey (Canada)	*Indirect approach*: Workshop with coaches, delivered by facilitator. Coaches delivered activities to team. *Type:* Various, selected by coach. *Theory:* Carron & Spink (1993) framework. *Description:* Introduction, conceptual, practical stages completed during a two-hour long workshop. Coaches delivered at least five team building sessions with athletes during the season. Researchers recommended practical strategies for coaches (e.g., rope challenge; balance beam activity).
Yukelson (1997): College Sport (Division I; USA)	*Direct approach*: Description of general approach of full-time consultant within a sport program. *Type:* Various, selected by team. *Theory:* Goals of intervention include aspirational group environment elements (e.g., shared vision, collaborative teamwork, accountability, positive team culture). *Description:* Four stages employed during season, including assessment (i.e., needs assessment), education (i.e., educating athletes and coaches about team development), brainstorm (i.e., athletes and coaches work with consultant to identify strategies), and implementation (i.e., consultant facilitates strategies).
Barker, Evans, Coffee, Slater, and McCarthy (2014): Elite cricket athletes (adolescent) during overseas tour (UK)	*Direct approach*: Team session led by sport psychology consultant. *Type:* Interpersonal relationships. *Theory:* Personal-disclosure mutual-sharing, focused on closeness generated through disclosures. *Description:* Teams participated in disclosure sessions during international tour. Following an initial session where athletes received a prompt to write a disclosure statement and were educated on the disclosure process, athletes attended two separate sessions—early and late in the tour—to complete speeches involving their disclosures to teammates (e.g., why they participate in elite sport; what they learned during tour).
McLaren, Eys, & Murray, (2015): Adolescent soccer teams (CAN)	*Indirect approach*: Training session with facilitator. Coaches used training when interacting with athletes. *Type:* Interpersonal relationships. Note that leadership training is also evident. *Theory:* Achievement goal theory. Focused on how coaches may enhance team climate through enhanced coaching and by defining success relative to personal development and effort. *Description:* Coaches attended a 1.5-hour presentation focused on several components (e.g., ideal use of reinforcement, using positive group norms, assigning team roles). Coaches also received a 30-page manual.
McEwan and Beauchamp (2018): Competitive team sport in adolescent, adult, and university-level contexts (CAN)	*Direct approach:* Workshop with facilitator. Athletes and coaches were encouraged to employ strategies. *Type:* Teamwork training, with goal-setting components (i.e., team building). *Theory:* Framework of teamwork (McEwan & Beauchamp, 2018). *Description:* Two 60-minute training sessions, spaced four weeks apart. Each session was preceded by a session to complete a teamwork survey. Training manuals were provided to teams. During sessions, members received feedback on survey responses and experienced tailored strategies (e.g., goal setting, simulations, debriefing worksheet)

Note. Type refers to types of team building intervention strategies (i.e., problem-solving, interpersonal relationships, role relationships, goal setting), or other types of team development (i.e., leadership development, teamwork training, debriefing).

building interventions importantly differ from the informal social activities commonly planned by coaches or team members in that they are systematically designed based on theory and because they focus on specific targets relating to the group environment. However, understanding the differences between existing interventions entails identifying the varying approaches they adopt.

Team building interventions are classified into types based on the focus of the activities in which members participate, with four types being most common (Lacerenza et al., 2018). In the first, the focus is on group goal setting. The coach or practitioner works with the team to establish collective goals and identify actions to achieve those goals. These goals are often set early in the season, alongside individual goals, and consistently evaluated and revised throughout the year, exemplified in the pilot intervention reported by Durdubas, Martin, and Koruc (2019).

The second type focuses on interpersonal relationships by engaging members in activities that bind members interpersonally or build understanding of members' values and perspectives. One example is personal-disclosure mutual-sharing (e.g., Barker, Evans, Coffee, Slater, & McCarthy, 2014), which is an activity where a facilitator leads team discussions about personal features such as their values and the meaning behind their sport involvement. The third type focuses on individual role involvement, including strategies to clarify members' roles, increase role acceptance and satisfaction, and otherwise prompt members to perform their roles. Problem solving comprises the fourth type, whereby members collectively face a novel challenge or activity.

Many of the activities recognized as teambuilding colloquially (i.e., outside of sport psychology) use problem-solving strategies. For example, the 2018 USA volleyball team reported on a team building activity led by Navy SEALs that resembled the notoriously challenging training that new SEALs must complete. Away from civilization for several days with little sleep, athletes faced extreme physical challenges along with demanding tasks involving cognitive effort and coordination, after which outside hitter Kelsey Robinson stated

> [In Volleyball] you fall into these roles naturally and they just become your roles. If we're successful, then those roles don't really change. But you get put in this environment where no one's been doing this forever and no one has experience and you rely on what people are good at ... I thought it was an awesome experience and we had some really funny moments and some really amazing moments where you're like, 'Our team is so, so rad, and these women are incredible.' (Price, 2018, para. 6)

Whereas these four approaches share similar outcomes, like group cohesion or role clarity, they entail differing assumptions about the path to reach those outcomes. For example, role development interventions are predicated on how members will be more likely to perform their role and be satisfied with the group when they understand their own role and those of others. In contrast, interpersonal relationship approaches come along with an assumption that affection and empathy will draw members together. Although these types are inclusive of most evidence-based team building interventions in sport, other types may emerge in the future.

Traditions of team building are further delineated across two ways of delivering protocols: indirect and direct. With the indirect approach, the facilitator or consultant works alongside a group leader or coach. The coach or leader then introduces the team building interventions to the team. As a result, the consultant may rarely, or never, take part in direct interactions with all members. Meanwhile, a direct approach refers to when the individual responsible for implementing the team building intervention works directly with the athletes. That individual could be the coach—as was the case with both Pat Riley's team building with the New York Knicks. Commonly, however, direct interventions refer to when a team building consultant enters the group to work directly with the team and aligns with the traditional role of a sport psychology consultant.

As an example of a direct approach, personal-disclosure mutual-sharing interventions rely on a skilled consultant to identify group needs, prepare members to contribute, and facilitate a meaningful group discussion. Yukelson (1997) also reported on his use of direct team building as the Penn State University sport psychology consultant. Yukelson (1997) outlined that promoting effective team environments was fundamental to his sport psychology consulting approach and advocated for consultants to embed themselves within the team and be accessible. Taking this role allows consultants to gain trust and respect and to adjust strategies to address new circumstances. Yukelson's (1997) approach is detailed in Exhibit 16.3.

Regardless of type or approach, all interventions could benefit from guidelines regarding the right environment. It is critical to establish rapport within a group and take the time to conduct an adequate assessment of group needs. Second, psychological safety is required for members to engage in team development activities. Ensuring that intervention activities convey respect and that activities are safe from added conflict is important. Third, activities should be sustainable. Although team development interventions need not span the life of the group, they should keep in mind how members can sustain the changes made in the intervention. Group leaders should continually focus on how the group environment is emerging, before and after interventions are completed. These changes will help ensure that the intervention fits well within the group and, perhaps most importantly, that group members buy-in to team building activities.

Carron and Colleagues' Indirect Team Building Approach

A detailed depiction of an indirect team building approach is a protocol developed through a series of team building investigations by Carron and colleagues (Carron, Spink, & Prapavessis, 1997; Carron & Spink, 1993; Prapavessis, Carron, & Spink, 1997; Spink & Carron, 1993). This work is also highly important. Notably, a review article that created a network using the citations of all team building research in sport revealed the value of this work for subsequent theory and team building interventions (Bruner et al., 2013). In a network where all citations (or references) from one research paper to another were "ties" between papers, the authors demonstrated that the vast majority of team building research within sport could be traced back through early work involving group cohesion and team building by Carron and Spink (Carron & Spink, 1993; Spink & Carron, 1993).

The team building intervention focused on developing coaches' skillset to regulate their team's environment. The intervention was designed to enhance the group for the season in which the intervention was delivered but was also designed to help coaches manage teams farther into the future. It involved stages that progressed sequentially, including introduction, conceptual, practical, and intervention stages. The first three stages occurred in a seminar/workshop conducted by a sport psychologist. The subsequent intervention stage was when the real 'action' took place, as coaches deployed team building strategies with the team.

Exhibit 16.4. Conceptual Framework Used as a Basis for the Implementation of a Team Building Program in Sport and Fitness Groups

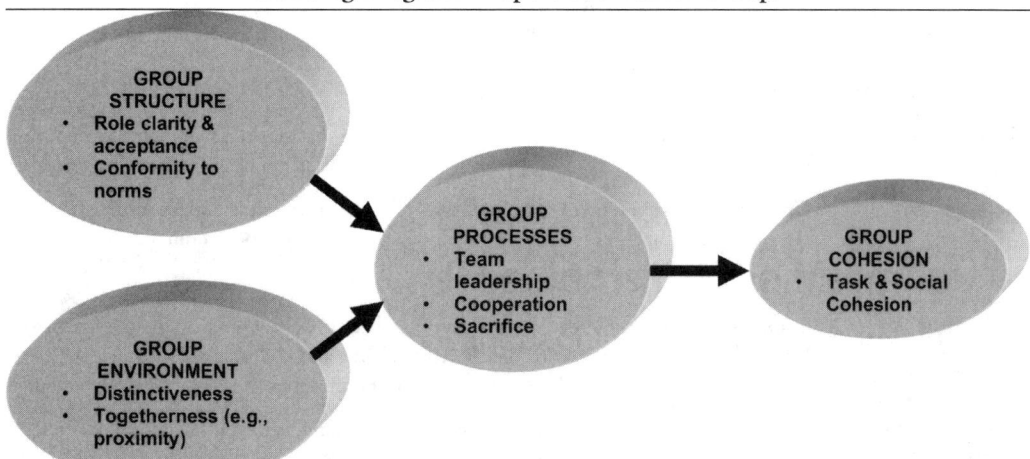

Source. "Team Building in Sport" by H. Prapavessis, A. V. Carron, K. S. Spink, 1997, *International Journal of Sport Psychology, 27,* 269–285.

In the introductory stage, the coach was provided with a brief overview of the general benefits of group cohesion (see Chapter 14) and the reasons for introducing team building. This stage may include findings from academic studies about links between group cohesion and valued outcomes, or broader anecdotal and theoretical justification for team building.

The conceptual stage was used to introduce a model to better understand group dynamics (see Exhibit 16.4). The conceptual model had three benefits. First, it facilitated communication with the coaches because the complex concepts were simplified and more readily described. Second, the interrelationship among the components of the team building protocol were highlighted. Third, the focus of the possible interventions was more easily distinguished.

The conceptual framework is linear—consisting of inputs, throughputs, and outputs. Cohesion (task and social) was presented as the product of three categories of factors:

- The team's environment (e.g., proximity and distinctiveness),
- The team's structure (e.g., group norms, leadership, and role clarity), and
- The team's processes (e.g., cooperation, sacrifices, cooperation, goals, and objectives).

As Exhibit 16.4 shows, a team's structure and its environment represents the inputs in the conceptual model. These two inputs are assumed to affect the throughput (i.e., team processes), which in turn is assumed to affect the output (i.e., group cohesion).

In the practical stage, the coaches engaged in brainstorming in an attempt to generate specific team building strategies for their specific situation. Representative examples of strategies listed in the sport brainstorming sessions are presented in Exhibit 16.5, alongside rationale provided to the coaches for including each of the factors.

In the intervention stage, the team building protocols were introduced to the team by their coaches. To ensure that the team building strategies were used, trained research assistants monitored the sessions on a weekly basis.

Exhibit 16.5. Examples of Specific Strategies Coaches Used to Enhance Group Cohesiveness

Category	Rationale (Cohesion is Enhanced By/When)	Strategies
Team Environment		
Distinctiveness	Feeling like a distinct unit.	Ensure that all team members have and use the identical training gear with team logos.
Togetherness	Group members are repetitively placed in close physical proximity.	Reserve a section of lockers in the same section in the locker room.
Team Structure		
Role clarity & acceptance	Team members clearly understand, accept their role, and are satisfied with their role.	Schedule weekly meetings with athletes to outline and reinforce their role responsibilities.
Conformity to team norms	Conformity to team social and task norms.	Have captains establish a behavioral code and have weekly sessions to discuss issues of noncompliance.
Group Processes		
Team leadership	A participative style of decision-making.	Establish an elected players' council to bring forward issues to discuss with the coach.
Individual sacrifices	High status team members make sacrifices for the group.	Request that team captains assume the responsibility for integrating rookies into the social network of the team.
Goals and objectives	Member participation in team goal setting.	Meet weekly with the total team to establish process, performance, and outcome goals for the upcoming week.
Cooperation	Cooperative behavior.	Have veterans provide individual instruction and assistance to athletes unfamiliar with the system.

Source. "Team Building in Sport" by H. Prapavessis, A. V. Carron, K. S. Spink, 1997, *International Journal of Sport Psychology, 27,* 269–285.

The Effectiveness of Team Building

What can we say about the effectiveness of team development? Also, how do we know which approaches work best? Which teams might be in the greatest need for team development? Addressing these questions, Martin et al. (2009) conducted a meta-analysis considering the effects of 17 sport interventions. They investigated team building interventions only, as other group intervention types are not common within sport (e.g., teamwork training, debriefing training, leadership training). The interventions reported positive outcomes such as increased team performance, improved attitudes toward one's role, enhanced task and social cohesion, and reduced competitive anxiety. The 17 studies they located differed from one another across several characteristics including type of team building program (e.g., goal setting, interpersonal relationship programs, combination programs, adventure programs), as well as the length of the intervention, and type of sport. The following is a summary of the findings about the types of interventions that were most effective:

- Goal setting was the most effective team building intervention,
- Interventions lasting longer than two weeks were more effective than shorter approaches, and
- Interventions were most effective with individual sport teams as opposed to team sport.

The Martin et al. (2009) review is useful for describing strategies that researchers, athletes, and coaches value and are willing to adopt. However, the studies it was based upon limit our understanding of effectiveness. In addition to a small number of studies, study samples were rarely big enough to identify whether or not true effects existed. Many studies included too few athletes or teams to be confident of the effects they reported. Studies also often lacked an adequate control condition (i.e., alternative team interventions) and teams were rarely randomly-assigned to conditions.

Studies within the organizational psychology literature produce a better barometer with regard to effectiveness. Indeed, initial reviews of the topic were not optimistic. Salas, Rozell, Mullen, and Driskell (1999) located 11 team building studies that met their criteria. Focused only on the link between team building and performance, Salas et al. (1999) concluded

> One of the most important results to emerge from the present analyses is the documentation of the overall nonsignificant and negligible effect of team building on performance. These results suggest that the enthusiastic testimonials on behalf of team building interventions should be interpreted with caution. (p. 323)

More recent research conveyed more optimism, but also more clarity regarding (a) the range of outcomes that may relate to team building and (b) the contrast between team building and team training. Specifically, DiazGranados, Shuffler, Wingate, and Salas (2017) summarized recent meta-analytic reviews that included the effects to team building as well as team training interventions. The outcomes of interest included performance along with cognitive outcomes (e.g., knowledge of team standards), affective outcomes (e.g., trust, satisfaction), and team processes (e.g., communication; teamwork). Although positive effects emerged in relation to all outcomes, team building had the strongest positive effects on affective as well as process outcomes. In comparison, teamwork training produces stronger positive effects related to cognitive outcomes and performance outcomes—findings that were again supported in a subsequent review (McEwan, Ruissen, Eys, Zumbo, & Beauchamp, 2017).

The resulting message is that team-building and teamwork training interventions are both effective strategies to develop groups but may have differing uses. Team building may continue to be ideal when the intended target entails enhancing teammate relationships as well as group processes like communication or coordination. Team building is also the sole approach that has been adopted with regularity within sport. Meanwhile, teamwork training also demonstrates effectiveness on these outcomes but may show particular strengths in relation to cognitive outcomes like helping members provide effective feedback, understand the team's mental model, and develop the skills needed to work together. In other words, team training may be preferable if the challenge facing their group is a deficiency in teamwork. In sum, it is possible to conduct interventions with lasting effects on the team environment.

References

Abdul-Jabbar, K., & Knobler, P. (1983). *Giant steps: The autobiography of Kareem Abdul-Jabbar.* Toronto, ON: Bantam House.

Adams, R. S., & Biddle, B. J. (1970). *Realities of teaching: Explorations with video tape.* New York: Holt, Rinehart, & Winston.

Agnew, G., & Carron, A. V. (1994). Crowd effects and the home advantage. *International Journal of Sport Psychology, 25,* 53–62.

Allen, M. (1987). *Jackie Robinson: A life remembered.* New York: Franklin Watts.

Allen, M. P., Panian, S. K., & Lotz, R. E. (1979). Managerial succession and organizational performance: A recalcitrant problem revisited. *Administrative Science Quarterly, 24,* 167–180.

Allen, M. S., Coffee, P., & Greenlees, I. (2012). A theoretical framework and research agenda for studying team attributions in sport. *International Review of Sport and Exercise Psychology, 5,* 121–144.

Allport, F. H. (1924). *Social psychology.* Cambridge, MA: Riverside.

Alsop, J. (1982). *FDR: A centenary remembrance.* New York: Viking Press.

Altman, I. (1975). *The environment and social behavior.* Monterey, CA: Brooks/Cole.

Alton, R. (2018, October 6). Teamwork? It's not the American way, even in the Ryder cup. *The Spectator.* Retrieved from https://www.spectator.co.uk/2018/10/teamwork-its-not-the-american-way-even-in-the-ryder-cup/.

Ames, N. (2018, June 5). What Iceland did next: How the tiny nation qualified for the World Cup. *ESPN.* Retrieved from https://www.espn.com/soccer/club/iceland/470/blog/post/3507356/how-iceland-qualified-for-the-world-cup

Anderson, C., Hildreth, J. A. D., & Howland, L. (2015). Is the desire for status a fundamental human motive? A review of the empirical literature. *Psychological Bulletin, 141,* 574–601.

Anderson, K. (1997, April 7). Surprise, surprise. Few people expected Tennessee to repeat as the women's champion, but guess what? *Sports Illustrated, 86,* 42–49.

Anderson, K. (2010, May 10). Crossover move. *Sports Illustrated, 112,* 26.

Anderson, L. R. (1978). Groups would do better without humans. *Personality and Social Psychology Bulletin, 4,* 557–558.

Andrews, B. (2017, July 12). Long snapper love. *Ticats.ca.* Retrieved from https://ticats.ca/long-snapper-love/

Anshel, M. H. (1995). Examining social loafing among elite female rowers as a function of task duration and mood. *Journal of Sport Behavior, 18,* 39-49.

Anshel, M. H., & Sailes, G. (1990). Discrepant attitudes of intercollegiate athletes as a function of race. *Journal of Sport Behavior, 13,* 87–101.

Arnold, G. E., & Straub, W.F. (1972). Personality and group cohesiveness as determinants of success among inter-scholastic basketball teams. In I. D. Williams & L. M. Wankel (Eds.), *Proceedings of the Fourth Canadian Symposium on Psycho-Motor Learning and Sport Psychology*, (pp. 346–352). Ottawa, ON: Fitness and Amateur Sport Directorate, Department of National Health and Welfare.

Arrow, H., Poole, M. S., Henry, K. B., Wheelan, S., & Moreland, R. (2004). Time, change, and development: The temporal perspective on groups. *Small Group Research, 35,* 73–105.

Arthur, C. A., Woodman, T., Ong, C. W., Hardy, L., & Ntoumanis, N. (2011). The role of athlete narcissism in moderating the relationship between coaches' transformational leader behaviors and athlete motivation. *Journal of Sport & Exercise Psychology, 33,* 3–19.

Asch, S. E. (1951). Effects of group pressure upon the modification and distortion of judgments. In H. Guetzkow (Ed.), *Groups, leadership, and men* (pp. 177–190). Pittsburgh, PA: Carnegie Press.

Associated Press. (2020, March 11). 'Our only virus is PSG': Fans defy coronavirus stadium closure in Paris. *Euronews.* Retrieved from https://www.euronews.com/2020/03/11/our-only-virus-is-psg-fans-defy-coronavirus-stadium-closure-in-paris

Audas, R., Dobson, S., & Goddard, J. (2002). The impact of managerial changes on team performance in professional sports. *Journal of Economics and Business, 54,* 633–650.

Bacharach, S. B., Bamberger, P., & Mundell, B. (1993). Status inconsistency in organizations: From social hierarchy to stress. *Journal of Organizational Behavior, 14,* 21–36.

Back, M. D., Küfner, A. C., Dufner, M., Gerlach, T. M., Rauthmann, J. F., & Denissen, J. J. (2013). Narcissistic admiration and rivalry: Disentangling the bright and dark sides of narcissism. *Journal of Personality and Social Psychology, 105,* 1013–1037.

Bailey, B., Benson, A. J., & Bruner, M. W. (2017). Investigating the organisational culture of CrossFit. *International Journal of Sport and Exercise Psychology,* 1–15.

Baker, P. (1981). The division of labor: Interdependence, isolation, and cohesion in small groups. *Small Group Behavior, 12,* 93–106.

Bales, R. F. (1966). Task roles and social roles in problem solving groups. In B. J. Biddle & E. J. Thomas (Eds.), *Role theory: Concepts and research* (pp. 254–262). New York: John Wiley.

Bales, R. F., & Slater, P. E. (1955). Role differentiation in small decision-making groups. In T. Parsons & R. F. Bales (Eds.), *The family socialization and interaction process* (pp. 259–306). Glencoe, IL: The Free Press.

Bales, R. F., & Strodtbeck, F. L. (1951). Phases in group problem solving. *Journal of Abnormal Social Psychology, 46,* 485–495.

Balish, S. M., Eys, M. A., & Schulte-Hostedde, A. I. (2013). Evolutionary sport and exercise psychology: Integrating proximate and ultimate explanations. *Psychology of Sport and Exercise, 14,* 413–422.

Balliet, D., Li, N. P., Macfarlan, S. J., & Van Vugt, M. (2011). Sex differences in cooperation: A meta-analytic review of social dilemmas. *Psychological Bulletin, 137,* 881–909.

Balmer, N. J., Nevill, A. M. & Williams, M. (2001). Home advantage in the Winter Olympics (1908–1998). *Journal of Sports Sciences, 19,* 129–139.

Balmer, N. J., Nevill, A. M., & Williams, M. (2003). Modelling home advantage in the Summer Olympic Games. *Journal of Sports Sciences, 21,* 469–478.

Bandura, A. (1982). Self-efficacy mechanism in human agency. *American Psychologist, 37,* 122–147.

Bandura, A. (1986). *Social foundations of thought and action: A social cognitive theory.* Englewood Cliffs, NJ: Prentice-Hill.

Bandura, A. (1997). *Self-efficacy: The exercise of control.* New York: W. H. Freeman & Co.

Barker, J. B., Evans, A. L., Coffee, P., Slater, M. J., & McCarthy, P. J. (2014). Consulting on tour: A dual-phase personal-disclosure mutual-sharing intervention and group functioning in elite youth cricket. *The Sport Psychologist, 28,* 186–197.

Barnett, V., & Hilditch, S. (1993). The effect of an artificial pitch surface on home team performance in football (soccer). *Journal of the Royal Statistical Society, 156,* 39–50.

Bass, B. M. (1960). *Leadership, psychology, and organizational behavior.* New York: Harper.

Bass, B. M., & Riggio, R. E. (2006). *Transformational leadership* (2nd ed.). Mahwah, NJ: Lawrence Erlbaum.

Baum, A., & Valins, S. (1977). *Architecture and social behavior: Psychological studies of social density.* Hillsdale, NJ: Erlbaum.

Baumeister, R. F. (1985, April). The championship choke. When a title is on the line, jubilant home crowds can root athletes on to win. *Psychology Today, 19,* 48–52.

Baumeister, R. F. (1995). Disputing the effects of championship pressures and home audiences. *Journal of Personality and Social Psychology, 68,* 644–648.

Baumeister, R. F., & Leary, M. R. (1995). The need to belong: Desire for interpersonal attachment as a fundamental human motivation. *Psychological Bulletin, 117,* 497–529.

Baumeister, R. F., & Steinhilber, A. (1984). Paradoxical effects of supportive audiences on performance under pressure: The home field disadvantage in sports championships. *Journal of Personality and Social Psychology, 47,* 85–93.

Beam, J. W., Serwatka, T. S., & Wilson, W. J. (2004). Preferred leadership of NCAA Division I and II intercollegiate student-athletes. *Journal of Sport Behavior, 27,* 3–17.

Beasley, A. H. (2015, October 12). Miami Dolphins interim coach Dan Campbell switches up locker assignments, X's and O's. *Miami Herald.* Retrieved from https://www.miamiherald.com/sports/nfl/miami-dolphins/article38842479.html

Beauchamp, M. R., & Bray, S. R. (2001). Role ambiguity and role conflict within interdependent teams. *Small Group Research, 32,* 133–157.

Beauchamp, M. R., Bray, S. R., Eys, M. A., & Carron, A. V. (2002). Role ambiguity, role efficacy, and role performance: Multidimensional and mediational relationships within interdependent sport teams. *Group Dynamics: Theory, Research, and Practice, 6,* 229–242.

Beauchamp, M. R., Bray, S. R., Eys, M. A., & Carron, A. V. (2003). The effect of role ambiguity on competitive state anxiety. *Journal of Sport & Exercise Psychology, 25,* 77–92.

Beauchamp, M. R., Bray, S. R., Eys, M. A., & Carron, A. V. (2005). Multidimensional role ambiguity and role satisfaction: A prospective examination using interdependent sport teams. *Journal of Applied Social Psychology, 35,* 2560–2576.

Beauchamp, M. R., Carron, A. V., McCutcheon, S., & Harper, O. (2007). Older adults' preferences for exercising alone versus in groups: Considering contextual congruence. *Annals of Behavioral Medicine, 33,* 200–206.

Bell, S. T. (2007). Deep-level composition variables as predictors of team performance: A meta-analysis. *Journal of Applied Psychology, 92,* 595–615.

Bell, S. T., Villado, A. J., Lukasik, M. A., Belau, L., & Briggs, A. L. (2011). Getting specific about demographic diversity variable and team performance relationships: A meta-analysis. *Journal of Management, 37,* 709–743.

Benjafield, J., Liddell, W. W., & Benjafield, I. (1989). Is there a home disadvantage in professional sports championships? *Social Behavior and Personality, 17,* 45–50.

Benson, A. J., Bruner, M. W., & Eys, M. (2017). A social identity approach to understanding the conditions associated with antisocial behaviors among teammates in female teams. *Sport, Exercise, and Performance Psychology, 6,* 129–142.

Benson, A. J., Evans, M. B., & Eys, M. A. (2016). Organizational socialization in team sport environments. *Scandinavian Journal of Medicine & Science in Sports, 26,* 463–473.

Benson, A. J., & Eys, M. A. (2017). Understanding the consequences of newcomer integration processes: The Sport Team Socialization Tactics Questionnaire. *Journal of Sport & Exercise Psychology, 39,* 13–28.

Benson, A. J., Eys, M., & Irving, P. G. (2016). Great expectations: How role expectations and role experiences relate to perceptions of team cohesion. *Journal of Sport & Exercise Psychology, 38,* 160–172.

Benson, A. J., Eys, M., Surya, M., Dawson, K., & Schneider, M. (2013). Athletes' perceptions of role acceptance in interdependent sport teams. *The Sport Psychologist, 27,* 269–280

Benson, A. J., Hardy, J., & Eys, M. (2016). Contextualizing leaders' interpretations of proactive followership. *Journal of Organizational Behavior, 37,* 949–966.

Benson, A. J., Šiška, P., Eys, M., Priklerová, S., & Slepička, P. (2016). A prospective multilevel examination of the relationship between cohesion and team performance in elite youth sport. *Psychology of Sport and Exercise, 27,* 39–46.

Benson, A. J., Surya, M., & Eys, M. A. (2014). The nature and transmission of roles in sport teams. *Sport, Exercise, and Performance Psychology, 3,* 228–240.

Berger, J., Ridgeway, C. L., & Zelditch, M. (2002). Construction of status and referential structures. *Sociological Theory, 20,* 157–179.

Berghorn, F. J., Yetman, N. R., & Hanna, W. E. (1988). Racial participation and integration in men's and women's intercollegiate basketball: Continuity and change. *Sociology of Sport Journal, 5,* 107–124.

Berglas, S., & Jones, E. E. (1978). Drug choice as a self-handicapping strategy in response to non-contingent success. *Journal of Personality and Social Psychology 36,* 405–417.

Berkowitz, L. (1954). Group standards, cohesiveness, and productivity. *Human Relations, 7,* 509–514.

Berkowitz, L. (1956). Group norms among bomber crews: Patterns of perceived crew attitudes, "active" crew attitudes, and crew liking related to air crew effectiveness in Far Eastern combat. *Sociometry, 19,* 141–153.

Bernthal, P. R., & Insko, C. A. (1993). Cohesiveness without groupthink: The interactive effects of social and task cohesion. *Group and Organizational Management, 18,* 66–87.

Bertrand, K. (2012, July 31). Olympic athletes' fierce friendship. *The Australian Women's Weekly.* Retrieved from https://www.nowtolove.co.nz/news/real-life/olympic-athletes-fierce-friendship-6322

Bien, L. (2018, July 17). How does a Tour de France team work? *SBNation.com.* Retrieved from https://www.sbnation.com/cycling/2018/7/17/17570042/tour-de-france-team-tactics-staff-support

Bird, A. M. (1977). Team structure and success as related to cohesiveness and leadership. *Journal of Social Psychology, 103,* 217–223.

Bird, A. M., Foster, C. D., & Maruyama, G. (1980). Convergent and incremental effects of cohesion on attributions for self and team. *Journal of Sport Psychology, 2,* 181–194.

Birrell, S., & Richter, D. M. (1994). Is a diamond forever? Feminist transformations of sport. In S. Birrell & C. L. Cole (Eds.), *Women, sport, and culture* (pp. 221–244). Champaign, IL: Human Kinetics.

Blount, R. (2018, February 9). Jessie Diggins, U.S. women's cross-country team apply lessons from Sochi in Pyeongchang. *Star Tribune Online*. Retrieved from http://www.startribune.com/jessie-diggins-u-s-women-s-cross-country-team-apply-lessons-from-sochi-in-pyeongchang/473488273/

Bond, R. (2005). Group size and conformity. *Group processes & Intergroup Relations, 8*, 331–354.

Bond, R., & Smith, P. B. (1996). Culture and conformity: A meta-analysis of studies using Asch's (1952b, 1956) line judgment task. *Psychological Bulletin, 119,* 111–137.

Bopp, T., & Sagas, M. (2014). Racial tasking and the college quarterback: Redefining the stacking phenomenon. *Journal of Sport Management, 28,* 136–142.

Boushey, H., & Glynn, S. J. (2012). There are significant costs to replacing employees. *Center for American Progress*. Retrieved from https://www.scribd.com/document/112707536/There-Are-Significant-Business-Costs-to-Replacing-Employees

Boroumand, S., Eys, M., & Benson, A. J. (2018). How status conflict undermines athletes' willingness to help new teammates. *Journal of Applied Sport Psychology, 30,* 358–365.

Bosselut, G., Heuzé, J., Eys, M. A., & Bouthier, D. (2010). Influence of task cohesion and role ambiguity on cognitive anxiety during a European Rugby Union Championship. *Athletic Insight, 2,* 17–34.

Bossetti, M. (2019, August 28). Jeremy Lin didn't give the Raptors much, but he gave them enough. *Fansided*. Retrieved from https://raptorsrapture.com/2019/08/28/toronto-raptors-jeremy-lin-beijing/

Boylen, R. (2018, March 14). Hurricanes coach concerned about culture of losing in Carolina. *SportsNet*. Retrieved from https://www.sportsnet.ca/hockey/nhl/hurricanes-coach-concerned-culture-losing-growing-carolina/

Brawley, L. R., Carron, A. V., & Widmeyer, W. N. (1987). Assessing the cohesion of teams: Validity of the Group Environment Questionnaire. *Journal of Sport Psychology, 9,* 275–294.

Brawley, L. R., Carron, A. V., & Widmeyer, W. N. (1992). The nature of group goals in sport teams: A phenomenological analysis. *The Sport Psychologist, 6,* 323–333.

Brawley, L. R., Carron, A. V., & Widmeyer, W. N. (1993). The influence of the group and its cohesiveness on perceptions of group-related variables. *Journal of Sport & Exercise Psychology, 15,* 245–260.

Brawley, L. R., & Paskevich, D. M. (1997). Conducting team building research in the context of sport and exercise. *Journal of Applied Psychology, 9,* 11–40.

Bray, S. R., Balaguer, I, & Duda, J. L. (2004). The relationship of task self-efficacy and role efficacy beliefs to role performance in Spanish youth soccer. *Journal of Sports Sciences, 22,* 429–437.

Bray, S. R., Beauchamp, M.R., Eys, M. A., & Carron, A. V. (2005). Need for clarity as a moderator of the role ambiguity – satisfaction relationship. *Journal of Applied Sport Psychology, 17,* 306–318.

Bray, S. R., Brawley, L. R. & Carron, A. V. (2002). Efficacy for interdependent role functions: Evidence from the sport domain. *Small Group Research, 33,* 644–666.

Bray, S., & Carron, A.V. (1993). The home advantage in alpine skiing. *The Australian Journal of Science and Medicine in Sport, 25,* 76–81.

Bray, S. R., Culos, S. N., Gyurcsik, N. C., Widmeyer, W. N., & Brawley, L. R. (1998). Athletes' causal perspectives on game location and performance: The home advantage? *Journal of Sport & Exercise Psychology, 20,* S100.

Bray, S. R. and Martin, K. A. (2003). The influence of competition location on individual sport athletes' performance and psychological states. *Psychology of Sport and Exercise, 4*, 117–123.

Bray, S. R., & Widmeyer, W. N. (1995). Athletes' perceptions of a home advantage in women's basketball. *Journal of Applied Sport Psychology, 7* (Suppl.), S43.

Breglio, J. (1976). *Formal structure and the recruitment of umpires in baseball organizations.* Paper presented at the American Sociological Association Annual Meeting, New York, NY.

Brewer, M. B. (1979). The role of ethnocentricism in intergroup conflict. In W.G. Austin & S. Worchel (Eds.), *The social psychology of intergroup relations* (pp.71–84). Belmont, CA: Wadsworth.

Brown, M. C. (1982). Administrative succession and organizational performance: The succession effect. *Administrative Science Quarterly, 27*, 1–16.

Brown, R. (1988). *Group processes: Dynamics within and between groups.* Oxford, UK: Blackwell.

Brown, R. W. (1965). *Social psychology.* New York: Free Press.

Brown Jr., T. D., Van Raalte, J. L., Brewer, B. W., Winter, C. R., & Cornelius, A. E. (2002). World Cup soccer home advantage. *Journal of Sport Behavior, 25*, 134–144.

Bruner, M. W., Boardley, I. D., Benson, A. J., Wilson, K. S., Root, Z., Turnnidge, J., . . . Côté, J. (2018). Disentangling the relations between social identity and prosocial and antisocial behavior in competitive youth sport. *Journal of Youth and Adolescence, 47*, 1113–1127.

Bruner, M. W., Carreau, J. M., Wilson, K. S., & Penney, M. (2014). Group norms in youth sport: Role of personal and social factors. *The Sport Psychologist, 28*, 323–333.

Bruner, M. W., Eys, M. A., Beauchamp, M. R., & Côté, J. (2013). Examining the origins of team building in sport: A citation network and genealogical approach. *Group Dynamics: Theory, Research, and Practice, 17*, 30–43.

Bruner, M. W., Eys, M. A., Wilson, K. S., & Côté, J. (2014). Group cohesion and positive youth development in team sport athletes. *Sport, Exercise, and Performance Psychology, 3*, 219–227.

Bruton, A. M., Shearer, D. A., & Mellalieu, S. D. (2019). Who said "there is no 'I' in team"? The effects of observational learning content level on efficacy beliefs in groups. *Psychology of Sport and Exercise, 45*, 101563. doi:10.1016/j.psychsport.2019.101563.

Buchanan, H. T., Blankenbaker, J., & Cotton, D. (1976). Academic and athletic ability as popularity factors in elementary school children. *Research Quarterly, 47*, 320–325.

Buehler, R., Messervey, D., & Griffin, D. (2005). Collaborative planning and prediction: Does group discussion affect optimistic biases in time estimation? *Organizational Behavior and Human Decision Processes, 97*, 47–63.

Burgoon, M., Heston, J. K., & McCroskey, J. (1974). *Small group communication: A functional approach.* New York: Holt, Rinehart & Winston.

Burke, C. S., Stagl, K. C., Klein, C., Goodwin, G. F., Salas, E., & Halpin, S. M. (2006). What type of leadership behaviors are functional in teams? A meta-analysis. *The Leadership Quarterly, 17*, 288–307.

Burns, J. M. (1978). *Leadership.* New York: Harper & Row.

Burnstein, E., & Vinokur, A. (1977). Persuasive argumentation and social comparison as determinant of attitude polarization. *Journal of Experimental Social Psychology, 13*, 315–332.

Burton, D., Weinberg, R., Yukelson, D., & Weigand, D. (1998). The goal effectiveness paradox in sport: Examining the goal practices of collegiate athletes. *The Sport Psychologist, 12*, 404–418.

Buton, F., Fontayne, P., Heuzé, J., Bosselut, G., & Raimbault, N. (2007). The QAG-a : An analog version of the Questionnaire sur l'Ambiance du Groupe for measuring the dynamic nature of group cohesion. *Small Group Research, 38,* 235–264.

Buys, C. J. (1978a). Humans would do better without groups. *Personality and Social Psychology Bulletin, 4,* 123–125.

Buys, C. J. (1978b). On groups would do better without groups: A final note. *Personality and Social Psychology Bulletin, 4,* 568.

Cantona, E., & Fynn, A. (1996). *Cantona on Cantona.* London: Deutsch.

Capel, S. A., Sisley, B. L., & Desertrain, G. S. (1987). The relationship between role conflict and role ambiguity to burnout in high school coaches. *Journal of Sport Psychology, 9,* 106–117.

Caplan-Bricker, N. (2017, June 23). The inextricable tie between eating disorders and endurance athletes. *Outside.* Retrieved from https://www.outsideonline.com/2191906/eating-disorders-are-more-common-you-think

Carig, M. (2010). Dallas Braden, unplugged: A's pitcher rips into Yankees star Alex Rodriguez. *NJ.com.* Retrieved from https://www.nj.com/yankees/2010/04/dallas_braden_unplugged_as_pit.html

Carli, L. L. (2001). Gender and social influence. *Journal of Social Issues, 57,* 725–741.

Caron, E. (2018, October 20). Toronto Raptors lay it all on the table in dramatic hype video. *Sports Illustrated.* Retrieved from https://www.si.com/nba/2018/10/20/toronto-raptors-pregame-hype-video-vs-celtics

Carp, S. (2018). No captain? No problem when it comes to leadership for Knights. *Las Vegas Review-Journal.* Retrieved from https://www.reviewjournal.com/sports/golden-knights-nhl/no-captain-no-problem-when-it-comes-to-leadership-for-knights/

Carron, A. V. (1978). Role behavior and coach-athlete interaction. *International Review of Sport Sociology, 13,* 51–65.

Carron, A. V. (1980). *Social psychology of sport.* Ithaca, NY: Mouvement.

Carron, A. V. (1981). Processes of group interaction in sport teams. *Quest, 33,* 245–270.

Carron, A. V., & Bennett, B. B. (1977). Compatibility in the coach-athlete dyad. *Research Quarterly, 48,* 671–679.

Carron, A. V., Brawley, L. R., & Widmeyer, W. N. (1998). The measurement of cohesiveness in sport groups. In J. L. Duda (Ed.), *Advancements in sport and exercise psychology measurement* (pp. 213–226). Morgantown, WV: Fitness Information Technology.

Carron, A. V., & Chelladurai, P. (1981). The dynamics of group cohesion in sport. *Journal of Sport Psychology, 3,* 123–139.

Carron, A. V., Colman, M. M., Wheeler, J., & Stevens, D. (2002). Cohesion and performance in sport: A meta-analysis. *Journal of Sport & Exercise Psychology, 24,* 168–188.

Carron, A. V., Loughead, T. M., & Bray, S. R. (2005). The home advantage in sport competitions: Courneya & Carron's (1992) conceptual framework a decade later. *Journal of Sport Sciences, 23,* 395–407.

Carron, A. V., Prapavessis, H., & Grove, J. R. (1994). Group effects and self-handicapping. *Journal of Sport & Exercise Psychology, 16,* 246–258.

Carron, A. V., & Spink, K. S. (1993). Team building in an exercise setting. *The Sport Psychologist, 7,* 8–18.

Carron, A. V., Spink, K. S., & Prapavessis, H. (1997). Team building and cohesiveness in the sport and exercise setting: Use of indirect interventions. *Journal of Applied Sport Psychology, 9,* 61–72.

Carron, A. V., Widmeyer, W. N., & Brawley, L. R. (1985). The development of an instrument to assess cohesion in sport teams: The group environment questionnaire. *Journal of Sport Psychology, 7,* 244–266.

Carron, A. V., Widmeyer, W. N., & Brawley, L. R. (1988). Group cohesion and individual adherence to physical activity. *Journal of Sport & Exercise Psychology, 10,* 119–126.

Carron, A. V., Widmeyer, W. N., & Brawley, L. R. (1989). Perceptions of ideal group size in sport team. *Perceptual and Motor Skills, 69,* 1368–1379.

Carron, A. V., Widmeyer, N. W., & Brawley, L. R. (1996). *Achievement and group size: Two toucans can but one toucan can too—and better.* Unpublished manuscript, University of Western Ontario, London, ON.

Cartwright, D., & Zander, A. (1968). *Group dynamics: Research and theory.* New York: Harper & Row.

Cattell, R. B. (1953). New concepts for measuring leadership in terms of group syntality. In D. C. Cartwright & A. Zander, (Eds.), *Group dynamics: Research and theory.* New York: Row & Peterson.

Chase, M. A., & Dummer, G. M. (1992). The role of sports as a social status determinant for children. *Research Quarterly for Exercise and Sport, 63,* 418–424.

Chelladurai, P. (1984). Leadership in sports. In J. M. Silva III & R. S. Weinberg (Eds.), *Psychological foundations of sport* (pp. 329–339). Champaign, IL: Human Kinetics.

Chelladurai, P. (1990). Leadership in sports: A review of relevant research. *International Journal of Sport Psychology, 21,* 328–354.

Chelladurai, P. (1993). Styles of decision making in coaching. In J. M. Williams (Ed.), *Applied sport psychology: Personal growth to peak performance* (pp. 99–109). Mountain View, CA: Mayfield.

Chelladurai, P., & Carron, A. V. (1977). A reanalysis of formal structure in sport. *Canadian Journal of Applied Sport Sciences, 2,* 9–14.

Chelladurai, P., & Carron, A. V. (1983). Athletic maturity and preferred leadership. *Journal of Sport Psychology, 5,* 371–380.

Chelladurai, P., & Haggerty, T. R. (1978). A normative model of decision styles in coaching. *Athletic Administrator, 13,* 6–9.

Chelladurai, P., & Saleh, S. D. (1978). Preferred leadership in sports. *Canadian Journal of Applied Sport Sciences, 3,* 85–92.

Cheng, J. T., Tracy, J. L., Foulsham, T., Kingstone, A., & Henrich, J. (2013). Two ways to the top: Evidence that dominance and prestige are distinct yet viable avenues to social rank and influence. *Journal of Personality and Social Psychology, 104,* 103–124.

Cherry, D., & Fischler, S. (1982). *Grapes: A vintage view of hockey.* Englewood Cliffs, NJ: Prentice-Hall.

Chow, G. M., & Feltz, D. L. (2014). Collective efficacy beliefs and sport. In M.R. Beauchamp & M. A. Eys (Eds.), *Group dynamics in exercise and sport psychology,* (pp. 298–315). New York: Routledge.

Cialdini, R. B., Reno, R. R., & Kallgren, C. A. (1990). A focus theory of normative conduct: recycling the concept of norms to reduce littering in public places. *Journal of Personality and Social Psychology, 58,* 1015–1026.

Clarey, C. (2019, June 23). France survives, sending Marta and Brazil to the exit. *The New York Times.* Retrieved from https://www.nytimes.com/2019/06/23/sports/soccer/france-brazil-world-cup.html

Clarke, S. R., & Norman, J. M. (1995). Home advantage of individual clubs in English soccer. *The Statistician, 44,* 509–521.

Clemente, F. M., Martins, F. M. L., & Mendes, R. S. (2015). There are differences between centrality levels of volleyball players in different competitive levels? *Journal of Physical Education and Sport, 15,* 272–276.

Clemente, F. M., Martins, F. M. L., Kalamaras, D., & Mendes, R. S. (2015). Network analysis in basketball: Inspecting the prominent players using centrality metrics. *Journal of Physical Education and Sport, 15,* 212–217.

Clemente, F. M., Martins, F. M. L., Wong, P. D., Kalamaras, D., & Mendes, R. S. (2015). Midfielder as the prominent participant in the building attack: A network analysis of national teams in FIFA World Cup 2014. *International Journal of Performance Analysis in Sport, 15,* 704–722.

Cohen, L. J., & DeBenedet, A. T (2012, July 17). Penn State Cover-up: Groupthink in Action. *Time Magazine.* Retrieved from http://ideas.time.com/2012/07/17/penn-state-cover-up-group-think-in-action/

Coleman, J. S. (1961). *The adolescent society.* New York: Free Press.

Coleman., T, Godfrey, M., Leo, F., Lopez-Gajardo, M., & Eys, M. (2019). *Do it for the team: Youth perceptions of team cohesion and role commitment in interdependent sport.* Manuscript submitted for publication.

Colman, M. M., & Carron, A. V. (2001). The nature of norms individual sport teams. *Small Group Research, 32,* 206–222.

Cooper, R., & Payne, R. (1967, January). Personality orientations and performance in football teams: Leaders and subordinates' orientations related to team success. *Organizational Psychology Group Report No. 1.*

Cooper, R., & Payne, R. (1972). Personality orientations and performance in soccer teams. *British Journal of Social and Clinical Psychology, 11,* 2–9.

Cope, C. J., Eys, M. A., Beauchamp, M. R., Schinke, R. J., & Bosselut, G. (2011). Informal roles on sport teams. *International Journal of Sport & Exercise Psychology, 9,* 19–30.

Cope, C. J., Eys, M. A., Schinke, R. J., & Bosselut, G. (2010). Coaches' perspectives of a negative informal role: The 'Cancer' within sport teams. *Journal of Applied Sport Psychology, 22,* 420–436.

Courneya, K. S., & Carron, A.V. (1990). Batting first versus last: Implications for the home advantage. *Journal of Sport & Exercise Psychology, 12,* 312–316.

Courneya, K. S., & Carron, A. V. (1992). The home advantage in sport competitions: A literature review. *Journal of Sport & Exercise Psychology, 14,* 13–27.

Cowan, S. (2018, December 5). Game day dress code isn't preferred fit for all Canadiens. *Montreal Gazette.* Retrieved from https://montrealgazette.com/sports/hockey/nhl/hockey-inside-out/stu-cowan-game-day-dress-code-isnt-preferred-fit-for-all-canadiens

Cresswell, S. L., & Eklund, R. C. (2003). The athlete burnout syndrome: A practitioner's guide. *New Zealand Journal of Sports Medicine, 31,* 4–9.

Cronin, L. D., Arthur, C. A., Hardy, J., & Callow, N. (2015). Transformational leadership and task cohesion in sport: The mediating role of inside sacrifice. *Journal of Sport & Exercise Psychology, 37,* 23–36.

Crosbie, P. V. (1975). Social exchange and power compliance: A test of humans' propositions. In P. V. Crosbie (Ed.), *Interaction in small groups* (pp. 356–373). New York: Macmillan.

Crothers, T. (1995, December 11). Little magic Canadian export Steve Nash doesn't get much TV time at Santa Clara, but he might be the best point guard in the country. *Sports Illustrated.* Retrieved from https://www.si.com/vault/1995/12/11/207115/little-magic-canadian-export-steve-nash-doesnt-get-much-tv-time-at-santa-clara-but-he-might-be-the-best-point-guard-in-the-country

Croxon, S. (2003). Preparing for Olympic glory. *Coaches Report, 9,* 7–11.

Crozier, A. J., & Benson, A. J. (2020). Group norms in youth sport. In M. W. Bruner, M. Eys, & L. Martin (Eds.), *The power of groups in youth sport* (pp. 17-31). Elsevier.

Crozier, A. J., & Spink, K. S. (2017). Examining the effects of normative messages on perceived effort in sport. *The Sport Psychologist, 31,* 56–64.

Crozier, A. J., & Spink, K. S. (2020). Coach and peer normative perceptions in relation to youth athlete effort. *International Journal of Sport and Exercise Psychology, 18,* 24-31.

Cunningham, I., & Eys, M. A. (2007). Role ambiguity and intra-team communication in interdependent sport teams. *Journal of Applied Social Psychology, 37,* 2220–2237.

Curhan, K. B., Levine, C. S., Markus, H. R., Kitayama, S., Park, J., Karasawa, M., ... & Ryff, C. D. (2014). Subjective and objective hierarchies and their relations to psychological well-being: A US/Japan comparison. *Social Psychological and Personality Science, 5,* 855–864.

Curtis, J. E., & Loy, J. W. (1978). Race/ethnicity and relative centrality of playing positions in team sports. In R. S. Hutton (Ed.), *Exercise and Sport Sciences Reviews* (Vol. 6, pp. 285–313). Philadelphia, PA: Franklin Institute Press.

Dauster, R. (2018, July 3). College basketball top 25: The pressing question for every team in our preseason rankings. *NBCSports.* Retrieved from https://collegebasketball.nbcsports.com/2018/07/03/college-basketball-top-25-pressing-question-preseason-ranking/

Davidson, N. (2015). What makes Canada's Christine Sinclair 'a perfect leader.' *The Globe and Mail.* Retrieved from https://www.theglobeandmail.com/sports/soccer/what-makes-canadas-christine-sinclair-a-perfect-leader/article25068860/

Davies, M. F. (1994). Personality and social characteristics. In A. P. Hare, H. H. Blemberg, M. F. Davies, & M. V. Kent (Eds.). *Small Group Research: A Handbook* (pp. 41–80). Norwood, NJ: Ablex.

Davis, L. J., Fodor, A., E. Pfahl, M., & Stoner, J. (2014). Team interdependence and turnover: evidence from the NFL. *American Journal of Business, 29,* 276–292.

Dawson, K. A., Bray, S. R., & Widmeyer, W. N. (2002). Goal setting by intercollegiate sport teams and athletes. *Avante, 8,* 14–23.

DeChurch, L. A., Mesmer-Magnus, J. R., & Doty, D. (2013). Moving beyond relationship and task conflict: Toward a process-state perspective. *Journal of Applied Psychology, 98,* 559–578.

Dennis, P. W. (1998). *Game location on ice hockey coaches and referees.* Unpublished Ph.D. Dissertation, University of Western Ontario, London, Ontario.

Dennis, P. W., & Carron, A. V. (1999). Strategic decisions of ice hockey coaches as a function of game location. *Journal of Sports Sciences, 17,* 263–268.

Dennis, P. W., Carron, A. V., & Loughead, T. M. (2002). The relationship between game location and decisions by National Hockey League officials. *Avante, 8,* 67–73.

DeRue, D. S., & Ashford, S. J. (2010). Who will lead and who will follow? A social process of leadership identity construction in organizations. *Academy of Management Review, 35,* 627–647.

DesJardins, N. M. L., Srivastava, S., Küfner, A. C., & Back, M. D. (2015). Who attains status? Similarities and differences across social contexts. *Social Psychological and Personality Science, 6,* 692–700.

Deutsch, M. (1949). A theory of cooperation and competition. *Human Relations, 2,* 129–152.

Di Salvo, V., Baron, R., Tschan, H., Calderon Montero, F. J., Bachl, N., & Pigozzi, F. (2007). Performance characteristics according to playing position in elite soccer. *International Journal of Sports Medicine, 28,* 222–227.

DiazGranados, D., Shuffler, M. L., Wingate, J. A., & Salas, E. (2017). Team development interventions. In E. Salas, R. Rico and J. Passmore (Eds.) *The Wiley Blackwell Handbook of the Psychology of Team Working and Collaborative Processes* (pp. 555–586). Oxford, UK: Wiley.

Dion, K. L. (1979). Intergroup conflict and intergroup cohesiveness. In W.G. Austin & S. Worchel (Eds.), *The social psychology of intergroup relations* (pp. 211–224). Belmont, CA: Wadsworth.

Dion, K. L. (2000). Group cohesion: From "field of forces" to multidimensional construct. *Group Dynamics: Theory, Research and Practice, 4,* 7–26.

Dodd, M. (1992). Job security remains elusive in pro sports. *USA Today,* February 20, 9C.

Donkers, J. L., Martin, L. J., & Evans, M. B. (2018). Psychological collectivism in youth athletes on individual sport teams. *International Journal of Sport and Exercise Psychology, 16,* 285–299.

Donnelly, P., Carron, A. V., & Chelladurai, P. (1978). *Group cohesion and sport.* Ottawa, ON: CAHPER Sociology of Sport Monograph Series.

Dosseville, F., Edoh, K. P., & Molinaro, C. (2016). Sports officials in home advantage phenomenon: A new framework. *International Journal of Sport and Exercise Psychology, 14,* 250–254.

Dovidio, J. F., Love, A., Schellhaas, F. M., & Hewstone, M. (2017). Reducing intergroup bias through intergroup contact: Twenty years of progress and future directions. *Group Processes & Intergroup Relations, 20,* 606–620.

Dowie, J. (1982). Why Spain should win the World Cup. *New Scientist, 94,* 693–695.

Driskell, J. E., & Mullen, B. (1990). Status, expectations, and behavior: A meta-analytic review and test of the theory. *Personality and Social Psychology Bulletin, 16,* 541–553.

Dryden, K. (1983). *The game: A thoughtful and provocative look at a life in hockey.* Toronto, ON: Macmillan.

Dryden, K., & Mulvoy, M. (1973). *Face-off at the summit.* Toronto, ON: Little, Brown & Co.

Duda, J. L. (1987). Toward a developmental theory of children's motivation in sport. *Journal of Sport Psychology, 9,* 130–145.

Duda, J. L. (1995). Motivation in sport settings: A goal perspective approach. In G. C. Roberts (Ed.), *Motivation in sport and exercise.* Champaign, IL, US: Human Kinetics. (p. 57–91).

Duffy, L. J. & Hinwood, D. P. (1997). Home field advantage: Does anxiety contribute? *Perceptual and Motor Skills, 84,* 283–286.

Dupuis, M., Bloom, G. A., & Loughead, T. M. (2006). Team captains' perceptions of athlete leadership. *Journal of Sport Behavior, 29,* 60–78.

Durdubas, D., Martin, L. J., & Koruc, Z. (2019). A season-long goal-setting intervention for elite youth basketball teams. *Journal of Applied Sport Psychology.* Advance Online Publication. doi:10.1080/10413200.2019.1593258.

Dyck, D. (2018, June 13). Supply and demand allowing Canadian offensive linemen in CFL to prosper. *The Globe and Mail*. Retrieved from https://www.theglobeandmail.com/sports/football/article-supply-and-demand-allowing-canadian-offensive-linemen-in-cfl-to/

Eagly, A. H., & Chin, J. L. (2010). Diversity and leadership in a changing world. *American Psychologist, 65*, 216–224.

Eagly, A. H., Johannesen-Schmidt, M. C., & Van Engen, M. L. (2003). Transformational, transactional, and laissez-faire leadership styles: A meta-analysis comparing women and men. *Psychological Bulletin, 129*, 569–591.

Eagly, A. H., & Johnson, B. T. (1990). Gender and leadership style: A meta-analysis. *Psychological Bulletin, 108*, 233–256.

Eagly, A. H., & Karau, S. J. (1991). Gender and the emergence of leaders: A meta-analysis. *Journal of Personality and Social Psychology, 60*, 685–710.

Eagly, A. H., Makhijani, M. G., & Klonsky, B. G. (1992). Gender and the evaluation of leaders: A meta-analysis. *Psychological Bulletin, 111*, 3–22.

Eccles, D. W., & Tenenbaum, G. (2004). Why an expert team is more than a team of experts: A social-cognitive conceptualization of team coordination and communication in sport. *Journal of Sport & Exercise Psychology, 26*, 542–560.

Edney, J. J., & Uhlig, S. R. (1977). Individual and small group territories. *Small Group Behavior, 8*, 457–468.

Eitzen, D. S. (1975). Group structure and group performance. In D. M. Landers, D. V. Harris, & R. W. Christina (Eds.), *Psychology of sport and motor behavior* (pp. 41–45). University Park, PA: College of HPER, Pennsylvania State University.

Eitzen, D. S. (1976). Sport and social status in American public secondary education. *Review of Sport and Leisure, 1*, 139–155.

Eitzen, D. S., & Furst, D. (1989). Racial bias in women's collegiate volleyball. *Journal of Sport and Social Issues, 13*, 46–51.

Eitzen, D. S., & Yetman, N. R. (1972). Managerial change, longevity, and organizational effectiveness. *Administrative Science Quarterly, 17*, 110–116.

Elsesser, K. M., & Lever, J. (2011). Does gender bias against female leaders persist? Quantitative and qualitative data from a large-scale survey. *Human Relations, 64*, 1555–1578.

Evans, M. B., & Eys, M. A. (2015). Collective goals and shared tasks: Interdependence structure and perceptions of individual sport team environments. *Scandinavian Journal of Medicine & Science in Sports, 25*, e139–e148.

Evans, M. B., Eys, M. A., & Bruner, M. W. (2012). Seeing the "we" in "me" sports: The need to consider individual sport team environments. *Canadian Psychology/Psychologie Canadienne, 53*, 301–308.

Evans, B., Eys, M., & Wolf, S. (2013). Exploring the nature of interpersonal influence in elite individual sport teams. *Journal of Applied Sport Psychology, 25*, 448–462.

Evans, L., & Hardy, L. (2002). Injury rehabilitation: A goal setting intervention study. *Research Quarterly for Exercise and Sport, 73*, 310–319.

Eys, M., Beauchamp, M. R., Godfrey, M., Dawson, K., Loughead, T. M., & Schinke, R. J. (2019). Role commitment and acceptance in a sport context. *Manuscript submitted for publication*.

Eys, M. A., & Carron, A. V. (2001). Role ambiguity, task cohesion, and task self-efficacy. *Small Group Research, 32*, 356–373.

Eys, M. A., Carron, A.V., Beauchamp, M. R., & Bray, S. R. (2003). Role ambiguity in sport teams. *Journal of Sport & Exercise Psychology, 25(4)*, 534–550.

Eys, M. A., Carron, A.V., Beauchamp, M. R., & Bray, S. R. (2005). Athletes' perceptions of the sources of role ambiguity. *Small Group Research, 36*, 383–403.

Eys, M. A., Carron, A. V., Bray, S. R., & Beauchamp, M. R. (2003). Role ambiguity and athlete satisfaction. *Journal of Sports Sciences, 21*, 391–401.

Eys, M. A., Carron, A. V., Bray, S. R., & Beauchamp, M. R. (2005). The relationship between role ambiguity and intention to return. *Journal of Applied Sport Psychology, 17*, 255–261.

Eys, M. A., Hardy, J., Carron, A. V., & Beauchamp, M. R. (2003). The relationship between task cohesion and competitive state anxiety. *Journal of Sport & Exercise Psychology, 25*, 66–76.

Eys, M. A., Loughead, T. M., Bray, S. R., & Carron, A. V. (2009a). Development of a cohesion questionnaire for youth: The Youth Sport Environment Questionnaire. *Journal of Sport & Exercise Psychology, 31*, 390–408.

Eys, M. A., Loughead, T. M., Bray, S. R., & Carron, A. V. (2009b). Perceptions of cohesion by youth sport participants. *The Sport Psychologist, 23*, 330–345.

Eys, M. A., Loughead, T. M., & Hardy, J. (2007). Athlete leadership dispersion and satisfaction in interactive sport teams. *Psychology of Sport and Exercise, 8*, 281–296.

Eys, M. A., Ohlert, J., Evans, B., Wolf, S., Martin, L., VanBussel, M., & Steins, C. (2015). Cohesion and performance for female and male sport teams. *The Sport Psychologist, 29*, 97–109.

Eys, M. A., Ritchie, S., Little, J., Slade, H., & Oddson, B. (2008). Leadership status congruency and cohesion in outdoor expedition groups. *Journal of Experiential Education, 30*, 78–94.

Eys, M., Surya, M., & Benson, A. J. (2017). Communicating within sport teams. In B. Jackson, J. Dimmock, and J. Compton (Eds.) *Persuasion and communication in sport, exercise, and physical activity* (pp. 217–232). New York, NY; Routledge.

Fabianic, D. (1984). Organizational effectiveness and managerial succession: An update of an old problem. *Journal of Sport Behavior, 7*, 139–152.

Fabianic, D. (1994). Managerial changed and organizational effectiveness in major league baseball: Findings for the eighties. *Journal of Sport Behavior, 17*, 135–147.

Farber, M. (1997a, January 13). Soaring. *Sports Illustrated, 86*, 52–54.

Farber, M. (1997b, March 24). The worst job in sports. *Sports Illustrated, 86*, 66–72.

Fasting, K., & Pfister, G. (2000). Female and male coaches in the eyes of female elite soccer players. *European Physical Education Review, 6*, 91–110.

Feinstein, J. (1987). *A season on the brink: A year with Bobby Knight and the Indiana Hoosiers.* New York, NY: Simon & Schuster.

Feld, N. D. (1959). Information and authority: The structure of military organization. *American Sociological Review, 24*, 15–22.

Feltz, D. L. (1978). Athletics in the status system of female adolescents. *Review of Sport and Leisure, 3*, 98–108.

Feltz, D. L., & Lirgg, C. D. (1998). Perceived team and player efficacy in hockey. *Journal of Applied Psychology, 83*, 557–564.

Festinger, L., Pepitone, A., & Newcomb, T. (1952). Some consequences of deindividuation in a group. *Journal of Abnormal and Social Psychology, 47*, 382–389.

Festinger, L., Schachter, S., & Back, K. (1963). *Social pressures in informal groups.* Stanford, CA: Stanford University Press. (Originally published in 1950).

Fiedler, F. E. (1954). Assumed similarity measures as predictors of team effectiveness. *Journal of Abnormal and Social Psychology, 49*, 381–388.

Fiedler, F. E. (1967). *A theory of leadership effectiveness.* New York: McGraw-Hill.

Fiedler, F. E., & Chemers, M. M. (1974). *Leadership and effective management.* Glenview, IL: Scott, Foresman & Co.

Fifa.com (2010, May 13). *Preliminary squads announced.* Retrieved from https://www.fifa.com/worldcup/news/preliminary-squads-announced-1210275

Filby, W. C., Maynard, I. W., & Graydon, J. K. (1999). The effect of multiple-goal strategies on performance outcomes in training and competition. *Journal of Applied Sport Psychology, 11,* 230–246.

Filho, E., Dobersek, U., Gershgoren, L., Becker, B., Tenenbaum, G. (2014). The cohesion-performance relationship in sport: A 10-year retrospective meta-analysis. *Sport Sciences for Health, 10,* 165–177.

Fisher, B., & Thomas, B. (1996). *Real dream teams: Seven practices used by world-class leaders to achieve extraordinary results.* Delray Beach, FL: St. Lucie.

Fitzsimons, G. M., Finkel, E. J., & Vandellen, M. R. (2015). Transactive goal dynamics. *Psychological Review, 122,* 648–661.

Fitzsimons, G. M., Sackett, E., & Finkel, E. J. (2016). Transactive goal dynamics theory: A relational goals perspective on work teams and leadership. *Research in Organizational Behavior, 36,* 135–155.

Fletcher, D., & Hanton, S. (2003). Sources of organizational stress in elite sports performers. *The Sport Psychologist, 17,* 175–195.

Fletcher, R. B., Wilkinson, H., Bladon, H., & Gargiulo, A. (2017). Developing a measure of collective efficacy for female netball using polytomous item response modeling and multilevel confirmatory analysis. *Group Dynamics: Theory, Research, and Practice, 21,* 61–72.

Fonti, F., & Maoret, M. (2016). The direct and indirect effects of core and peripheral social capital on organizational performance. *Strategic Management Journal, 37,* 1765–1786.

Forsyth, D. R. (2019). *Group dynamics* (7th ed.). Belmont, CA: Wadsworth, Cengage Learning.

Foulke, E., & Sticht, T. G. (1969). Review of research on the intelligibility and comprehension of accelerated speech. *Psychological Bulletin, 72,* 50–62.

Fransen, K., Decroos, S., Vanbeselaere, N., Vande Broek, G., De Cuyper, B., Vanroy, J., & Boen, F. (2015). Is team confidence the key to success? The reciprocal relation between collective efficacy, team outcome confidence, and perceptions of team performance during soccer games. *Journal of Sports Sciences, 33,* 219–231.

Fransen, K., Haslam, S. A., Mallett, C. J., Steffens, N. K., Peters, K., & Boen, F. (2016). Leadership from the centre: A comprehensive examination of the relationship between central playing positions and leadership in sport. *PLoS ONE, 11,* e0168150.

Fransen, K., Van Puyenbroeck, S., Loughead, T. M., Vanbeselaere, N., De Cuyper, B., Vande Broek, G. V., & Boen, F. (2015). Who takes the lead? Social network analysis as a pioneering tool to investigate shared leadership within sports teams. *Social Networks, 43,* 28–38.

Fransen, K., Vanbeselaere, N., De Cuyper, B., Vande Broek, G., & Boen, F. (2014). The myth of the team captain as principal leader: Extending the athlete leadership classification within sport teams. *Journal of Sports Sciences, 32,* 1389–1397.

Freedman, J. L., & Sears, D. O. (1965). Warning, distraction, and resistance to influence. *Journal of Personality and Social Psychology, 1,* 262–266.

French, J. R. P., & Raven, B. (1959). The bases of social power. In D. Cartwright (Ed.), *Studies in social power* (pp. 150–167). Ann Arbor, MI: Institute for Social Research.

Furley, P., Schweizer, G., & Memmert, D. (2018). Thin slices of athletes' nonverbal behavior give away game location: Testing the territoriality hypothesis of the home game advantage. *Evolutionary Psychology*. DOI: 10.1177%2F1474704918776456

Gammage, K. L., Carron, A. V., & Estabrooks, P. A. (2001). Team cohesion and individual productivity: The influence of the norm for productivity and the identifiability of individual effort. *Small Group Research, 32*, 3–18.

Gayton, W. F. & Coombs, R. (1995). The home advantage in high school basketball. *Perceptual and Motor Skills, 81*, 1344-1346.

Gayton, W. F., Matthews, G. R., & Nickless, C. J. (1987). The home field disadvantage in sports championships: Does it exist in hockey? *Journal of Sports Psychology, 9*, 183–185.

Gersick, C. J. G. (1988). Time and transition in work teams: Toward a new model of group development. *Academy of Management Journal, 31*, 9-41.

Gill, D. L. (1986). Competitiveness among females and males in physical activity classes. *Sex Roles, 15*, 233–247.

Godfrey, M., Kim, J., Eluère, M., & Eys, M. (2019). Diversity in cultural diversity research: a scoping review. *International Review of Sport and Exercise Psychology*. Advance online publication. doi:10.1080/1750984X.2019.1616316

Goff, S. (2019, August 28). Carli Lloyd 'not afraid' to kick in the NFL: 'There has got to be a first for everything'. *The Washington Post*. Retrieved from https://www.washingtonpost.com/sports/2019/08/28/carli-lloyd-not-afraid-kick-nfl-will-she-get-chance/.

Goldman, C. (2019, January 17). Patriots preparing for Arrowhead Stadium crowd noise with loud music during practice. *USA Today*. Retrieved from: https://chiefswire.usatoday.com/2019/01/17/patriots-music-preparations-for-arrowhead-stadium-crowd-noise-afc-championship/

Goldman, F. W., & Goldman, M. (1981). The effects of dyadic group experience in subsequent individual performance. *Journal of Social Psychology, 115*, 83–88.

Goldman, M., (1965). A comparison of individual and group performance for varying combinations of initial ability. *Journal of Personality and Social Psychology, 1*, 210–216.

Golembiewski, R. (1962). *The small group*. Chicago, IL: University of Chicago.

Gollwitzer, P. M. (1993). Goal achievement: The role of intentions. *European Review of Social Psychology, 4*, 141–185.

Goodger, K., Lavallee, D., Gorely, T., & Harwood, C. (2010). Burnout in sport: Understanding the process—from early warning signs to individualized intervention. In J. M. Williams (Ed.), *Applied sport psychology: Personal growth to peak performance* (6th ed., pp. 492–511). New York: McGraw-Hill.

Gorman, J. C. (2014). Team coordination and dynamics: Two central issues. *Current Directions in Psychological Science, 23*, 355–360.

Goyens, C., & Turowetz, A. (1986). Lions in winter. Scarborough, ON: Prentice-Hall.

Granito, V. J., & Rainey, D. W. (1988). Differences in cohesion between high school and college football teams and starters and nonstarters. *Perceptual and Motor Skills, 66*, 471-477.

Grant, A. (2019, March 14). Become friends with your rivals. *WorkLife with Adam Grant* [Audio podcast]. Transcript retrieved from: https://www.ted.com/talks/worklife_with_adam_grant_become_friends_with_your_rivals/transcript?language=en&referrer=playlist-worklife_with_adam_grant_mar_2019

Graupensperger, S., Benson, A. J., & Evans, M. B. (2018). Everyone else is doing it: The association between social identity and susceptibility to peer-influence in NCAA athletes. *Journal of Sport & Exercise Psychology, 40*, 117–127.

Graupensperger, S. A., Jensen, C. J., & Evans, M. B. (2018). A meta-analytic review of studies using the Prosocial and Antisocial Behavior in Sport Scale: Associations among intergroup moral behaviors. *Sport, Exercise, and Performance Psychology, 7,* 186–197.

Green, R. B., & Mack, J. (1978). Would groups do better without social psychologists? A response to Buys. *Personality and Social Psychology Bulletin, 4,* 561–563.

Greenlees, I. A., Graydon, J. K., & Maynard, I. W. (1999). The impact of collective efficacy beliefs on effort and persistence in a group task. *Journal of Sports Sciences, 17,* 151–158.

Greenlees, I. A., Graydon, J. K., & Maynard, I. W. (2000). The impact of individual efficacy beliefs on group goal selection and group goal commitment. *Journal of Sports Sciences, 18,* 451-459.

Greer, D. L. (1983). Spectator booing and the home advantage: A study of social influence in the basketball arena. *Social Psychology Quarterly, 46,* 252–261.

Greer, H. (2002). Five ways to motivate a team. *Coach and Athletic Director, 72,* 40–41.

Greer, L. L., de Jong, B. A., Schouten, M. E., & Dannals, J. E. (2018). Why and when hierarchy impacts team effectiveness: A meta-analytic integration. *Journal of Applied Psychology, 103,* 591–613.

Grégoire, M., & Monod, O. (2010). The French dejection: The sordid details behind the collapse and mutiny of France's national soccer team. *Slate.* Retrieved from http://www.slate.com/id/2257821

Griffin, R. (2004, October 17). Beware Rocket's red glare from mound. *Toronto Star,* p. E4.

Griffin, R. (2010, May 8). Steamed Ozzie has Cito's back. *Toronto Star,* p. S4.

Grijalva, E., Maynes, T. D., Badura, K. L., & Whiting, S. W. (2019). Examining the "I" in team: A longitudinal investigation of the influence of team narcissism composition on team outcomes in the NBA. *Academy of Management Journal.* Advance online publication.

Gross, N., & Martin, W. (1952). On group cohesiveness. *American Journal of Sociology, 57,* 533–546.

Grosz, M. P., Leckelt, M., & Back, M. D. (2020). Personality predictors of social status attainment. *Current Opinion in Psychology, 33,* 52–56.

Gruber, J. J., & Gray, G. R. (1982). Response to forces influencing cohesion as a function of player status and level of male varsity basketball competition. *Research Quarterly for Sport and Exercise, 53,* 27–36.

Grusky, O. (1963). Managerial succession and organizational effectiveness. *American Journal of Sociology, 69,* 21–31.

Guinote, A. (2017). How power affects people: Activating, wanting, and goal seeking. *Annual Review of Psychology, 68,* 353–381.

Habeeb, C. M., Eklund, R. C., & Coffee, P. (2019). Reciprocal relationships between efficacy and performance in athlete dyads: Self-, other-, and collective constructs. *Journal of Sport and Exercise Psychology, 41,* 147–158.

Hackman, J. R., & Oldham, G. R. (1980). *Work redesign.* Reading, MA: Addison-Wesley.

Hackman, J. R. (2012). From causes to conditions in group research. *Journal of Organizational Behavior, 33,* 428–444.

Halevy, N., Y. Chou, E., & D. Galinsky, A. (2011). A functional model of hierarchy: Why, how, and when vertical differentiation enhances group performance. *Organizational Psychology Review, 1,* 32–52.

Hallinan, C. J. (1991). Aborigines and positional segregation in Australian rugby league. *International Review of Sociology of Sport, 26,* 69–79.

Hampson, R., & Jowett, S. (2014). Effects of coach leadership and coach–athlete relationship on collective efficacy. *Scandinavian Journal of Medicine & Science in Sports, 24,* 454–460.

Hancock, D. J., Martin, L. J., Evans, M. B., & Paradis, K. F. (2018). Exploring perceptions of group processes in ice hockey officiating. *Journal of Applied Sport Psychology, 30,* 222–240.

Hardy, C. J., & Crace, R. K. (1997). Foundations of team building: Introduction to the Team Builder Primer. *Journal of Applied Sport Psychology, 9,* 1–10.

Hardy, C. J., & Latané, B. (1988). Social loafing in cheerleaders: Effects of team membership and competition. *Journal of Sport & Exercise Psychology, 10,* 109–114.

Hardy, J., Benson, A. J., & Boulter, M. (2020). *Personality and team effectiveness.* In H. Manly & R. Roberts (Eds.), *Encyclopaedia of sport psychology.* International Society of Sport Psychology

Hardy, J., Eys, M. A., & Carron, A. V. (2005). Exploring the potential disadvantages of high task cohesion in sport teams. *Small Group Research, 36,* 166–189.

Hardy, J., Eys, M.A., & Loughead, T. M. (2008). Does communication mediate the athlete leadership to cohesion relationship? *International Journal of Sport Psychology. 39,* 329–345.

Hardy, L., Arthur, C. A., Jones, G., Shariff, A., Munnoch, K., Isaacs, I., & Allsopp, A. J. (2010). The relationship between transformational leadership behaviours, psychological, and training outcomes in elite military recruits. *The Leadership Quarterly, 21,* 20–32.

Hare, A. P. (1976). *Handbook of small group research* (2nd ed.). New York: Free Press.

Hare, A. P. (1981). Group size. *American Behavioral Scientist, 24,* 695-708.

Hare, A. P. (1994). Types of roles in small groups: A bit of history and a current perspective. *Small Group Research, 25,* 433–448.

Hare, A. P., & Bales, R. F. (1963) Seating position and small group interaction. *Sociometry, 26,* 480–486.

Harenberg, S., Riemer, H. A., Dorsch, K. D., Karreman, E., & Paradis, K. F. (2019). Advancement of a conceptual framework for positional competition in sport: development and validation of the positional competition in team sports questionnaire. *Journal of Applied Sport Psychology.* Advanced Online Publication. doi:10.1080/10413200.2019.1631903

Harrison, D. A., & Klein, K. J. (2007). What's the difference? Diversity constructs as separation, variety, or disparity in organizations. *Academy of Management Review, 32,* 1199–1228.

Hausenblas, H. A., & Carron, A. V. (1996). Group cohesion and self-handicapping in female and male athletes. *Journal of Sport and Exercise Psychology, 18,* 132–143.

Hayhurst, D. (2014, May 2). The real secrets to team chemistry in baseball and how it can help a team. *Bleacher Report.* Retrieved from https://bleacherreport.com/articles/2044662-the-real-secrets-to-team-chemistry-in-baseball-and-how-it-can-help-a-team

Hayman, H. (1981). Minority group sports involvement in New Zealand: The New Zealand Maori. *Research Papers in Physical Education, 3,* 1–22.

Heaton, A. W., & Sigall, H. (1989). The "championship choke" revisited: The role of fear of acquiring a negative identity. *Journal of Applied Social Psychology, 19,* 1019–1033.

Heider, F. (1958). *The psychology of interpersonal relations.* New York: Wiley.

Hencken, C., & White, C. (2006). Anthropometric assessment of Premiership soccer players in relation to playing position. *European Journal Sport Science, 6,* 205–211.

Herman, M. (2013, December 16). Nadal and Williams raise the bar sky high. *Reuters*. Retrieved from https://ca.reuters.com/article/sportsNews/idCABRE9BG03B20131217

Heroux, D. (2019, August 19). Nick Nurse wants Canada's NBA-thin roster to reach for new heights at basketball World Cup. *CBC Sports*. Retrieved from https://www.cbc.ca/sports/basketball/nba/fiba-world-cup-canada-nick-nurse-1.5251476

Herring, C. (2018). The Warriors' dynasty is different. *FiveThirtyEight*. Retrieved from https://fivethirtyeight.com/features/the-warriors-dynasty-is-different/

Hersey, P., & Blanchard, K. H. (1969). Life style theory of leadership. *Training and Development Journal, 23,* 26–34.

Hersey, P., & Blanchard, K. H. (1982). Leadership style: Attitudes and behaviors. *Training and Development Journal, 36,* 50-52.

Herzog, W., & Horrigan, K. (1987). *White rat: A life in baseball.* New York: Harper & Row.

Heslin, R. (1964). Predicting group task effectiveness from member characteristics. *Psychological Bulletin, 62,* 248–256.

Heuzé, J., & Fontayne, P. (2002). Questionnaire sur l'Ambiance du Groupe: A French-language instrument for measuring group cohesion. *Journal of Sport & Exercise Psychology, 24,* 42–67.

Heuzé, J. P., Raimbault, N., & Fontayne, P. (2006). Relationships between cohesion, collective efficacy and performance in professional basketball teams: An examination of mediating effects. *Journal of Sport Sciences, 24,* 59–68.

Heuzé, J. P., Sarrazin, P., Masiero, M., Raimbault, N., & Thomas, J. P. (2006). The relationship of perceived motivational climate to cohesion and collective efficacy in elite female teams. *Journal of Applied Sport Psychology, 18,* 201–218.

Hill, A. P., Stoeber, J., Brown, A., & Appleton, P. R. (2014). Team perfectionism and team performance: A prospective study. *Journal of Sport & Exercise Psychology, 36,* 303–315.

Hodges, L., & Carron, A. V. (1992). Collective efficacy and group performance. *International Journal of Sport Psychology, 23,* 48–59.

Hoffman, M. D., Loughead, T. M., Dixon, J. C., & Crozier, A. J. (2017). Examining the home advantage in the National Hockey League: Comparisons among regulation, overtime, and the shootout. *Psychology of Sport and Exercise, 28,* 24–30.

Holder, R. L., & Nevill, A. M. (1997). Modelling performance at international tennis and golf tournaments: Is there a home advantage? *The Statistician, 46,* 551–559.

Holland, A., & Andre, T. (1999). Student characteristics and choice of high school remembrance role. *Adolescence, 34,* 315–338.

Hollander, E. P. (1961). Some effects of perceived status on responses to innovative behavior. *Journal of Abnormal and Social Psychology, 63,* 247–250.

Holt, J. E., Kinchin, G., & Clarke, G. (2012). Effects of peer-assessed feedback, goal setting and a group contingency on performance and learning by 10–12-year-old academy soccer players. *Physical Education & Sport Pedagogy, 17,* 231–250.

Homans, G. C. (1950). *The human group.* New York: Harcourt, Brace & World.

Hopkins, H. (2019, May 7). FIBA women's Eurobasket: Quarter Final Roundup. *SportingNews*. Retrieved from https://www.sportingnews.com/ca/fiba/news/fiba-womens-eurobasket-quarter-final-roundup/ej11ii6akfyd1gytgd0nsc9xf

Hopkins, T. K. (1964*). The silent language.* New York: Doubleday.

Hoption, C., Phelan, J., & Barling, J. (2014). Transformational leadership in sport. In M. Beauchamp, & M. Eys (Eds.), *Group dynamics advances in sport and exercise psychology: Contemporary themes* (pp. 45–62). Oxford: Routledge.

Horne, T., & Carron, A. V. (1985). Compatibility in coach-athlete relationships. *Journal of Sport Psychology, 7,* 137–149.

Horwitz, S. K., & Horwitz, I. B. (2007). The effects of team diversity on team outcomes: A meta-analytic review of team demography. *Journal of Management, 33,* 987–1015.

Humphrey, S. E., & LeBreton, J. M. (Eds.) (2018). *The handbook of multilevel theory, measurement, and analysis.* Washington, DC: American Psychological Association.

Humphreys, B. R., Paul, R. J., & Weinbach, A. P. (2016). Performance expectations and the tenure of head coaches: Evidence from NCAA football. *Research in Economics, 70,* 482–492.

Hunt, S. (2018, October 25). Strong chemistry helps make U.S. Women's Soccer the ultimate team. *TEAM USA.* Retrieved from: https://www.teamusa.org/News/2018/October/25/Strong-Chemistry-Helps-Make-US-Womens-Soccer-The-Ultimate-Team-presented-by-Ultimate-Software

Hunter, P. (2010, October 9). The Burke method. *Toronto Star,* Section 5, p. S5.

Isenberg, D. J. (1986). Group polarization: A critical review and meta-analysis. *Journal of Personality and Social Psychology, 50,* 1141–1151.

Jackson, B., Dimmock, J. A., Gucciardi, D. F., & Grove, J. R. (2010). Relationship commitment in athletic dyads: Actor and partner effects for Big Five self-and other-ratings. *Journal of Research in Personality, 44,* 641–648.

Jackson, D., Engstrom, E., & Emmers-Sommer, T. (2007). Think leader, think male and female: Sex vs. seating arrangement as leadership cues. *Sex Roles, 57,* 713–723.

Jackson, P. & Arkush, M. (2004). *The last season.* New York: Penguin Press.

Jackson, S. E., & Schuler, R. S. (1985). A meta-analysis and conceptual critique of research on role ambiguity and role conflict in work settings. *Organizational Behavior and Human Decision Process, 36,* 16-78.

Jacob, C. S., & Carron, A.V. (1996). Sources of status in sport teams. *International Journal of Sport Psychology, 27,* 369–382.

Jacob, C. S., & Carron, A. V. (1998). The association between status and cohesion in sport teams. *Journal of Sports Sciences, 16,* 187–198.

Jacobs, R. C., & Campbell, D. T. (1961). The perpetuation of an arbitrary tradition through several generations of a laboratory microculture. *The Journal of Abnormal and Social Psychology, 62,* 649–658.

Jambor, E. A., & Weekes, E. M. (1996). The nontraditional female athlete: A case study. *Journal of Applied Sport Psychology, 8,* 146–159.

Jamieson, J. P. (2010). The home field advantage in athletics: A meta-analysis. *Journal of Applied Social Psychology, 40,* 1819-1848.

Janis, I. L. (1972). *Victims of groupthink.* Boston, MA: Houghton-Mifflin.

Janis, I. L. (1982). *Groupthink: Psychological studies of policy decision and fiascoes* (2nd ed.). Boston, MA: Houghton Mifflin.

Janssens, L., & Nuttin, J. R. (1976). Frequency perception of individual and group successes as a function of competition, coaction, and isolation. *Journal of Personality and Social Psychology, 80,* 103–108.

Jason, L. A., Stevens, E., Ram, D., Miller, S. A., Beasley, C. R., & Gleason, K. D. (2016). Theories in the field of community psychology. *Global Journal of Community Psychology, 7,* 1–27.

Jeffery-Tosoni, S. M., Eys, M. A., Schinke, R. J., & Lewko, J. (2011). Youth sport status and perceptions of satisfaction and cohesion. *Journal of Sport Behavior, 34,* 150–159.

Jehue, R., Street, D., & Huizenga, R. (1993). Effect of time zone and game time changes on team performance: National Football League. *Medicine and Science in Sports and Exercise, 25,* 127–131.

Jimerson, J. B. (1999). "Who has next?": The symbolic, rational, and methodical use of norms in pickup basketball. *Social Psychology Quarterly, 62,* 136–156.

Johnson, D. W., & Johnson, R. (1989). *Cooperation and competition: Theory and research.* Edina, MN: Interaction Book Company.

Johnson, D. W., & Johnson, R. T. (2009). An educational psychology success story: Social interdependence theory and cooperative learning. *Educational Researcher, 38,* 365–379.

Johnson, T., Martin, A. J., Palmer, F. R., Watson, G., & Ramsey, P. (2012). Collective leadership: A case study of the All Blacks. *Asia-Pacific Management and Business Application, 1,* 53–67.

Johnson, K. E., & McRee, A. L. (2015). Health-risk behaviors among high school athletes and preventive services provided during sports physicals. *Journal of Pediatric Health Care, 29,* 17–27.

Johnson, S. K., Murphy, S. E., Zewdie, S., & Reichard, R. J. (2008). The strong, sensitive type: Effects of gender stereotypes and leadership prototypes on the evaluation of male and female leaders. *Organizational Behavior and Human Decision Processes, 106,* 39–60.

Jonas, R. (2019, June 28). Team unity, belief propel San Jose Earthquakes into playoff contender. *Pro Soccer USA.* Retrieved from https://www.prosoccerusa.com/mls/san-jose-earthquakes/matias-almeyda-team-unity-san-jose-earthquakes-mls-playoffs-contenders/

Jones, E. E., & Berglas, S. (1978). Control of attributions about the self through self-handicapping strategies: The appeal of alcohol and the role of underachievement. *Personality and Social Psychology Bulletin, 4,* 200–206.

Jones, G., Leonard, W. M. II, Schmitt, R. L., Smith, D. R., & Tolone, W. L. (1987). A loglinear analysis of stacking in college football. *Social Science Quarterly, 68,* 70–83.

Jones, G. R. (2001). *Organizational theory: Text and cases* (3rd ed). Upper Saddle River, NJ: Prentice Hall.

Jones, M. B. (1974). Regressing group on individual effectiveness. *Organizational Behavior and Human Performance, 11,* 426–451.

Jones, M. B. (2013). The home advantage in individual sports: An augmented review. *Psychology of Sport and Exercise, 14,* 397-404.

Jones, M. V., Bray, S. R., & Bolton, L. (2001). Do cricket umpires favour the home team? Officiating bias in English club cricket. *Perceptual and Motor Skills, 93,* 359–362.

Jowett, S. (2007). Coach-athlete relationships ignite a sense of groupness. In M.R. Beauchamp & M. A. Eys (Eds.), *Group dynamics in exercise and sport psychology,* (pp. 63–78). New York: Routledge.

Jowett, S. & Chaundy, V. (2004). An investigation into the impact of coach leadership and coach-athlete relationship on group cohesion. *Group Dynamics: Theory, Research & Practice, 8,* 302–311.

Judge, T. A., Bono, J. E., Ilies, R., & Gerhardt, M. W. (2002). Personality and leadership: a qualitative and quantitative review. *Journal of Applied Psychology, 87,* 765–780.

Juliano, J (2019, April 25). Penn women make history with first distance medley relay win at Penn Relays. *The Philadelphia Inquirer.* Retrieved from https://www.inquirer.com/college-sports/penn/penn-relays-quakers-distance-medley-relay-carnival-villanova-notre-dame-20190426.html

Juntumaa, B., Toms, M., Keskivaara, P., & Elovainio, M. (2007). Coaching and cohesion: The perceptions of adolescents, coaches, and team leaders in Finnish junior hockey. In E. M. Vargios (Ed.), *Educational psychology research focus*, (pp. 121–132). New York: Nova Science Publications.

Kahane, L., & Shmanske, S. (1997). Team roster turnover and attendance in major league baseball. *Applied Economics, 29*, 425–431.

Kahn, R. (1972). *The boys of summer*. New York: Harper & Row.

Kahn, R. L., Wolfe, D. M., Quinn, R. P., Snoek, J. D., & Rosenthal, R. A. (1964). *Occupational stress: Studies in role conflict and role ambiguity*. New York: Wily.

Kane, M. J. (1988). The female athletic role as a status determinant within the social systems of high school adolescents. *Adolescents, 23*, 253–264.

Karau, S. J., & Williams, K. D. (1993). Social loafing: A meta-analytic review and theoretical integration. *Journal of Personality and Social Psychology, 65*, 681–706.

Kelley, H. H., Berscheid, E., Christensen, A., Harvey, H. H., Huston, T. L., Levinger, G., McClintock, E., Peplau, L. A., & Peterson, D. R. (1983). *Close relationships*. New York: Freeman.

Kenny, D. A., & Garcia, R. L. (2012). Using the actor–partner interdependence model to study the effects of group composition. *Small Group Research, 43*, 468–496.

Kerlinger, F. N. (1986). *Foundations of behavioral research* (3rd ed.). New York: Holt, Rinehart & Winston.

Kernaghan, J. (1987, September 15). The best brings out the best. *The London Free Press*, p. C1.

Kerr, J. H. and Vanschaik, P. (1995). Effects of game venue and outcome on psychological mood states in rugby. *Personality and Individual Differences, 19*, 407-410.

Khrushchev, N. (1970). *Khrushchev remembers*. Toronto, ON: Little, Brown & Co.

Kiesler, C. A., & Kiesler, S. B. (1969). *Conformity*. Reading, MA: Addison-Wesley.

Kilduff, G. J., Willer, R., & Anderson, C. (2016). Hierarchy and its discontents: Status disagreement leads to withdrawal of contribution and lower group performance. *Organization Science, 27*, 373–390.

Kim, J., Coleman, T., Godfrey, M., Vierimaa, M., & Eys, M. (2020). The dynamics of informal role development within sport teams: A case study approach. *Psychology of Sport and Exercise, 48*, 101670.

Kim, J., Gardant, D., Bosselut, G., & Eys, M. (2018). Athlete personality characteristics and informal role occupancy in interdependent sport teams. *Psychology of Sport and Exercise, 39*, 193-203.

Kim, J., Godfrey, M., & Eys, M. (2019). The antecedents and outcomes of informal roles in interdependent sport teams. *Sport, Exercise, and Performance Psychology*. doi: https://psycnet.apa.org/doi/10.1037/spy0000179

Kim, M. S. (1992a). Changes in performance norms of Japanese school athletic teams mid- to postseason. *Perceptual and Motor Skills, 75*, 349–350.

Kim, M. S. (1992b) Types of leadership and performance norms in school athletic teams. *Perceptual and Motor Skills, 74*, 803–806.

Kim, M. S. (1995) Performance norms and performance by teams in basketball competition. *Perceptual and Motor Skills, 80*, 770.

Kim, M. S. (2001). Satisfaction and perception of performance norms of sport teams. *Perceptual and Motor Skills, 92*, 1201–1204.

Kim, M. S., & Cho, I. C. (1996). Self-monitoring and perception of performance norms of sport teams. *Perceptual and Motor Skills, 83*, 129–130.

King, L. A., & King, D. W. (1990). Role conflict and role ambiguity: A critical assessment of construct validity. *Psychological Bulletin, 107,* 48–64.

King, P. (2009, September 7). Hardest, riskiest, toughest, greatest job in sports. *Sports Illustrated, 111.* Retrieved from https://www.si.com/vault/2009/09/07/105854115/hardest-riskiest-toughest-greatest-job-in-sports

Klein, H. J., Molloy, J. C., & Brinsfield, C. T. (2012). Reconceptualizing workplace commitment to redress a stretched construct: Revisiting assumptions and removing confounds. *Academy of Management Review, 37,* 130–151.

Klein, M., & Christiansen, G. (1969). Group composition, group structure and group effectiveness of basketball teams. In J. W. Loy & G. S. Kenyon (Eds.), *Sport, culture and society* (pp. 397–408). New York: Macmillan.

Kleingeld, A., van Mierlo, H., & Arends, L. (2011). The effect of goal setting on group performance: A meta-analysis. *Journal of Applied Psychology, 96,* 1289–1300.

Klonsky, B. (1975). *The effects of formal structure and role skills on coaching recruitment and longevity: A study of professional basketball teams.* Unpublished paper, Department of Psychology, Fordham University.

Kluckhohn, C., & Murray, H. A. (1949). *Personality in nature, society and culture.* New York: Knopf.

Knight, H. (2019, January 16). We change women's hockey. *CBC Sports.* Retrieved from https://www.cbc.ca/playersvoice/entry/we-changed-womens-hockey

Koestner, R., Lekes, N., Powers, T. M., & Chicoine, E. (2002). Attaining personal goals: Self-concordance plus implementations equals success. *Journal of Personality and Social Psychology, 83,* 231–244.

Kogan, N., & Wallach, M. A. (1964). *Risk taking: A study of cognition and personality.* New York: Holt, Rinehart, & Winston.

Kornspan, A. S., Lerner, B. S., Ronayne, J., Etzel, E. F., & Johnson, S. (1995). The home disadvantage in the National Football League's conference championship games. *Perceptual and Motor Skills, 80,* 800–802.

Kozub, S. A., & McDonnell, J. F. (2000). Exploring the relationship between cohesion and collective efficacy in rugby teams. *Journal of Sport Behavior, 23,* 120–129.

Krane, V., Greenleaf, C. A., & Snow, J. (1997). Reaching for gold and the price of glory: A motivational case study of an elite gymnast. *The Sport Psychologist, 11,* 53–71.

Kravitz, D. A., Cohen, J. L., Martin, B., Sweeney, J., McCarty, J., Elliott, E., & Goldstein, P. (1978). Humans would do better without other humans. *Personality and Social Psychology Bulletin, 4,* 559–560.

Kravitz, D. A., & Martin, B. (1986). Ringelmann rediscovered: The original article. *Journal of Personality and Social Psychology, 50,* 936–941.

Krishnan, G. (2018, July 23). The team has understood importance of my role: Cheteshwar Pujara. *DNA.* Retrieved from https://www.dnaindia.com/cricket/interview-the-team-has-understood-importance-of-my-role-cheteshwar-pujara-2640491

Kristof-Brown, A. L., Zimmerman, R. D., & Johnson, E. C. (2005). Consequences of individuals' fit at work: A meta-analysis of person-job, person-organization, person-group, and person-supervisor fit. *Personnel Psychology, 58,* 281–342.

Krizan, Z., & Herlache, A. D. (2018). The narcissism spectrum model: A synthetic view of narcissistic personality. *Personality and Social Psychology Review, 22,* 3–31.

Kroshus, E., Kubzansky, L. D., Goldman, R. E., & Austin, S. B. (2014). Norms, athletic identity, and concussion symptom under-reporting among male collegiate ice hockey players: a prospective cohort study. *Annals of Behavioral Medicine, 49,* 95–103.

Kyllo, L. B., & Landers, D. M. (1995). Goal setting in sport and exercise: A research synthesis to resolve the controversy. *Journal of Sport & Exercise Psychology, 17,* 117–137.

Lacerenza, C. N., Marlow, S. L., Tannenbaum, S. I., & Salas, E. (2018). Team development interventions: Evidence-based approaches for improving teamwork. *American Psychologist, 73,* 517–532.

Ladyman, I. (2010, July 8). World Cup 2010: Beat Spain? It's hard enough to get the ball back, say defeated Germany. *Daily Mail.* Retrieved from: https://www.dailymail.co.uk/sport/worldcup2010/article-1293239/WORLD-CUP-2010-Beat-Spain-Its-hard-ball-say-Germany.html

Laios, A., Theodorakis, N., & Gargalianos, D. (2003). Leadership and power: Two important factors for effective coaching. *International Sports Journal, 7,* 150–154.

Lapchick, R. E. (2015a). *The 2015 racial and gender report card: Major League Baseball.* Orlando, FL: University of Central Florida, The Institute for Diversity and Ethics in Sport.

Lapchick, R. E. (2015b). *The 2015 racial and gender report card: National Football League.* Orlando, FL: University of Central Florida, The Institute for Diversity and Ethics in Sport.

Lapchick, R. E. (2018). *2018 racial and gender report card.* Orlando, FL: University of Central Florida, The Institute for Diversity and Ethics in Sport.

Latané, B., Williams, K., & Harkins, S. (1979). Many hands make light the work: The causes and consequences of social loafing. *Journal of Personality and Social Psychology, 37,* 822–832.

Latham, G. P., & Locke, E. A. (2007). New developments and directions for goal-setting research. *European Psychologist, 12,* 290–300.

Laughlin, P., Branch, L., & Johnson, H. (1969). Individual versus triadic performance on unidimensional complementary tasks as a function of initial ability level. *Journal of Personality and Social Psychology, 12,* 144–150.

Lavoie, M. (1989). Stacking, performance differentials, and salary discrimination in professional ice hockey: A survey of the evidence. *Sociology of Sport Journal, 6,* 17–35.

Lawrence, A. (2018). Packers reporter: Rodgers not grumpy. *CBS Sports.* Retrieved from https://cbssportsradio.radio.com/articles/packers-quarterback-aaron-rodgers-communicating-expectations-rookie-wide-receivers.

League Managers Association. (2013, June 14). LMA end of season statistics 2010. Retrieved from http://www.leaguemanagers.com/news.html

Leary, M. R., Tambor, E. S., Terdal, S. K., & Downs, D. L. (1995). Self-esteem as an interpersonal monitor: The sociometer hypothesis. *Journal of Personality and Social Psychology, 68,* 518–530.

Lehman, D. R., & Reifman, A. (1987). Spectator influence on basketball officiating. *Journal of Social Psychology, 127,* 673–675.

Leo, F. M., González-Ponce, I., García-Calvo, T., & Sánchez-Oliva, D. (2019). The relationship among cohesion, transactive memory systems, and collective efficacy in professional soccer teams: A multilevel structural equation analysis. *Group Dynamics: Theory, Research, and Practice, 23,* 44–52.

Leo, F. M., González-Ponce, I., Sánchez-Miguel, P. A., Ivarsson, A., & García-Calvo, T. (2015). Role ambiguity, role conflict, team conflict, cohesion and collective efficacy in sport teams: A multilevel analysis. *Psychology of Sport and Exercise, 20,* 60–66.

Leonard, W. M. (1987). "Stacking" in college basketball: A neglected analysis. *Sociology of Sport Journal, 4,* 403–409.

Leonard, W. M. (1989). The "home advantage": The case of the modern Olympiads. *Journal of Sport Behavior, 12,* 227-241.

Levine, J. M., & Moreland, R. L. (1991). Culture and socialization in work groups. In L. B. Resnick, J. M. Levine, & S. D. Teasley (Eds.), *Perspectives on socially shared cognition* (pp. 257–282). Washington, DC, American. Psychological Association.

Lewin, K. (1935). *A dynamic theory of personality.* New York: McGraw-Hill.

Lewin, K. (1936). *Principles of topological psychology.* York, PA: The Maple Press Co.

Lewin, K. (1947). Frontiers in group dynamics: Concept, method and reality in social science; social equilibria and social change. *Human Relations, 1,* 5-41.

Lewis, G. H. (1972). Role differentiation. *American Sociological Review, 37,* 424-434.

Liardi, V. L. & Carron, A. V. (2011). An analysis of National Hockey League face-offs: Implications for the home advantage. *International Journal of Sport and Exercise Psychology, 9,* 102-109.

Lisi, C. (2018, June 20). How Óscar Tabárez used philosophy and Garra Charrúa to return Uruguay to the top table. *These Football Times.* Retrieved from https://thesefootball-times.co/2018/06/20/how-oscar-tabarez-used-philosophy-and-garra-charrua-to-return-uruguay-to-the-top-table/

Llopis, G. (2019, February 6). The New England Patriots: The mastery of teamwork in a climate of constant change. *Forbes.* Retrieved from https://www.forbes.com/sites/glennllopis/2019/02/06/the-new-england-patriots-the-mastery-of-teamwork-in-a-climate-of-constant-change/#4b32251112a9

Locke, E. A. (1976). The nature and causes of job satisfaction. In M. D. Dunnette (Ed.), *Handbook of industrial and organizational psychology.* Chicago, IL: Rand McNally.

Locke, E. A., & Latham, G. P. (1984). *Goal setting: A motivational technique that works.* Englewood Cliffs, NJ: Prentice-Hall.

Locke, E. A., & Latham, G. P. (1985). The application of goal setting to sports. *Journal of Sport Psychology, 7,* 205-222.

Locke, E. A., & Latham, G. P. (2002). Building a practically useful theory of goal setting and task motivation. *American Psychologist, 57,* 705–717.

Locke, E. A., Shaw, K. N., Saari, L. M., & Latham, G. P. (1981). Goal setting and task performance: 1969–1980. *Psychological Bulletin, 90,* 125–152.

Looney, D. S. (1988, January 11). Why, oh why did Pat stand pat? *Sports Illustrated, 68,* 22–23.

Lott, A. J., & Lott, B. E. (1965). Group cohesiveness as interpersonal attraction: A review of relationships with antecedent and consequent variables. *Psychological Bulletin, 64,* 259–309.

Loughead, T. M., Carron, A. V., Bray, S. R., & Kim, A. (2003). Facility familiarity and the home advantage in professional sports. *International Journal of Sport Psychology and Exercise Psychology, 1,* 264-274.

Loughead, T. M., & Hardy, J. (2005). A comparison of coach and peer leader behaviors in sport. *Psychology of Sport and Exercise, 6,* 303–312.

Loughead, T. M., Hardy, J., & Eys, M. A. (2006). The nature of athlete leadership. *Journal of Sport Behavior, 29,* 142–158.

Loy, J. W., & McElvogue, J. F. (1970). Racial integration in American sport. *International Review of Sport Sociology, 5*, 5–24.

Loy, J. W., & Sage, J. N. (1968). *The effects of formal structure on organizational leadership: An investigation of interscholastic baseball teams.* Paper presented at the 2nd International Congress of Sport Psychology, Washington, D.C.

Loy, J. W., Theberge, N., Kjeldsen, E., & Donnelly, P. (1975). *An examination of hypothesized correlates of replacement processes in sport organizations.* Paper prepared for presentation at the International Seminar for the Sociology of Sport, University of Heidelberg.

Ludwig, J. (1972). *Hockey night in Moscow.* Toronto, ON: McClelland & Stewart.

Mabry, E. A., & Barnes, R. E. (1980). *The dynamics of small group communication.* Englewood Cliffs, NJ: Prentice-Hall.

MacLachlan, J. (1982). Listener perception of time-compressed spokespersons. *Journal of Advertising Research, 22*, 47–51.

MacLachlan, J., & Siegel, M. H. (1980). Reducing the costs of TV commercials by use of time compressions. *Journal of Marketing Research, 17*, 52–57.

Madden, J., & Anderson, D. (1986). *One knee equals two feet: (And everything else you need to know about football).* New York: Jove Books.

Magee, J. C., & Galinsky, A. D. (2008). Social hierarchy: The self-reinforcing nature of power and status. *The Academy of Management Annals, 2*, 351–398.

Maguire, J. (1988). Race and position assignment in English soccer: A preliminary analysis of ethnicity and sport in Britain. *Sociology of Sport Journal, 5*, 257–269.

Magyar, T. M., Feltz, D. L., & Simpson, I. P. (2004). Individual and crew level determinants of collective efficacy in rowing. *Journal of Sport & Exercise Psychology, 26*, 136–153.

Maitland, A., & Gervis, M. (2010). Goal-setting in youth football. Are coaches missing an opportunity? *Physical Education and Sport Pedagogy, 15*, 323–343.

Mann, R. D. (1959). A review of the relationship between personality and performance in small groups. *Psychological Bulletin, 56*, 241–270.

Mannix, C. (2010, March 8). Sputtering Spur. *Sports Illustrated.* Retrieved from http://sportsillustrated.cnn.com/vault/article/ magazine/MAG1166772 /index.htm

Martens, R. (1970). Influence of participation motivation on success and satisfaction in team performance. *Research Quarterly, 41*, 510–518.

Martens, R., Landers, D. M., & Loy, J. W. (1972). *Sport cohesiveness questionnaire.* Washington, DC: AAHPERD Publications.

Martens, R., & Peterson, J. (1971). Group cohesiveness as a determinant of success and member satisfaction in team performance. *International Review of Sport Sociology, 6*, 49–71.

Martin, B., & Pepe, P. (1987). *Billyball.* Garden City, NY: Doubleday & Co.

Martin, D. (2017, July 19). Pickleball, tennis dispute packs Courtenay council chambers. *Comox Valley Record.* Retrieved from https://www.comoxvalleyrecord.com/home2/pickleball-tennis-dispute-packs-courtenay-council-chambers/

Martin, L. J., Carron, A. V., & Burke, S. M. (2009). Team building interventions in sport: A meta-analysis. *International Review of Sport and Exercise Psychology, 5*, 3–18.

Martin, L. J., Carron, A. V., Eys, M. A., & Loughead, T. (2012). Development of a cohesion questionnaire for children's sport teams. *Group Dynamics: Theory, Research, and Practice, 16*, 68–79.

Martin, L. J., Evans, M. B., & Spink, K. S. (2016). Coach perspectives of "groups within the group": An analysis of subgroups and cliques in sport. *Sport, Exercise, and Performance Psychology, 5*, 52–66.

Martin, L. J., & Eys, M. A. (2019). Setting the conditions for success: A case study involving the selection process for the Canadian Forces Snowbird Demonstration Team. *Journal of Applied Sport Psychology, 31,* 116–133.

Martin, L. J., Wilson, J., Evans, M. B., & Spink, K. S. (2015). Cliques in sport: Perceptions of intercollegiate athletes. *The Sport Psychologist, 29,* 82–95.

Massengale, J., & Farrington, S. (1977). The influence of playing position centrality on the careers of college football coaches. *Review of Sport and Leisure, 2,* 107–115.

Mathieu, J. E., Heffner, T. S., Goodwin, G. F., Salas, E., & Cannon-Bowers, J. A. (2000). The influence of shared mental models on team process and performance. *Journal of Applied Psychology, 85,* 273–282.

Matsui, T., Kakuyama, T., & Onglatco, M. L. (1987). Effects of goals and feedback on performance in groups. *Journal of Applied Psychology, 72,* 407-415.

McAndrew, F. T., (1993). The home advantage in individual sports. *Journal of Social Psychology, 133,* 401

McCallum, J. (1996, November 25). The man. By speaking his mind, Grant Hill had demonstrated that he's the guy who now drives the Pistons. *Sports Illustrated, 85,* 40–48.

McEwan, D. (2019). A home advantage? Examining 100 years of team success in National Hockey League playoff overtimes games. *Psychology of Sport and Exercise, 43,* 195–199.

McEwan, D., & Beauchamp, M. R. (2014). Teamwork in sport: A theoretical and integrative review. *International Review of Sport and Exercise Psychology, 7,* 229–250.

McEwan, D., & Beauchamp, M. R. (2020). Teamwork training in sport: A pilot intervention study. *Journal of Applied Sport Psychology, 32*(2), 220–236.

McEwan, D., Ruissen, G. R., Eys, M. A., Zumbo, B. D., & Beauchamp, M. R. (2017). The effectiveness of teamwork training on teamwork behaviors and team performance: A systematic review and meta-analysis of controlled interventions. *PloS one, 12,* e0169604.

McGrath, J. E. (1962). The influence of positive interpersonal relations on adjustment and effectiveness in rifle teams. *Journal of Abnormal and Social Psychology, 65,* 365–375.

McGrath, J. E. (1984). *Groups: Interaction and performance.* Englewood Cliffs, NJ: Prentice-Hall.

McGuire, E.J., Courneya, K.S., Widmeyer, W.N., & Carron, A.V. (1992). Aggression as a potential mediator of the home advantage in professional ice hockey. *Journal of Sport & Exercise Psychology, 14,* 148-158.

McLaren, C. D., Eys, M. A., & Murray, R. A. (2015). A coach-initiated motivational climate intervention and athletes' perceptions of group cohesion in youth sport. *Sport, Exercise, and Performance Psychology, 4,* 113–121.

McLaren, C. D., & Spink, K. S. (2018). Team member communication and perceived cohesion in youth soccer. *Communication & Sport, 6,* 111–125.

McMahan, I. (2018, October 26). How sleep and jet-lag influences success in the travel-crazy NBA. *The Guardian.* Retrieved from https://www.theguardian.com/sport/2018/oct/26/sleep-nba-effects-basketball

McMenamin, D. (2018, June 1). JR Smith on dribbling out clock: 'I thought we were going to take a timeout'. *ESPN.com.* Retrieved from https://www.espn.com/nba/story/_/id/23665905/jr-smith-cleveland-cavaliers-says-knew-score-was-tied-thought-team-was-going-take-out

McNamee, M., Jones, C., Cooper, S. M., Bingham, J., North, J., & Finley, V. (2007). British spectators' perceptions of the values and norms in selected professional sports: A comparative ethical survey. *Leisure Studies, 26,* 23–45.

McPherson, B. D. (1976a). Involuntary turnover: A characteristic process of sport organizations. *International Review of Sport Sociology, 4,* 5–16.

McPherson, B. D. (1976b). Involuntary turnover and organizational effectiveness in the National Hockey League. In R. S. Gruneau & J. G. Albinson (Eds.), *Canadian sport: Sociological perspectives* (pp. 259–264). Don Mills, ON: Addison-Wesley.

McTeer, W., White, P. G., & Persad, S. (1995). Manager/coach midseason replacement and team performance in professional team sport. *Journal of Sport Behavior, 18,* 58–68.

Mellalieu, S. D., & Juniper, S. W. (2006). A qualitative investigation into experiences of the role episode in soccer. *The Sport Psychologist, 20,* 399-418.

Melnick, M. J. (1982). Six obstacles to effective team performance: Small group considerations. *Journal of Sport Behavior, 5,* 114-123.

Melnick, M. J. (1988). Racial segregation by playing position in English football league: Some preliminary observations. *Journal of Sport and Social Issues, 12,* 122–130.

Melnick, M. J. (1996). Maori women and positional segregation in New Zealand netball: Another test of the Anglocentric hypothesis. *Sociology of Sport Journal, 13,* 259–273.

Melnick, M. J., & Loy, J. W. (1996). The effects of formal structure on leadership recruitment: An analysis of team captaincy among New Zealand provincial rugby teams. *International Review for Sociology of Sport, 31,* 91–107.

Mennecke, B. E., Hoffer, J. A., & Wynne, B. E. (1992). The implications of group development and history for group support system theory and practice. *Small Group Research, 23,* 524–572.

Meyer, J. P., & Allen, N. J. (1991). A three-component conceptualization of organizational commitment. *Human Resource Management Review, 1,* 61–98.

Miesing, P., & Preble, J. F. (1985). Group processes and performance in a complex business simulation. *Small Group Behavior, 16,* 325–338.

Mikalachki, A. (1969). *Group cohesion reconsidered.* London, ON: School of Business Administration, University of Western Ontario.

Mills, T. M. (1984). *The sociology of small groups* (2nd ed.). Englewood Cliffs, NJ: Prentice-Hall.

Miranda, A. M. (1994). Avoidance of groupthink: Meeting management using group support systems. *Small Group Research, 25,* 105–136.

Mishna, F., Kerr, G., McInroy, L. B., & MacPherson, E. (2019). Student athletes' experiences of bullying in intercollegiate sport. *Journal for the Study of Sports and Athletes in Education, 13,* 53–73.

Mohr, P. B. & Larsen, K. (1998). Ingroup favoritism in umpiring decisions in Australian football. *Journal of Social Psychology, 138,* 495–504.

Moore, J. (2018, April 13). At least the NFL isn't pretending it's not blackballing Colin Kaepernick. *The Guardian.* Retrieved from https://www.theguardian.com/sport/2018/apr/13/kaepernick-reid-blackballed-nfl-kneeling-anthem.

Moore, J. C., & Brylinsky, J. A. (1995). Facility familiarity and the home advantage. *Journal of Sport Behavior, 18,* 302–311.

Moran, M. M., & Weiss, M. R. (2006). Peer leadership in sport: Links with friendship, peer acceptance, psychological characteristics, and athletic ability. *Journal of Applied Sport Psychology, 18,* 97–113.

Morgan, P. B., Fletcher, D., & Sarkar, M. (2013). Defining and characterizing team resilience in elite sport. *Psychology of Sport and Exercise, 14,* 549–559.

Morgan-Lopez, A. A., Fals-Stewart, W., & Cluff, L. A. (2009). Capturing the impact of membership turnover in small groups via latent class growth analysis: Modeling the rise of the New York Knicks of the 1960s and 1970s. *Group Dynamics: Theory, Research, and Practice, 13*, 120–132.

Morse, A. L., Shapiro, S. L., McEvoy, C. D., & Rascher, D. A. (2008). The effects of roster turnover on demand in the National Basketball Association. *International Journal of Sport Finance, 3*, 8–18.

Mott, P. E. (1965). *The organization of society*. Englewood Cliffs, NJ: Prentice Hall.

Mravic, M., & O'Brien, R. (1999, April). An age-old problem. *Sports Illustrated, 90*, 31–32.

Mullen, B., & Copper, C. (1994). The relation between group cohesiveness and performance: An integration. *Psychological Bulletin, 115*, 210–227.

Munroe, K., Estabrooks, P., Dennis, P., & Carron, A. (1999). A phenomenological analysis of group norms in sport teams. *The Sport Psychologist, 13*, 171–182.

Munroe-Chandler, K. J., & Hall, C. R. (2004). Enhancing the collective efficacy of a soccer team through motivational general-mastery imagery. *Imagination, Cognition and Personality, 24*, 51–67.

Murayama, K., & Elliot, A. J. (2012). The competition–performance relation: A meta-analytic review and test of the opposing processes model of competition and performance. *Psychological Bulletin, 138*, 1035-1070.

Murray, C. (2017, September 21). New turf fight has U.S. Soccer and women's team at odds again. *The New York Times*. Retrieved from https://www.nytimes.com/2017/09/21/sports/soccer/uswnt-us-soccer-artificial-turf.html

Murray, M. C., & Mann, B. L. (1993). Leadership effectiveness. In J. M. Williams (Ed.), *Applied sport psychology: Personal growth to peak performance* (pp. 82–98). Mountain View, CA: Mayfield.

Myers, A. (1962). Team competition, success, and adjustment of team members. *Journal of Abnormal and Social Psychology, 65*, 325–332.

Myers, N. D., Payment, C. A., & Feltz, D. L. (2004). Reciprocal relationships between collective efficacy and team performance in women's ice hockey. *Group Dynamics: Theory, Research and Practice, 8*, 182–195.

Naquin, C. E., & Tynan, R. O. (2003). The team halo effect: Why teams are not blamed for their failures. *Journal of Applied Psychology, 88*, 332–340.

Neave, N., & Wolfson, S. (2003). Testosterone, territoriality, and the 'home advantage'. *Physiology & Behavior, 78*, 269-275.

Nevill, A. M., Balmer, N. J., & Williams, A. M. (2002). The influence of crowd noise and experience upon refereeing decisions in football. *Psychology of Sport and Exercise, 3*, 261–272.

Nevill, A. M., Newell, S. M., & Gale, S. (1996). Factors associated with home advantage in English and Scottish soccer matches. *Journal of Sports Sciences, 14*, 181–186.

Newcomb, T. M. (1951). Social psychological theory. In J. H. Rohrer & M. Sherif (Eds.), *Social psychology at the crossroads*. New York: Harper.

Newin, J., Bloom, G. A., & Loughead, T. M. (2008). Youth ice hockey coaches' perceptions of a team-building intervention program. *The Sport Psychologist, 22*, 54–72.

Ngabo, G., & Miller, J. (2019). Fans flock to stores to snag Raptors championship gear. *Toronto Star*. Retrieved from https://www.thestar.com/news/gta/2019/06/14/fans-flock-to-stores-to-snag-raptors-championship-gear.html

Nord, W. R. (1969). Social exchange theory: An integrative approach to social conformity. *Psychological Bulletin, 71,* 174–208.

Olympiou, A. Jowett, S., Duda, J. L. (2008). The interface of the coach-created motivational climate and the coach-athlete relationship. *The Sport Psychologist, 22,* 423–431.

Ong, C. W., Roberts, R., Arthur, C. A., Woodman, T., & Akehurst, S. (2016). The leader ship is sinking: A temporal investigation of narcissistic leadership. *Journal of Personality, 84,* 237–247.

Orlick, T. (1986). *Psyching for sport: Mental training for athletes.* Champaign, IL: Human Kinetics.

Orwell, G. (1949). *Nineteen eighty-four.* New York: Harcourt, Brace, & World.

Osborn, K. A., Irwin, B. C., Skogsberg, N. J., & Feltz, D. L. (2012). The Köhler effect: Motivation gains and losses in real sports groups. *Sport, Exercise, and Performance Psychology, 1,* 242–253.

Pace, A., & Carron, A.V. (1992). Travel and the home advantage. *Canadian Journal of Sport Sciences, 17,* 60-64.

Parkhouse, B. L., & Williams, J. M. (1986). Differential effects of sex and status on evaluation of coaching ability. *Research Quarterly for Exercise and Sport, 57,* 53–59.

Partridge, J., & Stevens, D. E. (2002). Group dynamics: The influence of the team in sport. In J. M. Silva & D. E. Stevens (Eds.), *Psychological foundations of sport.* (pp.272–290). Boston, MA: Allyn & Bacon.

Paskevich, D. M. (1995). *Conceptual and measurement factors of collective efficacy in its relationship to cohesion and performance outcome* (Unpublished doctoral dissertation). University of Waterloo, Canada.

Paskevich, D. M., Estabrooks, P. A., Brawley, L. R. & Carron, A. V. (2001). Group cohesion in sport and exercise. In R. N. Singer, H. A. Hausenblas, & C. M. Janelle (Eds.), *Handbook of sport psychology* (2nd ed., pp. 472–496). New York: Wiley.

Paulus, P. B., Annis, A. B., Seta, J. J., Schkade, J. K., & Matthews, R. W. (1976). Density does effect task performance. *Journal of Personality and Social Psychology, 34,* 248-253.

Pearsall, M. J., & Venkataramani, V. (2015). Overcoming asymmetric goals in teams: The interactive roles of team learning orientation and team identification. *Journal of Applied Psychology, 100,* 735–749.

Pease, D. A., Locke, L. F., & Burlingame, M. (1971). Athletic exclusion: A complex phenomenon. *Quest, 16,* 42-46.

Penrod, S. (1986). *Social psychology.* Englewood Cliffs, NJ: Prentice-Hall.

Petitta, L., Jiang, L., & Palange, M. (2015). The differential mediating roles of task, relations, and emotions collective efficacy on the link between dominance and performance: A multilevel study in sport teams. *Group Dynamics: Theory, Research, and Practice, 19,* 181–190.

Pfeffer, J., & Davis-Blake, A. (1986). Administrative succession and organizational performance: How administrator experience mediates the succession effect. *Academy of Management Journal, 29,* 72–83.

Pike, B. E., Kilduff, G. J., & Galinsky, A. D. (2018). The long shadow of rivalry: Rivalry motivates performance today and tomorrow. *Psychological Science, 29,* 804–813.

Pina, M. (2019). LeBron James has never had a teammate as perfect as Anthony Davis. *SB Nation.* Retrieved from

Plunkett, J., & Newhouse, D. (1981). *The Jim Plunkett story: The saga of a man who cameback.* New York: Arbor House.

Pollard, R. (1986). Home advantage in soccer: A retrospective analysis. *Journal of Sport Sciences, 4,* 237-248.

Pollard, R. (2002). Evidence of a reduced home advantage when a team moves to a new stadium. *Journal of Sports Sciences, 20,* 969–973.

Pollard, R., & Armatas, V. (2017). Factors affecting home advantage in football World Cup qualification. *International Journal of Performance Analysis in Sport, 17,* 121–135.

Pollard, R., & Pollard, G. (2005). Long-term trends in home advantage in professional team sports in North America and England (1876–2003). *Journal of Sport Sciences, 23,* 337–350.

Pollard, R., Prieto, J., & Gómez, M-A. (2017). Global differences in home advantage by country, sport, and sex. *International Journal of Performance Analysis in Sport, 17,* 586–599.

Ponzo, M., & Scoppa, V. (2018). Does the home advantage depend on crowd support? Evidence from same-stadium derbies. *Journal of Sports Economics, 19,* 562–582.

Potter, A. (2019, June 20). Women's World Cup fiascos show video review has no place in soccer. *The Telegram.* Retrieved from https://www.thetelegram.com/sports/soccer/andrew-potter-womens-world-cup-fiascos-show-video-review-has-no-place-in-soccer-324662/

Prapavessis, H., & Carron, A. V. (1996). The effect of group cohesion on competitive state anxiety. *Journal of Sport & Exercise Psychology, 18,* 64-74.

Prapavessis, H., & Carron, A. V. (1997a). Cohesion and work output. *Small Group Research, 28,* 294–301.

Prapavessis, H., & Carron, A. V. (1997b). Sacrifice, cohesion, and conformity to norms in sport teams. *Group Dynamics, 1,* 231–240.

Prapavessis, H., Carron, A. V., & Spink, K. S. (1997). Team building in sport. *International Journal of Sport Psychology, 27,* 269–285.

Prapavessis, H., & Gordon, S. (1991). Coach/player relationships in tennis. *Canadian Journal of Sport Sciences, 16,* 229-233.

Prelutsky, J. (1983). *Zoo doings.* New York: Greenwillow Books.

Price, S. L. (2001). Lords of discipline. *Sports Illustrated, 95,* 78–82.

Price, K. (2018, August 2). Secretive Navy SEAL-Inspired Camp Provides Ultimate Bonding Experience for U.S. Women's Volleyball Team. *TeamUSA.* Retrieved from https://www.teamusa.org/News/2018/August/02/Secretive-Navy-SEAL-Inspired-Camp-Provides-Ultimate-Bonding-Experience-For-US-Womens-Volleyball-Team

Price, M. S., & Weiss, M. R. (2013). Relationships among coach leadership, peer leadership, and adolescent athletes' psychosocial and team outcomes: A test of transformational leadership theory. *Journal of Applied Sport Psychology, 25,* 265–279.

Rail, G. (1987). Perceived role characteristics and executive satisfaction in voluntary sport associations. *Journal of Sport Psychology, 9,* 376–384.

Rainey, D. W., & Larsen, J. D. (1988). Balls, strikes, and norms: Rule violation and normative rules among baseball umpires. *Journal of Sport & Exercise Psychology, 10,* 75–80.

Recht, L. D., Lew, R. A., & Schwartz, W. J. (1995). Baseball teams beaten by jet lag. *Nature, 377,* 583.

Rees, C. R., & Segal, M. W. (1984). Role differentiation in groups: The relationship between instrumental and expressive leadership. *Small Group Behavior, 15,* 109–123.

Ren, Y., & Argote, L. (2011). Transactive memory systems 1985–2010: An integrative framework of key dimensions, antecedents, and consequences. *Academy of Management Annals, 5,* 189–229.

Ridgeway, C. L. (2001). Gender, status, and leadership. *Journal of Social Issues, 57,* 637–655.

Riley, P. (1993). *The winner within: A life plan for team players*. New York: Berkeley Books.

Riots erupt in Vancouver after Canucks loss. (2011, June 15). *CBC News*. Retrieved from https://www.cbc.ca/news/canada/british-columbia/riots-erupt-in-vancouver-after-canucks-loss-1.993707

Robertson, G. (2018, February 12). How Patrick Chan's teammates helped him rebuild his confidence at the Olympics. *Globe and Mail*. Retrieved from https://www.theglobeandmail.com/sports/olympics/2018-pyeongchang-winter-olympics-patrick-chan/article37956475/

Roloff, M. E. (1981). *Interpersonal communication: The social exchange approach*. Beverly Hills, CA, Sage.

Rovio, E., Eskola, J., Kozub, S. A., Duda, J. L., & Lintunen, T. (2009). Can high group cohesion be harmful? A case study of a junior ice-hockey team. *Small Group Research, 40*, 421–435.

Roy, G. (1974). *The relationship between centrality and mobility: The case of the National Hockey League*. Unpublished master's thesis, University of Waterloo, Waterloo, Canada.

Rushin, S. (2003). Can this marriage be saved? *Sports Illustrated, 99*, 21.

Ryan, J. (1995). *Little girls in pretty boxes: The making and breaking of elite gymnasts and figure skaters*. Doubleday: New York.

Rybaltowski, M. (2018, January 18). Vegas Golden Knights GM George McPhee credits teamwork, depth for historic start. *Forbes*. Retrieved from https://www.forbes.com/sites/mattrybaltowski/2018/01/18/vegas-golden-knights-gm-george-mcphee-credits-teamwork-depth-for-historic-start/#500dbfda6d20

Sabo, D., & Veliz, P. (2008). *Go out and play: Youth sports in America*. East Meadow, NY: Women's Sports Foundation.

Sack, A. L., Singh, P., & Thiel, R. (2005). Occupational segregation on the playing field: The case of Major League Baseball. *Journal of Sport Management, 19*, 300–318.

Sage, G. H. (1974). *The effects of formal structure on organizational leadership: An investigation of collegiate football teams*. Paper presented at the Annual Meeting of the American Association for Health, Physical Education, & Recreation, Anaheim, CA.

Sage, G. H. (1998). *Power and ideology in American sport: A critical perspective* (2nd ed.). Champaign, IL: Human Kinetics.

Sage, G. H., Loy, J. W., & Ingham, A. G. (1970). *The effects of formal structure on organizational leadership: An investigation of collegiate baseball teams*. Paper presented at the Annual Meetings of the American Association for Health, Physical Education, and Recreation, Seattle, WA.

Salas, E., Rozell, D., Mullen, B., & Driskell, J. (1999). The effect of team building on performance: An Integration. *Small Group Research, 30*, 309–329.

Sarri, R. C., & Galinsky, M. J. (1974). A conceptual framework for group development. In P. Glasser, R. Sarri, & R. Vinter, (Eds.), *Individual change through small groups* (pp. 71–88). New York: Free Press.

Schachter, S., Ellertson, N., McBride, D., & Gregory, D. (1951). An experimental study of cohesiveness and productivity. *Human Relations, 4*, 229–238.

Schlenker, B. R., & Miller, R. S. (1977b). Group cohesiveness as a determinant of egocentric perceptions in cooperative groups. *Human Relations, 30*, 1039–1055.

Schlenker, B. R., Phillips, S. T., Boniecki, K. A., & Schlenker, D. R. (1995). Where is the home choke? *Journal of Personality and Social Psychology, 68*, 649-652.

Schutz, W. C. (1966). *The interpersonal underworld* (5th ed.). Palo Alto, CA: Science & Behavior Books.

Schwartz, B., & Barsky, S. F. (1977). The home advantage. *Social forces, 55,* 641-661.

Schwartz, G. (1973). *A comparative analysis of succession, size, and success among professional sport organizations.* Unpublished paper, University of Massachusetts Amherst, Amhert, MA.

Scott, A. (2017). Dallas stars have fallen victim to ebb and flows of NHL season. *Fansided.* Retrieved from https://blackoutdallas.com/2017/12/11/dallas-stars-fallen-victim-ebb-flows/

Senécal, J., Loughead, T. M., & Bloom, G. A. (2008). A season-long team-building intervention: Examining the effect of team goal setting on cohesion. *Journal of Sport & Exercise Psychology, 30,* 186–199.

Shaffer, L. S. (1978). On the current confusion of group-related behavior and collective behavior: A reaction to Buys. *Personality and Social Psychology Bulletin, 4,* 564-567.

Shakespeare, W. (1896). *As you like it.* Boston, MA: Houghton.

Shapcott, K. M., & Carron, A. V. (2010). Development and validation of a team attribution style questionnaire. *Group Dynamics: Theory, Research & Practice, 14,* 93–113.

Shapcott, K. M., Carron, A.V., Greenlees, I., & El Hakim, Y. (2008). Do member attributions for team outcomes represent a collective belief? *Psychology of Sport and Exercise, 9,* 487–492.

Shaw, M. E. (1981). *Group dynamics: The psychology of small group behavior* (3rd ed.). New York: McGraw-Hill.

Shaw, M. E., & Webb, J. N. (1982). When compatibility interferes with group effectiveness. Facilitation of learning in small groups. *Small Group Behavior, 13,* 555–564.

Sherif, M. (1936). *The psychology of social norms.* New York: Harper & Row.

Sherif, M., Harvey, O. J., White, B. J., Hood, W. R., & Sherif, C. W. (1961). *Intergroup cooperation and conflict: The Robbers Cave Experiment.* Norman, OK: Institute of Group Relations.

Sherif, M., & Sherif, C. W. (1956). *An outline of social psychology* (Rev. ed.). New York: Harper & Row.

Sherif, M., & Sherif, C. W. (1969). *Social psychology.* New York: Harper & Row.

Shields, D. L., Bredemeier, B. J., Gardner, D. E., & Boston, A. (1995). Leadership, cohesion, and team norms regarding cheating and aggression. *Sociology of Sport Journal, 12,* 324–336.

Shields, D. L., Funk, C. D., & Bredemeier, B. L. (2015). Contesting orientations: Measure construction and the prediction of sportspersonship. *Psychology of Sport and Exercise, 20,* 1–10.

Shields, D. L., LaVoi, N. M., Bredemeier, B. L., & Power, F. C. (2007). Predictors of poor sportspersonship in youth sports: Personal attitudes and social influences. *Journal of Sport & Exercise Psychology, 29,* 747–762.

Shinn, P. (2018) *World Class; The making of the U.S. Women's cross-country ski team.* Lebanon, NH; Fore Edge.

Sieber, J., & Ziegler, R. (2019). Group polarization revisited: A processing effort account. *Personality and Social Psychology Bulletin, 45*(10), 1482–1498. doi:10.1177/0146167219833389

Silva, J. M. III (1983). The perceived legitimacy of rule violating behavior in sport. *Journal of Sport Psychology, 5,* 438–448.

Silver, M. (1995, September 4). The key link: At its best, the relationship between a coach and his quarterback can elevate a team. At its worst, it can destroy an entire season. *Sports Illustrated, 83,* 84–90.

Silver, M. (2001). No forward progress. *Sports Illustrated, 95,* 38.

Silverman, I. W., & Stone, J. M. (1972). Modifying cognitive functioning through participation in a problem-solving group. *Journal of Educational Psychology, 63,* 603–608.

Sistrunk, F., & McDavid, J. W. (1971). Sex variable in conforming behavior. *Journal of Personality and Social Psychology, 17,* 200–207.

Slusher, A., Van Dyke, J., & Rose, G. (1972). Technical competence of group leaders, managerial role, and productivity in engineering design groups. *Academy of Management Journal, 15,* 197–204.

Smith, D. (2017, December 28). Backups have each other's backs. *Toronto Star,* S4.

Smith, D. (2018). Raptors clicking in record time. *Toronto Star.* Retrieved from https://www.thestar.com/sports/raptors/opinion/2018/10/27/raptors-clicking-in-record-time.html

Smith, D. R., Ciacciarelli, A., Serzan, J., & Lambert, D. (2000). Travel and the home advantage in professional sports. *Sociology of Sport Journal, 17,* 364–385.

Smith, R. E., Smoll, F. L., & Curtis, B. (1978). Coaching behaviors in Little League baseball. In F. L. Smoll & R. E. Smith (Eds.), *Psychological perspectives in youth sports.* Washington, DC: Hemisphere.

Smith. R. E., Smoll, F. L., & Hunt, E. (1977). A system for the behavioral assessment of athletic coaches. *Research Quarterly, 48,* 401–407.

Smoll, F. L., & Smith, R. E. (1979). *Improving relationship skills in youth sport coaches.* East Lansing, MI: Institute for the Study of Youth Sports.

Snyder, E. E., & Purdy, D. A. (1987). Social control in sport: An analysis of basketball officiating. *Sociology of Sport Journal, 4,* 394–402.

Sommer, R. (1969). *Personal space.* Englewood Cliffs, NJ: Prentice-Hall.

Sorrentino, R. M., & Sheppard, B. H. (1978). Effects of affiliation-related motives on swimmers in individual versus group competition: A field experiment. *Journal of Personality and Social Psychology, 7,* 704–714.

Soto, C. J., & John, O. P. (2017). The next Big Five Inventory (BFI-2): Developing and assessing a hierarchical model with 15 facets to enhance bandwidth, fidelity, and predictive power. *Journal of Personality and Social Psychology, 113,* 117–143.

Sparkman, G., & Walton, G. M. (2017). Dynamic norms promote sustainable behavior, even it is counternormative. *Psychological Science, 28,* 1663–1674.

Spense, E. (1980). *The relative contributions of ability cohesion, and participation motivation to team performance outcome in women's intramural basketball.* Unpublished undergraduate thesis, University of Waterloo, Waterloo, ON, Canada.

Spink, K. S. (1990). Group cohesion and collective efficacy of volleyball teams. *Journal of Sport & Exercise Psychology, 12,* 301–311.

Spink, K. S. (1995). Cohesion and intention to participate of female sport team athletes. *Journal of Sport & Exercise Psychology 17,* 417–427.

Spink, K. S. (1998). Mediational effects of social cohesion on the leadership behavior-intention to return relationship in sport, *Group Dynamics: Theory, Research, and Practice 2,* 92–100.

Spink, K. S., & Carron, A. V. (1993). The effects of team building on the adherence patterns of female exercise participants. *Journal of Sport & Exercise Psychology, 15,* 39–49.

Spink, K. S., Crozier, A. J., & Robinson, B. (2013). Examining the relationship between descriptive norms and perceived effort in adolescent athletes: Effects of different reference groups. *Psychology of Sport and Exercise, 14*, 813–818.

Spink, K. S., Wilson, K. S., & Odnokon, P. (2010). Examining the relationship between cohesion and return to team in elite athletes. *Psychology of Sport and Exercise, 11*, 6–11.

Sportsnet. (Producer). (2019). *Kawhi Leonard attributes Raptors' chemistry to team's success*. [online video interview]. Available from https://www.sportsnet.ca/basketball/nba/kawhi-leonard-attributes-raptors-chemistry-teams-success/

Sridhar, S. (2018, February 26). Klopp wants Liverpool to stay angry for home stretch. *Reuters*. Retrieved from https://www.euronews.com/2018/02/26/klopp-wants-liverpool-to-stay-angry-for-home-stretch.

Stajkovic, A. D., Lee, D., & Nyberg, A. J. (2009). Collective efficacy, group potency, and group performance: Meta-analyses of their relationships, and test of a mediation model. *Journal of Applied Psychology, 94*, 814–828.

Stanne, M. B., Johnson, D. W., & Johnson, R. T. (1999). Does competition enhance or inhibit motor performance: A meta-analysis. *Psychological Bulletin, 125*, 133–154.

Staufenbiel, K., Lobinger, B., & Strauss, B. (2015). Home advantage in soccer–A matter of expectations, goal setting and tactical decisions of coaches? *Journal of Sports Sciences, 33*, 1932–1941.

Steiner, I. D. (1972). *Group processes and group productivity*. New York: Academic.

Steinzor, B. (1955). The spatial factor in face-to-face discussion groups. In A. P. Hare, E. F. Borgatta, & R. F. Bales (Eds.), *Small groups: Studies in social interaction* (pp. 348–352). New York: Alfred A. Knopf.

Stengel, S. (2010). *Inspiring quotes and stories*. Retrieved from http://www.inspiring-quotes-and-stories.com/teamwork-quotes-1.html

Stogdill, R. M. (1964). *Team achievement under high motivation*. Columbus, Ohio: The Bureau of Business Research, College of Commerce and Administration, Ohio State University.

Strashin, J. (2017, April 4). NHL players risk their careers if they opt for Olympics, sports lawyer says. *CBC Sports*. Retrieved from https://www.cbc.ca/sports/hockey/nhl/nhl-players-risk-their-careers-if-they-opt-for-olympics-1.4055477

Strauss, B., & Welberg, M. (2008). Der Heimvorteil bei Kontinentalmeisterschaften im Fußball. [Home advantage in the Continental Championship tournaments in Soccer]. *Spectrum der Sportwissenschaft, 20*, 64–73.

Strodtbeck, F. L., & Hook, L. H. (1961). The social dimension of a twelve-man jury table. *Sociometry, 24*, 397–415.

Sullivan, P., & Feltz, D. L. (2001). The relationship between intrateam conflict and cohesion within hockey teams. *Small Group Research, 32*, 342–355.

Sullivan, P., & Feltz, D. L. (2003). The preliminary development of the Scale for Effective Communication in Team Sports (SECTS). *Journal of Applied Social Psychology, 33*, 1693–1715.

Sumner, J., & Mobley, M. (1981). Are cricket umpires biased? *New Scientist, 91*, 29–31.

Surya, M., Benson, A. J., Balish, S. M., & Eys, M. A. (2015). The influence of injury on group interaction processes. *Journal of Applied Sport Psychology, 27*, 52-66.

Sussman, S., Pokhrel, P., Ashmore, R. D., & Brown, B. B. (2007). Adolescent peer group identification and characteristics: A review of the literature. *Addictive Behaviors, 32*, 1602–1627.

Tajfel, H. (1981). *Human groups and social categories: Studies in social psychology.* Cambridge, England: Cambridge University Press.

Tajfel, H., & Turner, J. (1979). An integrative theory of intergroup conflict. In W. G. Austin & S. Worchel (Eds.), *The social psychology of intergroup relations* (pp. 33–48). Belmont, CA: Wadsworth.

Tannenbaum, A. J. (1960). *Adolescents' attitudes toward academic brilliance* (Doctoral dissertation, Columbia University).

Terborg, J., Castore, C., & DeNinno, J. (1976). A longitudinal field investigation of the impact of group composition on group performance and cohesion. *Journal of Personality and Social Psychology, 6*, 782–790.

Terry, P. C., Carron, A. V., Pink, M. J., Lane, A. M., Jones, G. J. W. & Hall, M. P. (2000). Perceptions of group cohesion and mood in sport teams. *Group Dynamics, 4*, 244-253.

Terry, P. C., Walrond, N., & Carron, A. V. (1998). The influence of game location on athletes' psychological states. *Journal of Science and Medicine in Sport, 1*, 29-37.

Tharp, R. G., & Gallimore, R. (1976, April). What a coach can teach a teacher. *Coaching Association of Canada Bulletin, 13*, 8–10.

Theberge, N., & Loy, J. W. (1976). Replacement processes in sport organizations: the case of professional baseball. *International Review of Sport Sociology, 11*, 73–93.

Thomas, L. (2019, August 27). Pain and resentment and the inspiring retirement of Andrew Luck. *The New Yorker.* Retrieved from https://www.newyorker.com/sports/sporting-scene/pain-and-resentment-and-the-inspiring-retirement-of-andrew-luck.

Thürmer, J. L., Wieber, F., & Gollwitzer, P. M. (2017). Planning and performance in small groups: collective implementation intentions enhance group goal striving. *Frontiers in psychology, 8*, 603.

Timmerman, T. A. (2000). Racial diversity, age diversity, interdependence, and team performance. *Small Group Research, 31*, 592–606.

Tjosvold, D. (1998). Cooperative and competitive goal approach to conflict: Accomplishments and challenges. *Applied Psychology, 47*, 285-313.

Tjosvold, D., West, M. A., & Smith, K. G. (2003). Teamwork and cooperation: Fundamentals of organizational effectiveness. In M. A. West, D. Tjosvold, and K. G. Smith (Eds.) *International handbook of organizational teamwork and cooperative learning* (p. 2-24). West Sussex, U.K.; Wiley.

Tropp, K. J., & Landers, D. M. (1979). Team interaction and the emergence of leadership and interpersonal attraction in field hockey. *Journal of Sport Psychology, 3*, 228-240.

TSN.ca (2019, March 6). Backes: 'Calculated decision' to become enforcer. *TSN.ca.* Retrieved from https://www.tsn.ca/backes-calculated-decision-to-become-enforcer-1.1268719.

Tucker, L. W., & Parks, J. B. (2001). Effects of gender and sport type on intercollegiate athletes' perceptions of the legitimacy of aggressive behaviors in sport. *Sociology of Sport Journal, 18*, 403–413.

Tuckman, B. W. (1965). Developmental sequences in small groups. *Psychological Bulletin, 63*, 384–399.

Tuckman, B. W. & Jensen, M. A. C. (1977). Stages of small group development revisited. *Group and Organizational Studies, 2*, 419–427.

Turner, J. C. (1982). Towards a cognitive redefinition of the social group. In H. Tajfel (Ed.), *Social identity and intergroup relations.* Cambridge, UK: Cambridge University Press.

Tutko, T. A., & Richards, J. W. (1977). *Psychology of coaching.* Boston, MA: Allyn and Bacon.

Tychkowski, R. (2019, March 5). Edmonton Oilers playoff hopes rest at Rogers Place. *Edmonton Sun*. Retrieved from https://edmontonsun.com/sports/hockey/nhl/edmonton-oilers/edmonton-oilers-playoff-hopes-rest-at-rogers-place

Uhl-Bien, M., Riggio, R. E., Lowe, K. B., & Carsten, M. K. (2014). Followership theory: A review and research agenda. *The Leadership Quarterly, 25*, 83–104.

Van Maanen, J. (2011). *Tales of the field: On writing ethnography*. University of Chicago Press.

Van Maanen, J., & Schein, E. H. (1979). Toward a theory of organizational socialization. *Research in Organizational Behavior, 1*, 209-264.

van Ours, J. C., & van Tuijl, M. A. (2016). In-season head-coach dismissals and the performance of professional football teams. *Economic Inquiry, 54*, 591–604.

Varca, P. E. (1980). An analysis of home and away game performance of male college basketball teams. *Journal of Sport Psychology, 2*, 245–257.

Vargas-Tonsing, T. M., & Guan, J. (2007). Athletes' preference for informational and emotional pre-game speech content. *International Journal of Sports Science & Coaching, 2*, 171–180.

Verducci, T. (1996, February 26). A new fresh: The rebuilding is nearly complete (once again) in San Diego, where the Padres look like contender. *Sports Illustrated, 84*, 68–71.

Vigne, G., Gaudino, C., Rogowski, I., Alloatti, G., & Hautier, C. (2010). Activity profile in elite Italian soccer team. *International Journal of Sports Medicine, 31*, 304–310.

Vignoles, V. L., Regalia, C., Manzi, C., Golledge, J., & Scabini, E. (2006). Beyond self-esteem: influence of multiple motives on identity construction. *Journal of Personality and Social Psychology, 90*, 308–333.

Vincent, D. (2005, January 9). Old Fish helping young Warriors. *Toronto Star*, p. B2

Volp, A., & Keil, U. (1987). The relationship between performance, intention to drop out, and interpersonal conflict in swimmers. *Journal of Sport Psychology, 9*, 358–375.

Vrentas, J. (2017). The tale of Tom Brady and Johnny Foxborough. *Sports Illustrated*. Retrieved from https://www.si.com/mmqb/2017/01/18/nfl-tom-brady-bill-belichick-new-england-patriots

Wageman, R. (1995). Interdependence and group effectiveness. *Administrative Science Quarterly, 40*, 145–180.

Wagstaff, C. R., Gilmore, S., & Thelwell, R. C. (2016). When the show must go on: Investigating repeated organizational change in elite sport. *Journal of Change Management, 16*, 38–54.

Waldron, J. J. (2015). Predictors of mild hazing, severe hazing, and positive initiation rituals in sport. *International Journal of Sports Science & Coaching, 10*, 1089–1101.

Walsh, B. (1990). *Building a champion: On football and the making of the 49ers*. New York, NY: St. Martin's.

Watson, C. B., Chemers, M. M., & Preiser, N. (2001). Collective efficacy: A multilevel analysis. *Personality and Social Psychology, 27*, 1057–1068.

Webb, T., Dicks, M., Thelwell, R., & Nevill, A. (2018). The impact of referee training: Reflections on the reduction of home advantage in association football. *Soccer & Society, 19*, 1024–1037.

Weinberg, R., Burton, D., Yukelson, D., & Weigand, D. (2000). Perceived goal setting practices of Olympic athletes: An exploratory investigation. *The Sport Psychologist, 14*, 279–295.

Weinberg, R., Reveles, M., & Jackson, A. (1984). Attitudes of male and female athletes toward male and female coaches. *Journal of Sport Psychology, 6*, 448–453.

Weiss, M. R., & Friedrichs, W. D. (1986). The influence of leader behaviors, coach attributes, and institutional variables on performance and satisfaction of collegiate basketball teams. *Journal of Sport Psychology, 8,* 332–346.

Weldon, E., & Weingart, L. R. (1993). Group goals and group performance. *British Journal of Social Psychology, 32,* 307–334.

Wertheim, J. (2004, March). Good job. You're fired. *Sports Illustrated, 100,* 54–63.

Wertheim, J. (2019, June). The talent and mindset behind the Golden State Warriors' dynasty. *CBS News.* Retrieved from https://www.cbsnews.com/news/golden-state-warriors-the-talent-and-mindset-behind-the-nba-reigning-dynasty-60-minutes-2019-06-02/

Westre, K. R., & Weiss, M. R. (1991). The relationship between perceived coaching behaviors and group cohesion in high school football teams. *Sport Psychologist, 5,* 41–54.

Wheelan, S. A. (1999). *Creating effective teams: A guide for members and leaders.* Thousand Oaks, CA: SAGE Publications, Inc.

Widmeyer, W. N. (1971). *The size of sport groups with special implications for the triad.* Unpublished paper, University of Illinois, Champaign, IL.

Widmeyer, W. N. (1990). Group composition in sport. *International Journal of Sport Psychology, 21,* 264–285.

Widmeyer, W. N., Brawley, L. R., & Carron, A. V. (1985). *The measurement of cohesion in sport teams: The Group Environment Questionnaire.* London, ON: Sports Dynamics.

Widmeyer, W. N., Brawley, L. R., & Carron, A. V. (1988). How many should I carry on my team? Consequences of group size. *Psychology of Motor Behavior and Sport: Abnstracts 1988.* Knoxville, TN: North American Society for the Psychology of Sport and Physical Activity.

Widmeyer, W. N., Brawley, L. R., & Carron, A. V. (1990). The effects of group size in sport. *Journal of Sport & Exercise Psychology, 12,* 177–190.

Widmeyer, W. N., & Gossett, D. M. (1978). *The relative contributions of ability and cohesion to team performance outcome in intramural basketball.* Paper presented at the Annual Meeting of the North American Society for the Psychology of Sport and Physical Activity, Tallahassee, FL.

Widmeyer, W. N., & Loy, J. W. (1989). Dynamic duos: An analysis of the relationships between group composition and group performance in women's doubles tennis. In R. Bolton (Ed.), *Studies in Honor of J. M. Roberts.* New Haven: Human Relations Area Files.

Widmeyer, W. N., & Loy, J. W., & Roberts, J. (1980). The relative contribution of action styles and ability to the performance outcomes of doubles tennis teams. In C. Nadeau, W. Halliwell, K. Newell, & G. Roberts (Eds.), *Psychology of Motor Behavior and Sport-1979* (pp. 209–218). Champaign, IL: Human Kinetics.

Widmeyer, W. N., Silva, J. M., & Hardy, C. J. (1992, October). *The nature of group cohesion in sport teams: A phenomenological approach.* Paper presented at Association for the Advancement of Applied Sport Psychology Conference, Colorado Springs, CO.

Wiese, B. S., & Freund, A. M. (2005). Goal progress makes one happy, or does it? Longitudinal findings from the work domain. *Journal of Occupational and Organizational Psychology, 78,* 287–304.

Williams, J. M., & Hacker, C. M. (1982). Causal relationships among cohesion, satisfaction and performance in women's intercollegiate field hockey teams. *Journal of Sport Psychology, 4,* 324–337.

Williams, K. D. (2007). Ostracism. *Annual Review of Psychology, 58,* 425-452.

Wilson, D., & Ramchandani, G. (2017a). Home advantage in the Winter Paralympic Games 1976-2014. *Sport Sciences for Health, 13,* 355–363.

Wilson, D., & Ramchandani, G. (2017b). An investigation of home advantage in the Summer Paralympic Games. *Sport Sciences for Health, 13,* 625–633.

Winfield, K. (2018). Dwane Casey won Coach of the Year for the team that fired him. *SB Nation.* Retrieved from https://www.sbnation.com/nba/2018/6/25/17504606/dwane-casey-coach-of-the-year-fired-raptors-pistons

Wolf, S. A., Eys, M. A., & Kleinert, J. (2015). Predictors of the precompetitive anxiety response: Relative impact and prospects for anxiety regulation. *International Journal of Sport and Exercise Psychology, 13,* 344–358.

Wolf, S. A., Eys, M. A., Sadler, P., & Kleinert, J. (2015). Appraisal in a team context: Perceptions of cohesion predict competition importance and prospects for coping. *Journal of Sport & Exercise Psychology, 37,* 489–499.

Wolff, A., & Spear, G. (1995, November 27). Chemistry 101. Here's the reason that the most talented teams don't always win NCAA's. *Sports Illustrated Canada, 2,* 34–43.

Woodcock, M., & Francis, D. (1994). *Teambuilding strategy.* Cambridge, UK: University Press.

Woodward, J. R. (2004). Professional football scouts: An investigation of racial stacking. *Sociology of Sport Journal, 21,* 356–375.

Worchel, S. (1979). Cooperation and the reduction of intergroup conflict: Some determining factors. In W.G. Austin & S. Worchel (Eds.), *The social psychology of intergroup relations* (pp. 174–187). Belmont, CA: Wadsworth.

Worchel, S. (1994). You can go home again: Returning group research to the group context with an eye on developmental issues. *Small Group Research, 25,* 205-223.

Worchel, S., Cooper, J., & Goethals, G. R. (1991). *Understanding social psychology* (5th ed.). Belmont, CA, US: Thomson Brooks/Cole Publishing Co.

Wright, E. F., Jackson, W., Christie, S. D., McGuire, G. R., & Wright, R. D. (1991). The home-course disadvantage in golf championships: Further evidence for the undermining effect of supportive audiences on performance under pressure. *Journal of Sport Behavior, 14,* 51–60.

Wright, E. F., Voyer, D., Wright, R. D., & Roney, C. (1995). Supporting audiences and performance under pressure: The home disadvantage in hockey championships. *Journal of Sport Behavior, 18,* 21–29.

Yetman, N. R., & Berghorn, F. J. (1993). Racial participation and integration in intercollegiate basketball: A longitudinal perspective. *Sociology of Sport Journal, 10,* 301–314.

Yukelson, D. (1993). Communicating effectively. In J. M. Williams (Ed.). *Applied sport psychology. Personal growth to peak performance* (2nd ed.) (pp. 122–136). Mountain View, CA: Mayfield.

Yukelson, D. (1997). Principles of effective team building interventions in sport: A direct services approach at Penn State University. *Journal of Applied Sport Psychology, 9,* 73–96.

Yukelson, D., Weinberg, R., & Jackson, A. (1984). A multidimensional group cohesion instrument for intercollegiate basketball. *Journal of Sport Psychology, 6,* 103–117.

Zaccaro, S. J., Blair, V., Peterson, C., & Zazanis, M. (1995). Collective efficacy. In J. Maddux (Ed.), *Self-efficacy, adaptation, and adjustment* (pp. 305–328). New York, NY: Plenum.

Zander, A. (1971). *Motives and goals in groups.* New York: Academic Press.

Zander, A. (1982). *Making groups effective.* San Francisco: Jossey-Bass.

Zimmerman, E. (1985). Almost all you wanted to know about status inconsistency but never dared to measure: Theoretical deficits on status inconsistency. *Social Behavior and Personality, 13,* 195–214.

Index

3+1 Cs Conceptual Model, 92–93

A

Abdul-Jabbar, Kareem, 148, 149,
Ability, 78–93,
  individual, 78–83
  member, 90–93
Adaptive response models, 38
Additive tasks, 77
Adherence, 17, 86, 128, 138, 140, 169, 237
Adversity, 208, 248, 253, 256, 258
Affect/Affection, 5, 35, 55–56, 90, 91, 92, 119, 123, 148, 149, 169, 199, 200, 225, 226, 240, 259, 260, 263, 267
  cohesion and, 236–237
Age, 10, 16, 22, 148, 151, 154–155, 168, 169, 170, 185, 210, 230, 231
  group resources and age variability, 85–86
Aggression, 9–10, 70, 142
Alden, Mike, 43
Allport, Fred, 5–6
Alonso, Xabi, 214
Altman, Irwin, 58–60
Ambiguity
  degree of, 138
  role, 27-28, 116–120, 240
  socioemotional, 116
  task, 116
Anglocentric hypothesis, 107
Anxiety, 69, 119, 236–237, 254, 266
  state anxiety, 69, 236, 237
Assimilating, 217
Asgeirsson, Sveinn, 5

Attitude, 3, 75, 76, 86, 132, 139, 143, 145, 210, 212, 217, 232, 235, 261, 260
Attitude change, 143, 145–146
Attributions, 235
Auburn University, 219
Authority, 90, 123, 149, 151, 153, 165, 178
Autocratic decision style, 177, 181

B

Backes, David, 117
Balance theory, 192
Bales, R. F., 112–113
Bandura, A., 248, 250, 253
Barker, Jim, 99
Baumeister, R. F., 3, 4, 5, 71–73, 236–237
Bay of Pigs, 8
Belichick, Bill, 127, 165
Bell, George, 79, 81, 84, 86
Berenson, Red, 31
Big Five Personality Taxonomy, 80
Blanchard, K., 166–167
Bloom, Gordon A., 262
Boston Bruins, 8, 117, 120, 121
Boston Celtics, 156
Bowman, Scotty, 148, 149
Brady, Tom, 165
Brawley, L. R., 179, 203–204
Brazilian National Women's Soccer Team, 47
Brooklyn Dodgers, 75
Bryant, Kobe, 154
Burke, Brian, 109
Buys, Christian, 8–9, 244

C

Calgary Stampeders, 99
Campbell, Dan, 105–106
Canadian Football League, 95, 96, 99
Cantona, Eric, 231
Carolina Hurricanes, 133
Carrington, Lisa, 97
Carson, Essence, 31
Casey, Dwane, 43, 234
Chan, Patrick, 256
Charrúa, Garra, 159
Chase, Melissa A., 157
Checketts, Dave, 261
Chelladurai, P., 168–169, 254–255
Chicago Bulls, 261
Chicago White Sox, 45
Choice Dilemma Inventory (Kogan and Wallach), 218
Churchill, Winston, 75
Clark, Monte, 148
Clemens, Roger, 66
Cleveland Cavaliers, 43, 209
Coach-athlete compatibility, 89. 91–93, 239, 255
Coaching behavior, 27, 163, 168, 169, 238, 239, 255
   assessment of, 163–164
   consequences of, 170
   member characteristics and, 169–170
   situational characteristics and, 170
Coaching Behavior Assessment System, 27, 163–164
Coercive power, 148, 162
Cognitions, 3, 56, 92, 123, 125, 132, 228
   cohesion and, 235–236
   individual cognitions, 55–56, 119
Cognitive restructuring, 125–126
Cohesion, 4, 21–22, 23, 26, 27, 29, 31–32, 37–38, 89, 93, 140, 159–160, 204, 210, 211, 215, 223–246
   collective efficacy and, 14, 160, 240, 254
   communication and, 172
   conceptual model of, 229–230
   conformity to group norms and, 138, 140–141
   decision making and, 179–180
   definitions of, 224–226
   group cohesion, 140, 254
   group size and, 55
   leadership factors and, 238–239
   measurement of in sport teams, 226–227
   measurement of in work groups, 224–225
   meta-analysis of, 242
   moderators of cohesion-performance relationship, 242
   negative aspects of, 244–247
   personal factors and, 234–238
   situational factors and, 233–234
   task cohesion, 27–28, 120, 171
   team factors and, 239–241
   team success and, 241–244
Collective efficacy, 13, 14, 28, 69, 159, 240–241, 247–257
   group cohesion, 254
   group leadership, 254–255
   motivational climate, 255
   nature of, 248–249
   overlaps with self-efficacy, 255–257
   performance and, 249–250
   prior performance, 250–253
   situational specificity of, 249
   verbal persuasion, 253
   vicarious experiences, 253
Commonsense vs science, 19–20
Communication, 143–145, 209–221
   cohesion and, 172
   group size and, 57
   of role responsibilities, 115
   See also Group communication
Compatibility, 88–91
   between people, 91
   and FIRO theory, 90
   with group roles, 91
   of member abilities, 90–91
Competition, 183–197
   inter- and intra-group competition, 185–191, 191–194
   nature of, 184–185
   consequences of, 190–191
   See also Robbers Cave Experiment

Conceptual frameworks, 13–18
   for group effectiveness, 14–16
   for the nature of groups, 16–18
   for sports team, 18
Conflict, 36–38, 125–126, 151–152, 211, 241
   interrole, 121
   intrasender, 120–121
   person-role, 121
   role, 120–122
Conformity, 4, 8, 133, 214, 244–245
   cohesion and, 237
   group/team norms and, 134–139
   individual, 240
   personal factors, 136–138
   situational factors and, 138–139
Conjunctive tasks, 78
Consultative decision style, 177
Contingency theory of leadership, 165–166
Control, 20, 29, 35, 58–59, 90, 92, 148, 164, 203, 224
Cooperation, 183–197
   between-group, 194–195
   consequences of, 190–191
   intergroup competition, 185–191, 191–194
   nature of, 184–185
   within-group, 194
   See also Robbers Cave Experiment
Cragg, Amy, 189
Crowding, 50
   density and, 56–57
Croxon, Sheilagh, 250–251
Culture, 10, 26, 32, 54, 127, 133, 148, 154–155, 207, 238
   coaching behavior and, 169

D

Dallas Stars, 34
Davis, Anthony, 89
Debriefing, 221, 259
Decision-making, 13, 57, 66, 92, 100, 126, 139, 169, 171, 173, 177, 215
   cohesion and, 179–180
   flaws in groups, 216–217
   leadership and, 177–179
   normative model of, 180–183

Decision styles, 177–183
   autocratic, 177–178
   consultative, 177–178
   delegative, 178
   effectiveness of, 179
   participative (democratic), 178
Deindividuation, 8–9, 244
Demographics and cohesion, 234–235
Density, 62, 64
   crowd density, 65
   crowding and, 56–57
   group size and, 14
   home advantage and, 25
   transactive, 206–207
Detroit Pistons, 154
Diggins, Jessie, 247
Dilfer, Trent, 178
Disjunctive Tasks, 77
Distribution of rewards, 103
Diversity, 77, 84–88
   disparity, 85
   in ability, 87–88
   in age and team tenure, 85–86
   in racial identity/ethnicity, 86
   in sex, 85
   in social psychological characteristics, 86–87
   separation, 84–85
   variety, 84
Djokovic, Novak, 7
Dolan, Steve, 5
Domenech, Raymond, 239
Donovan, Ann, 31
Dortmund, Borussia, 49
Dryden, Ken, 36–37
Duke University, 191, 212
Dumars, Joe, 147, 154
Dundon, Tom, 133
Durant, Kevin, 78, 137
Dye, Pat, 219

E

Eagly, A., 174–177
Edmonton Oilers, 71
Ellis, Bo, 152
Ellis, Jill, 3

Enjoyment, 55, 150, 172, 227, 244, 258
    crowding and, 56
    gender and, 85
Esposito, Phil, 206
Ewing, Patrick, 260, 261
Exercise classes, 86
Experimental protocols, 28–29
Expert power, 148–149, 162

F

Feedback, coaching behavior and, 50, 54, 124, 169, 170, 194, 200, 203, 220, 238, 239, 244, 255, 256, 259, 267
Feinstein, John, 36–37
Fiedler, F. E., 165–166
    See also Contingency theory of leadership
FIFA World Cup, *See* World Cup
FIRO theory, 90
Fisher, Derek, 144
Flanagan, Shalane, 189
Followership, 172–174
Formal roles, 110–111, 119
France, Anatole, 21
Fraschilla, Fran, 42
French Soccer Team, 143

G

Gender,
    cohesion and, 242–243
    conformity and, 137
    leadership and, 174–177
    status and, 156–157
Geography/Geographic location, 99
Golden State Warriors, 43, 78, 137, 144, 152
Goals/Goal setting, 197–209
    components of effective individual, 199–200
    effective goal setting, 198–199
    group or team goal setting, 203–204
    individual goal setting, 201–203
    individual versus team goal setting, 204–207
    in industry, 207–209
    performance and, 199
    reasons for success of, 199–200
    in sports, 201–207
    why goal setting works, 200–201
    youth development and, 203
Green Bay Packers, 130
Green, Danny, 96
Group communication, 209–223
    coordination and, 212–213
    decision-making flaws in, 216–217
    downfalls of, 214–220
    effective, 211–214
    heterogeneity versus homogeneity and, 210
    improving of, 220–222
        accounting for biases, 221
        creating a positive environment, 220
        proactive approaches to, 220
        strategic ways to convey information, 220
        training in group situations, 221–222
    nature of, 145, 210–211
    principles of, 210
    sources of, 143–145
    See also Group polarization, groupthink, and transactive memory
Group composition, 76–77, 80, 86, 210
    definition of, 76
    Widmeyer and Loy perspective of, 80
Group development, 31–47
    definition of, 31–32
    managing new members, 39–40
    membership turnover, 40
    replacement of managers and coaches, 42–47
    See also Group development theories, and turnover
Group development theories, 32–38
    adaptive response models, 38
    punctuated equilibrium models, 38
    repeating cycles (pendulum) perspective, 34–38
    robust equilibrium models, 38
    sequential stage (linear) perspective, 32–34

Group dynamics, 1, 5, 19, 21–24, 26, 28, 31, 39, 47, 81, 82, 85, 87, 93, 107, 149, 165, 173, 226, 227–228, 231, 232, 242, 243, 245, 265
   definition of, 13
   experimental protocols concerning, 28
Group effectiveness, 76–78, 82, 86, 153, 245, 258–259
   conceptual framework for, 14–16
Group Environment Questionnaire (GEQ), 227–231
Group interaction processes, 16–18
   definition, 16
Group integration-task, 28, 230, 237, 240
Group member attributes, 75–93
Group membership changes, 39–40
Group members, psychosocial attributes of, 79–83
Group norms, 11, 96, 127–147, 237, 240, 262, 265
   attitude change and, 143
   beyond sport teams, 141–143
   cohesion and, 138–139, 227, 237, 240
   conformity to, 134–139
   dynamic, 146
   emergence of, 131–132
   functions of, 132–133
   modification of, 143–147
   nature of, 139–143
   permissive, 130–131
   personal factors related to conformity and, 136–138
   preference, 130, 131
   prescribed, 129, 130
   proscribed, 129–130
   rule violations and, 141–142
   situational factors and, 138–139
   sport teams and, 139–141
   stability of, 133–134
   types of, 129–131
Group polarization, 217–220
   cautious shift, 217
   risky shift, 217
Group position, 99–109
   group processes and, 105–106
   importance of, 100–101

   interactional centrality, 100
   spatial centrality, 100
   sport teams and, 101
   See also Positional stacking
Group processes and group position, 105–106
Group resources, 77–93
   amount of, 77–83
      individual ability, 78
   compatibility and, 88–93
      between the coach and the athlete, 91–93
      group roles, 91
      member abilities, 90–91
   diversity of, 83–88
      ability, 87–88
      age and team tenure, 85–86
      racial identity and ethnicity, 86
      sex, 85
      social psychological characteristics, 86–87
   variability and, 84–85
   See also Group members, psychosocial attributes of
Group roles, 91, 109–126
   communicating responsibility for, 114–115
   development of, 112–116
   formal, 110–111, 114–115
   informal, 110–111, 115–116
   nature and correlates of the elements of, 116–124
   passive, 91
   role clarity, 116–120
   role commitment and acceptance, 122–123
   role conflict, 120–122
   role efficacy, 122
   role performance, 116, 124–125
   role satisfaction, 123–124
   social vs task, 111–112
   types of, 110–112
Group size, 21, 49–57
   cohesion and, 55
   collective efficacy and, 253, 258
   communication and, 57
   conformity and, 138
   crowding/density and, 56–57

individual affect and, 55
individual cognitions and, 55–56
leadership and, 175
optimal sport team size, 50–52
outcomes related to, 52–57
productivity/performance and, 52–53
psychosocial outcomes and, 57
social loafing and, 53–55
Group structure, 16–17, 95–158
competition and cooperation as, 186–188
norms and, 127–146
physical structure, 95–96
position and, 99–108
psychological structure, 95–96
roles and, 109–126
status and, 147–158
Group territory. *See* Territory/Territoriality
Groups,
cohesion and, 223–246
communication in, 209–222
conceptual framework for, 13–18
cooperation and competition in, 183–196
definitions of, 9–13
development of, 31–46
effectiveness of, 14–15
goal setting in, 197–208
importance of positions in, 99–108
leadership in, 161–182
minimal groups, 193
nature of, 3–18
norms in, 127–146
positions in, 99–108
reality of, 5–7
reasons for influence and importance, 4
resources in, 75–94
roles in, 109–126
size of, 49–57
social hierarchy in, 147–158
study of, 19–30
utility of, 7–8
Groupthink, 8, 215–216, 221, 245
antecedents of, 215
concurrence seeking and, 216
decision-making and, 216–217
examples of, 215
nature of, 215
symptoms of, 215
Grusky, O., 102–103
Guillen, Ozzie, 45
Gyan, Asamoah, 235

H

Hayhurst, Dirk, 243
Henderson, Ricky, 41
Hersey, P., 166–167
Heterogeneity versus homogeneity, 84, 87–88
communication and, 210
Heuzé, J., 230
Hierarchies, 147–159
attributes and, 154–155
benefits vs detriments of, 152–154
conflict perspective on, 151–152
functional perspective on, 149–151
nature of, 148–156
sport involvement and, 156–159
situational characteristics and, 155–156
status and, 148–149
Hill, Grant, 147, 154, 212
Holmgren, Mike, 178
Home advantage, 25, 60–63
causes of, 63–71
game location factors and, 64–69
in individual sports, 63
in professional and international team sport, 61–63
psychological factors and, 69–72
Home disadvantage, 71–75
Houston Astros, 66
Houston Rockets, 42
"Humans Would Do Better Without Groups" (Buys), 7
Hurley, Bobby, 212

I

Iceland National Soccer Team, 5
Idiosyncrasy credit, 136–137
indirect team building approach, 264–266

Indiana University, 37, 113
Implementation intentions, 207–208
Individual ability and group success, 78–79
Individual goal setting, 125, 201, 205
Individual roles, 114, 116, 118
Informal roles, 110, 115, 119, 161
Ingroups versus outgroups, 185, 192–195
Intelligence, 77
Interactional centrality, 100
Interdependence, 101–102, 152, 189, 191, 194
   definition of, 185
Intergroup contact, 194–195

J

Jackson, Phil, 162, 171, 241
Jacob, C. S., 154–155
James, LeBron, 43, 89, 209
Janis, Irving, 216–217
Jefferson, Richard, 116, 117
Johnson, Larry, 87
Johnson, Magic, 83
Jones, Jerry, 129
Jordan, Michael, 191
Jowett, S., 92–93

K

Kaepernick, Colin, 128–129
Kahn, R. L., 116
Kansas City Chiefs, 58
Karolyi, B., 183
Keenan, Mike, 6, 7
Kent State University, 37
Klopp, Juergen, 225
Knight, Bobby, 113
Krzyzewski, Mike, 212

L

Laettner, Christian, 212
Landers, D. M., 202
Las Vegas Golden Knights, 5, 172
Latham, Gary, 197, 199–200

Leaders, 161–183
   decision making and, 179–183
   decision styles and, 177–179
   emergent, 161
   prescribed, 161
   See also Leadership
Leadership, 161–183
   cohesion and, 179–180, 238–239
   collective efficacy and, 251, 254
   contingency theory and, 165–166
   effectiveness of, 162–166
   evaluation of in relation to gender, 176–177
   gender and, 174–177
   group leadership, 161–183
   impartial and autocratic, 215
   life cycle theory and, 166–168
   multidimensional model of, 168–170
   peer, 171–172
   person-focused, 164–165
   process model, 172–174
   situational approaches to, 165–170
   task-focused, 164
   transactional, 170
   transformational, 170–171
   universal approaches to, 162–165
Leadership Scale for Sports (LSS), 169
Lee, Butch, 152
Leveling, 217
Lewin, K., 19
Life cycle theory of leadership, 166–168
Likert, Rensis, 205
Lin, Jeremey, 96, 123
Lloyd, Carli, 117, 122
Locke, E. A., 198–200
Looney, D. S., 219
Lopez, Felipe, 87
Los Angeles Lakers, 89, 144, 154, 162, 241
Loughead, T., 171–172, 262
Lowry, Kyle, 83
Loy, J. W., 80, 88, 106
Lucas, Maurice, 152
Luck, Andrew, 117, 121

M

MacPherson, Dick, 219

Madden, John, 149
Major League Baseball, 20, 40, 43, 61, 67, 68, 103, 105, 107, 234
Major League Soccer, 108, 132
Marquette University, 152
Martin, Billy, 41
Mattingly, Don, 41
McGrath, J. E., 10, 11, 16, 17
McGuire, Al, 152
McNair, Bob, 129
McPhee, 5
Melnick, M. J., 107
Miami Dolphins, 105
Mickelson, Phil, 243
Mills, Phoebe, 183
Moir, 256
Montreal Canadiens, 60, 130, 156
Motivation, 41, 82, 86–87
    achievement, 87
    affiliation, 87
    climate, 93, 255
    definition, 82
    inspirational, 171
    source of, 151
Multidimensional Sport Cohesion Instrument (MSCI), 227
Mulvey, Paul, 122
Mulvoy, Mark, 36–37

N

Nadal, Rafael, 7
Nash, Steve, 197
National Basketball Association, 25, 42, 43, 61, 67, 81, 83, 96, 105, 116, 162
National Collegiate Athletic Association, 27, 36, 43, 88, 163, 179, 201, 212, 216
National Football League, 25, 44, 58, 61, 68, 73, 105, 117, 121, 122, 128, 130, 178, 258
National Hockey League, 5, 8, 25, 36, 60, 61, 65, 67, 70, 71, 72, 105, 109, 117, 122, 133, 149, 172, 233
Navy SEALs, 263
New England Patriots, 58, 127, 165
New York Knicks, 68
New York Liberty, 31
New York Yankees, 156
New Zealand All Blacks, 161
Nigerian Soccer Team, 143
Nogueira, Lucas, 234
Nonexperimental protocols, 24–28
Norms. *See* Group norms
Northwestern University, 148
Nurse, Nick, 223
Nwogwugwu, Uchechi, 5

O

O'Neill, Shaquille, 154
Olympic Games, 25, 36, 62, 189, 233, 247, 250, 254
Ordering, 147, 217
Orr, Bobby, 206
Orwell, George, 8
Outgroup rejection, 193
Outgroups versus ingroups, 185, 192–195, 216

P

Paris Saint-Germain, 49
Parks, Cherokee, 212
Pendulum perspective of group development, 32, 34–38
Penn Relays, 5
Performance
    cohesion and, 242–244
    collective efficacy and, 249–250, 250–253
    cooperation and competition and, 189–192, 198
    group goals and, 116, 202–203
    individual/personal performance, 7, 17, 52, 54, 71, 169, 254
    performance norms, 140–141
    team performance, 14, 22, 23, 28, 42, 43, 45, 77, 78–82, 84, 85, 86, 88, 147, 152, 164, 165, 168, 169, 190, 204, 211, 230, 231, 237, 240–241, 242, 244, 250, 257, 266
See also Role performance.

Penn State University, 216
Perry, Don, 122
Personality traits, 76, 77, 80–81, 155, 162, 163, 204
    Big Five traits, 79–81, 86, 155, 162
Persuasive arguments approach, 219–220
Phillips, Kristie, 183
Pittsburgh Steelers, 97
Poeltl, Jakob, 234
Poindexter, Cappie, 31
Polarization in groups, 217–220
Pollard, G., 25, 61–62
Pollard, R., 25, 61–62
Positional stacking, 105–106
Powell, Norman, 234
Power, 148–149
    coercive, 148, 149, 162
    expert, 148–149
    groups and, 34
    legitimate, 148, 149
    power position, 165–166
    reference, 148, 149
    regulatory, 59
    reward, 148, 149
    statistical, 24, 25
Prelutsky, Jack, 50
Productivity, 8, 15, 79, 165, 167, 176, 198–199, 229
    actual productivity, 15, 79
    norms and, 129, 132, 133, 140–141
    performance and, 52–53
    potential productivity, 15, 79
Psychological structure of groups, 96–97, 186
Pujara, Cheteshwar, 124
Punctuated equilibrium models, 32, 38

R

Race, 234, 235
    positional stacking by race, 106–109
    variability in, 86
Rail, G., 124
Randall, Kikkan, 247, 251
Rank, 97, 154–156
    personal attributes associated with, 154–155
    situational characteristics and, 155–156

Raven, B., 148
Rees, C. R., 111–112
Reid, Eric, 128–129
Renard, Wendie, 143
Repeating cycles perspective, 34–38
Research Protocols, 24–29
    Experimental, 28–29
    Nonexperimental, 24-28
Reward
    exchange of, 170
    power, 148, 149, 162
Riley, Pat, 83–84, 260–261
Robbers Cave Experiment, 184, 185, 192, 195
Robinson, Jackie, 75, 76, 234
Robinson, Kelsey, 263
Robust equilibrium models, 38
Rodgers, Aaron, 130
Roethlisberger, Ben, 97
Role acceptance, 14, 114, 122, 125, 240, 263
Role clarity, 14, 114, 116–120, 125, 240, 261, 263, 265, 266
Role conflict, 117, 120–122, 125, 126
Role efficacy, 117, 122
Role performance, 28, 110, 116, 117, 119, 122, 124–126, 240
Role satisfaction, 117, 123–124
Roosevelt, Franklin, 75
Rules, 13, 57, 63, 95, 99, 128, 130, 141–142, 233, 258
    as a game location factor, 68–69
Rutgers University, 31
Ryder Cup, 243

S

Sacrifice
    role of, 237
    individual, 266
Saint John's University, 87
Saint Louis Cardinals, 66
San Antonio Spurs, 117
San Francisco 49ers, 157
San Jose Earthquakes, 132
Sandusky, Jerry, 216
Scale for Effective Communication in Sport Teams (SECT), 211

Saukrates, 203
Schlenker, B. R., 73
Schutz, William, 35
Schefter, Adam, 128
Science vs commonsense, 19–20
Scientific method, 20–22
    formulating a hypothesis, 21
    generating a research question, 21
    ruling out alternative explanations and replication, 22
    testing a hypothesis, 21–22
Secord, Al, 120, 121
Segregation of positions by race, 106–108
Self, Bill, 88
Self-deception, 244
Sequential stage (linear) perspective, 32–34
Shakespeare, William, 124
Shared beliefs, 248
Shared mental models, 213–214
Sharpening, 217
Shoshanna, Brenda, 154
Siakem, 234
Silva, J. M., 141
Sinclair, Christine, 166
Sinden, Harry, 37, 120, 121
Smith, J. R., 209
Smith, Kohn, 113
Smoll, F. L., 163–164
Snyder, Dan, 129
Social categorization, 193
Social comparison, 192–193
Social comparison process, 219–220
Social hierarchies, *See* Hierarchies
Social identity, 137–138, 192
    theory, 192
Social loafing, 53–54, 83, 201, 257
    cohesion and, 238, 244
Social norms, 123, 132, 138
Socialization, 39–40
    organizational, 39
    Sport Team Socialization Tactics Questionnaire, 40
Sommer, R. R., 105–106
Spatial centrality, 100
Spink, Kevin S., 140, 264–266
Sport teams,
    attributions in, 235
    cohesion and, 223–247
    communication and, 209–223
    compatibility issues in, 88–95
    conceptual framework for, 17
    definition of, 12–13
    group norms in, 127–147
    group size and, 49–52
    importance of positions in, 101–105
    research protocols in the study of, 24–29
    social loafing and, 53–54
    special considerations in the study of, 22–24
    status in, 156–159
Stacking by Race/Ethnicity, 105–106
Stalin, Joseph 75
Stallworth, Donté, 165
Stanford University, 135
Stanley Cup, 8, 60, 172
Status, 147–159
    age and, 148, 151, 154–155
    personal attributes and, 154–155
    rank and, 155
    situational characteristics and, 155–156
    sources of in sport teams, 154–155
    sport involvement and social status, 156–158
Steiner, Ivan, 15–16, 52–53
    task typology of, 77–78
Steinzor, B., 100
Stewart, Norm, 43
Synchronized swimming, 11, 249, 250–251, 254
Syracuse University, 219

T

Tabárez, Oscar, 159
Task(s), 54, 77–78, 137, 190–191, 249
    Group Integration-Task, 28
    Steiner's task typology, 78
Task ability, 113–114
Task cohesion, 22, 27, 28, 55, 120, 171, 204, 211, 229, 233, 235–245, 254
Task dependence, 101, 103
Task versus social roles, 111–112
Task-oriented individuals, 112, 165
Taylor, Erin, 97

Team building, 23, 29, 143, 204
  benefits of, 259–261
  definition of, 259
  direct and indirect team-building interventions, 264–266
  effectiveness of, 266–269
  general strategies for, 257–267
Team-building interventions, 29, 115, 259, 261–264, 266–267
Team-building programs in sport, 261–266
Team Canada, 36–38, 166, 216
Team development, 257–268
  benefits of, 259–261
  definition of, 259
  leveraging for health-related outcomes, 260
  nature of, 257–259
Team goals. *See* Goals/Goal setting
Team identifty, 211
Team success, 29, 38, 79
  athlete turnover and, 40–42
  cohesion and, 241–244
  manager turnover and, 43–44
Teamwork, 5, 227, 259, 262
  training, 259, 267
Territory/Territoriality,
  group territory, 57–75
  marking of, 60
  nature of, 58
  primary territory, 58–59
  public territory, 58–60
  secondary territory, 58–59
  types of, 58–60
  See also Home advantage
Tharp, R. G., 27
Thomas, Daryl, 113
Thomas, Jesse, 135, 148
Title IX, 157
Toronto Argonauts, 99
Toronto Maple Leafs, 109
Toronto Raptors, 59, 83, 96, 117, 123, 203, 234
Transactive density, 206–207
Transactive memory, 213–214, 221–223
Tuchel, Thomas, 49
Tuckman, Bruce, 32–35

Turnover, 28, 39–46
  advantages and disadvantages of, 40
  athlete turnover and team success, 40–42
  cause versus effect interpretations of, 45–46
  manager turnover and team success, 43–45

U

UCLA, 163
USSR, 216
United States Women's Soccer team, 3
University of Kansas, 88
University of Missouri, 43
University of Pennsylvania, 5
University of Tennessee, 197
Uruguay Men's National Soccer Team, 159

V

Vadnais, Carol, 206
Van Gundy, Jeff, 42
Vancouver Canucks, 8
VanVleet, Fred, 234
Varca, P. E., 70
Variability in group resources, 83–88
  age and, 85–86
  gender and, 85
  members' ability and, 87–88
  race/ethnicity and, 86
  social-psychological characteristics and, 86–87
Vaughn, Kia, 31
Verbal persuasion, 240, 250, 251
  collective efficacy and, 253
Vicarious experiences, 240, 250, 251, 253
Volp, A., 125
Vonn, Lindsey, 191

W

Walker, Randy, 148, 149
Walsh, Bill., 257–258

Watson, Tom, 243
Whiffen, Trevor, 233
Widmeyer, W. N., 55–57, 80
Widmeyer/Loy perspective, 80
Williams, Serena, 191
Winfield, Dave, 41
WNBA, 39, 105, 108
Woodcock, M., 260
Wooden, John, 27, 148–149, 240
Worchel, S., 35

World Cup, 3, 5, 36, 47, 62, 63, 68, 83, 95, 96, 117, 142, 166, 228, 235, 247, 251
World Series, 71, 73

Y

Yukelson, D., 262

Z

Zaccaro, S. J., 248–249

About the Authors

Mark Eys, Ph.D., is a professor in the Departments of Kinesiology/Physical Education and Psychology (joint) at Wilfrid Laurier University. Dr. Eys is the Laurier Research Chair in Group Dynamics and Physical Activity (2019–present), and he previously held a Tier II Canada Research Chair (2009–2019). His research projects consider the social environments within sport and exercise and focus on topics such as cohesion within youth sport teams (SSHRC 2005–2008; Ontario Ministry of Research and Innovation Early Researcher Award, 2007–2012) and role commitment and acceptance in groups (SSHRC 2013–2017). Most recently, Dr. Eys leads a Partnership Development initiative (SSHRC 2019–2022) to facilitate physical activity participation for New Canadian women and children. He has published his work in top sport and exercise psychology journals, and he is a co-editor of *Group Dynamics in Exercise and Sport Psychology* (2nd edition, 2014) and *The Power of Groups in Youth Sport* (2020). Finally, in 2001, he was named Canadian Interuniversity Sport Women's Soccer Coach of the Year.

M. Blair Evans, PhD, joined the Kinesiology Department at Penn State in his current role of assistant professor in 2015. His educational pathway includes doctoral studies in social psychology at Wilfrid Laurier University (2014), along with Master's education from the University of Lethbridge and undergraduate education from Laurentian University. He also completed a postdoctoral fellowship at Queen's University in the School of Kinesiology and Health Studies. Research conducted by Dr. Evans and his students in the Team Lab focuses on how our peers within small groups can influence our wellbeing and health behaviors. Although this research spans varying contexts, developmental stages, and populations, he focuses on young athletes and individuals with disabilities. His research is published in leading journals related to sport and health psychology and is supported by sport-related research foundations, as well as federal funding bodies in Canada and the United States. He lives with his wife and two young children in State College, Pennsylvania.

Alex Benson, PhD, joined the Department of Psychology at Western University as an assistant professor in 2017—bridging the cluster areas of Industrial/Organizational Psychology and Social, Personality and Developmental Psychology. He completed all of his formal education at Wilfrid Laurier University, beginning with a Bachelor's and Master's degrees in Kinesiology before going on to complete his doctoral studies in social psychology. He was awarded a Social Sciences and Humanities Research Council postdoctoral fellowship to investigate group dynamics in youth sport teams at Nipissing University. Dr. Benson is the director of the Group Experiences Laboratory, where he and his students integrate a variety of theoretical and methodological approaches to better understand the conditions and processes that shape people's experiences in teams. Reflecting the interdisciplinary nature of his work, he has published in top-tier journals in the areas of sport psychology, organizational behaviour, social psychology, and personality psychology. His lab's research is supported by funds from the Social Sciences and Humanities Research Council of Canada, Canada Foundation for Innovation, and Mitacs.